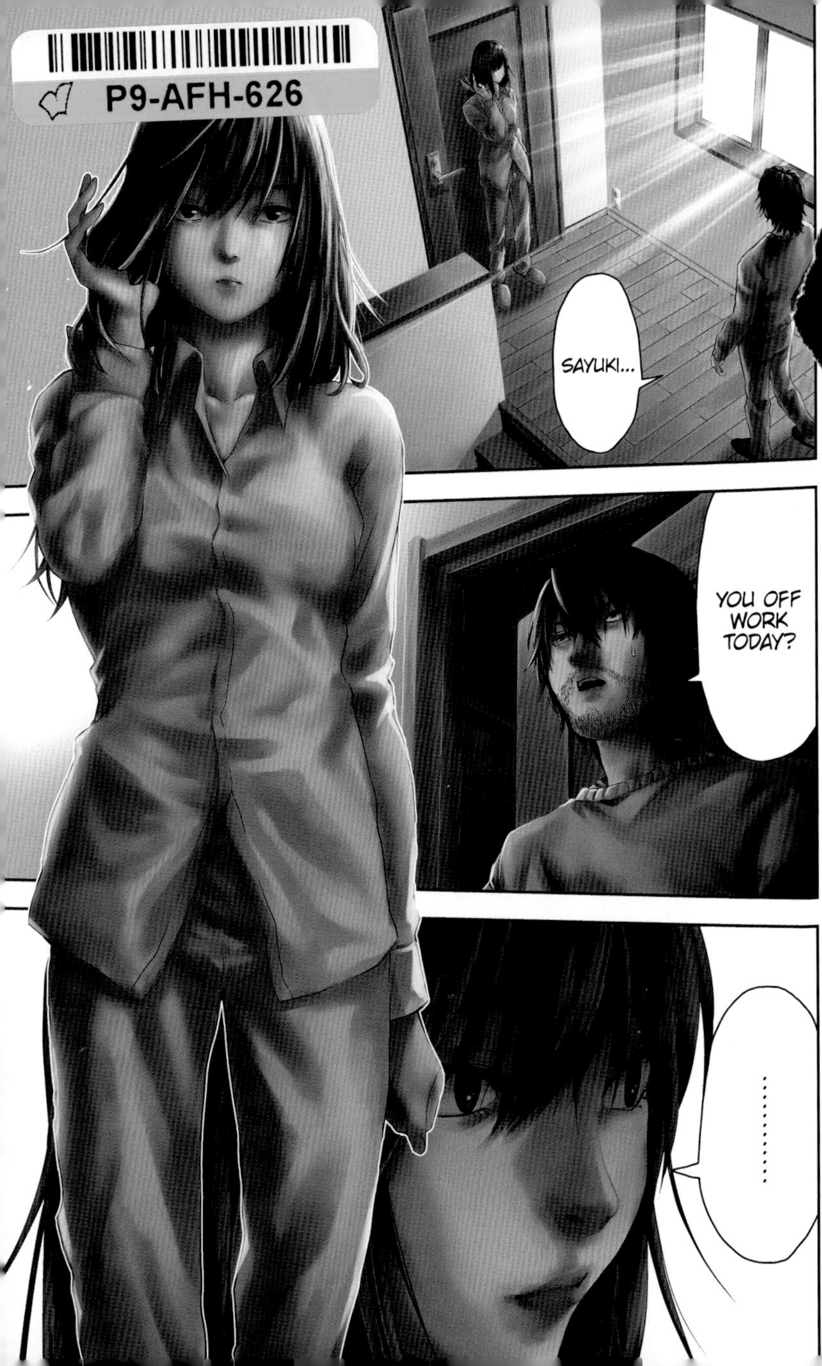
SAYUKI...
YOU OFF WORK TODAY?
....

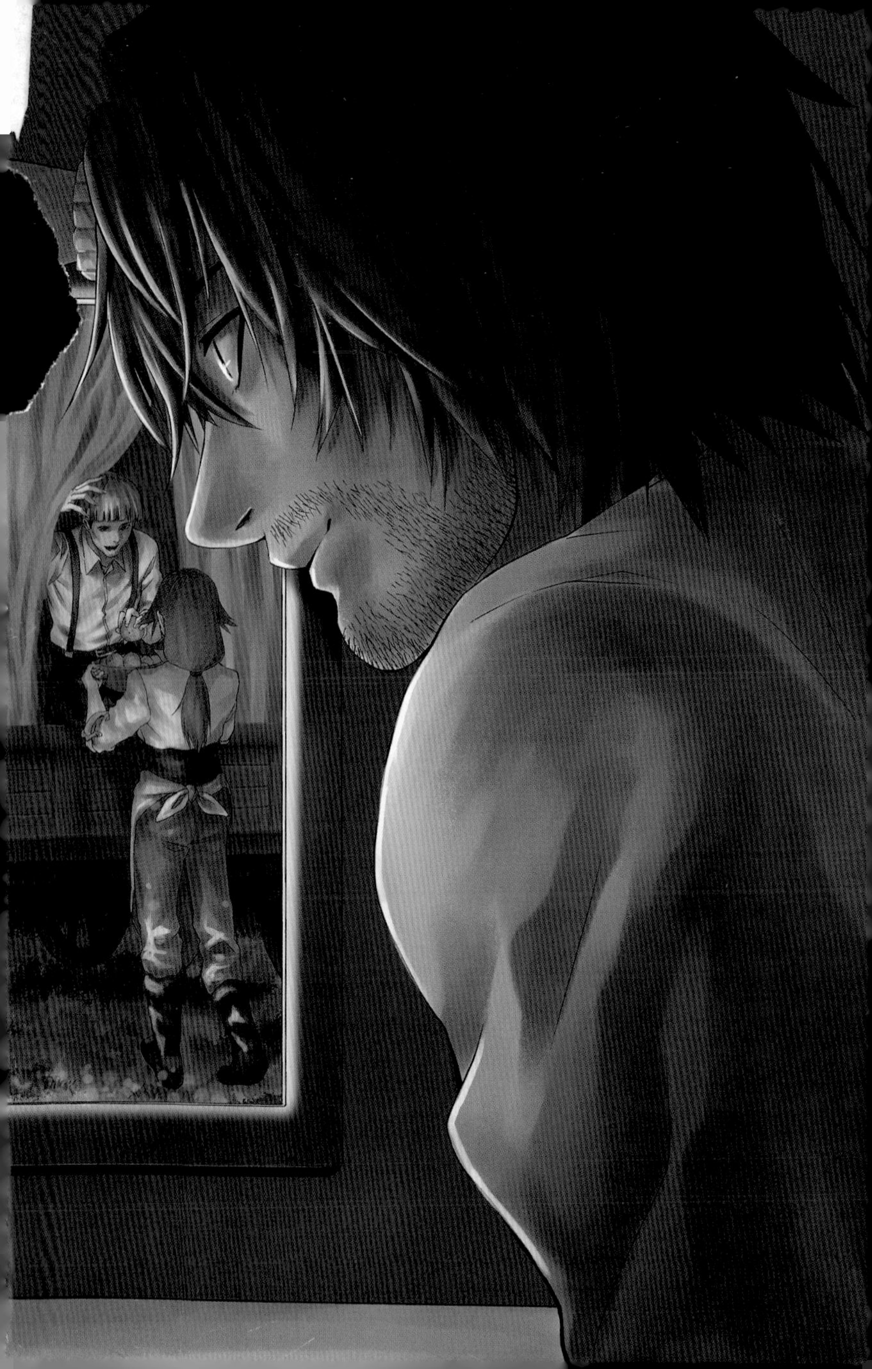

HE NPCs IN THIS [redacted]LAGE SIM GAME [redacted]JST BE REAL! 2

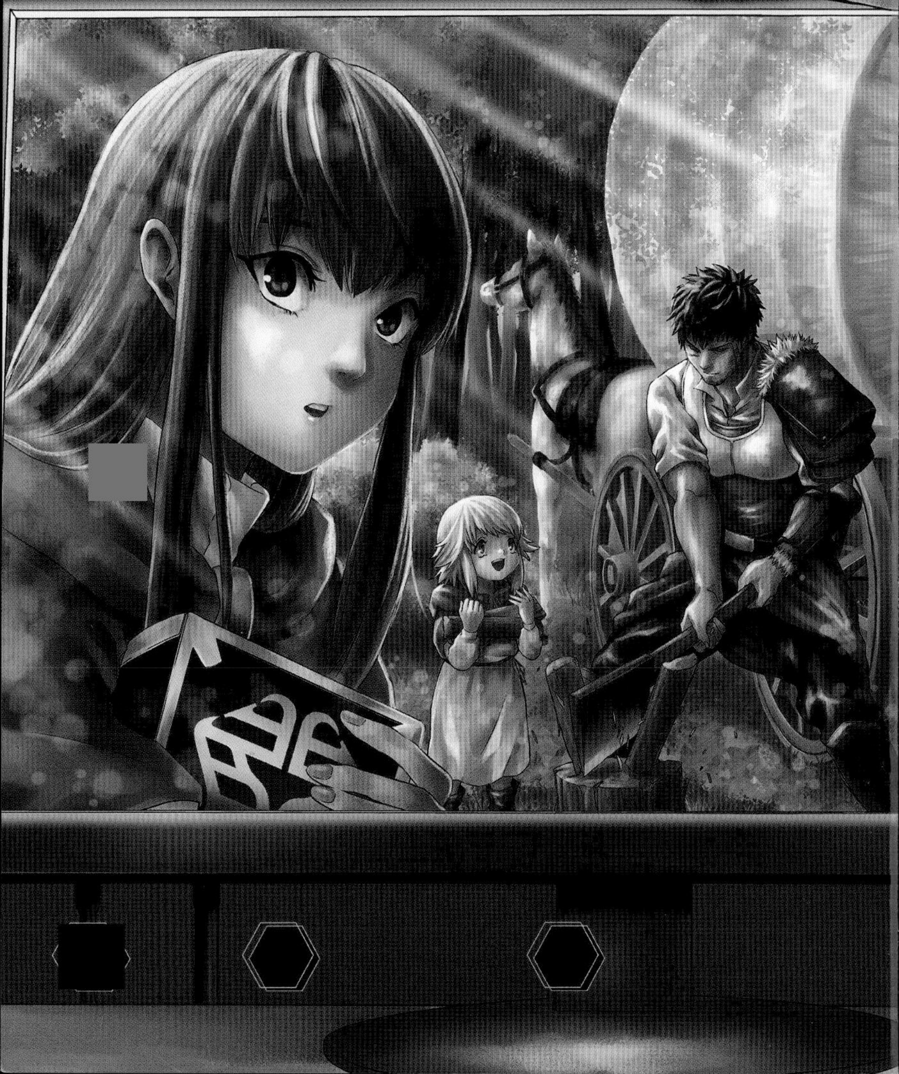

THE NPCs IN THIS VILLAGE SIM GAME MUST BE REAL! ↵

2

CONTENTS

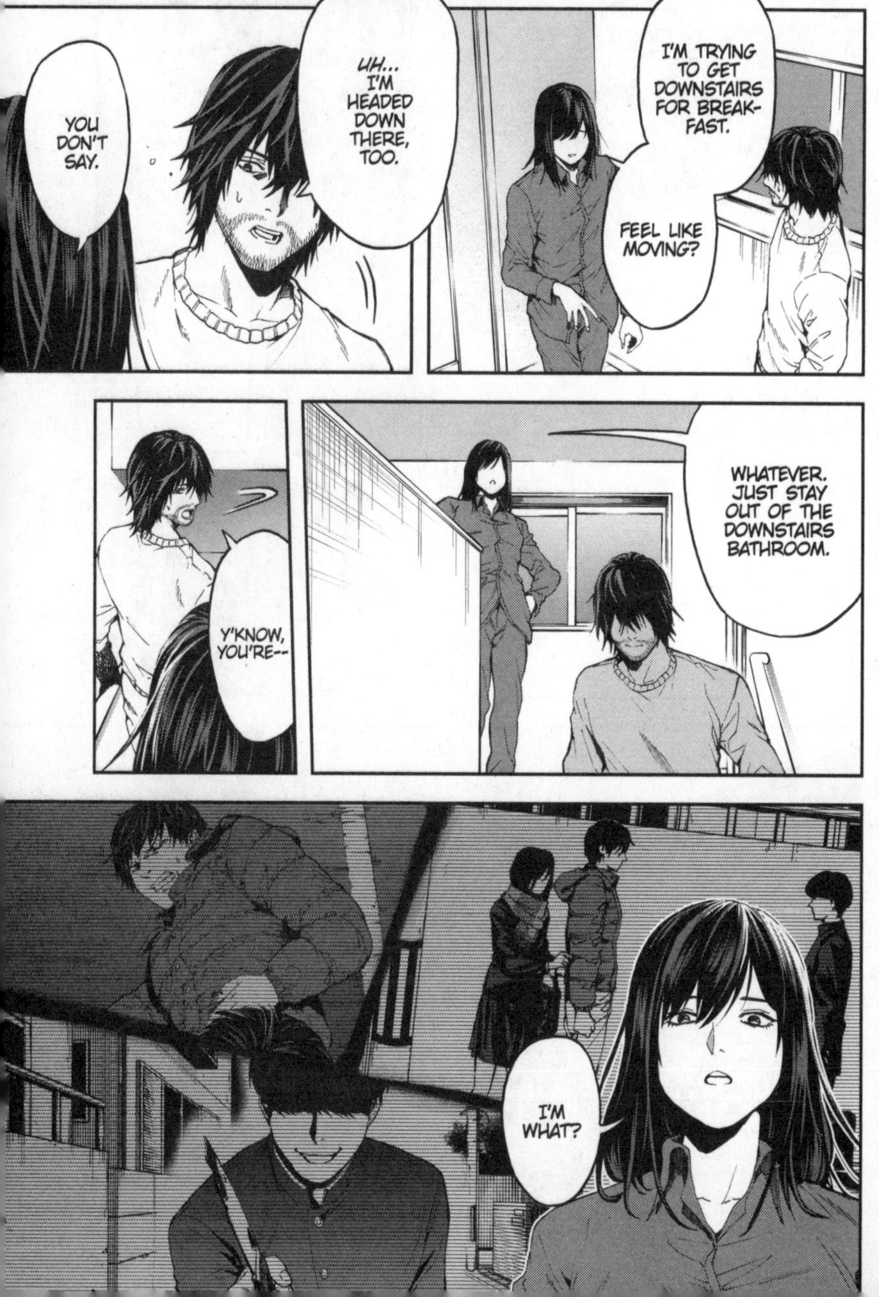
I'M TRYING TO GET DOWNSTAIRS FOR BREAK-FAST.
FEEL LIKE MOVING?
UH... I'M HEADED DOWN THERE, TOO.
YOU DON'T SAY.
WHATEVER. JUST STAY OUT OF THE DOWNSTAIRS BATHROOM.
Y'KNOW, YOU'RE--
I'M WHAT?

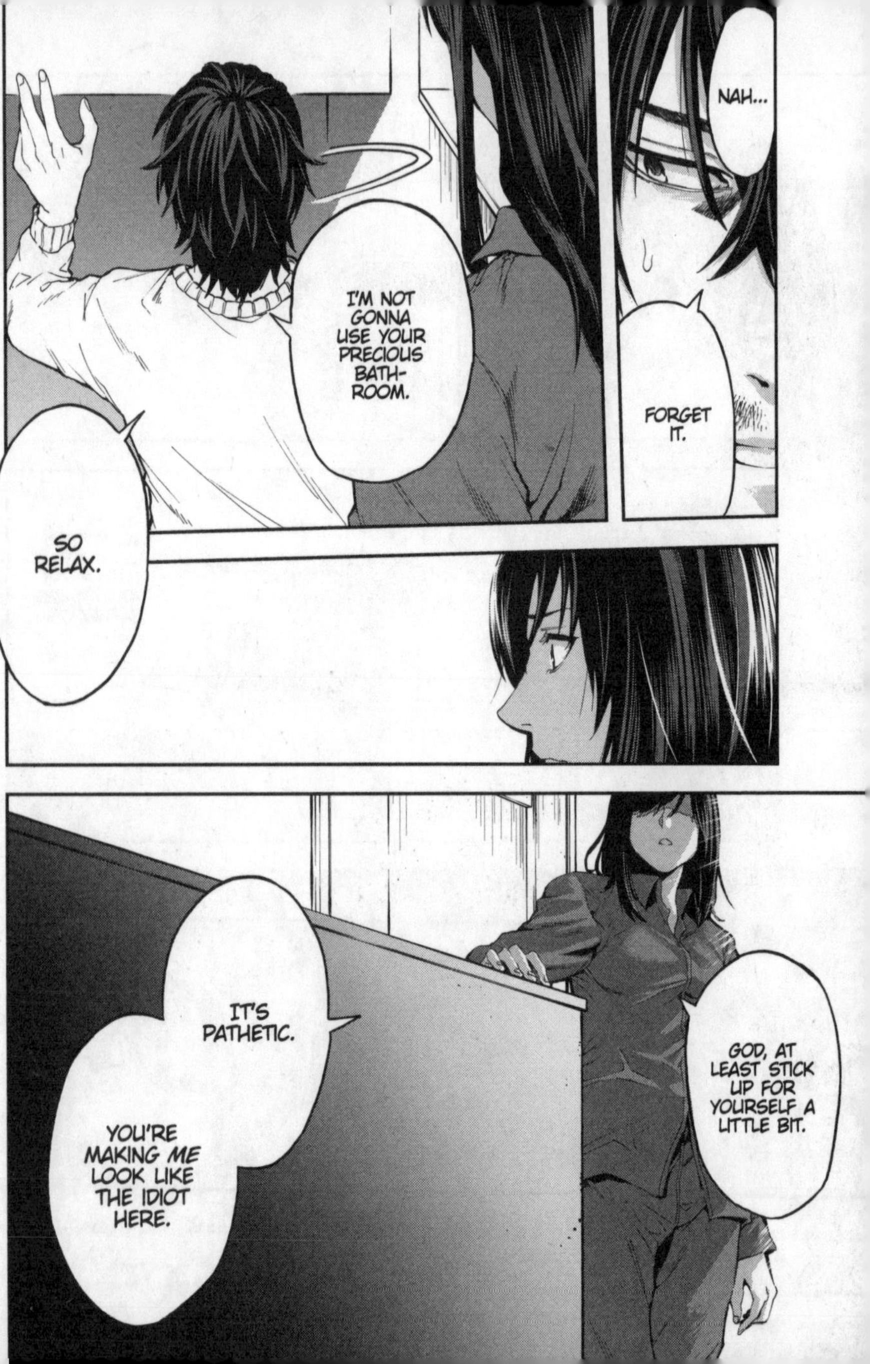
NAH...
FORGET IT.
I'M NOT GONNA USE YOUR PRECIOUS BATH-ROOM.
SO RELAX.
GOD, AT LEAST STICK UP FOR YOURSELF A LITTLE BIT.
IT'S PATHETIC.
YOU'RE MAKING *ME* LOOK LIKE THE IDIOT HERE.

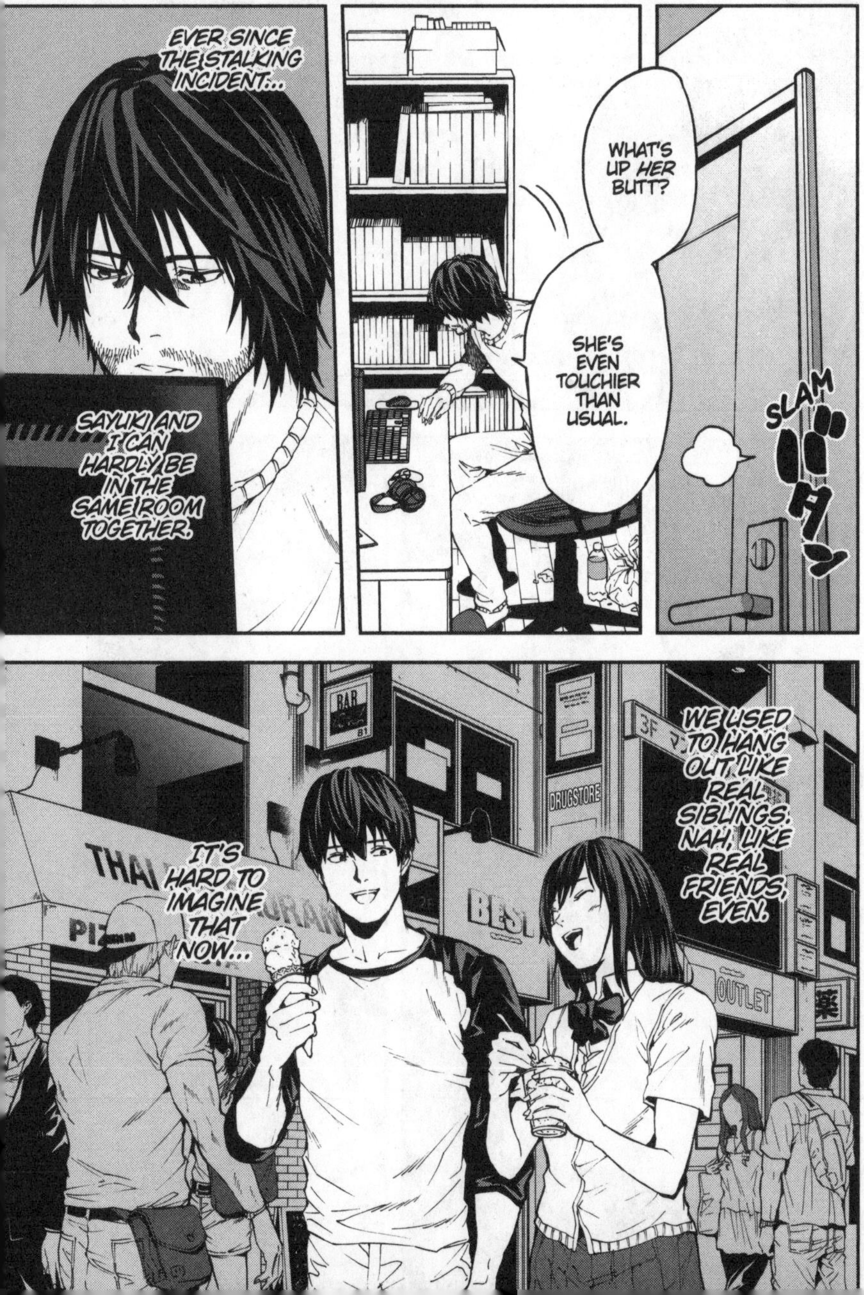
SLAM
バタン
WHAT'S UP HER BUTT?
SHE'S EVEN TOUCHIER THAN USUAL.
EVER SINCE THE STALKING INCIDENT...
SAYUKI AND I CAN HARDLY BE IN THE SAME ROOM TOGETHER.
WE USED TO HANG OUT LIKE REAL SIBLINGS. NAH, LIKE REAL FRIENDS, EVEN.
IT'S HARD TO IMAGINE THAT NOW...
BAR
DRUGSTORE
OUTLET

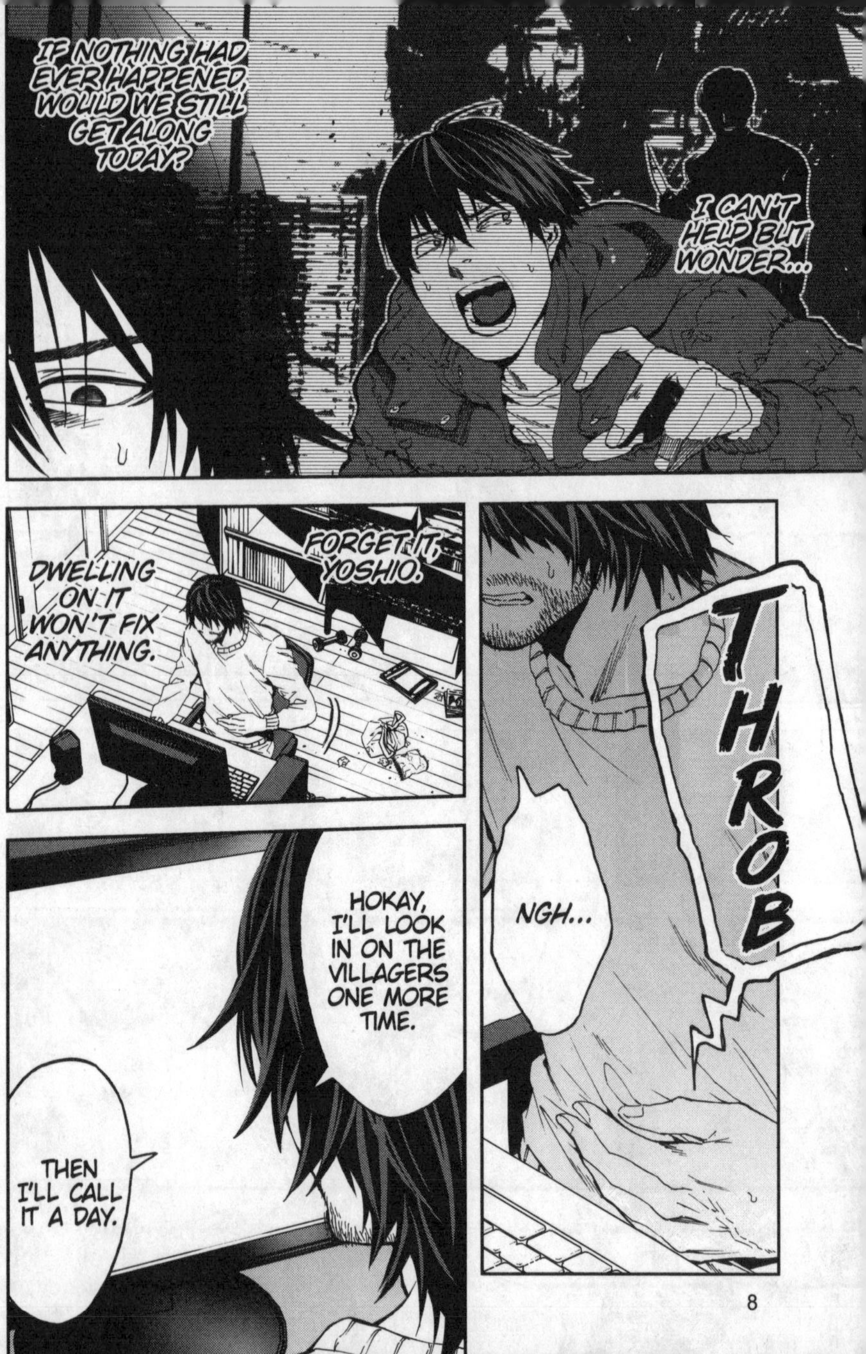
IF NOTHING HAD EVER HAPPENED, WOULD WE STILL GET ALONG TODAY?
I CAN'T HELP BUT WONDER...
THROB
NGH...
FORGET IT, YOSHIO.
DWELLING ON IT WON'T FIX ANYTHING.
HOKAY, I'LL LOOK IN ON THE VILLAGERS ONE MORE TIME.
THEN I'LL CALL IT A DAY.

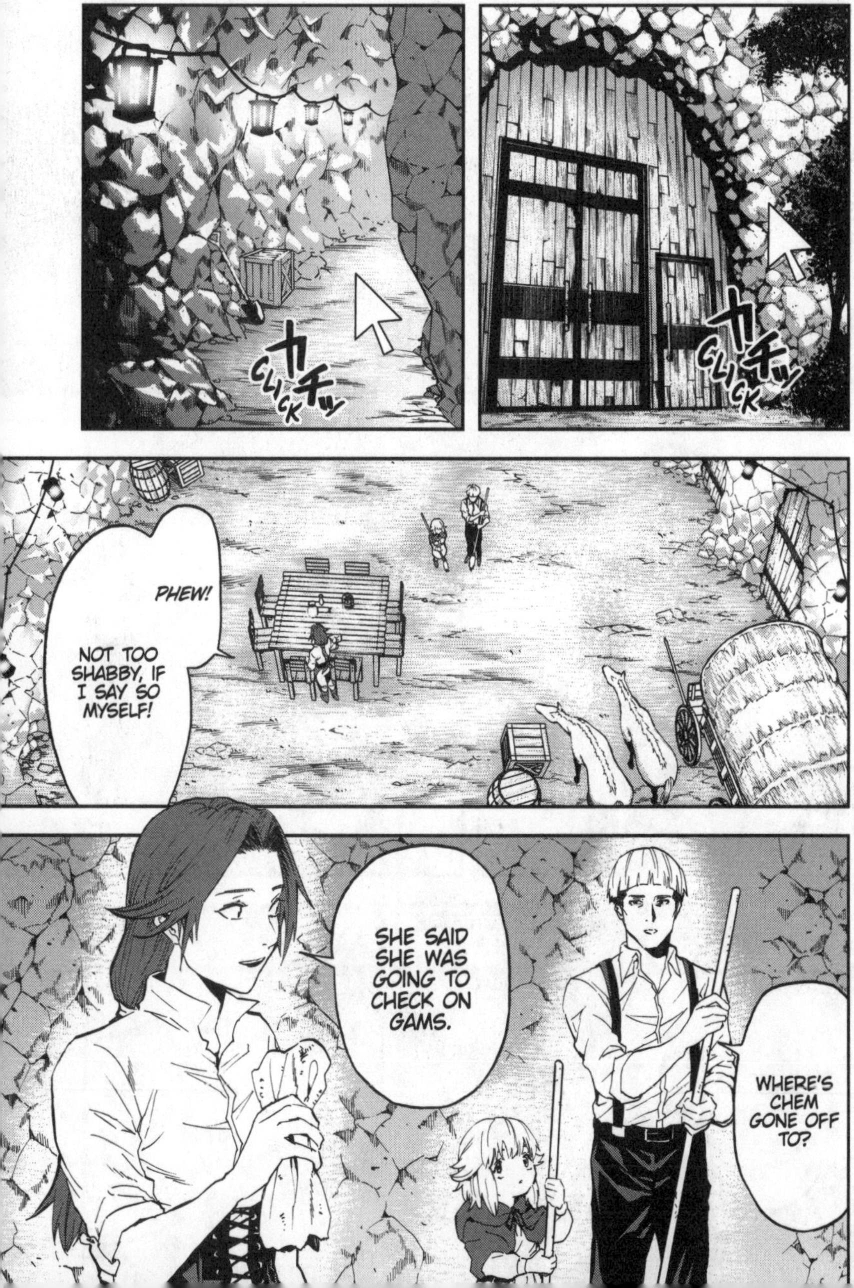
カチッ
CLICK
カチッ
CLICK
PHEW!
NOT TOO SHABBY, IF I SAY SO MYSELF!
WHERE'S CHEM GONE OFF TO?
SHE SAID SHE WAS GOING TO CHECK ON GAMS.

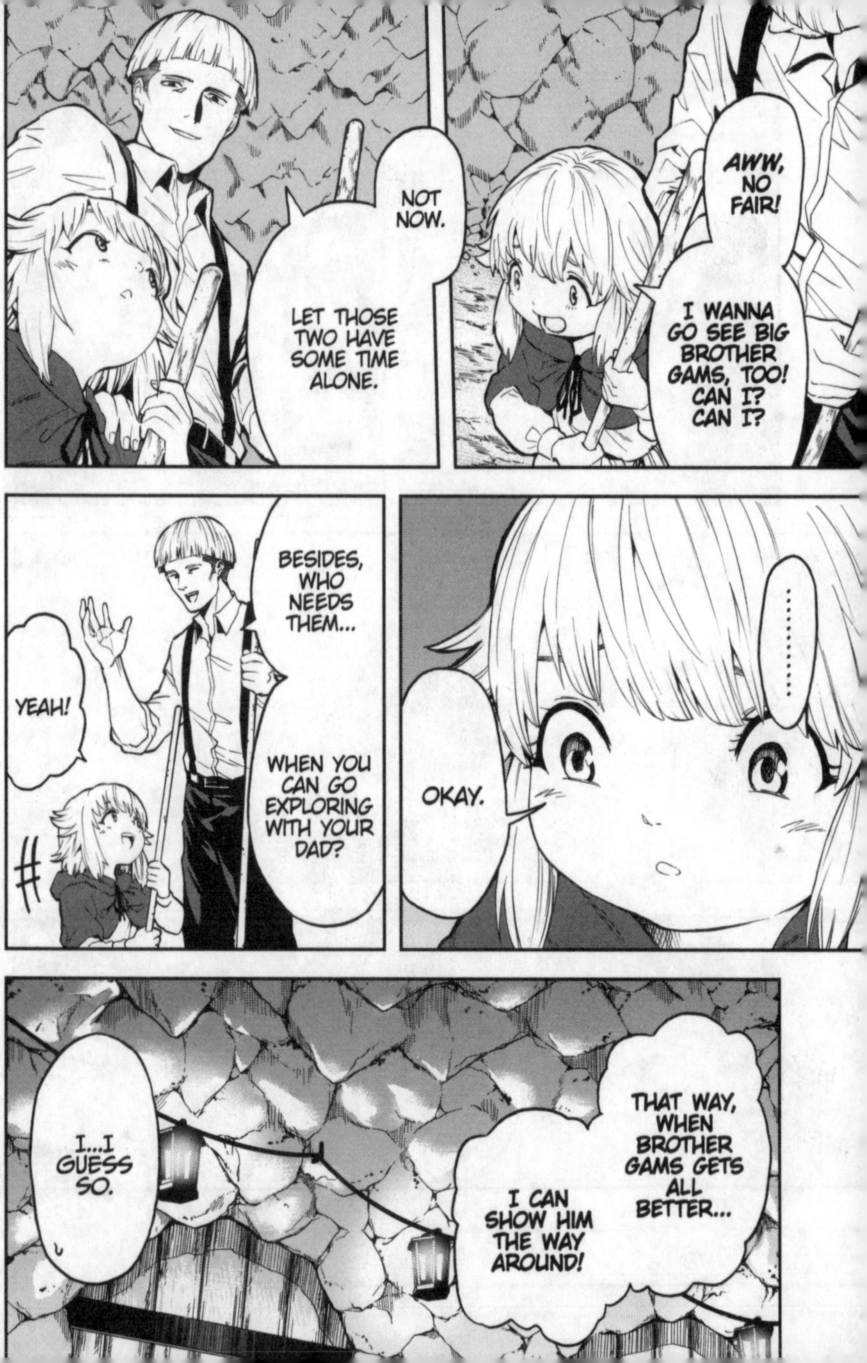
AWW, NO FAIR!
I WANNA GO SEE BIG BROTHER GAMS, TOO! CAN I? CAN I?
NOT NOW.
LET THOSE TWO HAVE SOME TIME ALONE.
......
OKAY.
BESIDES, WHO NEEDS THEM...
WHEN YOU CAN GO EXPLORING WITH YOUR DAD?
YEAH!
THAT WAY, WHEN BROTHER GAMS GETS ALL BETTER...
I CAN SHOW HIM THE WAY AROUND!
I...I GUESS SO.

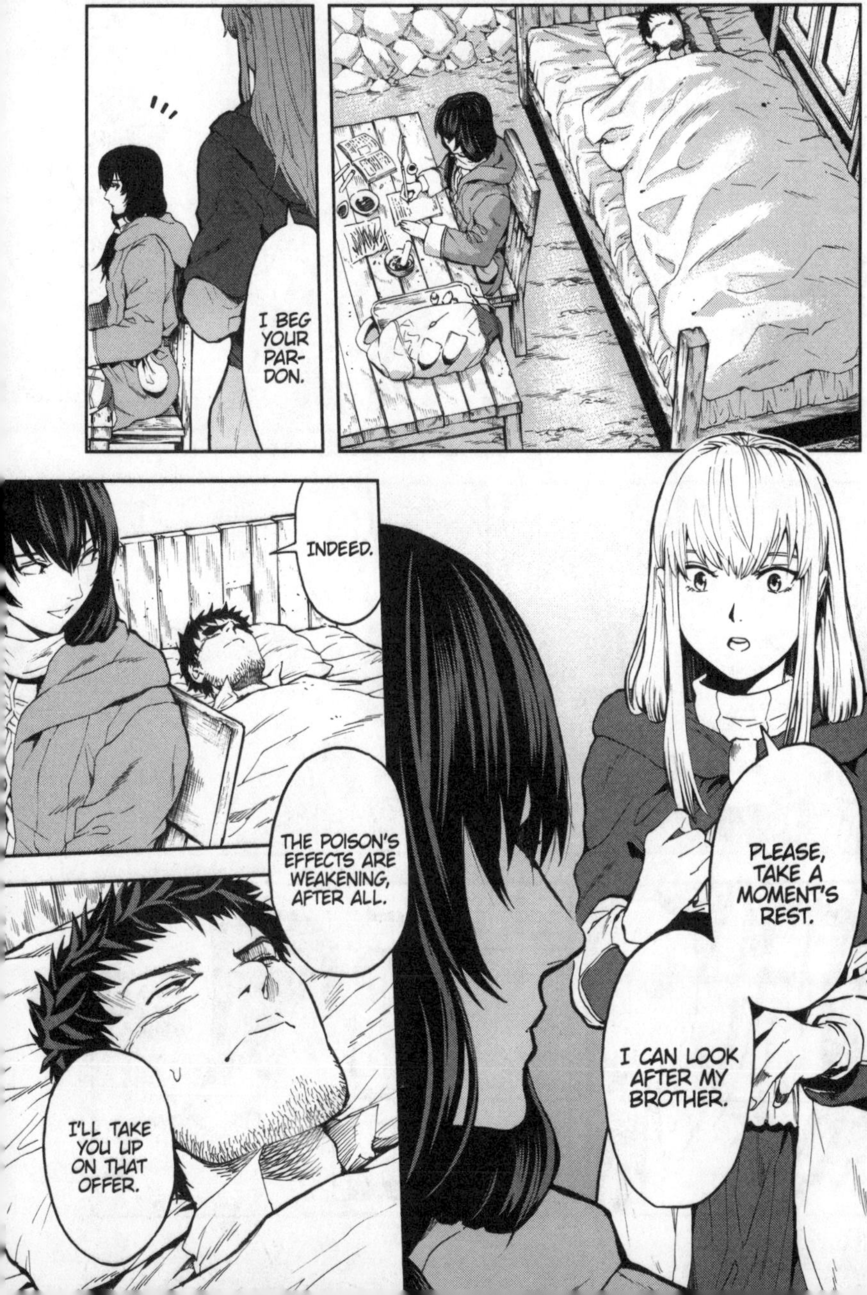
I BEG YOUR PARDON.
PLEASE, TAKE A MOMENT'S REST.
I CAN LOOK AFTER MY BROTHER.
INDEED.
THE POISON'S EFFECTS ARE WEAKENING, AFTER ALL.
I'LL TAKE YOU UP ON THAT OFFER.

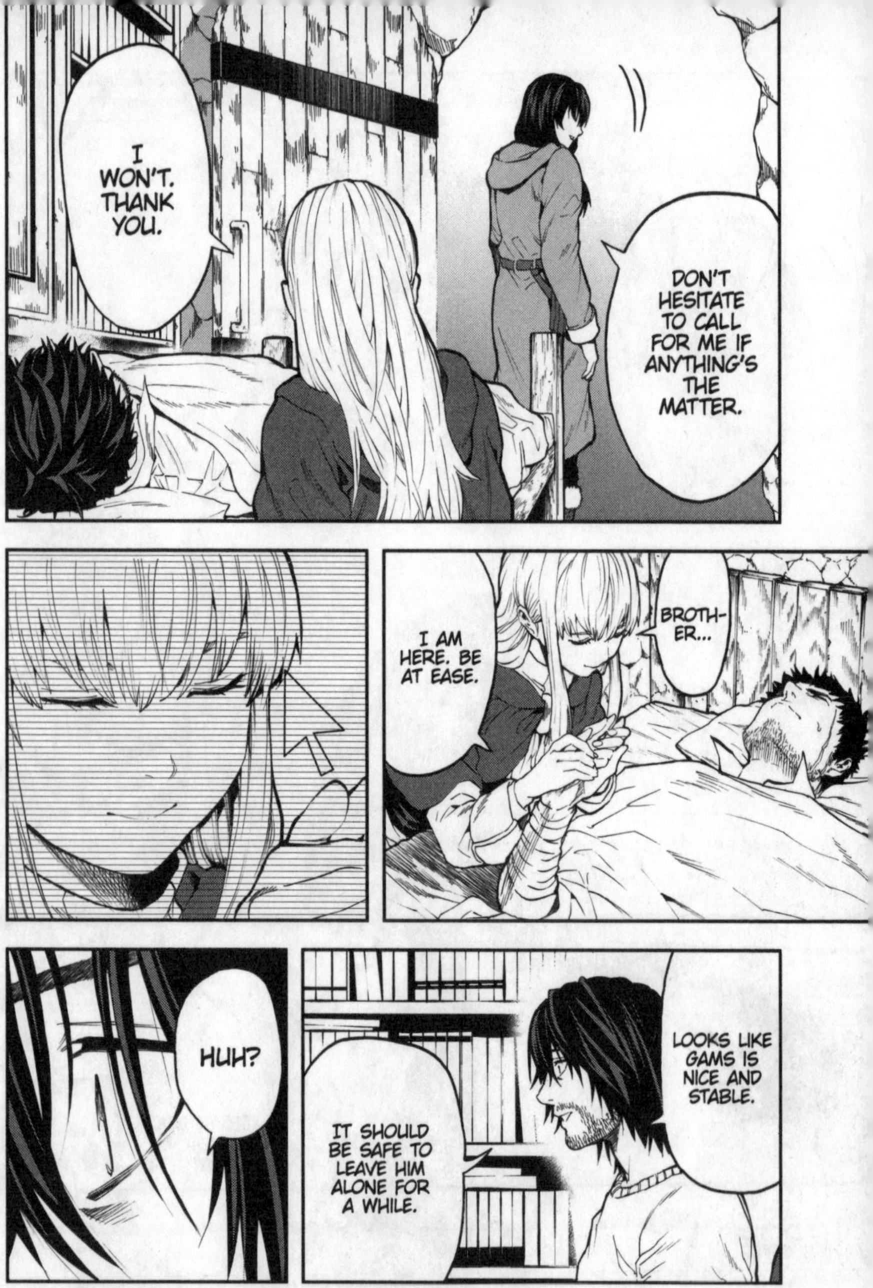
DON'T HESITATE TO CALL FOR ME IF ANYTHING'S THE MATTER.
I WON'T. THANK YOU.
BROTHER...
I AM HERE. BE AT EASE.
LOOKS LIKE GAMS IS NICE AND STABLE.
IT SHOULD BE SAFE TO LEAVE HIM ALONE FOR A WHILE.
HUH?

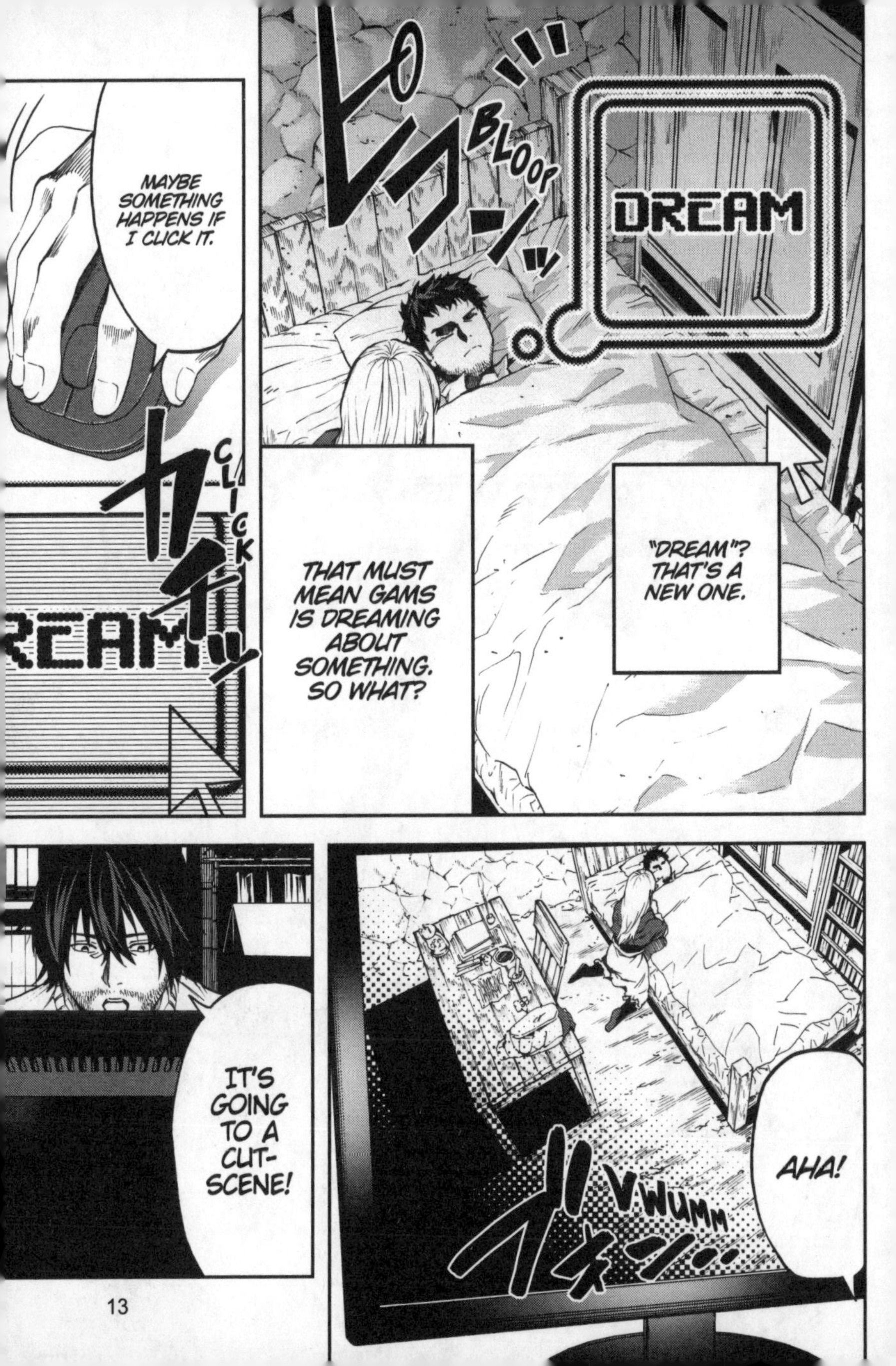
DREAM
BLOOOP
"DREAM"? THAT'S A NEW ONE.
THAT MUST MEAN GAMS IS DREAMING ABOUT SOMETHING. SO WHAT?
MAYBE SOMETHING HAPPENS IF I CLICK IT.
CLICK
REAM
AHA!
VWUMM
IT'S GOING TO A CUT-SCENE!

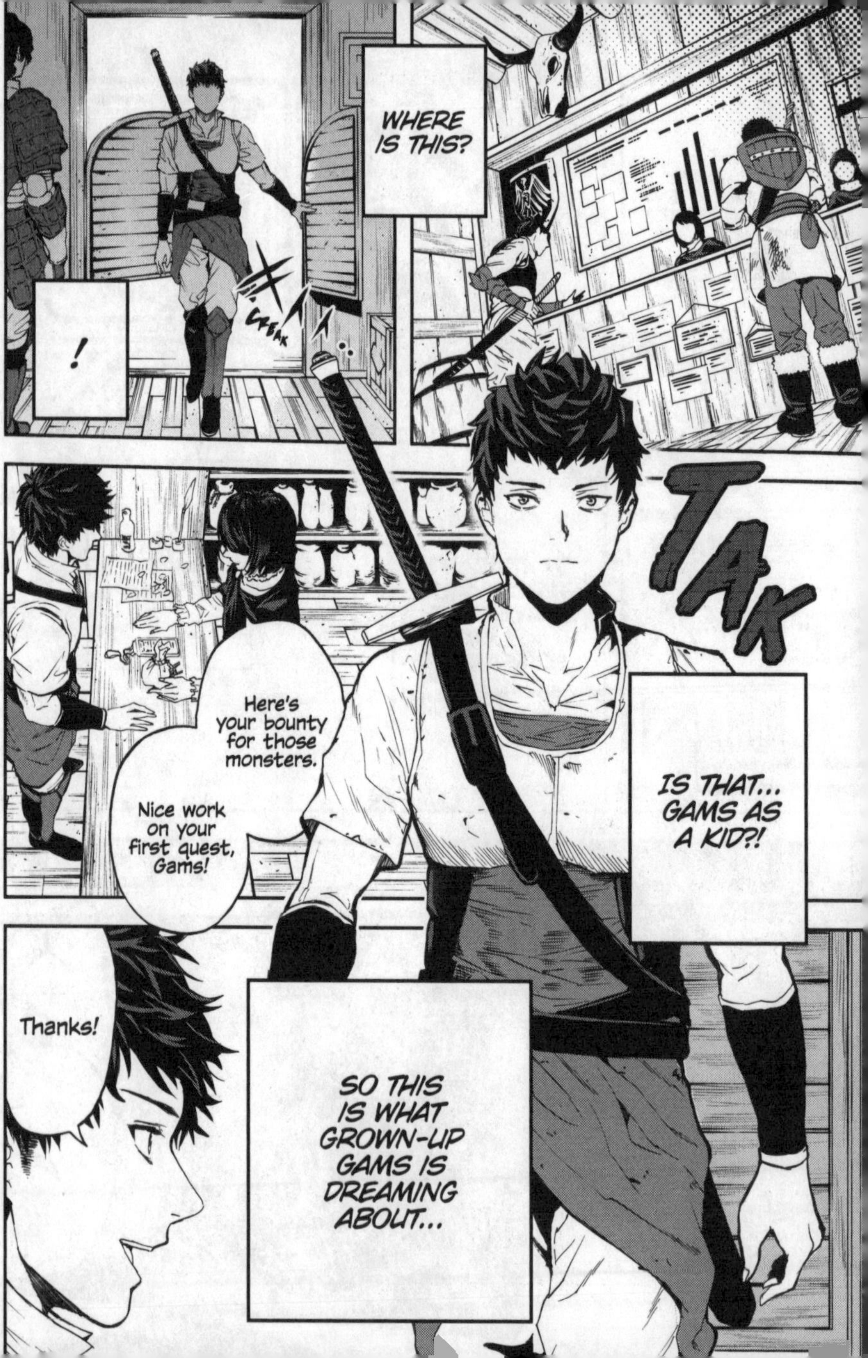
WHERE IS THIS?
CREAK
!
TAK
IS THAT... GAMS AS A KID?!
Here's your bounty for those monsters.
Nice work on your first quest, Gams!
SO THIS IS WHAT GROWN-UP GAMS IS DREAMING ABOUT...
Thanks!

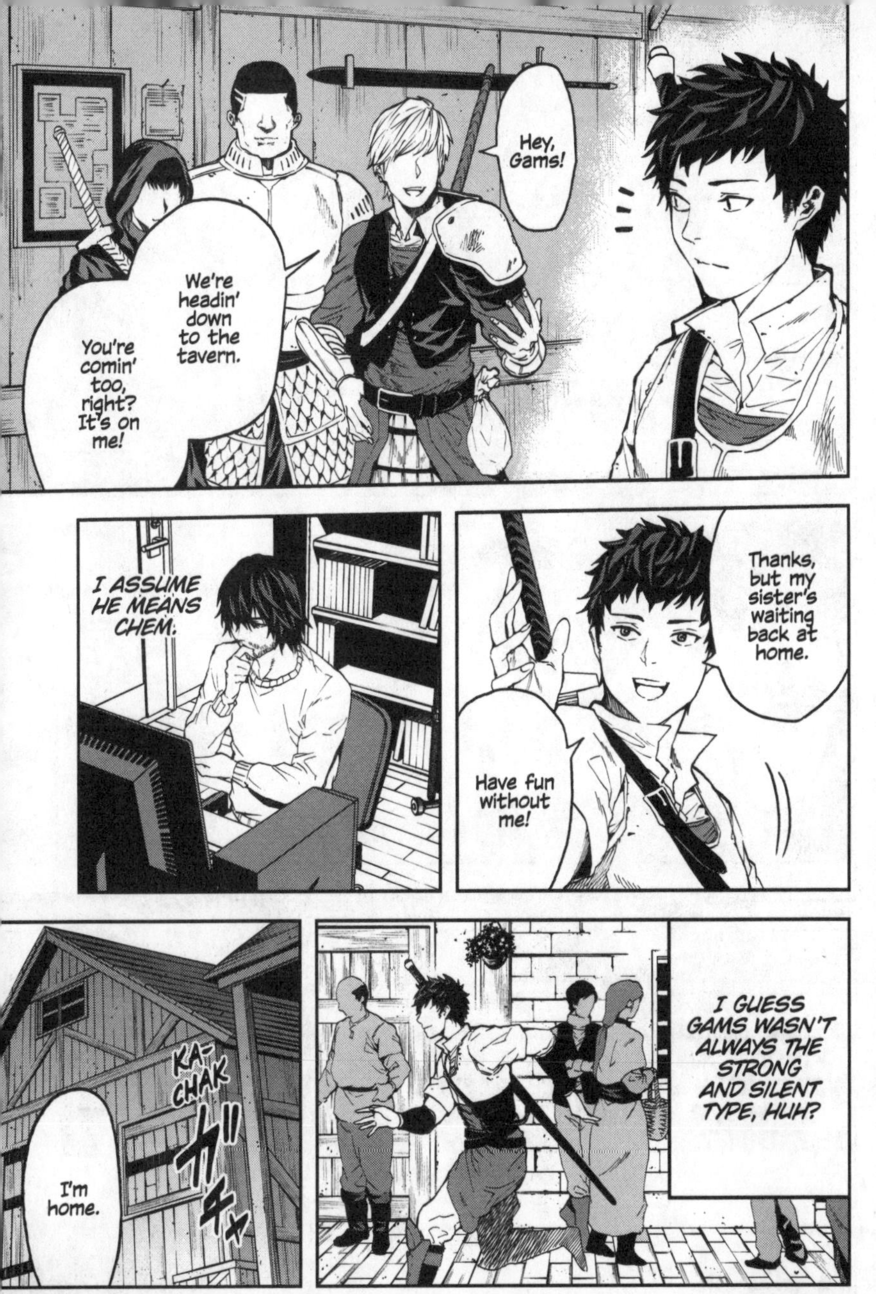
Hey, Gams!
We're headin' down to the tavern.
You're comin' too, right? It's on me!
Thanks, but my sister's waiting back at home.
Have fun without me!
I ASSUME HE MEANS CHEM.
I GUESS GAMS WASN'T ALWAYS THE STRONG AND SILENT TYPE, HUH?
KA-CHAK
ガチャ
I'm home.

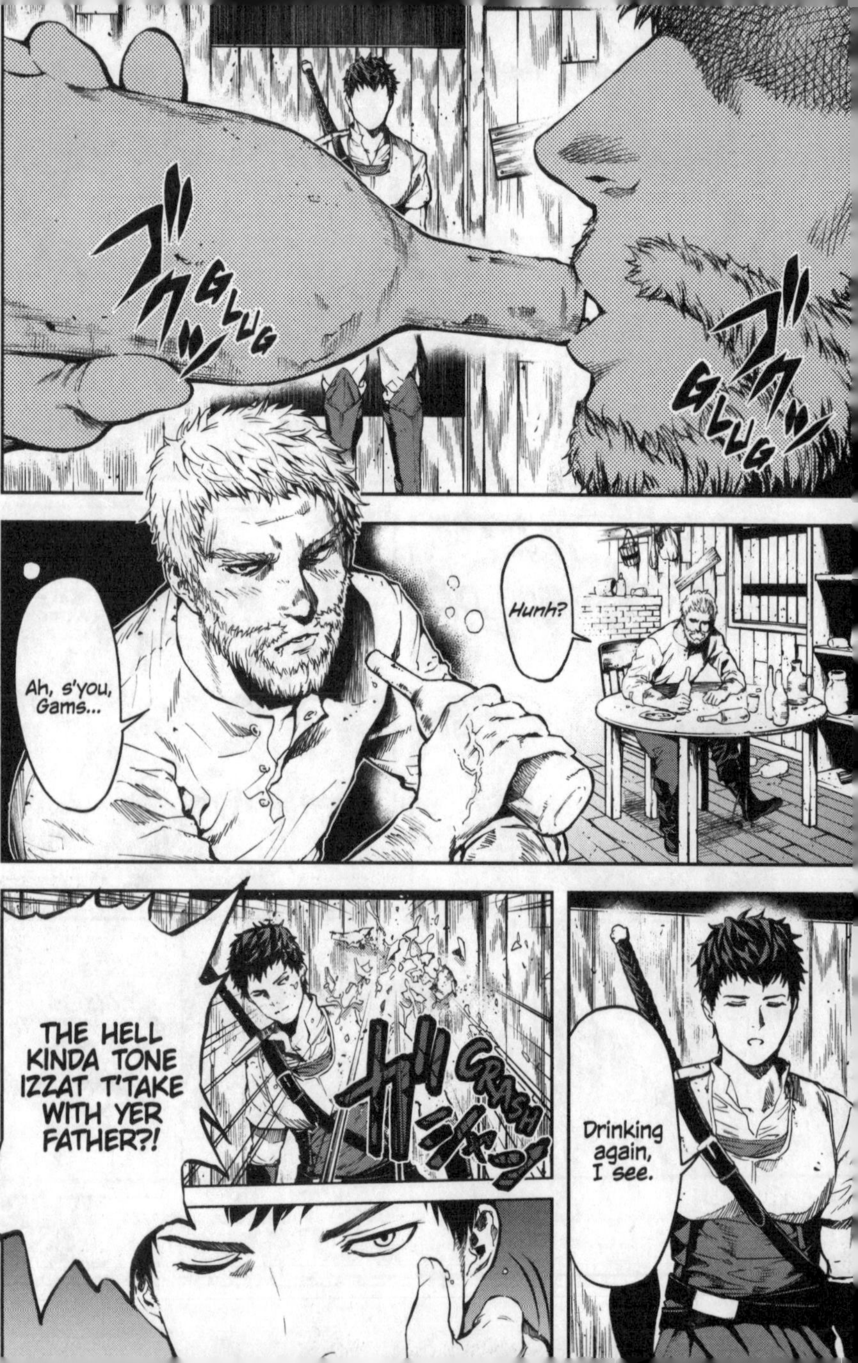

ゴクッ
GLUG
ゴクッ
GLUG
Hunh?
Ah, s'you, Gams...
Drinking again, I see.
THE HELL KINDA TONE IZZAT T'TAKE WITH YER FATHER?!
CRASH

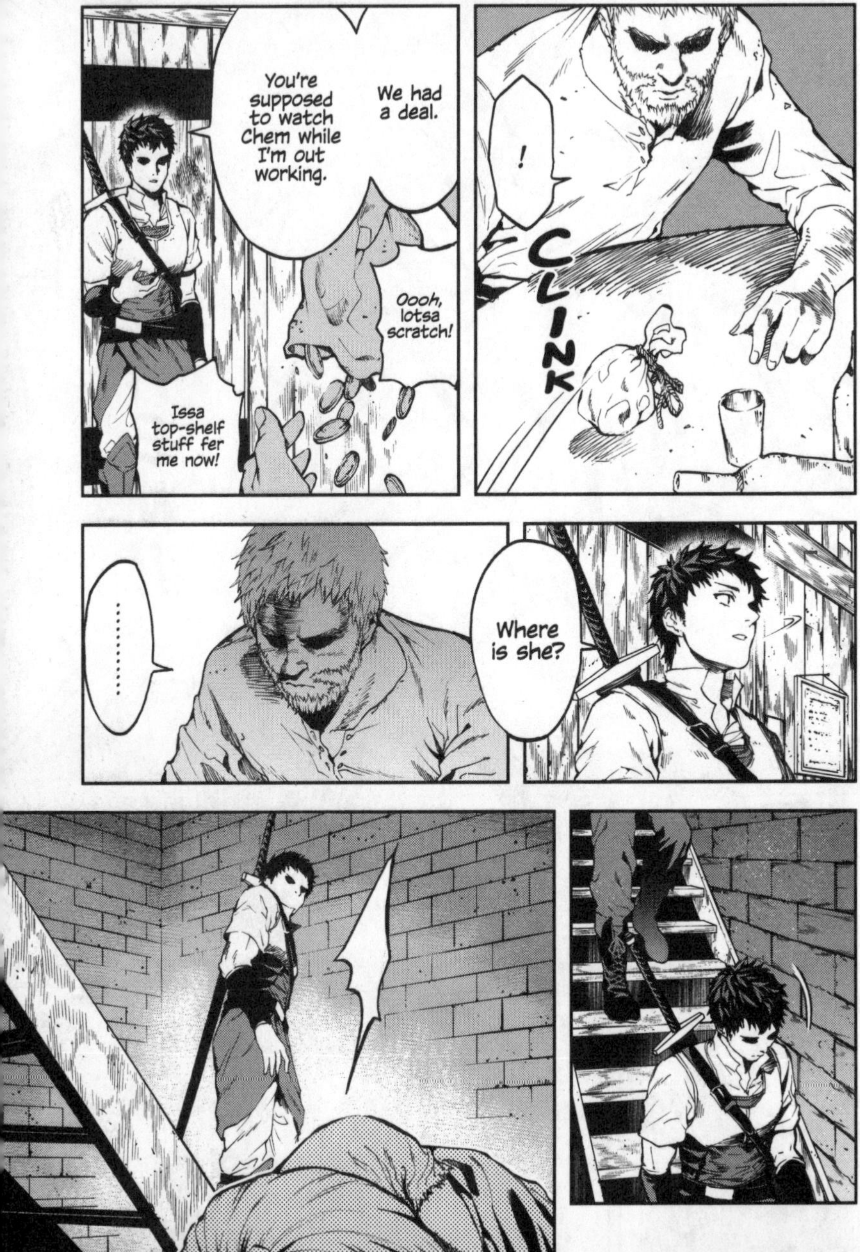
!
CLINK
We had a deal.
You're supposed to watch Chem while I'm out working.
Oooh, lotsa scratch!
Issa top-shelf stuff fer me now!
Where is she?
....

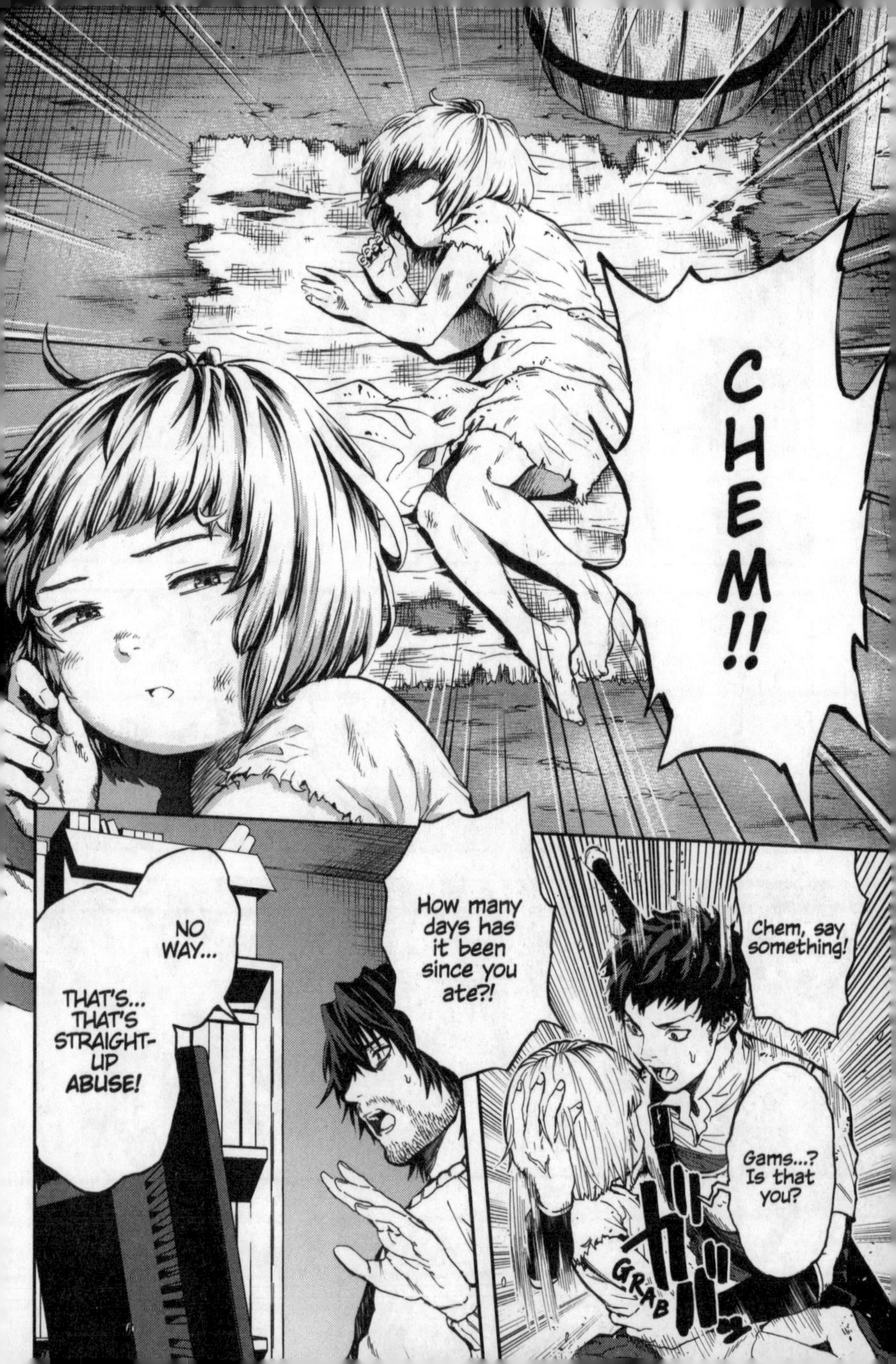
CHEM!!
Chem, say something!
Gams...? Is that you?
GRAB
How many days has it been since you ate?!
NO WAY...
THAT'S... THAT'S STRAIGHT-UP ABUSE!

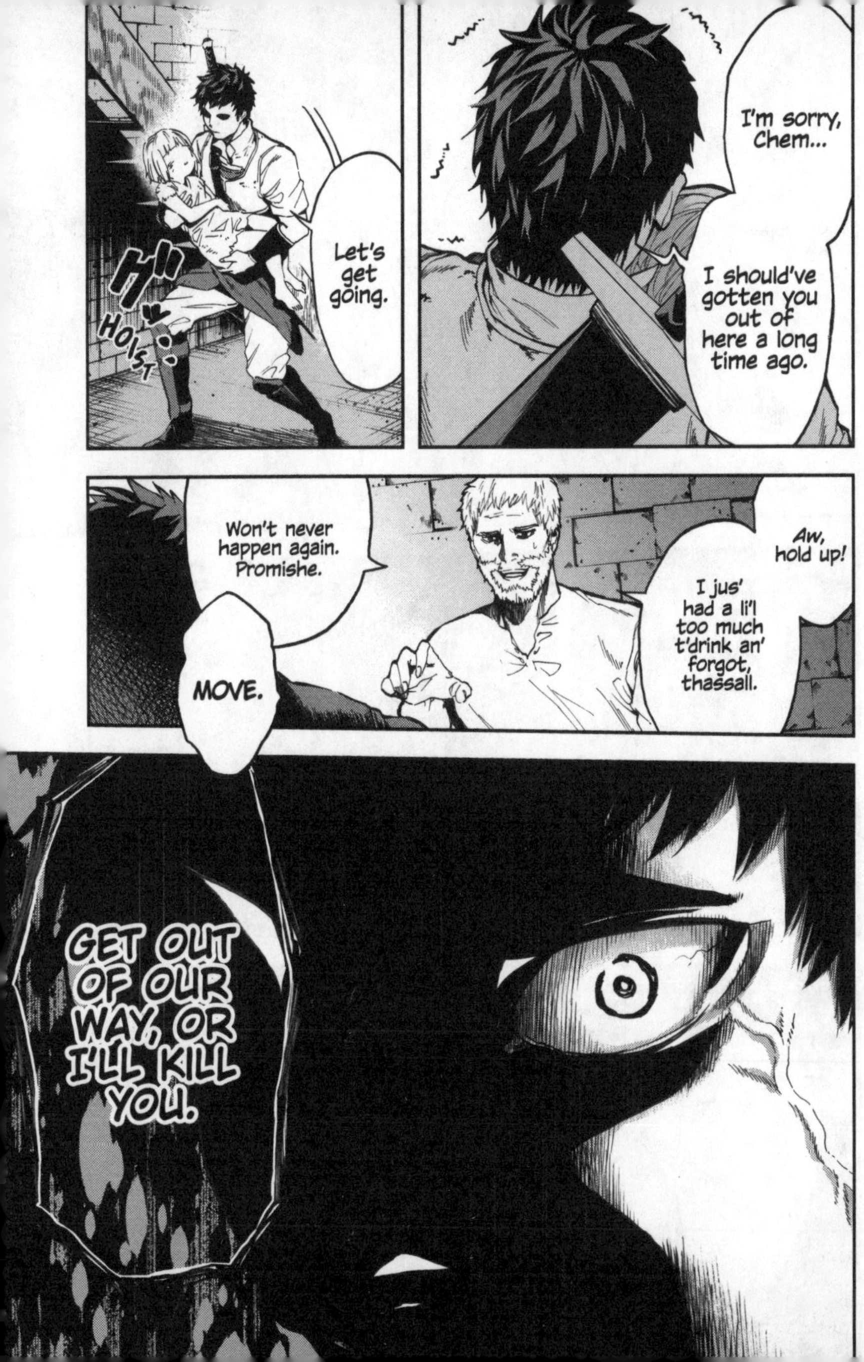
I'm sorry, Chem...
I should've gotten you out of here a long time ago.
HOIST
Let's get going.
Aw, hold up!
I jus' had a li'l too much t'drink an' forgot, thassall.
Won't never happen again. Promishe.
MOVE.
GET OUT OF OUR WAY, OR I'LL KILL YOU.

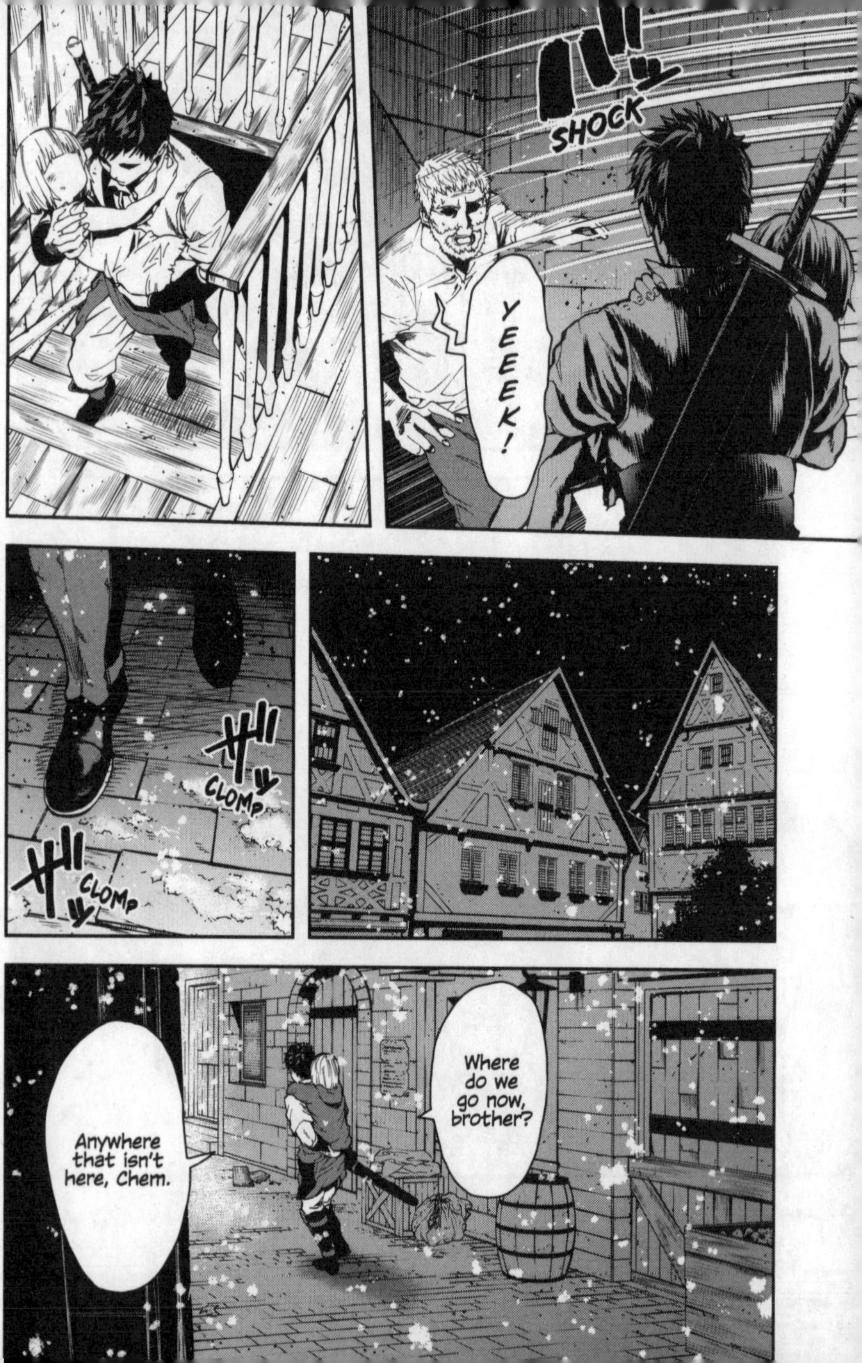
SHOCK
YEEEEK!
CLOMP
CLOMP
Where do we go now, brother?
Anywhere that isn't here, Chem.

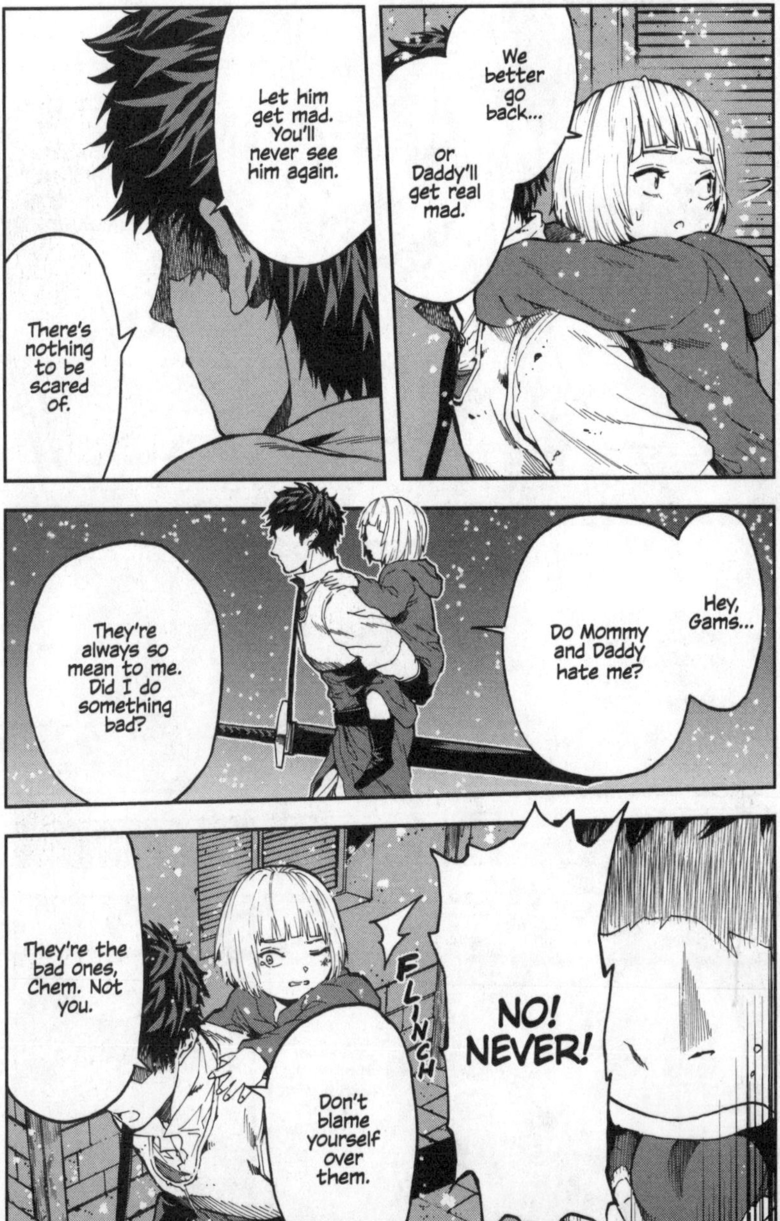
We better go back...
or Daddy'll get real mad.
Let him get mad. You'll never see him again.
There's nothing to be scared of.
Hey, Gams...
Do Mommy and Daddy hate me?
They're always so mean to me. Did I do something bad?
NO! NEVER!
FLINCH
They're the bad ones, Chem. Not you.
Don't blame yourself over them.

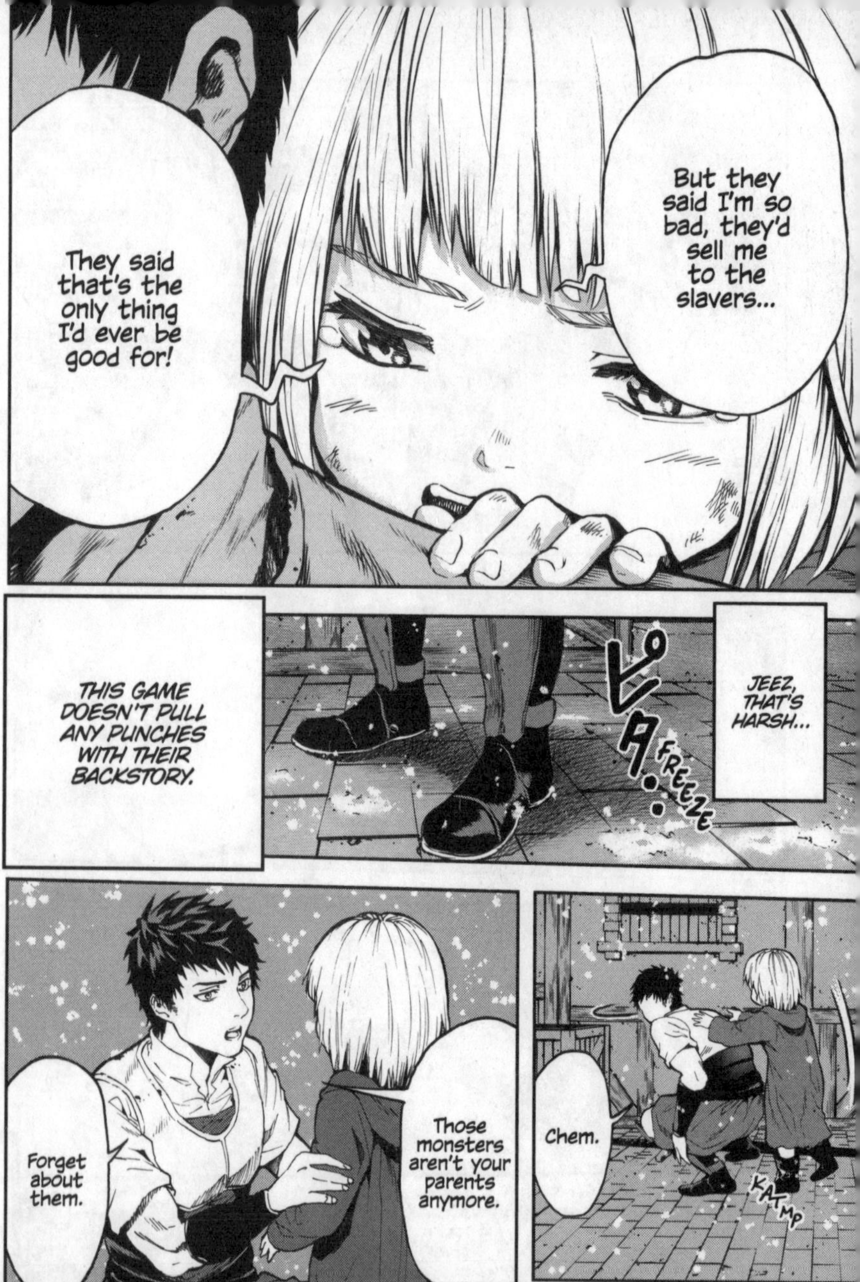
But they said I'm so bad, they'd sell me to the slavers...
They said that's the only thing I'd ever be good for!
JEEZ, THAT'S HARSH...
ピタ
FREEZE
THIS GAME DOESN'T PULL ANY PUNCHES WITH THEIR BACKSTORY.
Chem.
KATMP
Those monsters aren't your parents anymore.
Forget about them.

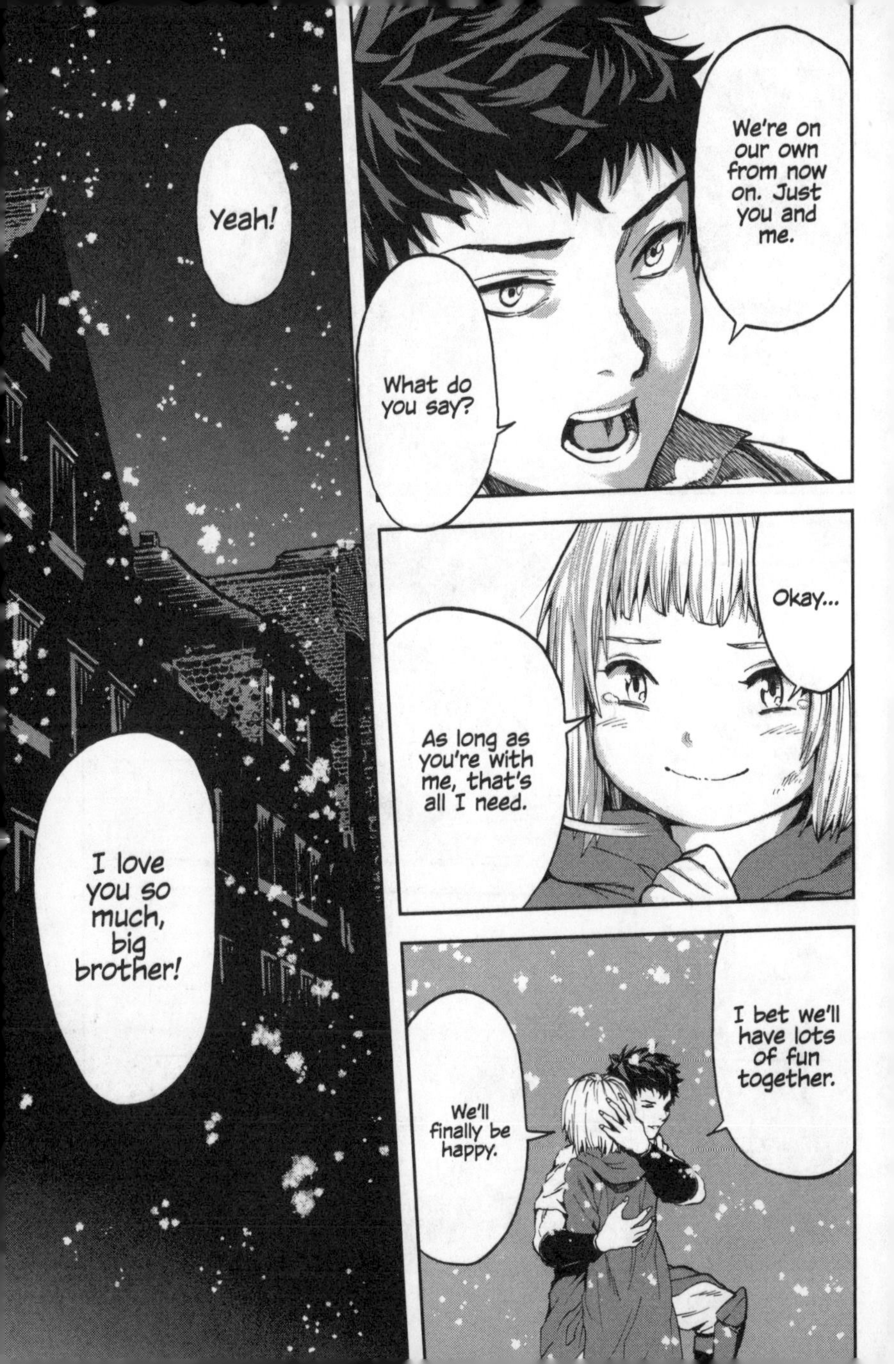
We're on our own from now on. Just you and me.
What do you say?
Okay...
As long as you're with me, that's all I need.
I bet we'll have lots of fun together.
We'll finally be happy.
Yeah!
I love you so much, big brother!

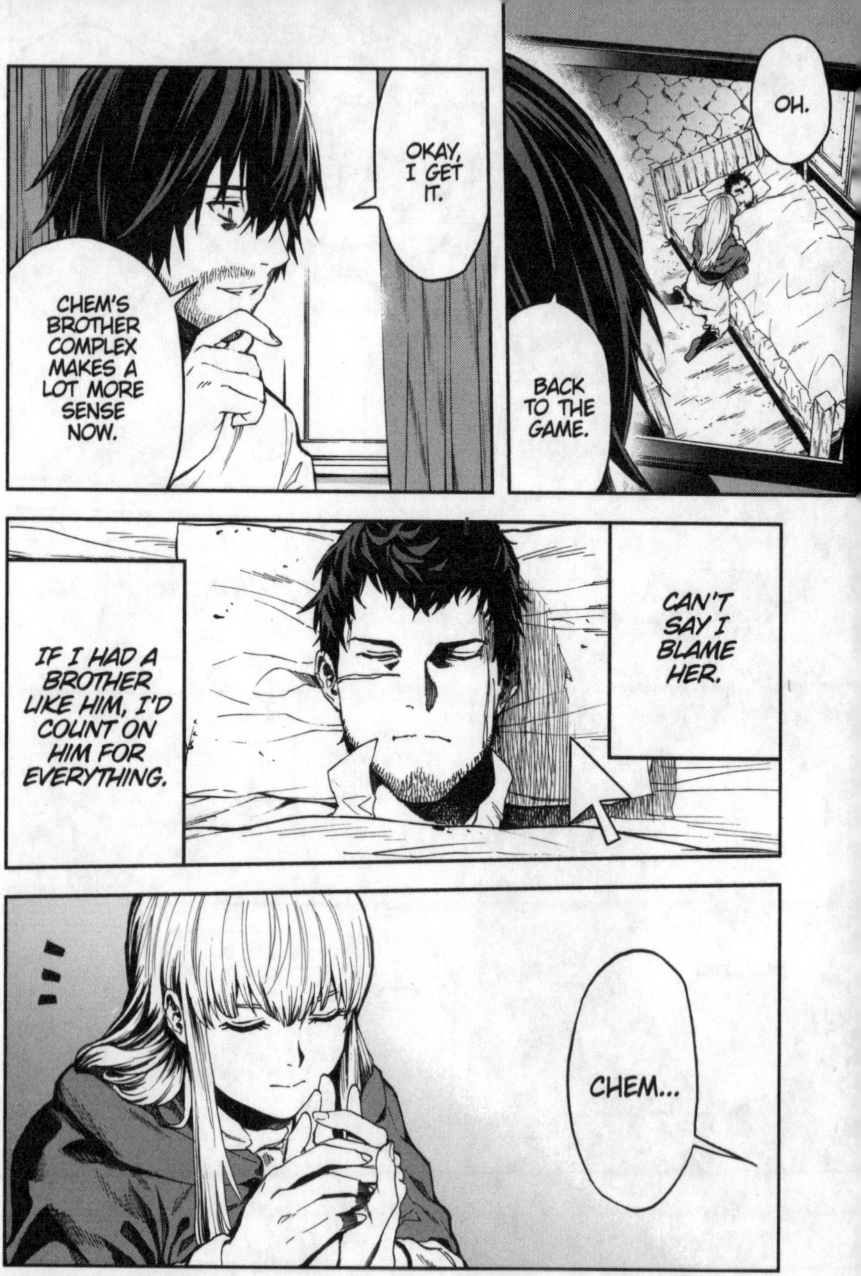
OH.
BACK TO THE GAME.
OKAY, I GET IT.
CHEM'S BROTHER COMPLEX MAKES A LOT MORE SENSE NOW.
CAN'T SAY I BLAME HER.
IF I HAD A BROTHER LIKE HIM, I'D COUNT ON HIM FOR EVERYTHING.
CHEM...

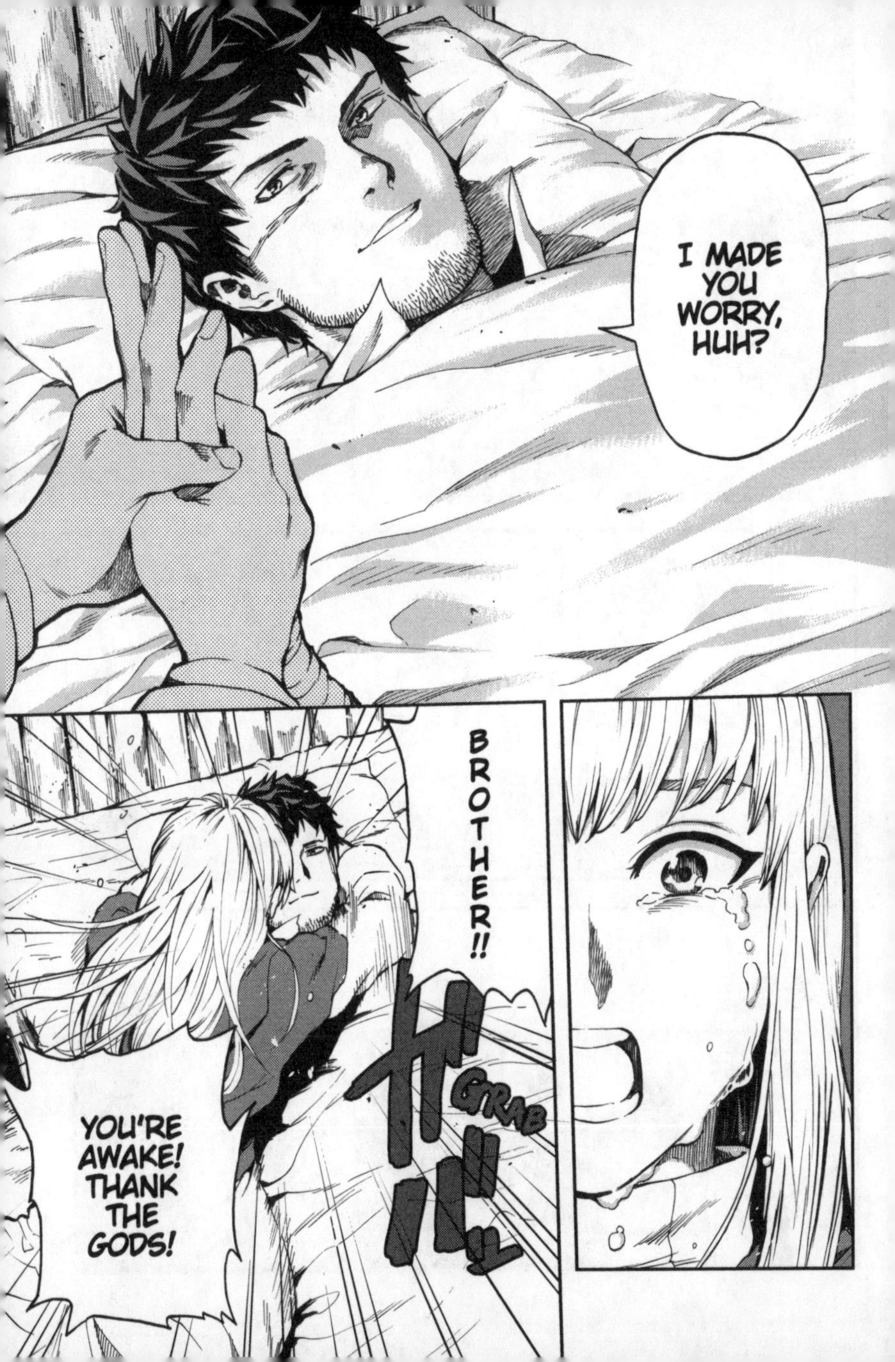
I MADE YOU WORRY, HUH?
BROTHER!!
GRAB
YOU'RE AWAKE! THANK THE GODS!

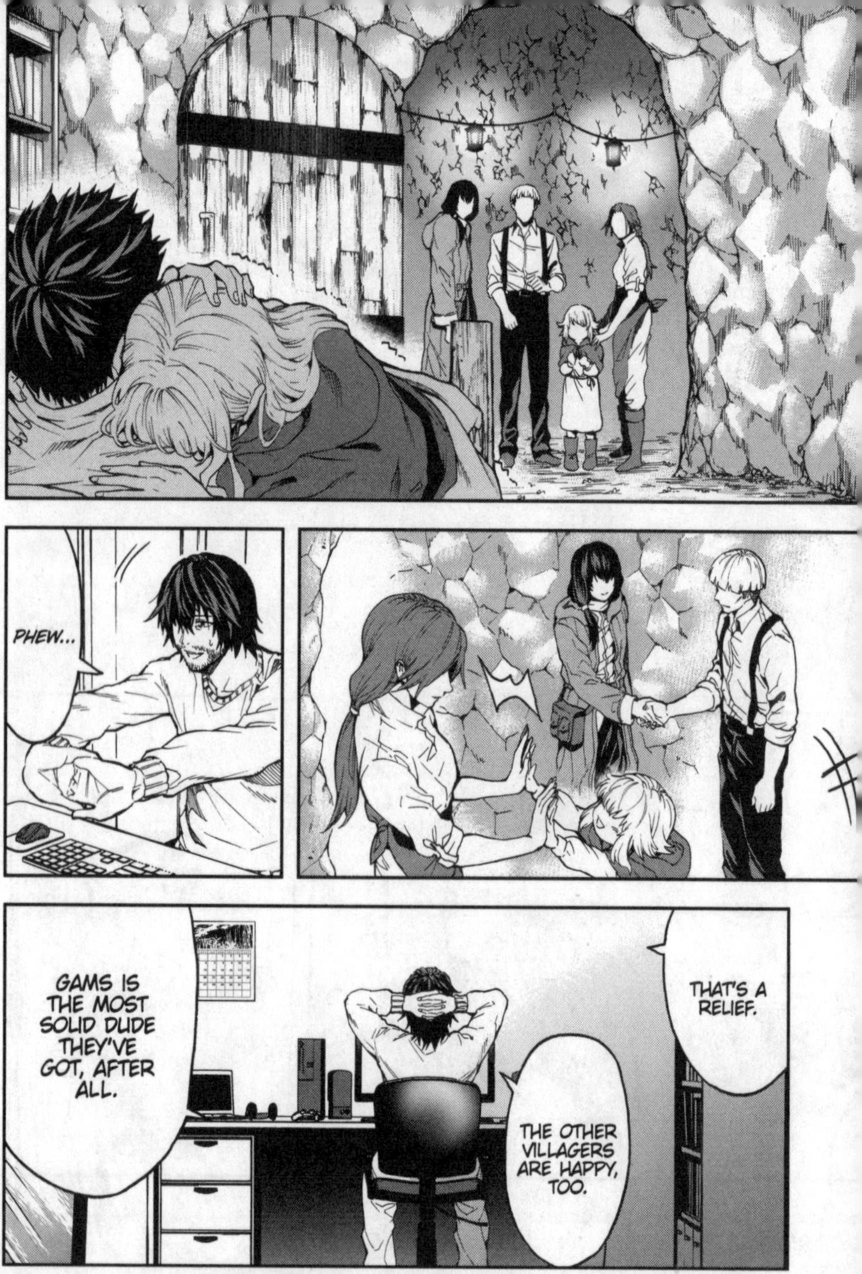
PHEW...
THAT'S A RELIEF.
THE OTHER VILLAGERS ARE HAPPY, TOO.
GAMS IS THE MOST SOLID DUDE THEY'VE GOT, AFTER ALL.

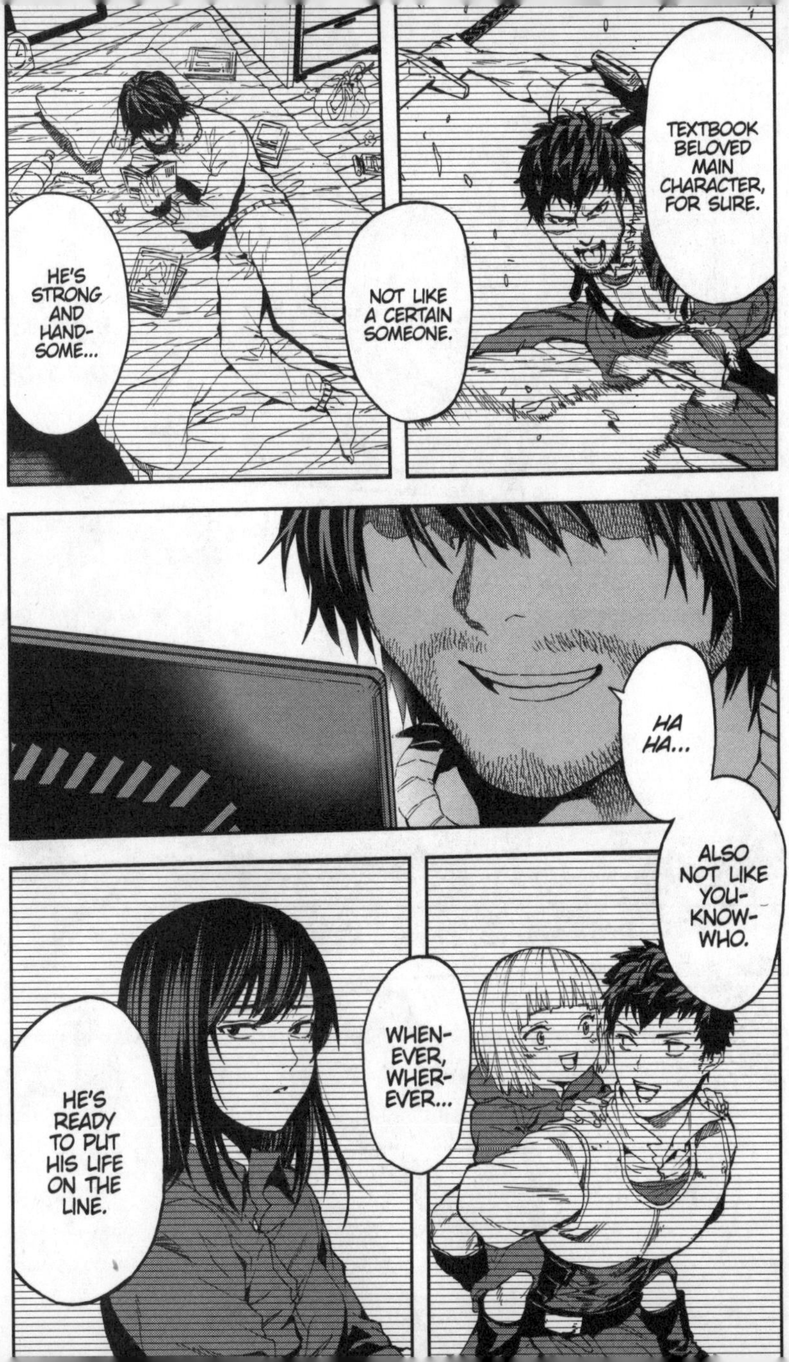
TEXTBOOK BELOVED MAIN CHARACTER, FOR SURE.
NOT LIKE A CERTAIN SOMEONE.
HE'S STRONG AND HAND-SOME...
HA HA...
ALSO NOT LIKE YOU-KNOW-WHO.
WHEN-EVER, WHER-EVER...
HE'S READY TO PUT HIS LIFE ON THE LINE.

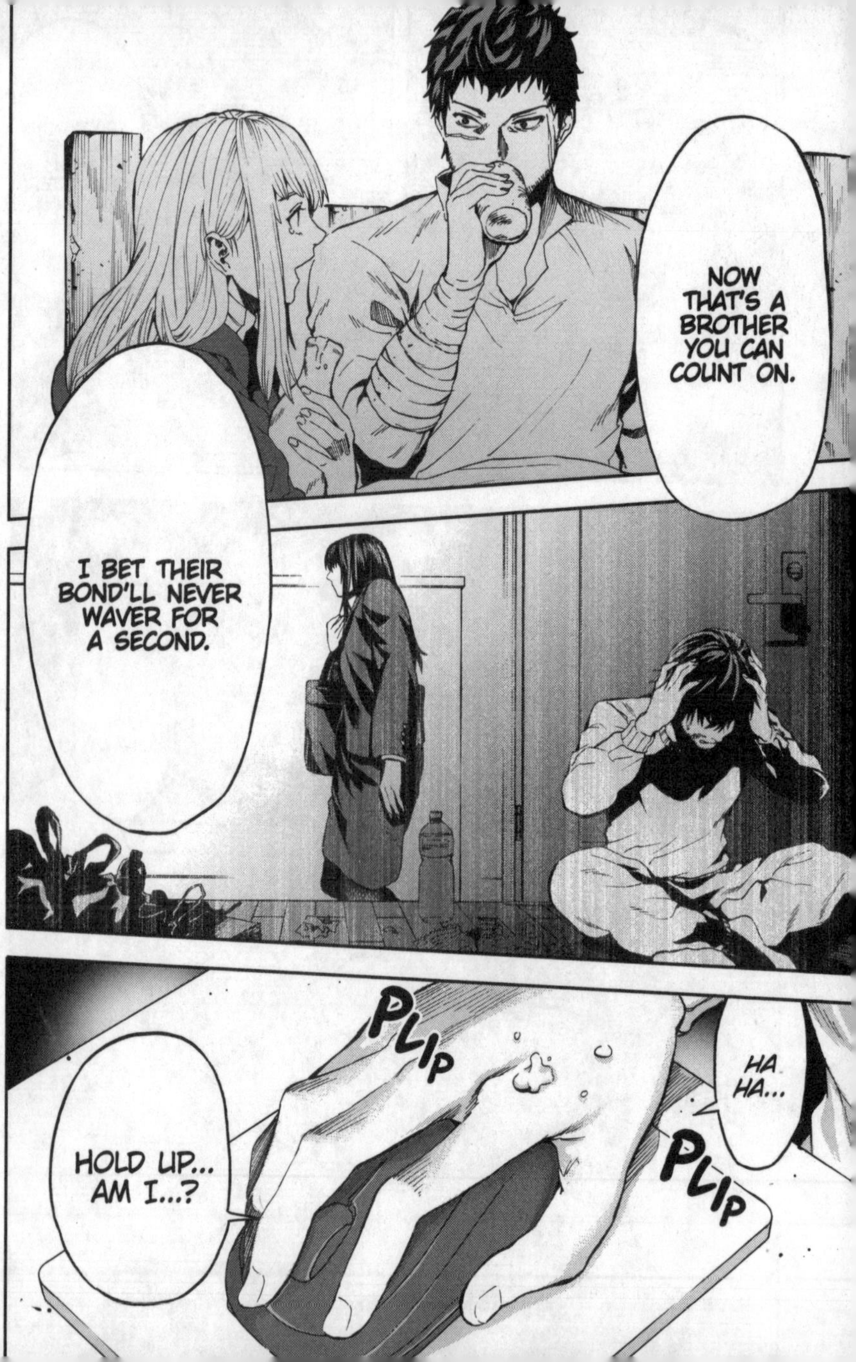
NOW THAT'S A BROTHER YOU CAN COUNT ON.
I BET THEIR BOND'LL NEVER WAVER FOR A SECOND.
HA HA...
PLIP
PLIP
HOLD UP... AM I...?

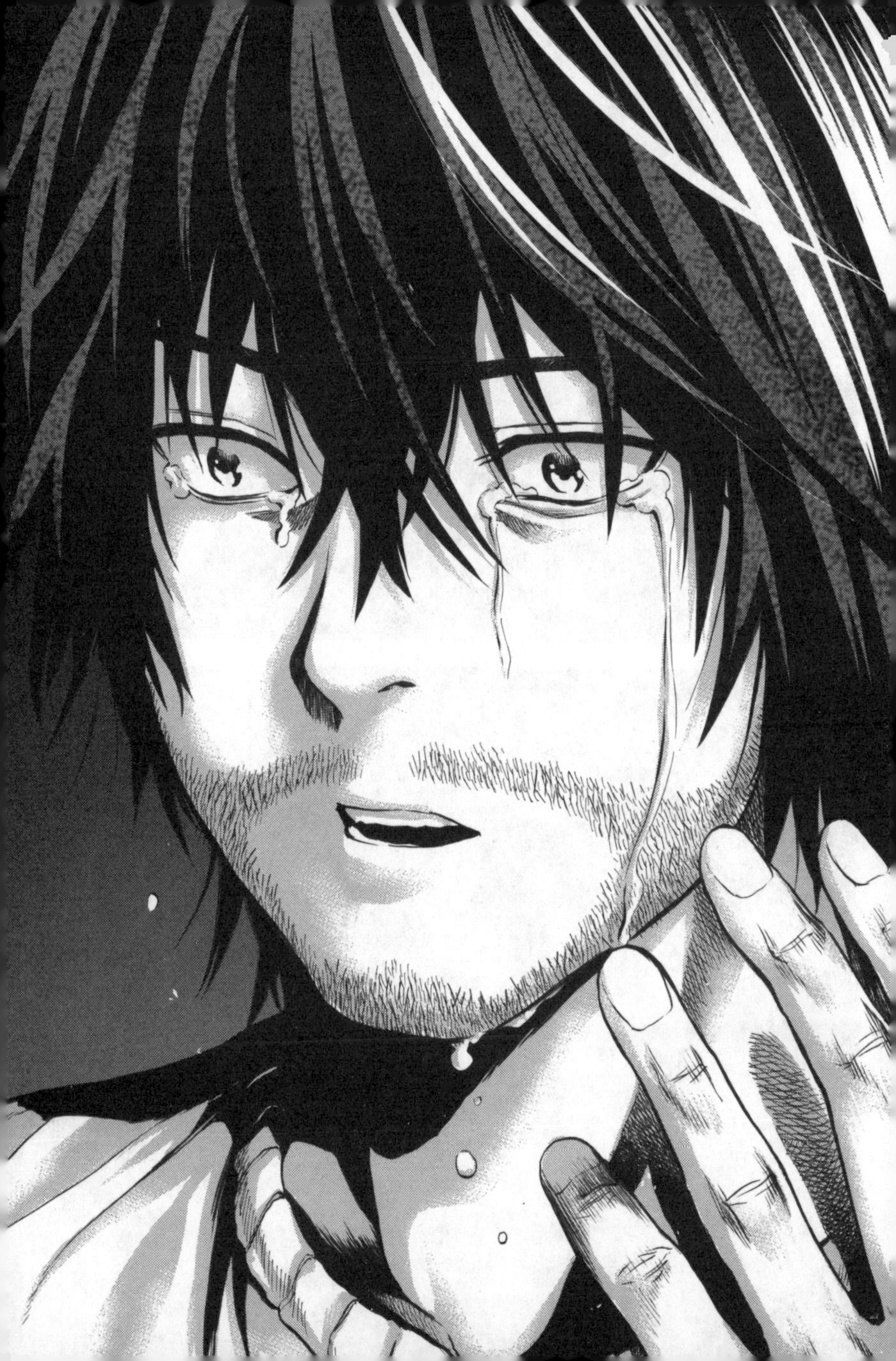

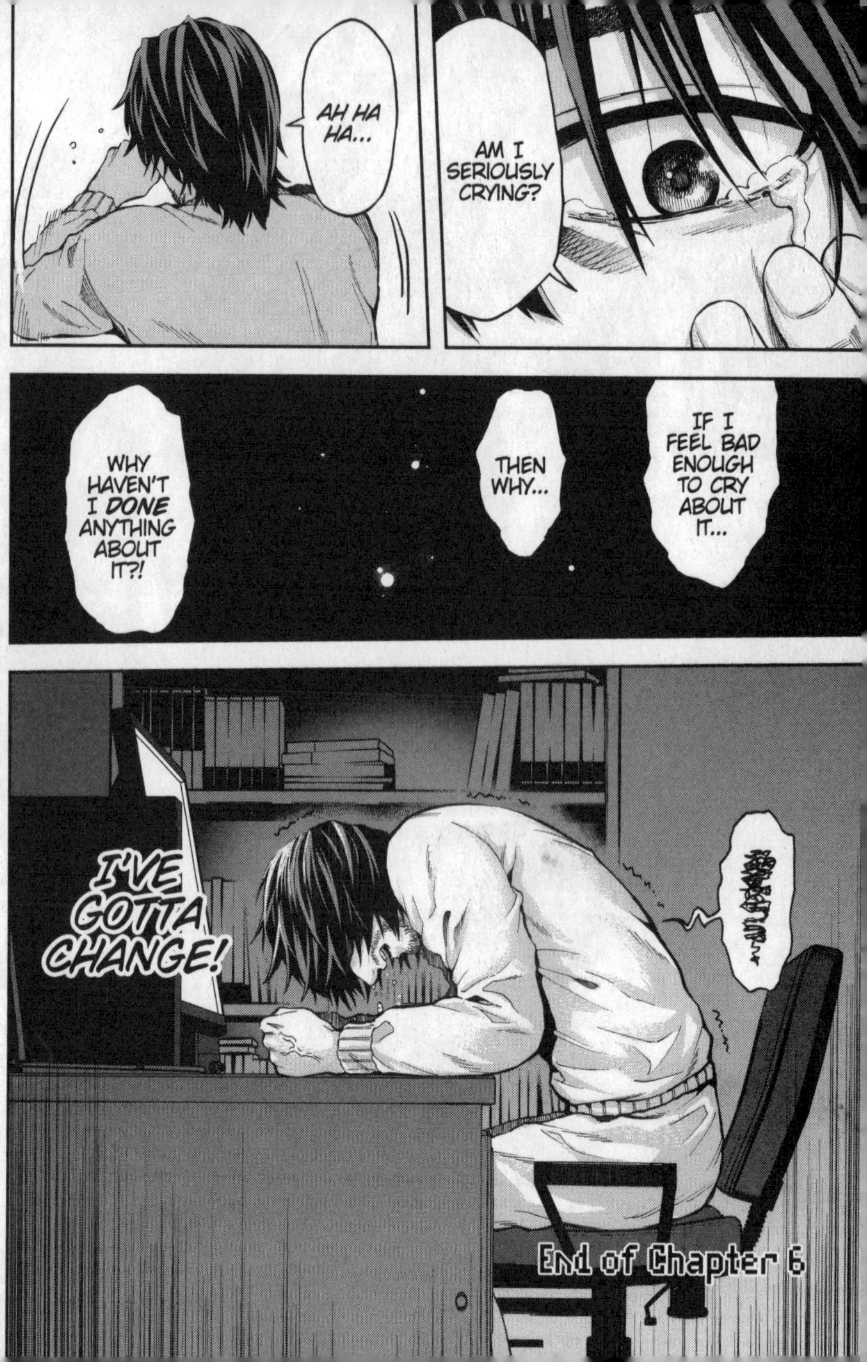
AM I SERIOUSLY CRYING?
AH HA HA...
IF I FEEL BAD ENOUGH TO CRY ABOUT IT...
THEN WHY...
WHY HAVEN'T I *DONE* ANYTHING ABOUT IT?!
I'VE GOTTA CHANGE!
End of Chapter 6

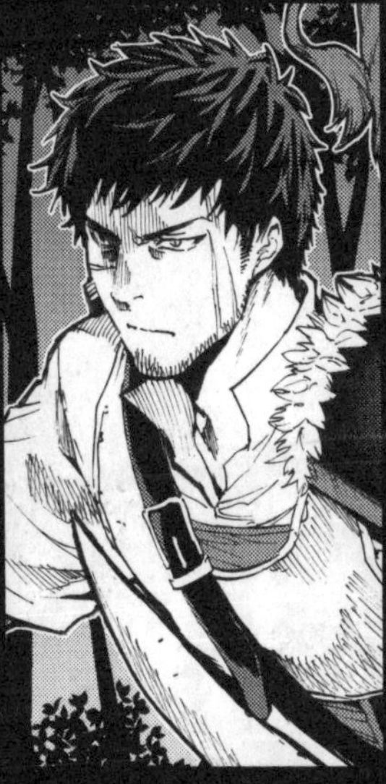

Character

Gams

▶ Gender: Male

Class: Swordsman

E : Longsword

E : Leather Armor

E : Brotherly Love

THE NPCs IN THIS VILLAGE SIM GAME MUST BE REAL!

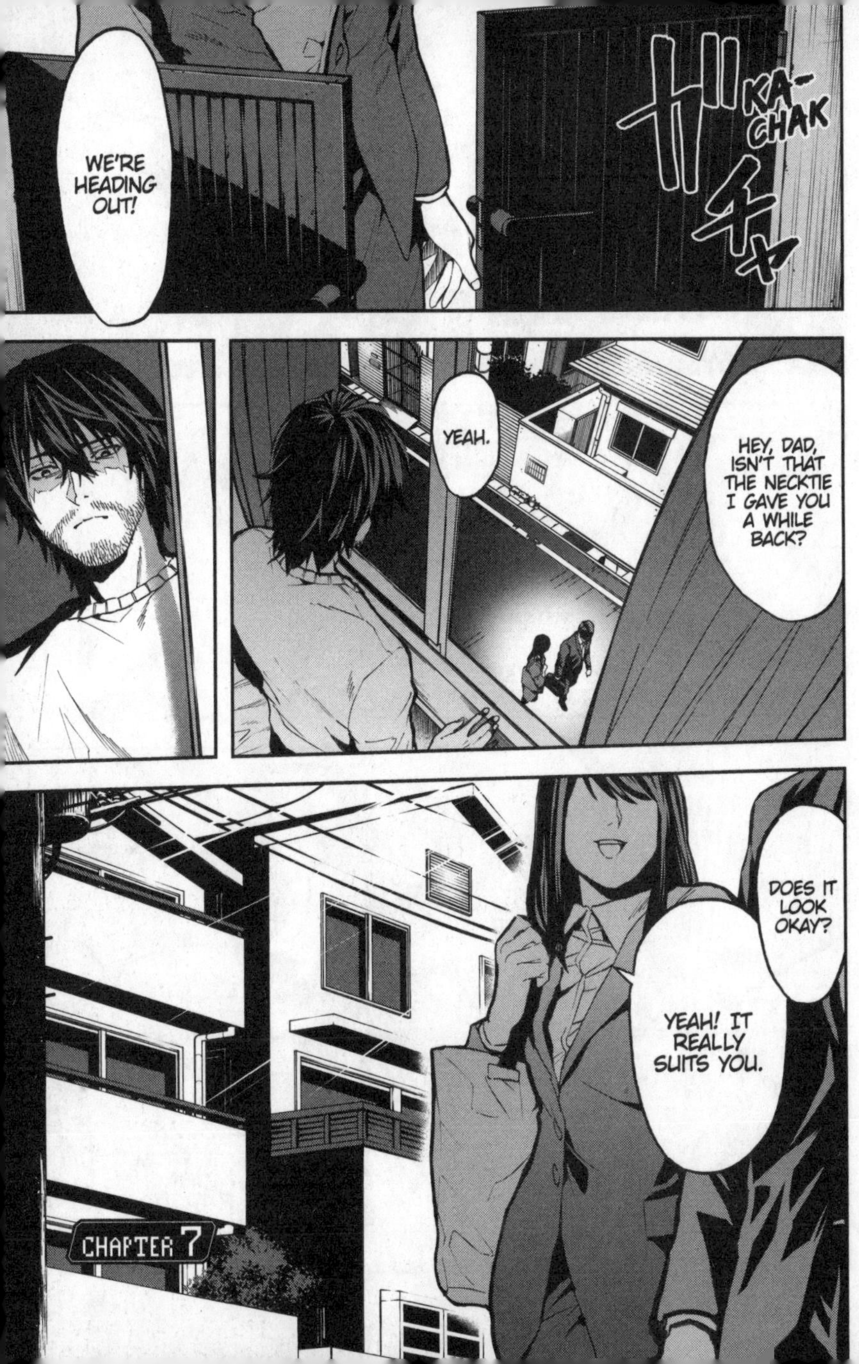
KA-CHAK
WE'RE HEADING OUT!
HEY, DAD, ISN'T THAT THE NECKTIE I GAVE YOU A WHILE BACK?
YEAH.
DOES IT LOOK OKAY?
YEAH! IT REALLY SUITS YOU.
CHAPTER 7

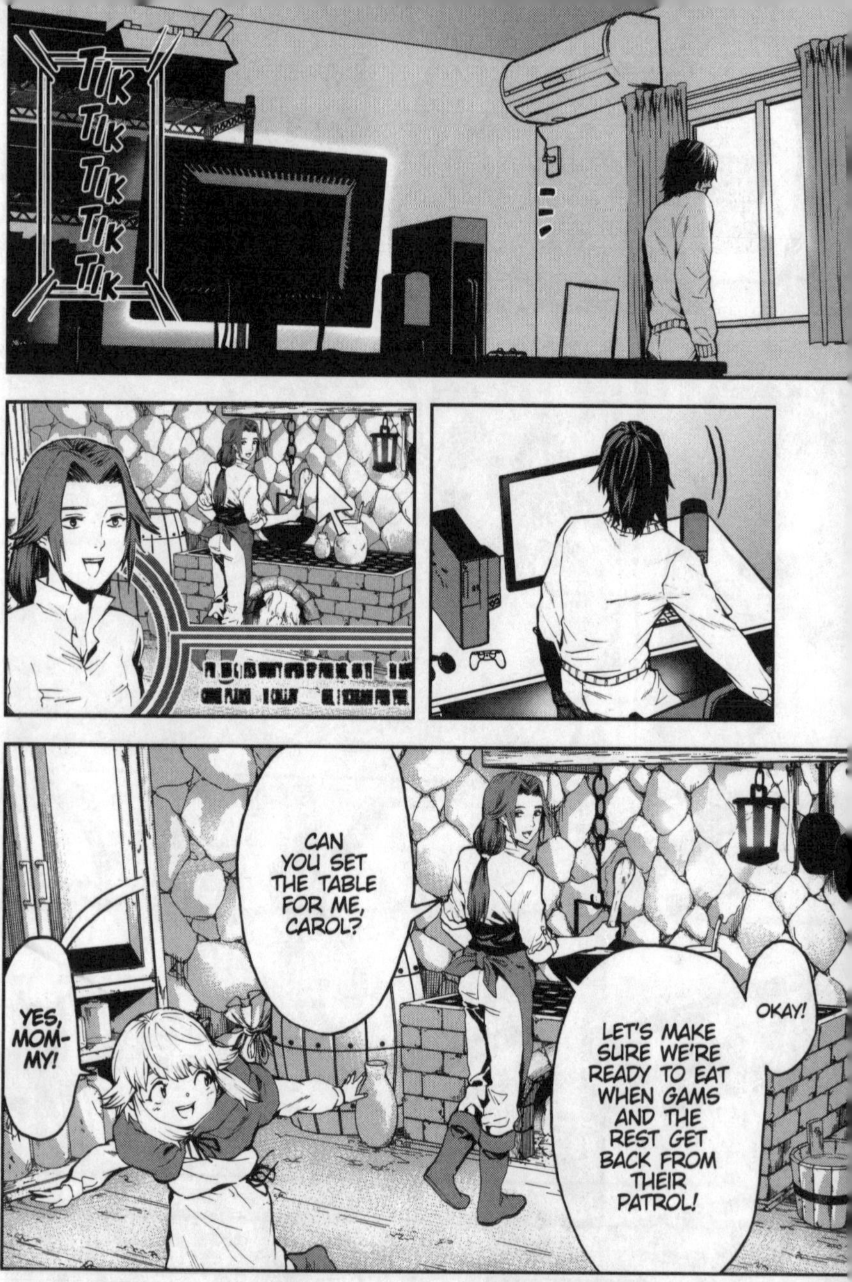
TIK
TIK
TIK
TIK
TIK
CAN YOU SET THE TABLE FOR ME, CAROL?
YES, MOM-MY!
OKAY!
LET'S MAKE SURE WE'RE READY TO EAT WHEN GAMS AND THE REST GET BACK FROM THEIR PATROL!

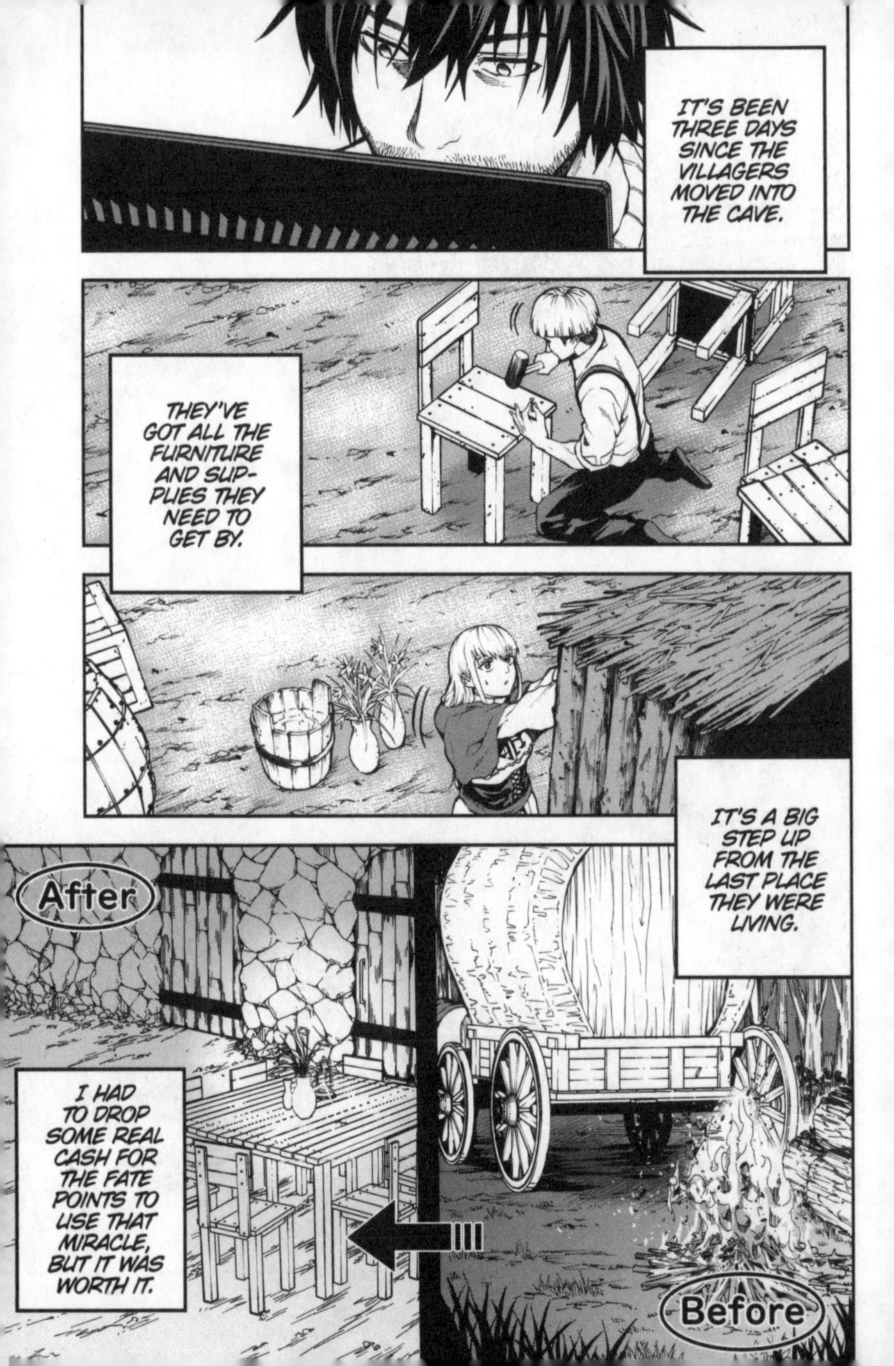
IT'S BEEN THREE DAYS SINCE THE VILLAGERS MOVED INTO THE CAVE.
THEY'VE GOT ALL THE FURNITURE AND SUPPLIES THEY NEED TO GET BY.
IT'S A BIG STEP UP FROM THE LAST PLACE THEY WERE LIVING.
Before
After
I HAD TO DROP SOME REAL CASH FOR THE FATE POINTS TO USE THAT MIRACLE, BUT IT WAS WORTH IT.

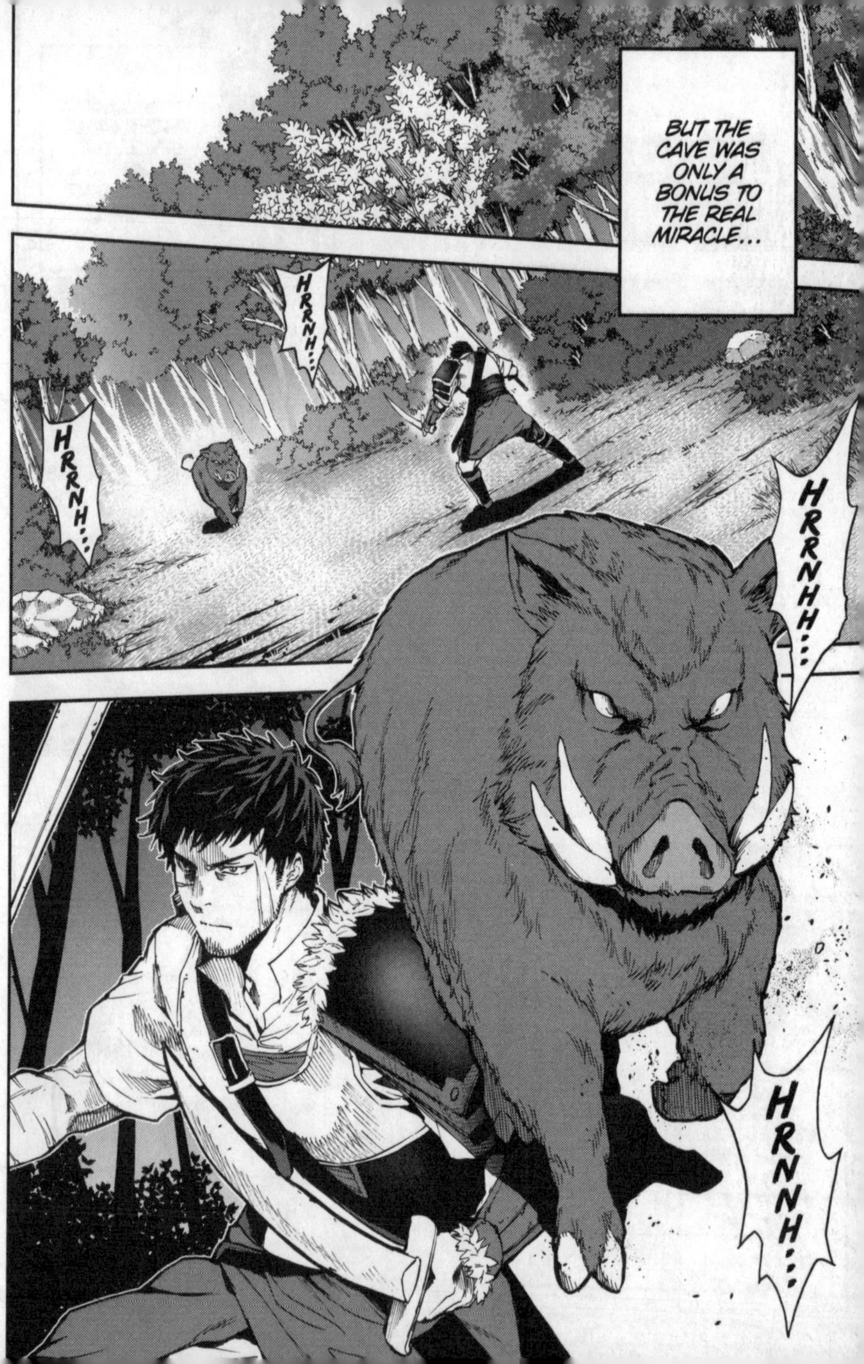

BUT THE CAVE WAS ONLY A BONUS TO THE REAL MIRACLE...
HRRNH...
HRRNH...
HRRNHH...
HRNNH...

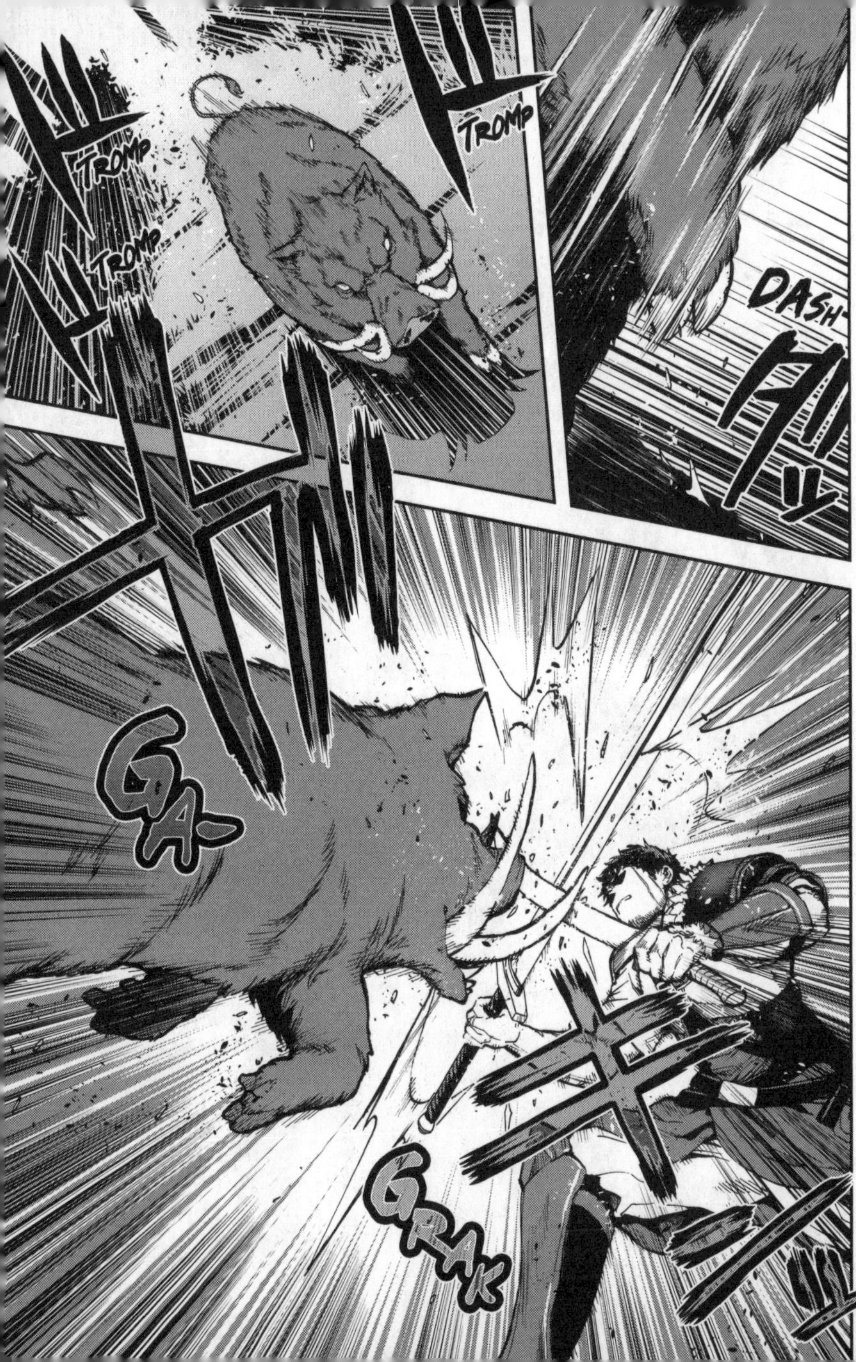
DASH
TROMP
TROMP
TROMP
GA
GRAK

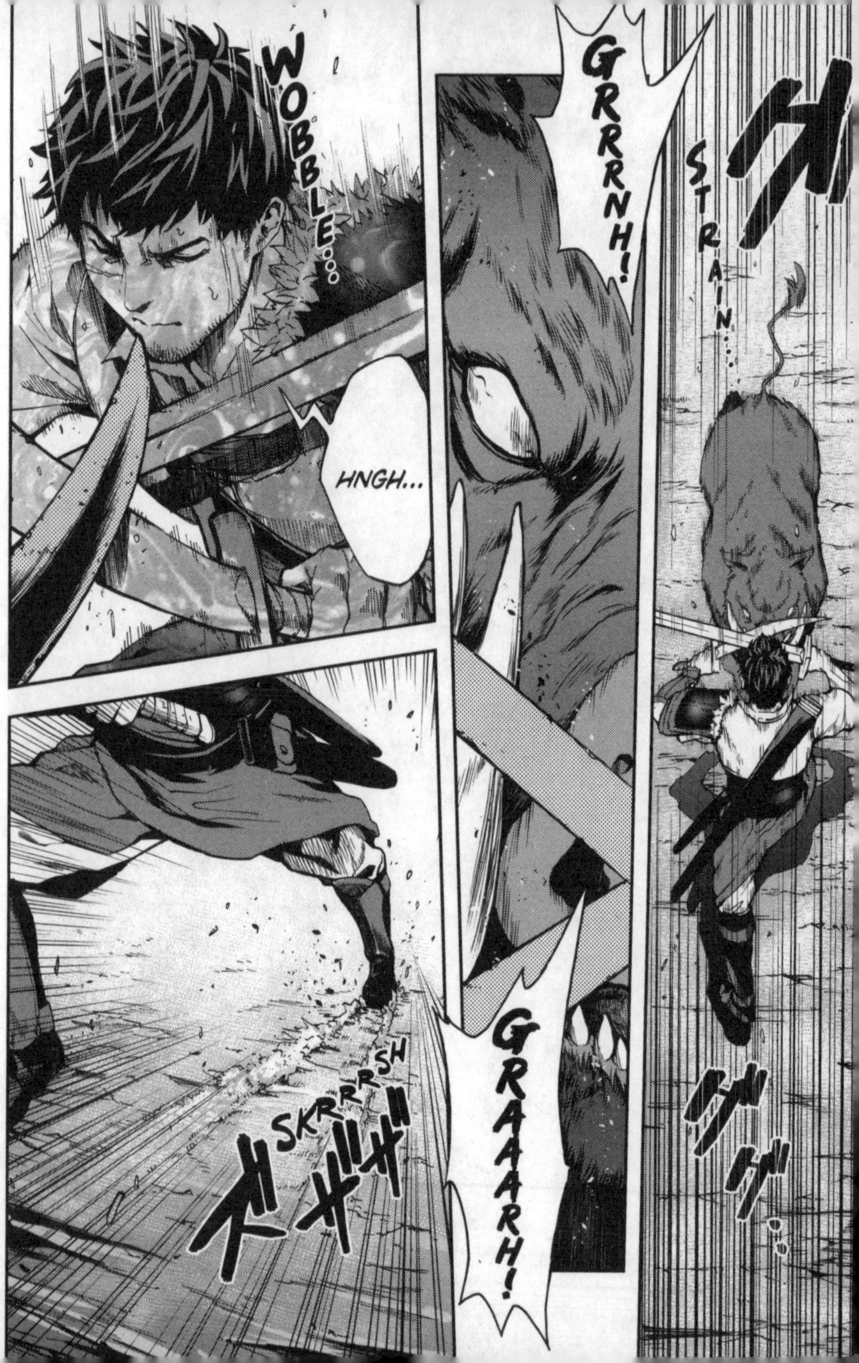
STRAIN...
GRRRNH!
GRAAAARH!
WOBBLE...
HNGH...
SKRRRSH

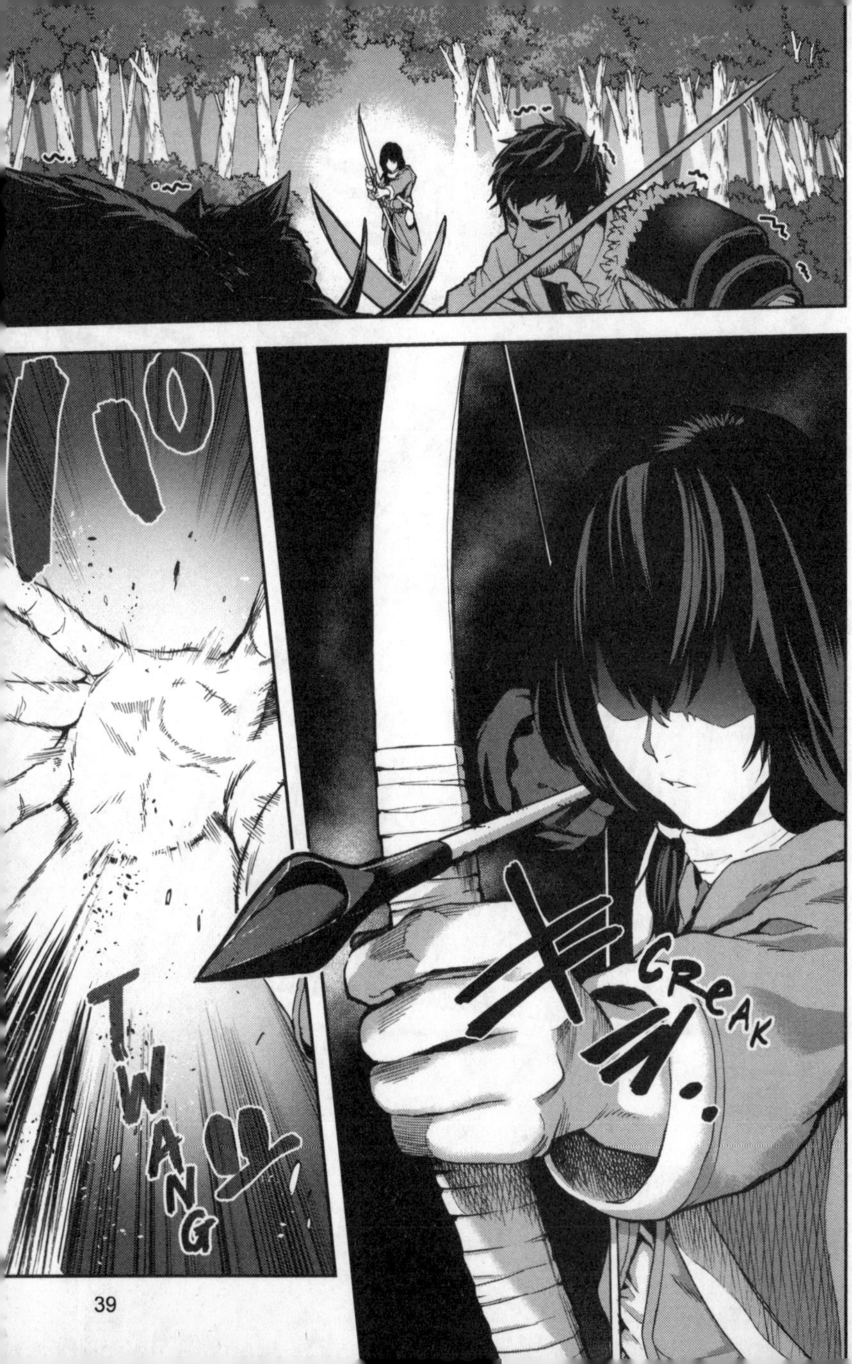
CREAK
TWANG

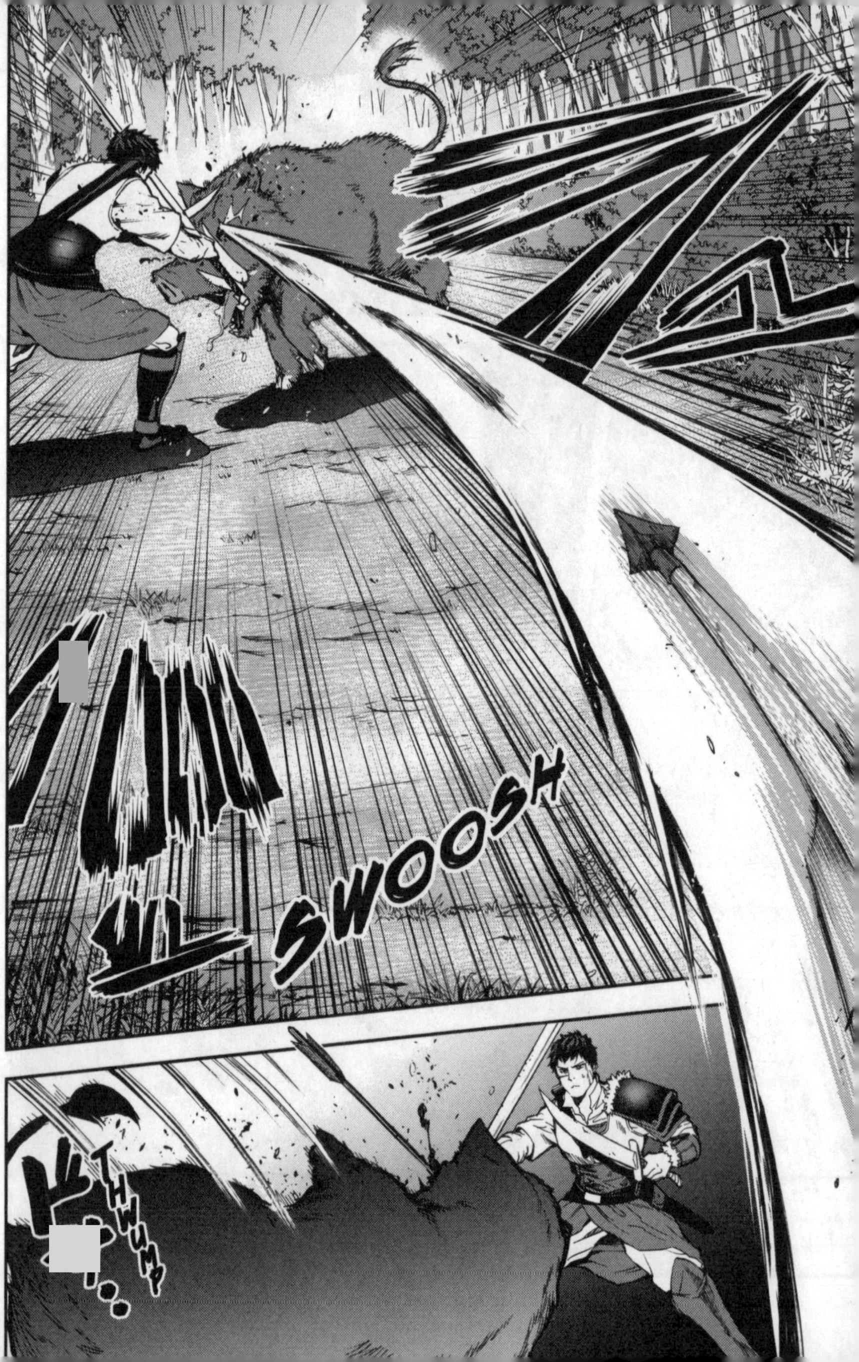
SWOOSH
THWUMP...

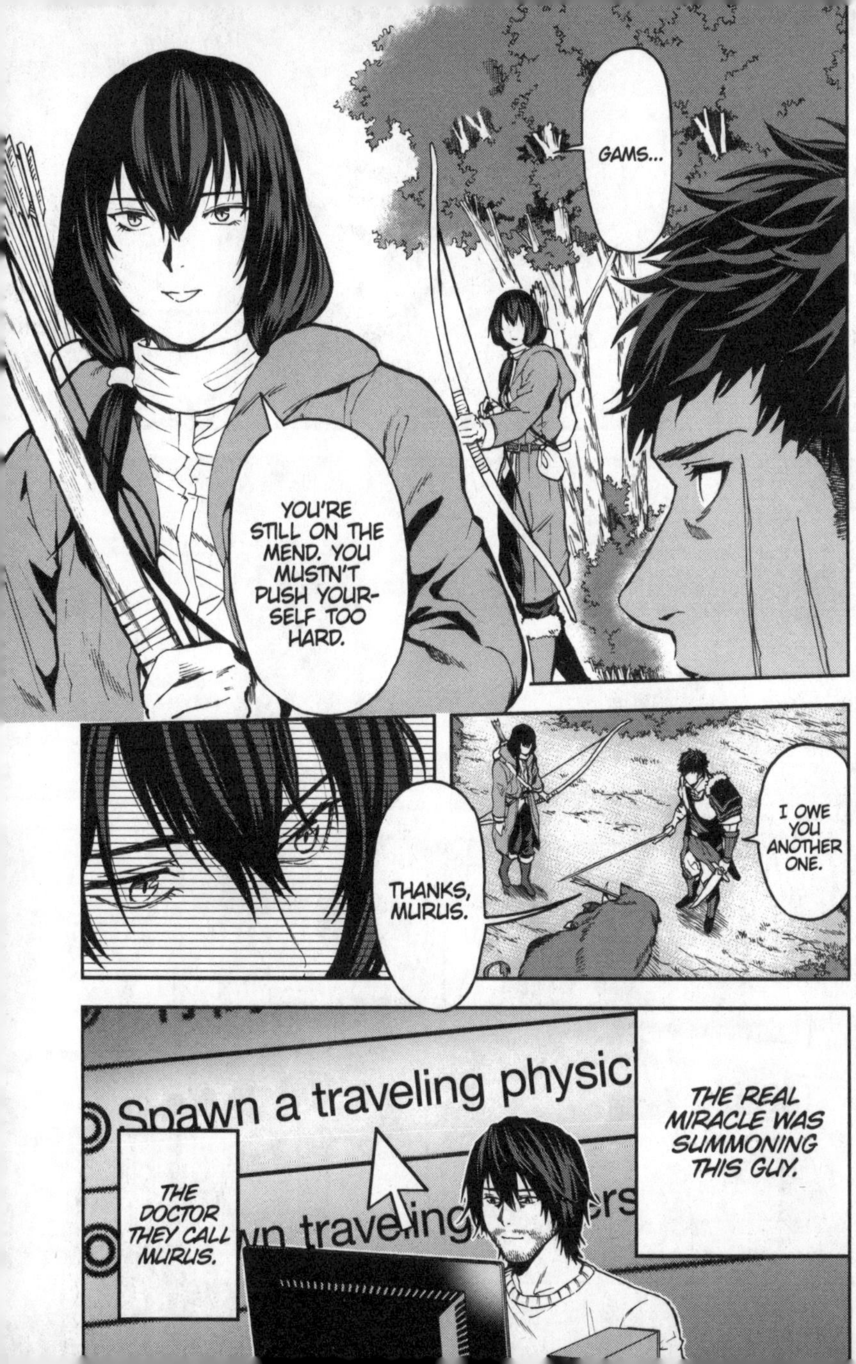
GAMS...
YOU'RE STILL ON THE MEND. YOU MUSTN'T PUSH YOURSELF TOO HARD.
I OWE YOU ANOTHER ONE.
THANKS, MURUS.
THE REAL MIRACLE WAS SUMMONING THIS GUY.
Spawn a traveling physic
wn traveling
THE DOCTOR THEY CALL MURUS.

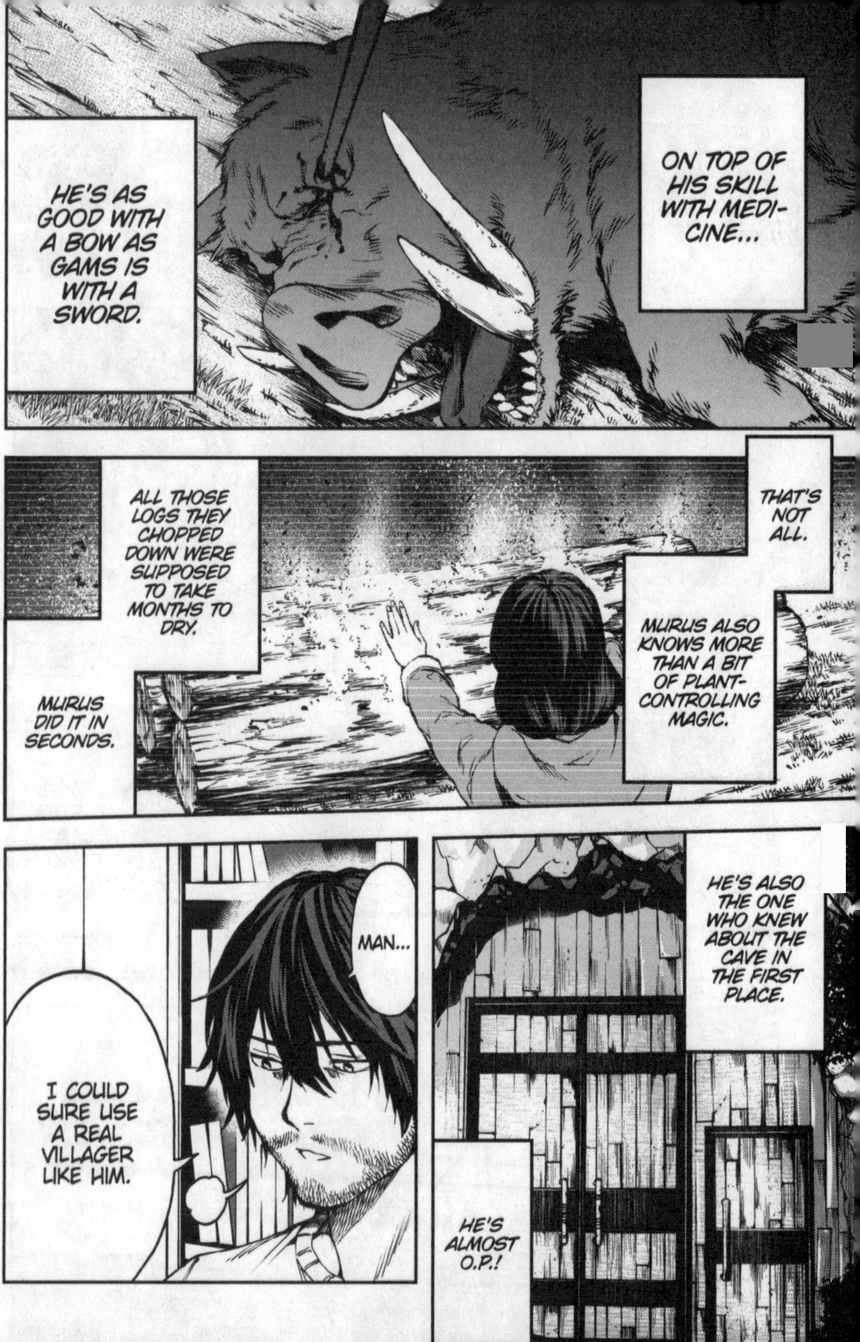
ON TOP OF HIS SKILL WITH MEDICINE...
HE'S AS GOOD WITH A BOW AS GAMS IS WITH A SWORD.
THAT'S NOT ALL.
MURUS ALSO KNOWS MORE THAN A BIT OF PLANT-CONTROLLING MAGIC.
ALL THOSE LOGS THEY CHOPPED DOWN WERE SUPPOSED TO TAKE MONTHS TO DRY.
MURUS DID IT IN SECONDS.
HE'S ALSO THE ONE WHO KNEW ABOUT THE CAVE IN THE FIRST PLACE.
HE'S ALMOST O.P.!
MAN...
I COULD SURE USE A REAL VILLAGER LIKE HIM.

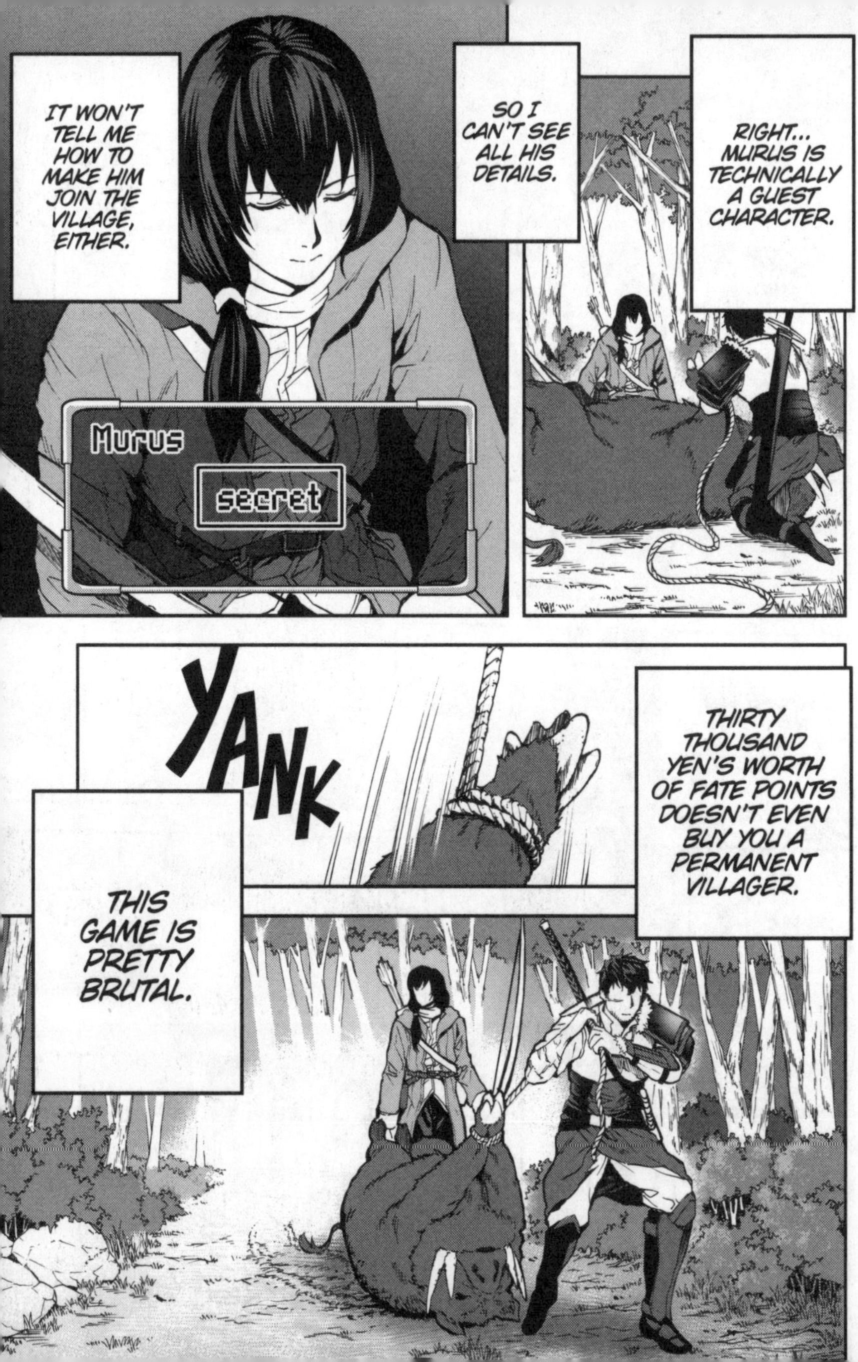
RIGHT... MURUS IS TECHNICALLY A GUEST CHARACTER.
SO I CAN'T SEE ALL HIS DETAILS.
IT WON'T TELL ME HOW TO MAKE HIM JOIN THE VILLAGE, EITHER.
Murus
secret
THIRTY THOUSAND YEN'S WORTH OF FATE POINTS DOESN'T EVEN BUY YOU A PERMANENT VILLAGER.
YANK
THIS GAME IS PRETTY BRUTAL.

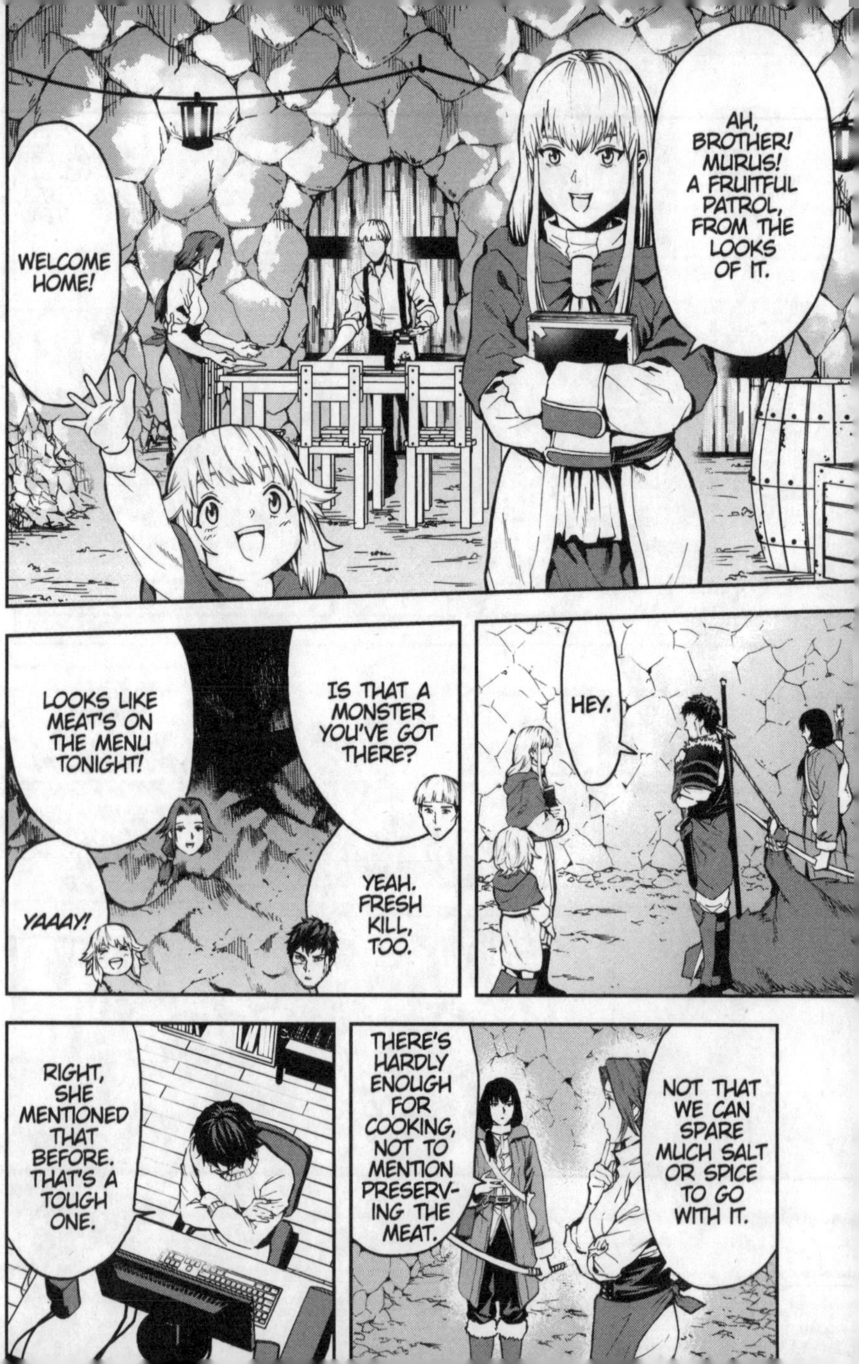
AH, BROTHER! MURUS! A FRUITFUL PATROL, FROM THE LOOKS OF IT.
WELCOME HOME!
HEY.
IS THAT A MONSTER YOU'VE GOT THERE?
LOOKS LIKE MEAT'S ON THE MENU TONIGHT!
YEAH. FRESH KILL, TOO.
YAAAY!
NOT THAT WE CAN SPARE MUCH SALT OR SPICE TO GO WITH IT.
THERE'S HARDLY ENOUGH FOR COOKING, NOT TO MENTION PRESERV-ING THE MEAT.
RIGHT, SHE MENTIONED THAT BEFORE. THAT'S A TOUGH ONE.

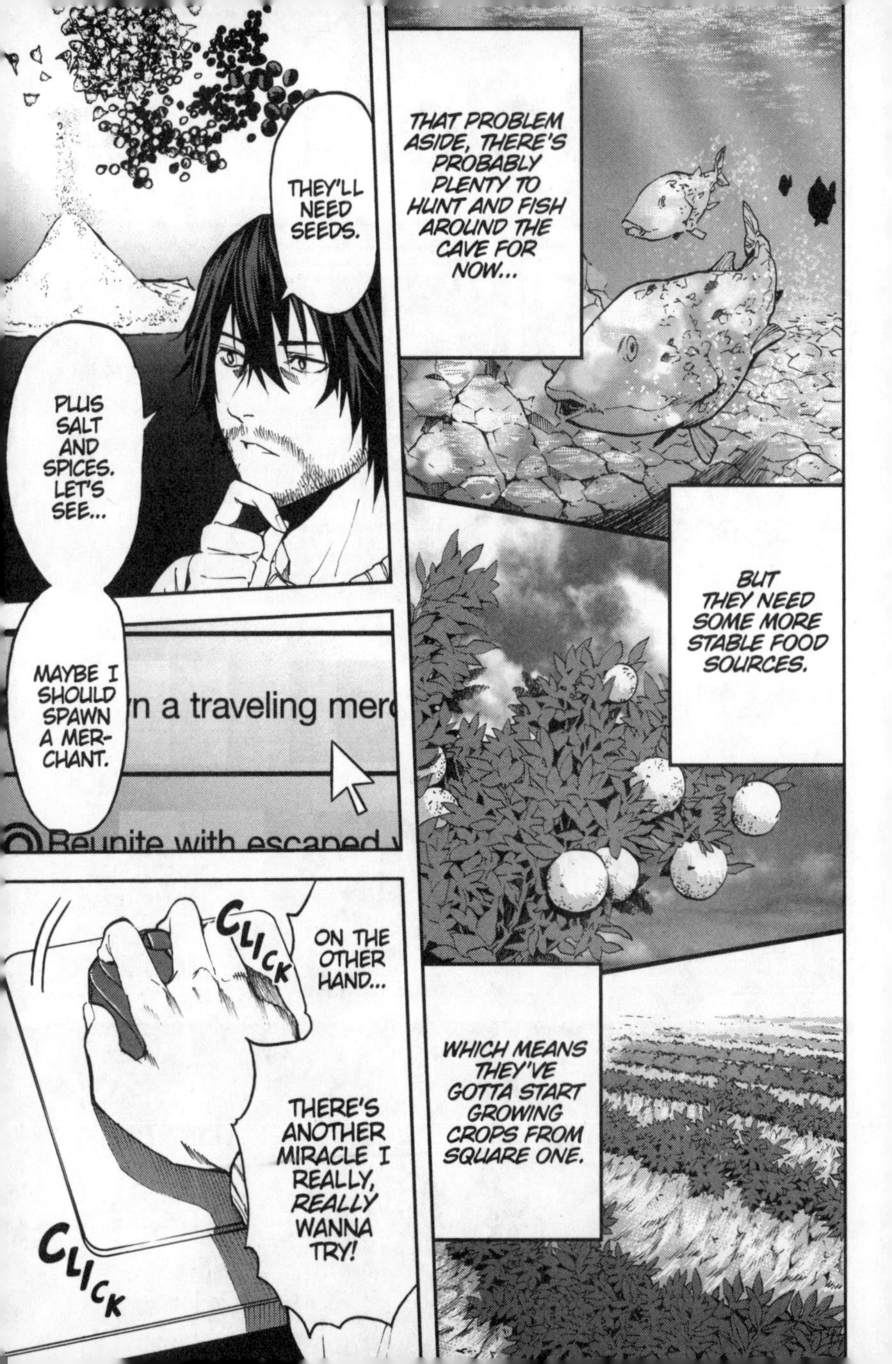

THAT PROBLEM ASIDE, THERE'S PROBABLY PLENTY TO HUNT AND FISH AROUND THE CAVE FOR NOW...
BUT THEY NEED SOME MORE STABLE FOOD SOURCES.
WHICH MEANS THEY'VE GOTTA START GROWING CROPS FROM SQUARE ONE.
THEY'LL NEED SEEDS.
PLUS SALT AND SPICES. LET'S SEE...
MAYBE I SHOULD SPAWN A MER-CHANT.
n a traveling merc
Reunite with escaped
CLICK
ON THE OTHER HAND...
THERE'S ANOTHER MIRACLE I REALLY, *REALLY* WANNA TRY!
CLICK

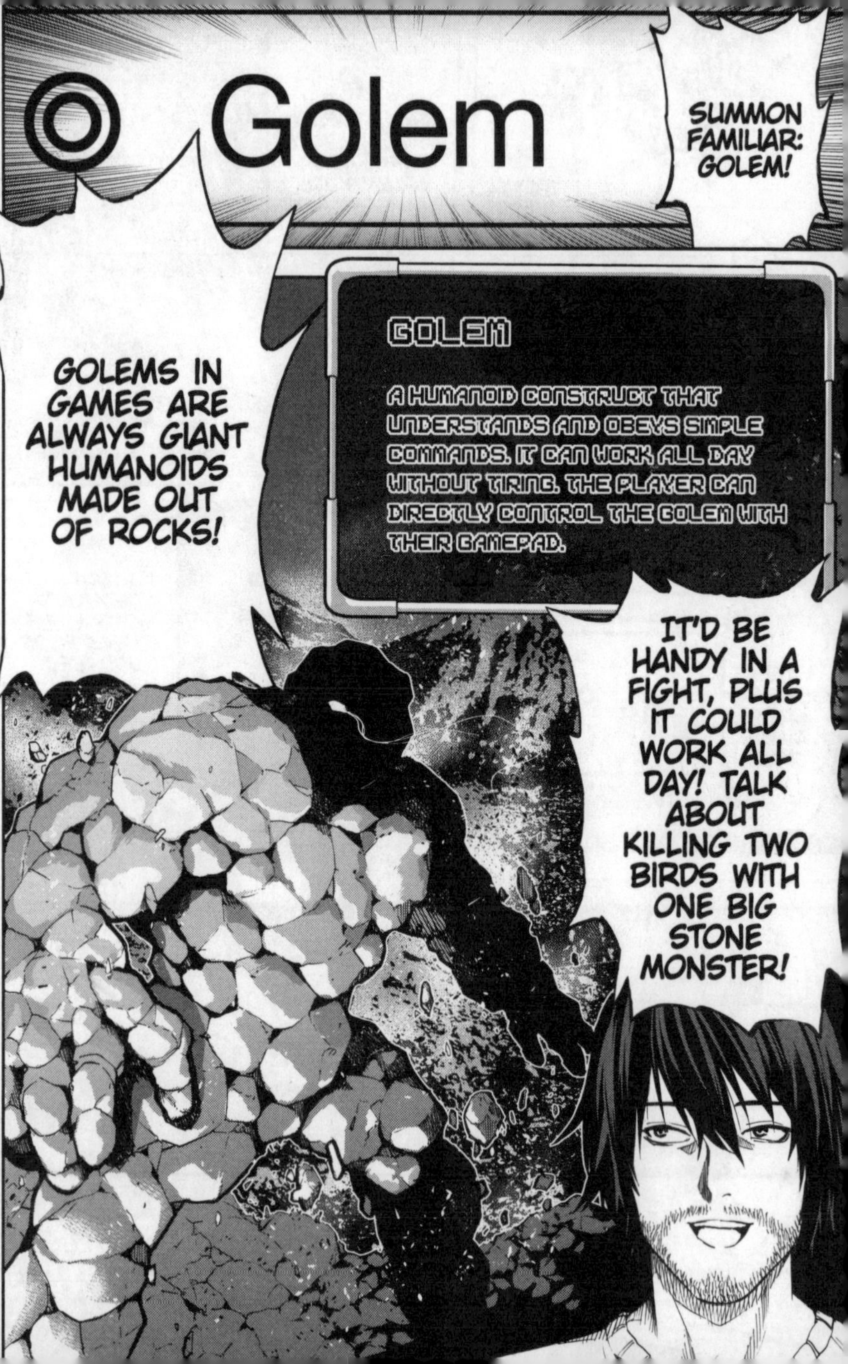
SUMMON FAMILIAR: GOLEM!
Golem
GOLEM
A HUMANOID CONSTRUCT THAT UNDERSTANDS AND OBEYS SIMPLE COMMANDS. IT CAN WORK ALL DAY WITHOUT TIRING. THE PLAYER CAN DIRECTLY CONTROL THE GOLEM WITH THEIR GAMEPAD.
GOLEMS IN GAMES ARE ALWAYS GIANT HUMANOIDS MADE OUT OF ROCKS!
IT'D BE HANDY IN A FIGHT, PLUS IT COULD WORK ALL DAY! TALK ABOUT KILLING TWO BIRDS WITH ONE BIG STONE MONSTER!

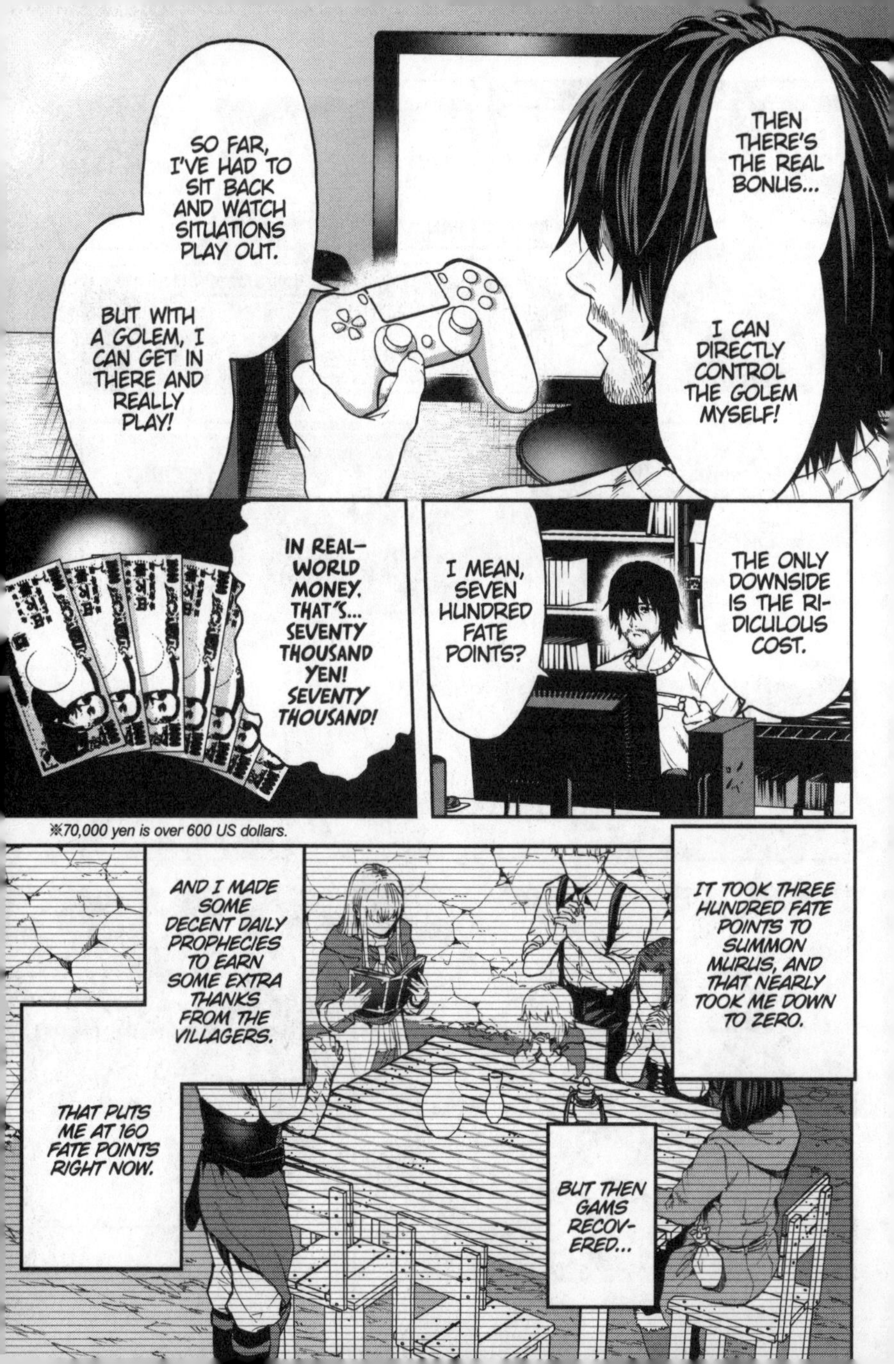
THEN THERE'S THE REAL BONUS...
I CAN DIRECTLY CONTROL THE GOLEM MYSELF!
SO FAR, I'VE HAD TO SIT BACK AND WATCH SITUATIONS PLAY OUT.
BUT WITH A GOLEM, I CAN GET IN THERE AND REALLY PLAY!
THE ONLY DOWNSIDE IS THE RI-DICULOUS COST.
I MEAN, SEVEN HUNDRED FATE POINTS?
IN REAL-WORLD MONEY. THAT'S... SEVENTY THOUSAND YEN! SEVENTY THOUSAND!
IT TOOK THREE HUNDRED FATE POINTS TO SUMMON MURUS, AND THAT NEARLY TOOK ME DOWN TO ZERO.
AND I MADE SOME DECENT DAILY PROPHECIES TO EARN SOME EXTRA THANKS FROM THE VILLAGERS.
BUT THEN GAMS RECOV-ERED...
THAT PUTS ME AT 160 FATE POINTS RIGHT NOW.

※70,000 yen is over 600 US dollars.

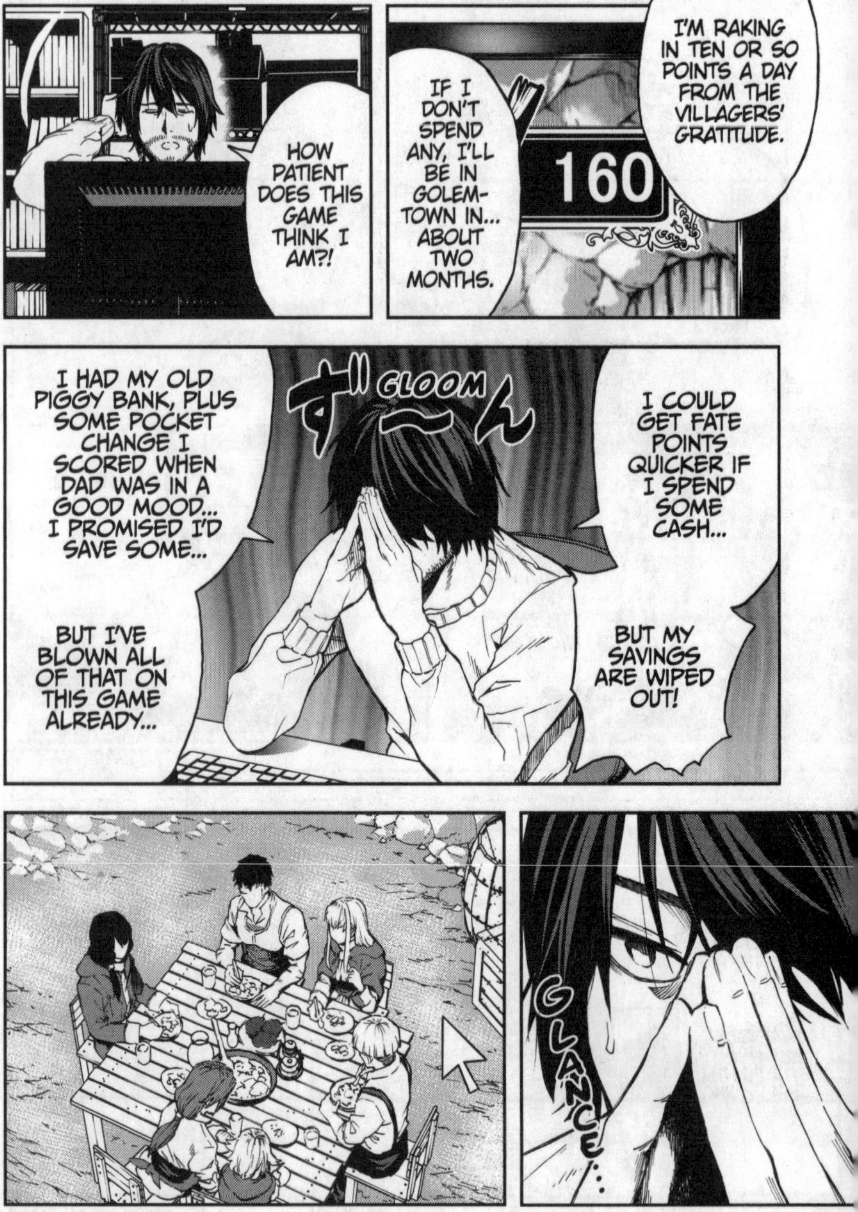
I'M RAKING IN TEN OR SO POINTS A DAY FROM THE VILLAGERS' GRATITUDE.
160
IF I DON'T SPEND ANY, I'LL BE IN GOLEM-TOWN IN... ABOUT TWO MONTHS.
HOW PATIENT DOES THIS GAME THINK I AM?!
I COULD GET FATE POINTS QUICKER IF I SPEND SOME CASH...
ず〜ん GLOOM
I HAD MY OLD PIGGY BANK, PLUS SOME POCKET CHANGE I SCORED WHEN DAD WAS IN A GOOD MOOD... I PROMISED I'D SAVE SOME...
BUT MY SAVINGS ARE WIPED OUT!
BUT I'VE BLOWN ALL OF THAT ON THIS GAME ALREADY...
GLANCE...

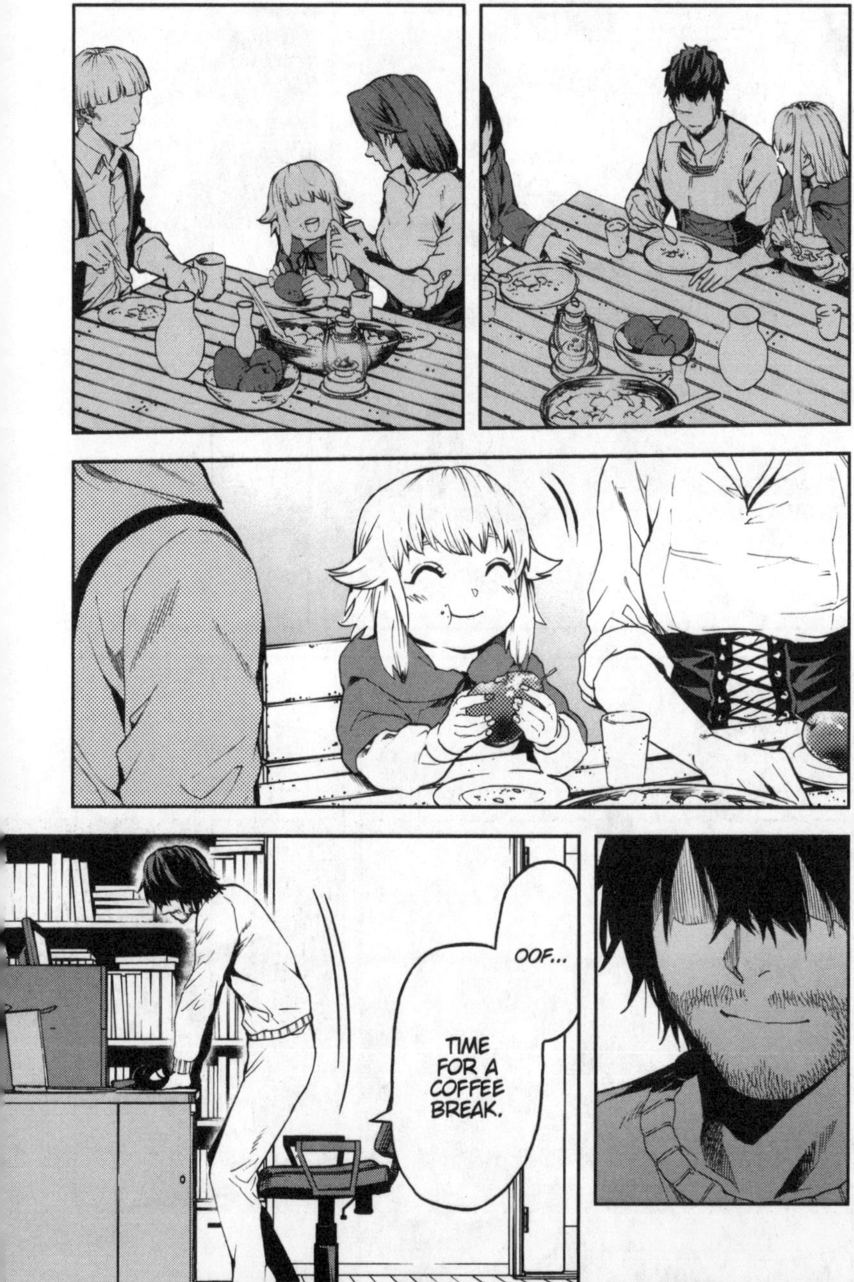
OOF...
TIME FOR A COFFEE BREAK.

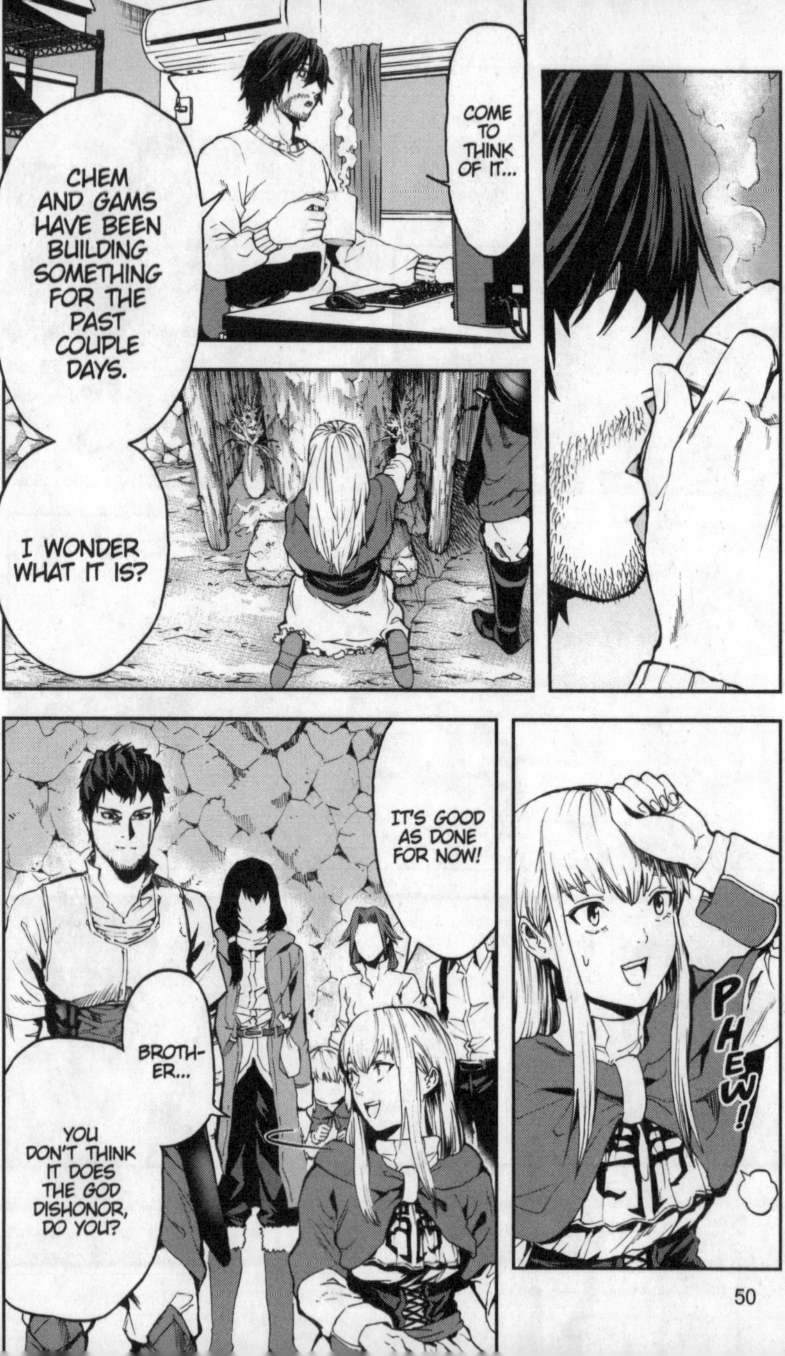
COME TO THINK OF IT...
CHEM AND GAMS HAVE BEEN BUILDING SOMETHING FOR THE PAST COUPLE DAYS.
I WONDER WHAT IT IS?
PHEW!
IT'S GOOD AS DONE FOR NOW!
BROTH-ER...
YOU DON'T THINK IT DOES THE GOD DISHONOR, DO YOU?

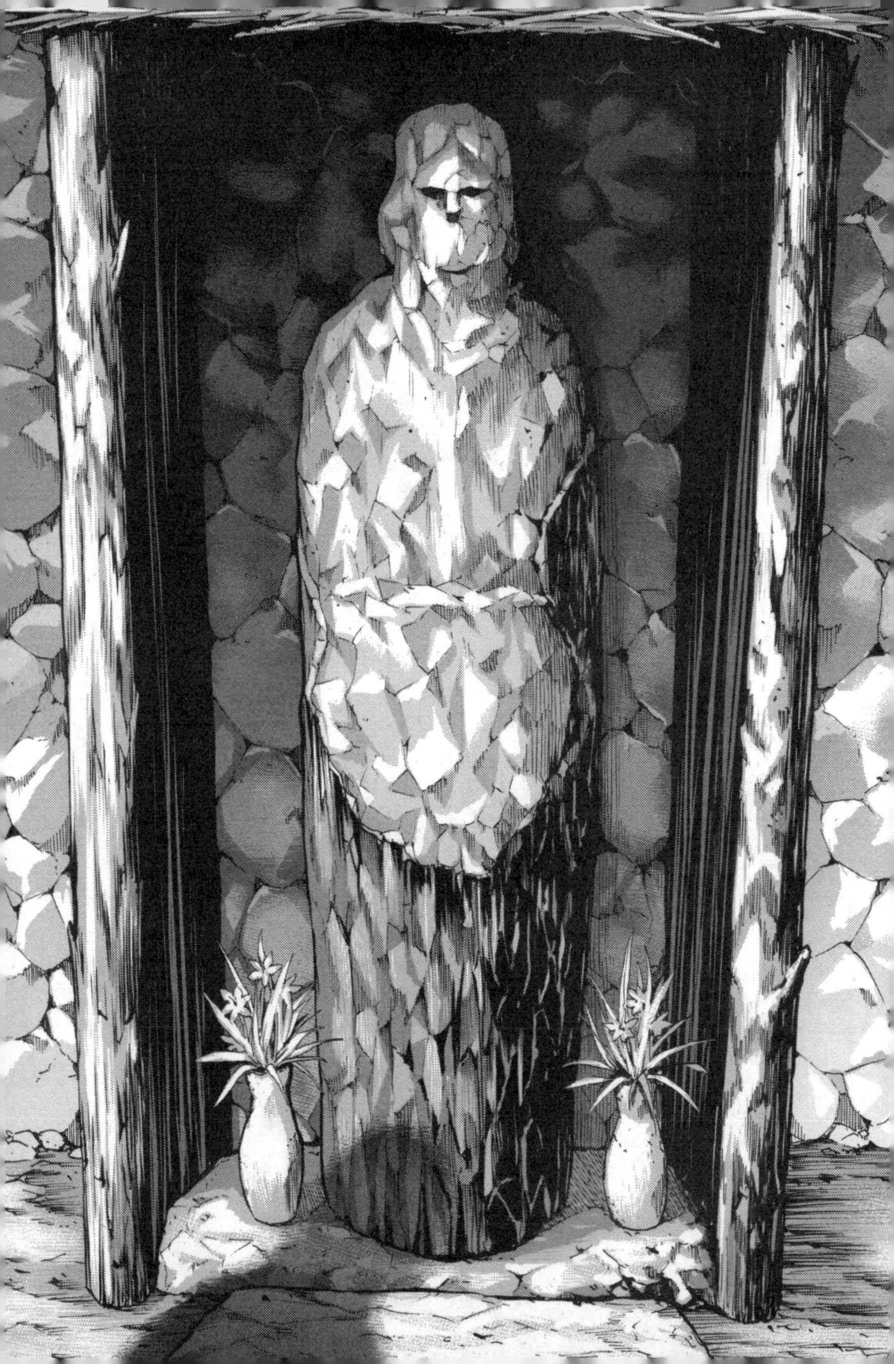

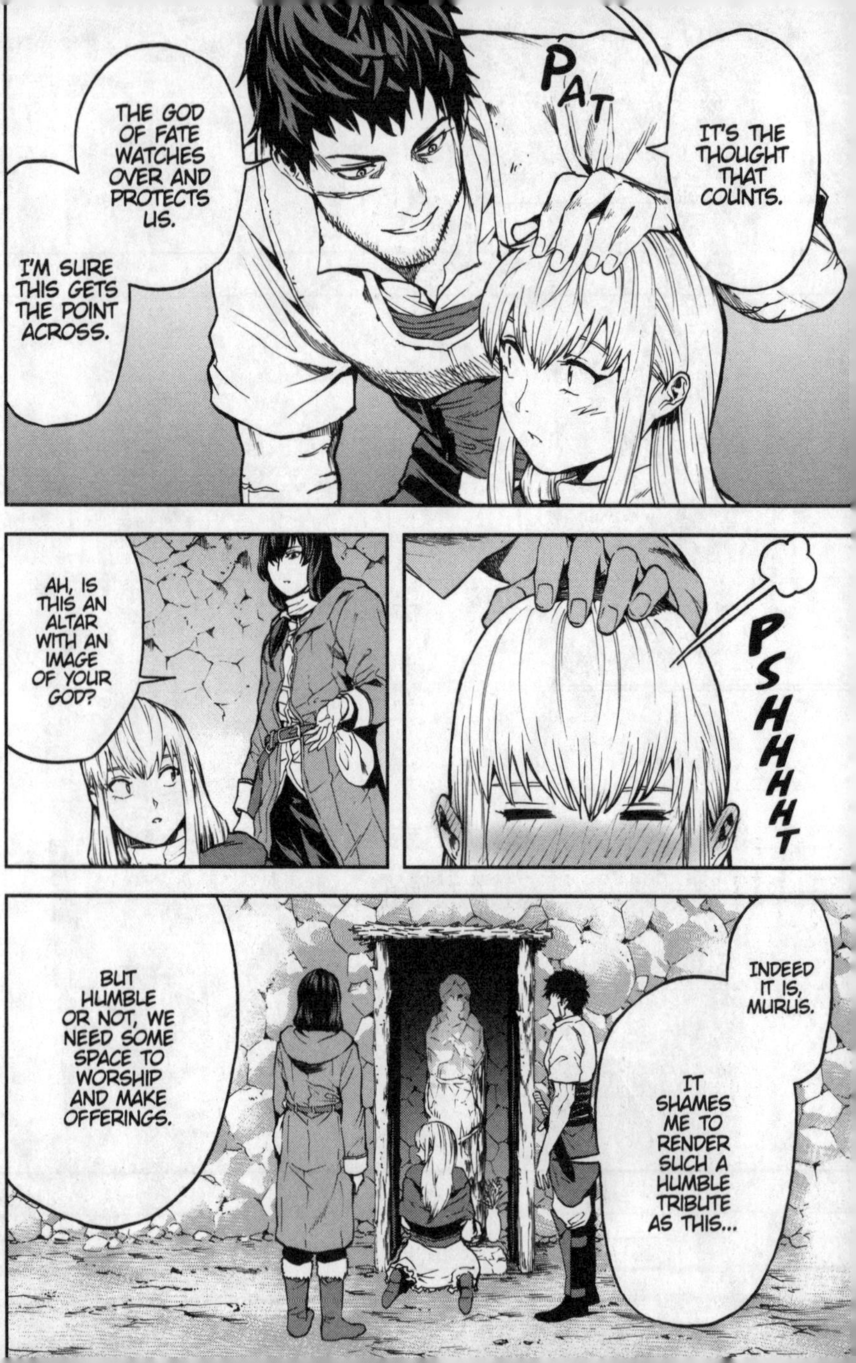

PAT
IT'S THE THOUGHT THAT COUNTS.
THE GOD OF FATE WATCHES OVER AND PROTECTS US.
I'M SURE THIS GETS THE POINT ACROSS.
PSHHHHT
AH, IS THIS AN ALTAR WITH AN IMAGE OF YOUR GOD?
INDEED IT IS, MURUS.
IT SHAMES ME TO RENDER SUCH A HUMBLE TRIBUTE AS THIS...
BUT HUMBLE OR NOT, WE NEED SOME SPACE TO WORSHIP AND MAKE OFFERINGS.

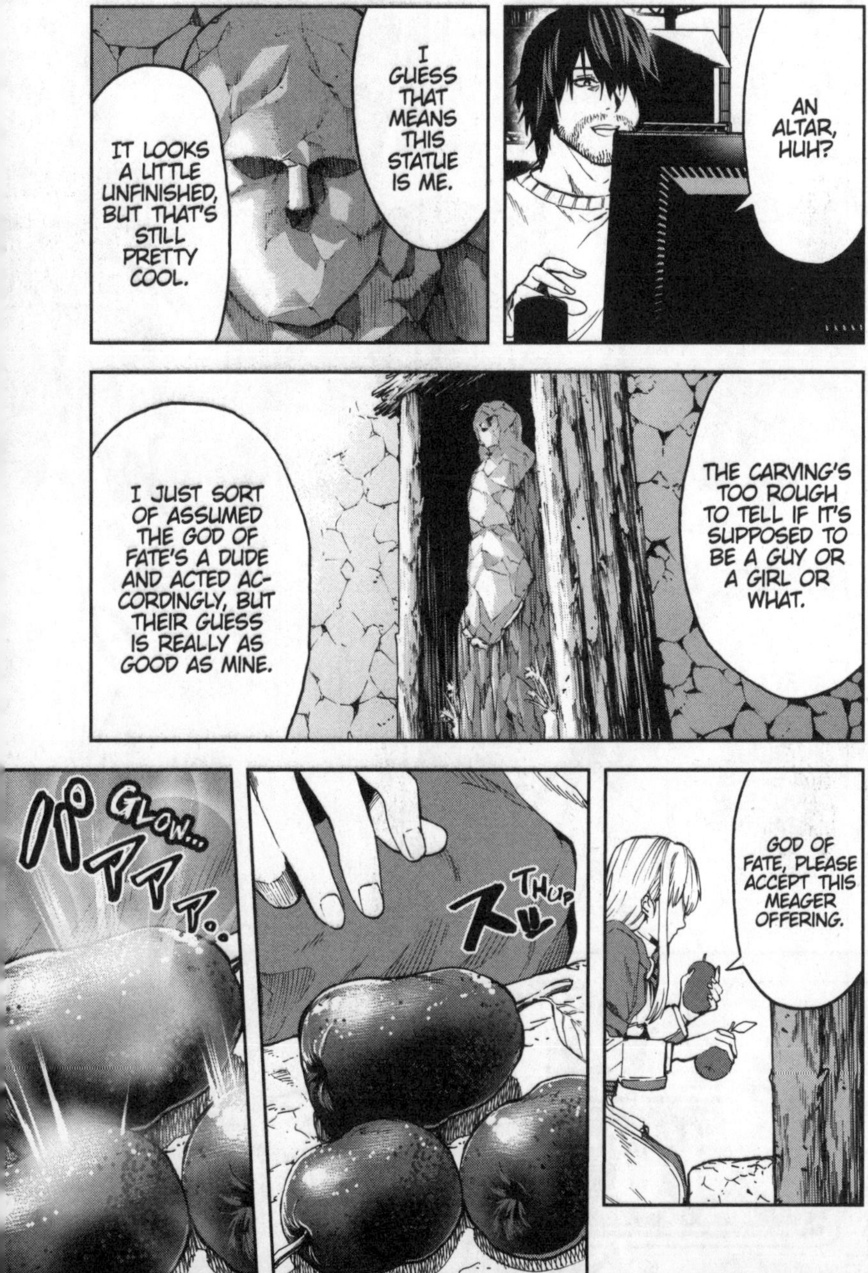
AN ALTAR, HUH?
I GUESS THAT MEANS THIS STATUE IS ME.
IT LOOKS A LITTLE UNFINISHED, BUT THAT'S STILL PRETTY COOL.
THE CARVING'S TOO ROUGH TO TELL IF IT'S SUPPOSED TO BE A GUY OR A GIRL OR WHAT.
I JUST SORT OF ASSUMED THE GOD OF FATE'S A DUDE AND ACTED AC-CORDINGLY, BUT THEIR GUESS IS REALLY AS GOOD AS MINE.
GOD OF FATE, PLEASE ACCEPT THIS MEAGER OFFERING.
スッ
THUP
パァァァ..
GLOW...

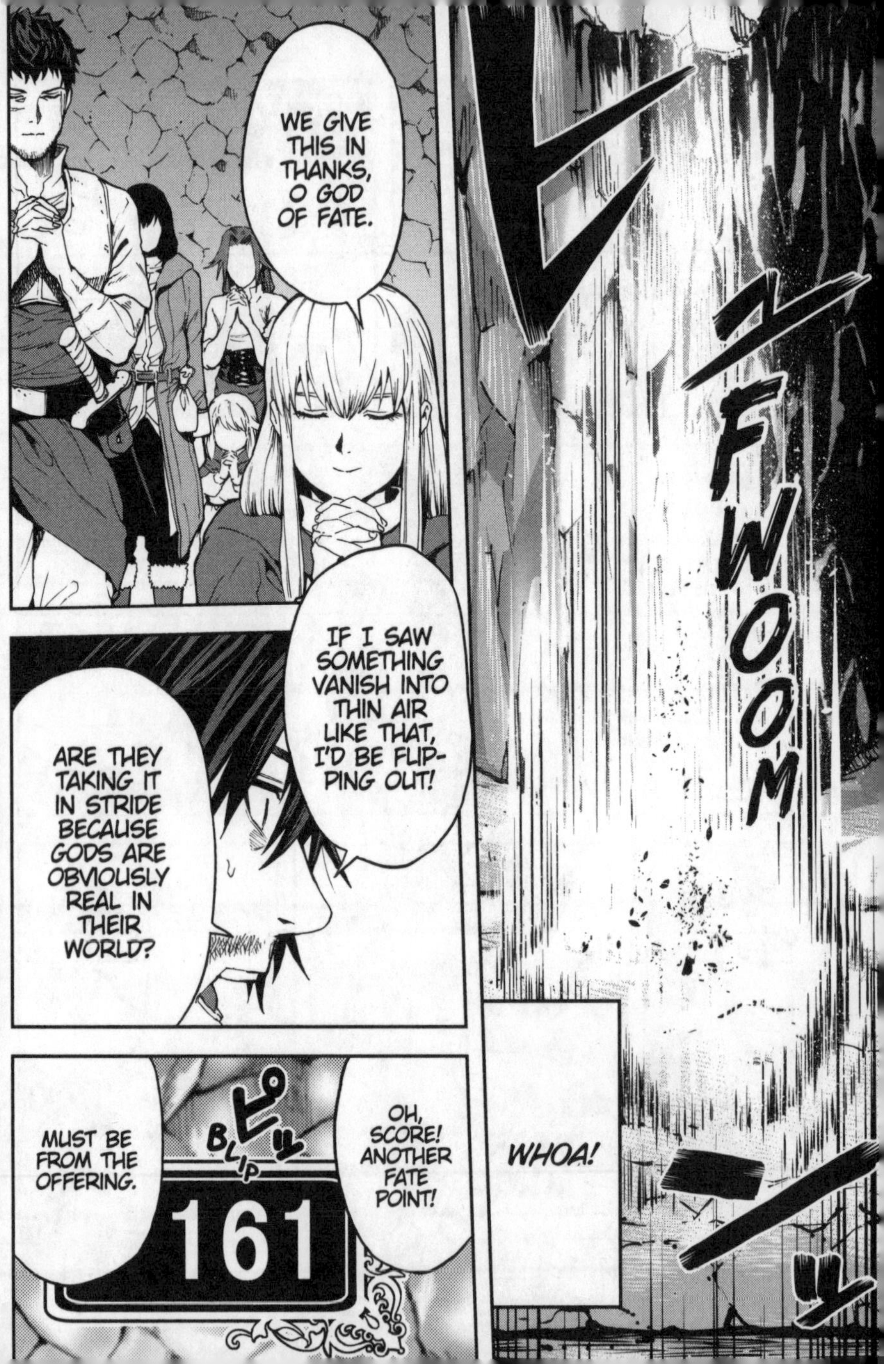
FWOOM
WHOA!
WE GIVE THIS IN THANKS, O GOD OF FATE.
IF I SAW SOMETHING VANISH INTO THIN AIR LIKE THAT, I'D BE FLIP-PING OUT!
ARE THEY TAKING IT IN STRIDE BECAUSE GODS ARE OBVIOUSLY REAL IN THEIR WORLD?
OH, SCORE! ANOTHER FATE POINT!
BLIP
161
MUST BE FROM THE OFFERING.

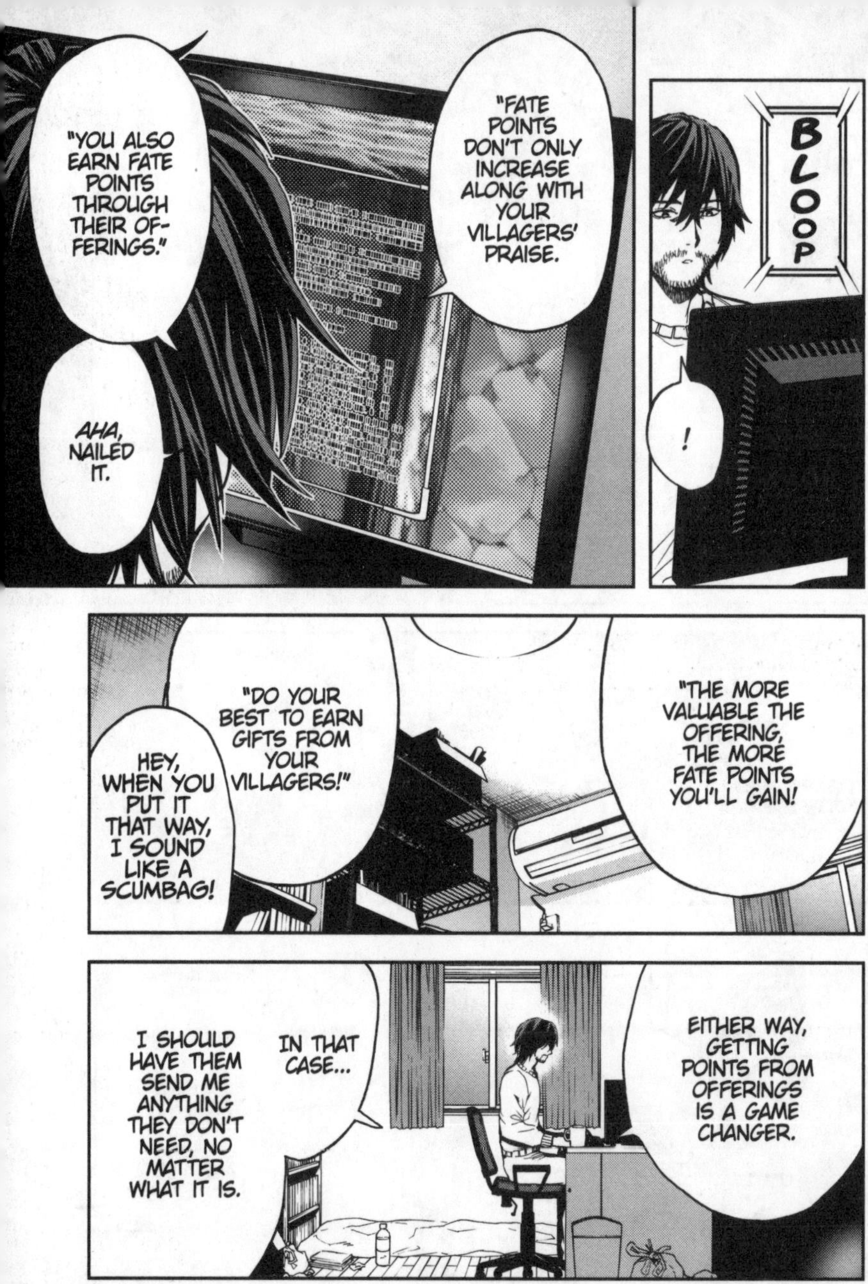
BLOOP
!
"FATE POINTS DON'T ONLY INCREASE ALONG WITH YOUR VILLAGERS' PRAISE.
"YOU ALSO EARN FATE POINTS THROUGH THEIR OF-FERINGS."
AHA, NAILED IT.
"THE MORE VALUABLE THE OFFERING, THE MORE FATE POINTS YOU'LL GAIN!
"DO YOUR BEST TO EARN GIFTS FROM YOUR VILLAGERS!"
HEY, WHEN YOU PUT IT THAT WAY, I SOUND LIKE A SCUMBAG!
EITHER WAY, GETTING POINTS FROM OFFERINGS IS A GAME CHANGER.
IN THAT CASE...
I SHOULD HAVE THEM SEND ME ANYTHING THEY DON'T NEED, NO MATTER WHAT IT IS.

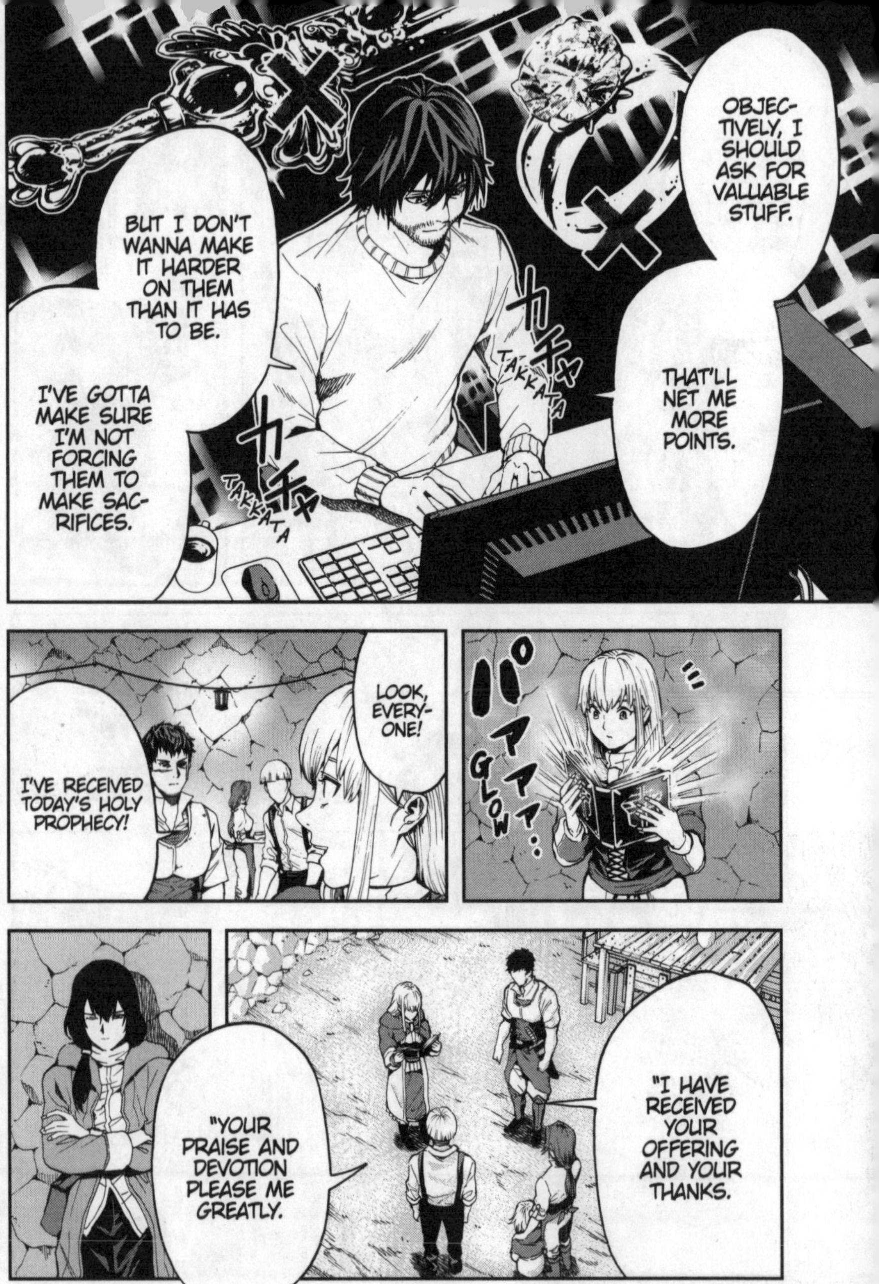
OBJECTIVELY, I SHOULD ASK FOR VALUABLE STUFF.
THAT'LL NET ME MORE POINTS.
カチャ TAKKATA
BUT I DON'T WANNA MAKE IT HARDER ON THEM THAN IT HAS TO BE.
I'VE GOTTA MAKE SURE I'M NOT FORCING THEM TO MAKE SACRIFICES.
カチャ TAKKATA
パァァ… GLOW
LOOK, EVERYONE!
I'VE RECEIVED TODAY'S HOLY PROPHECY!
"I HAVE RECEIVED YOUR OFFERING AND YOUR THANKS.
"YOUR PRAISE AND DEVOTION PLEASE ME GREATLY.

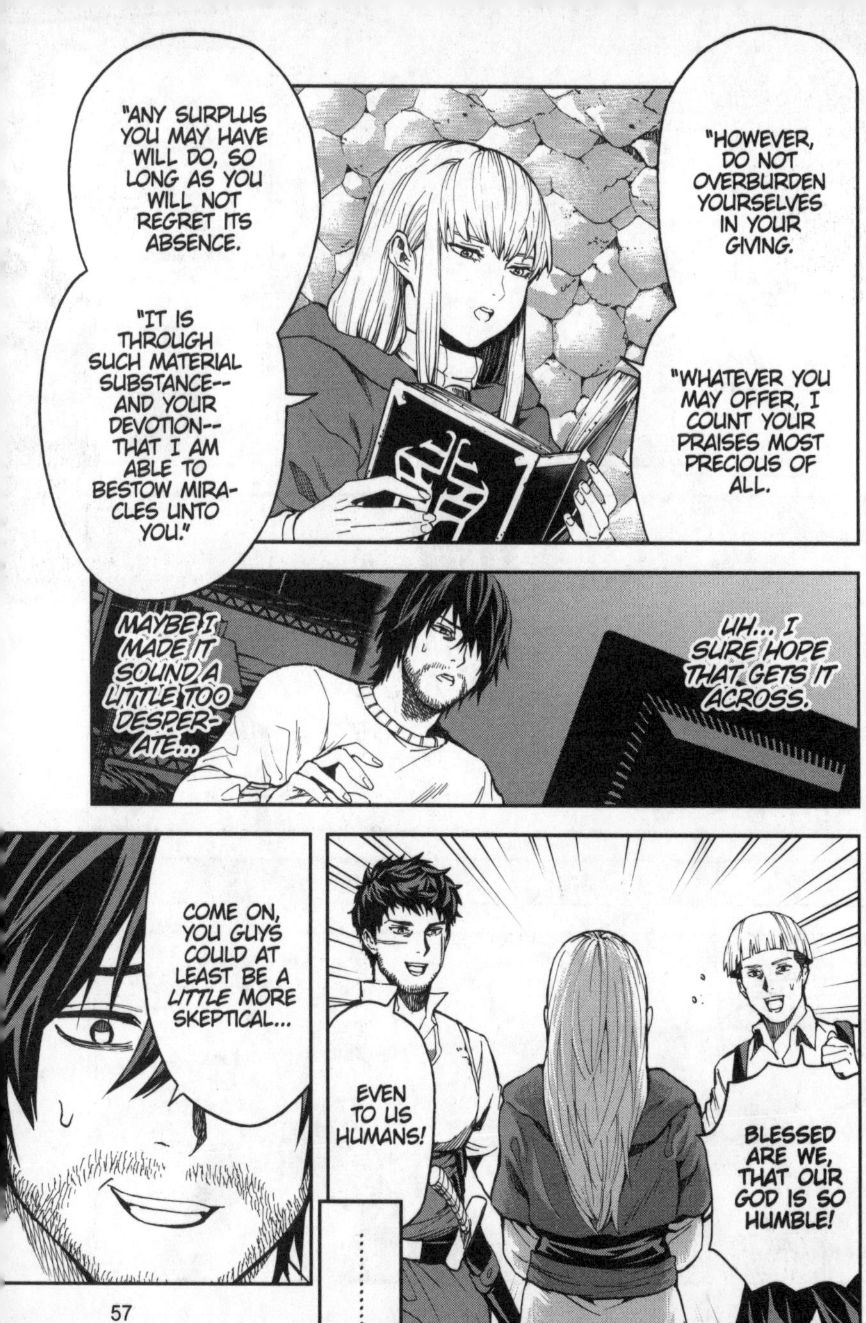
"HOWEVER, DO NOT OVERBURDEN YOURSELVES IN YOUR GIVING.
"ANY SURPLUS YOU MAY HAVE WILL DO, SO LONG AS YOU WILL NOT REGRET ITS ABSENCE.
"WHATEVER YOU MAY OFFER, I COUNT YOUR PRAISES MOST PRECIOUS OF ALL.
"IT IS THROUGH SUCH MATERIAL SUBSTANCE--AND YOUR DEVOTION--THAT I AM ABLE TO BESTOW MIRACLES UNTO YOU."
UH... I SURE HOPE THAT GETS IT ACROSS.
MAYBE I MADE IT SOUND A LITTLE TOO DESPERATE...
BLESSED ARE WE, THAT OUR GOD IS SO HUMBLE!
EVEN TO US HUMANS!
......
COME ON, YOU GUYS COULD AT LEAST BE A LITTLE MORE SKEPTICAL...

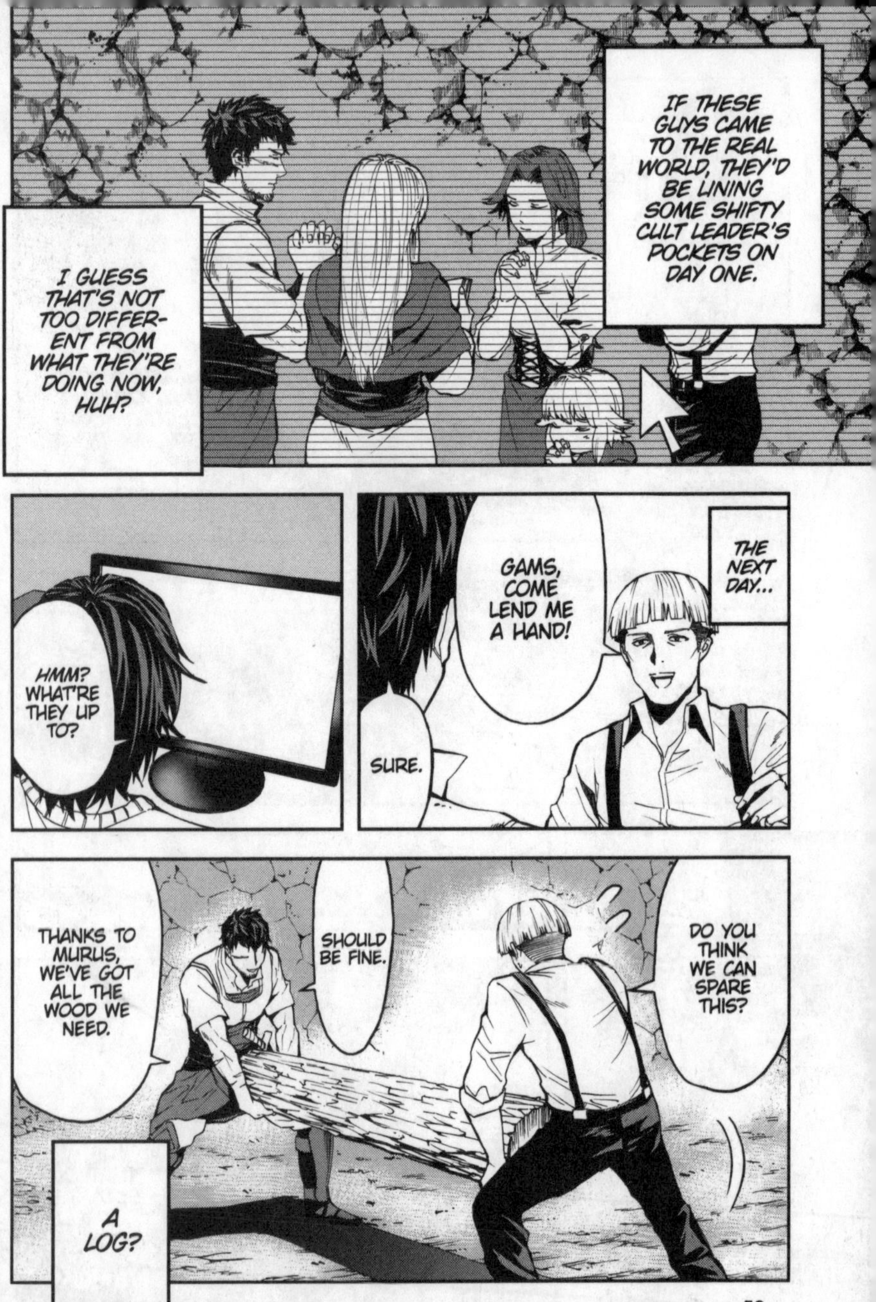
IF THESE GUYS CAME TO THE REAL WORLD, THEY'D BE LINING SOME SHIFTY CULT LEADER'S POCKETS ON DAY ONE.
I GUESS THAT'S NOT TOO DIFFERENT FROM WHAT THEY'RE DOING NOW, HUH?
THE NEXT DAY...
GAMS, COME LEND ME A HAND!
SURE.
HMM? WHAT'RE THEY UP TO?
DO YOU THINK WE CAN SPARE THIS?
SHOULD BE FINE.
THANKS TO MURUS, WE'VE GOT ALL THE WOOD WE NEED.
A LOG?

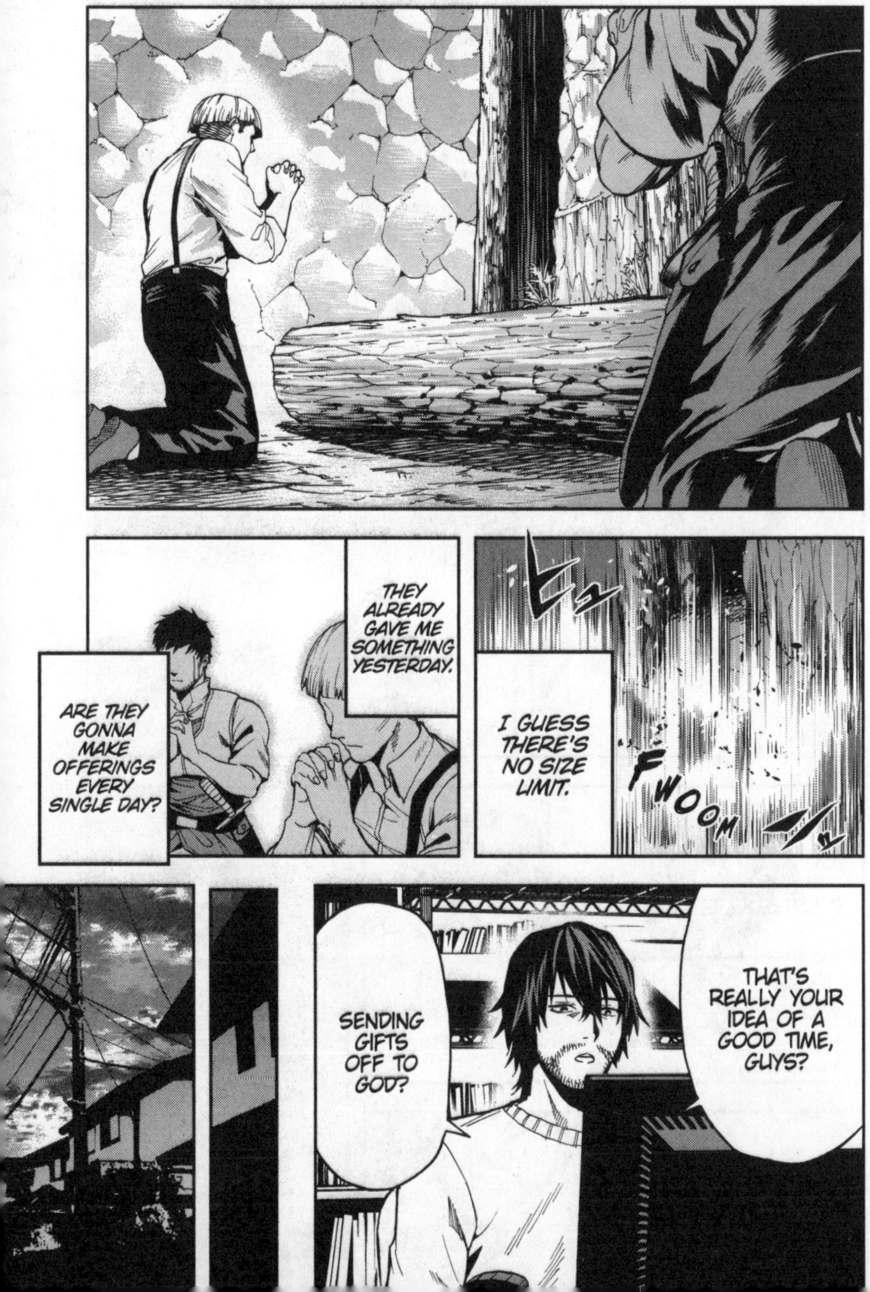
I GUESS THERE'S NO SIZE LIMIT.
FWOOM
THEY ALREADY GAVE ME SOMETHING YESTERDAY.
ARE THEY GONNA MAKE OFFERINGS EVERY SINGLE DAY?
THAT'S REALLY YOUR IDEA OF A GOOD TIME, GUYS?
SENDING GIFTS OFF TO GOD?

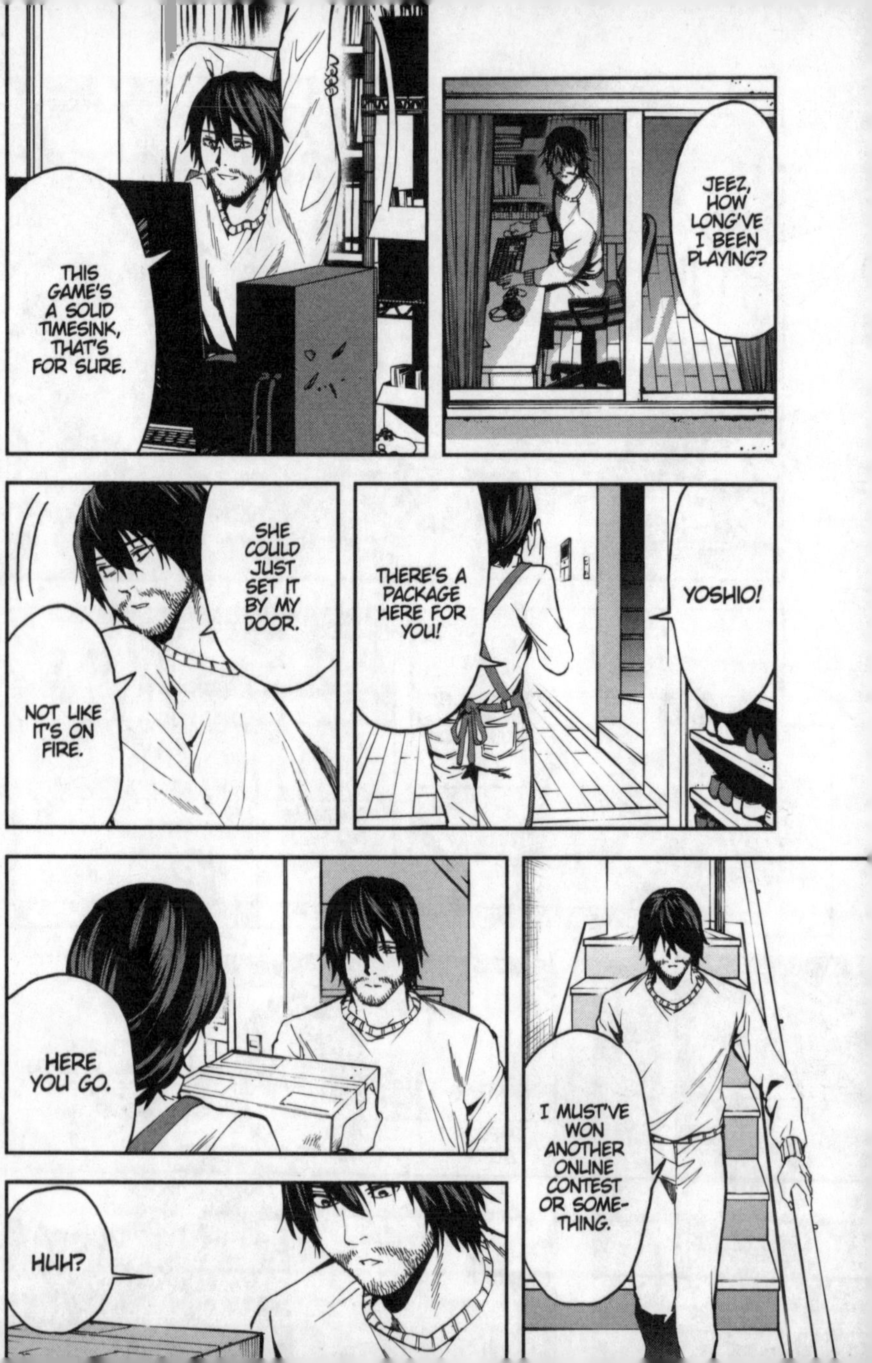
JEEZ, HOW LONG'VE I BEEN PLAYING?
THIS GAME'S A SOLID TIMESINK, THAT'S FOR SURE.
YOSHIO!
THERE'S A PACKAGE HERE FOR YOU!
SHE COULD JUST SET IT BY MY DOOR.
NOT LIKE IT'S ON FIRE.
I MUST'VE WON ANOTHER ONLINE CONTEST OR SOME-THING.
HERE YOU GO.
HUH?

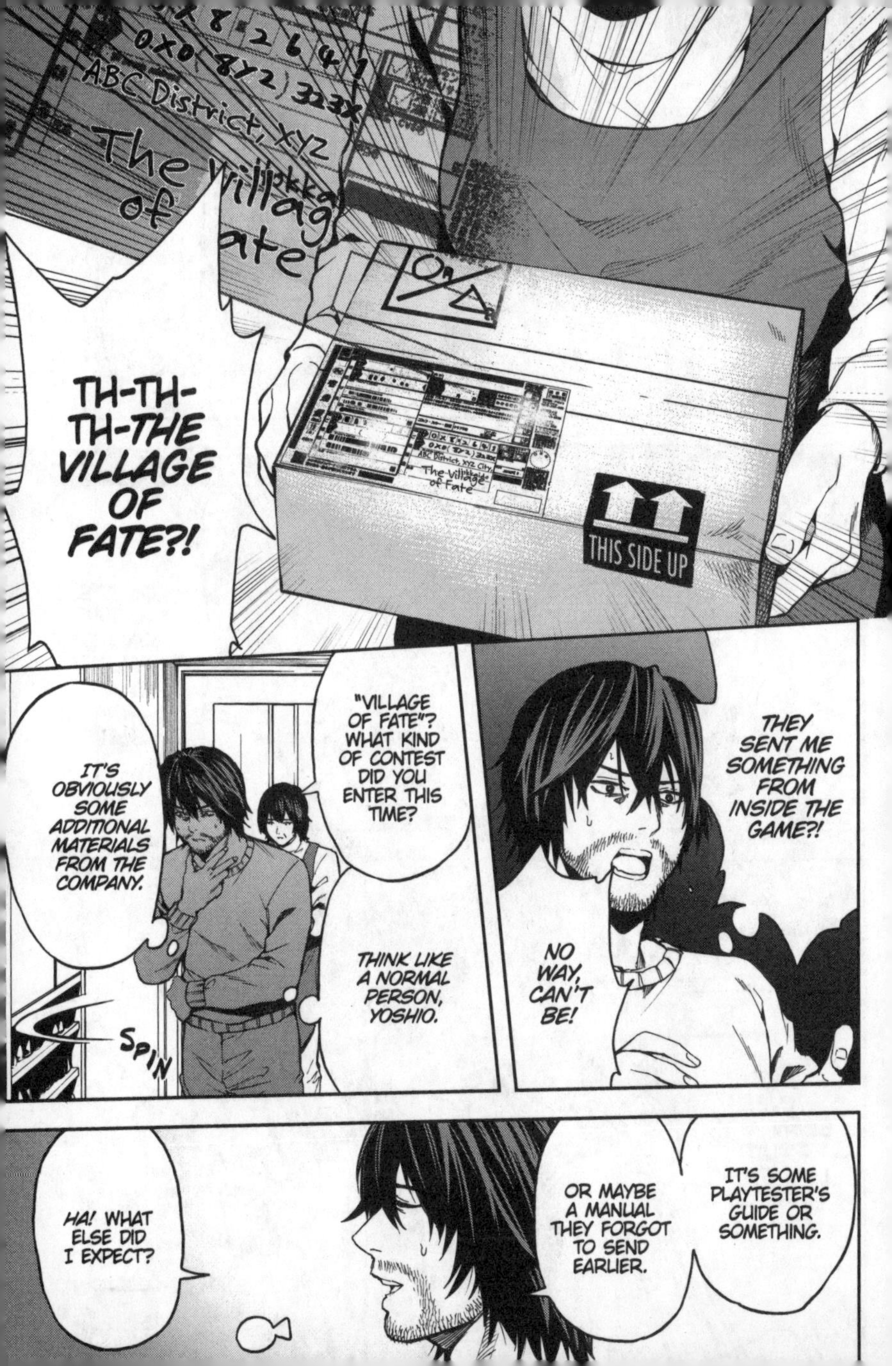
ABC District, XYZ City
The Village of Fate
THIS SIDE UP
TH-TH-TH-*THE* VILLAGE OF FATE?!
THEY SENT ME SOMETHING FROM INSIDE THE GAME?!
NO WAY, CAN'T BE!
"VILLAGE OF FATE"? WHAT KIND OF CONTEST DID YOU ENTER THIS TIME?
IT'S OBVIOUSLY SOME ADDITIONAL MATERIALS FROM THE COMPANY.
THINK LIKE A NORMAL PERSON, YOSHIO.
SPIN
IT'S SOME PLAYTESTER'S GUIDE OR SOMETHING.
OR MAYBE A MANUAL THEY FORGOT TO SEND EARLIER.
HA! WHAT ELSE DID I EXPECT?

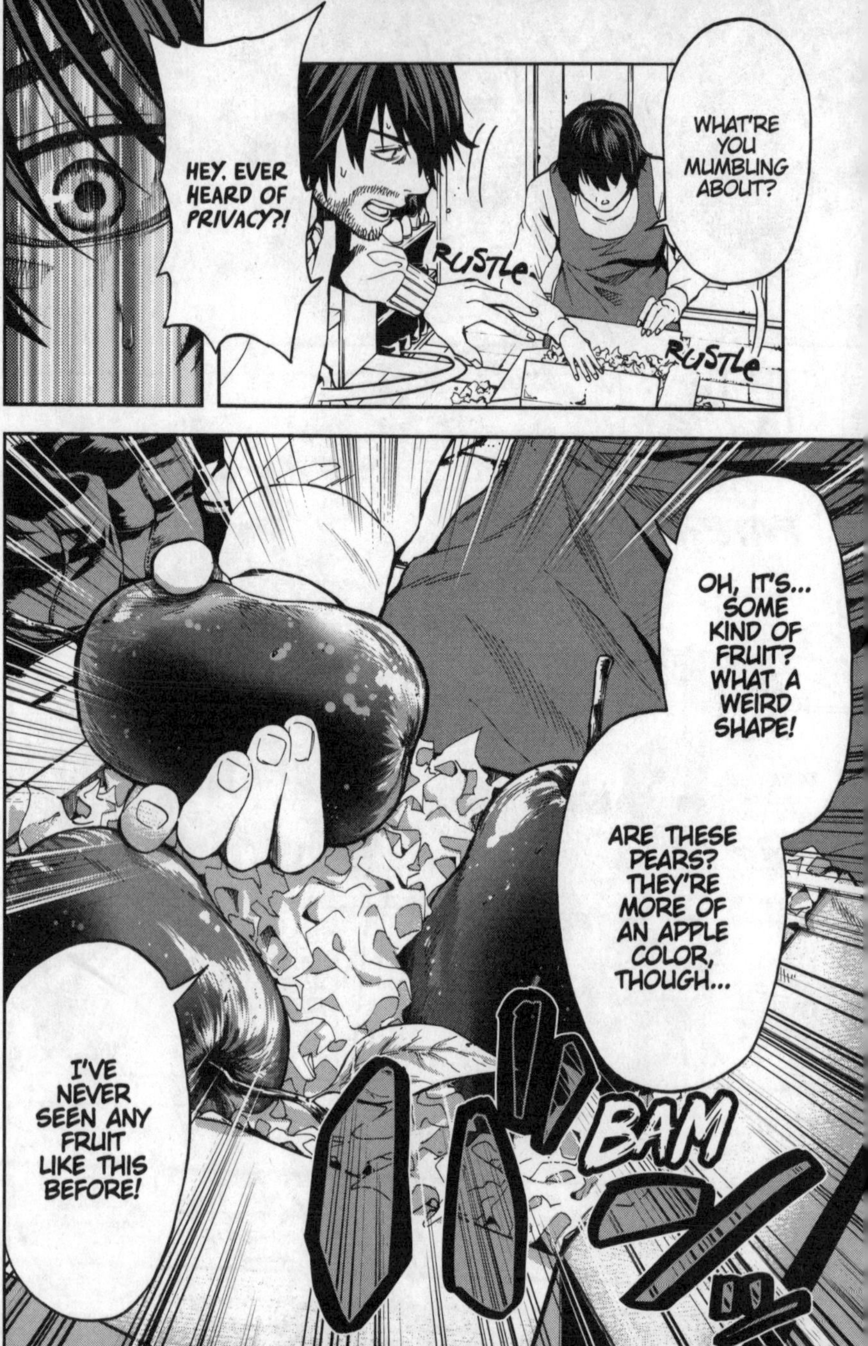
WHAT'RE YOU MUMBLING ABOUT?
RUSTLE
RUSTLE
HEY. EVER HEARD OF PRIVACY?!
OH, IT'S... SOME KIND OF FRUIT? WHAT A WEIRD SHAPE!
ARE THESE PEARS? THEY'RE MORE OF AN APPLE COLOR, THOUGH...
I'VE NEVER SEEN ANY FRUIT LIKE THIS BEFORE!
BAM

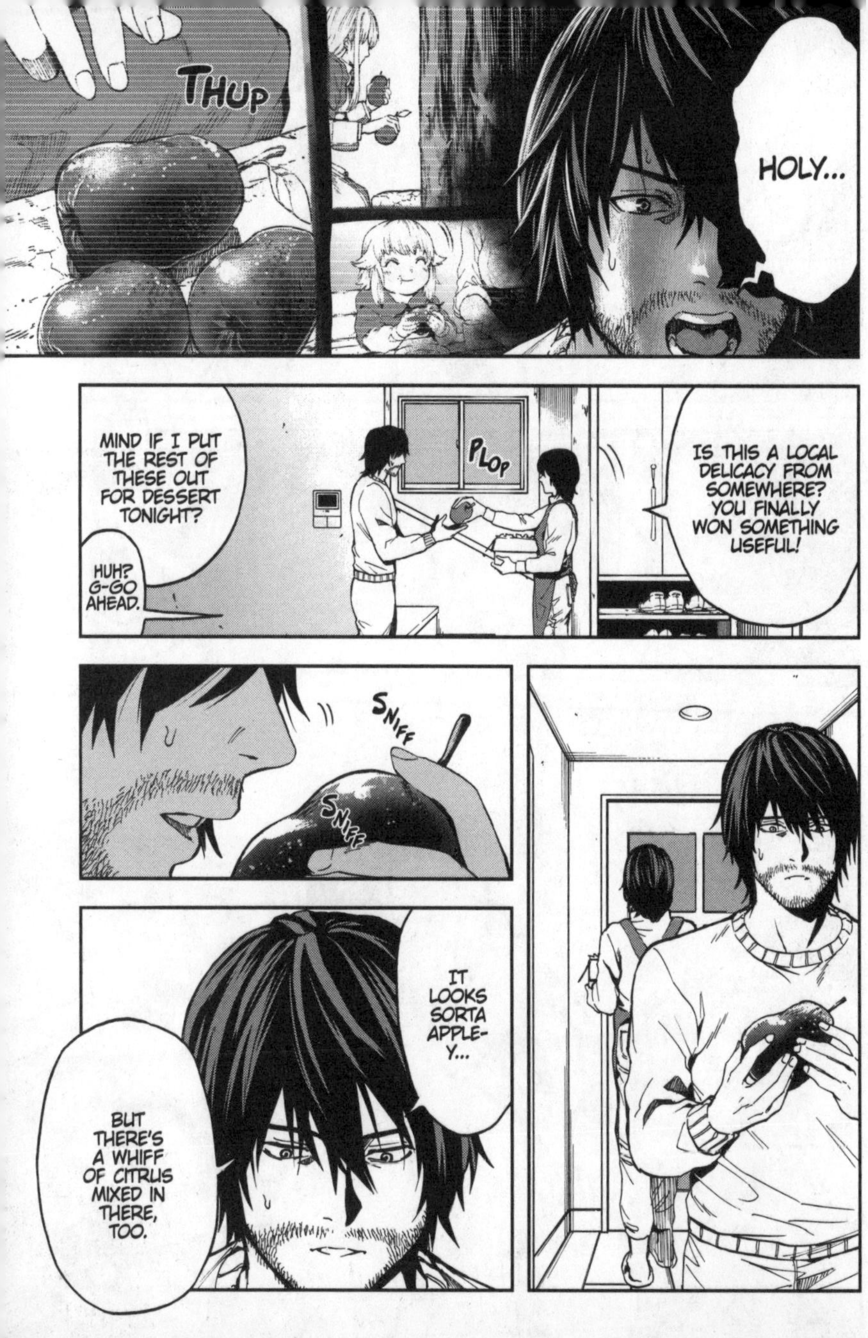
HOLY...
THUP
IS THIS A LOCAL DELICACY FROM SOMEWHERE? YOU FINALLY WON SOMETHING USEFUL!
PLOP
MIND IF I PUT THE REST OF THESE OUT FOR DESSERT TONIGHT?
HUH? G-GO AHEAD.
SNIFF
SNIFF
IT LOOKS SORTA APPLE-Y...
BUT THERE'S A WHIFF OF CITRUS MIXED IN THERE, TOO.

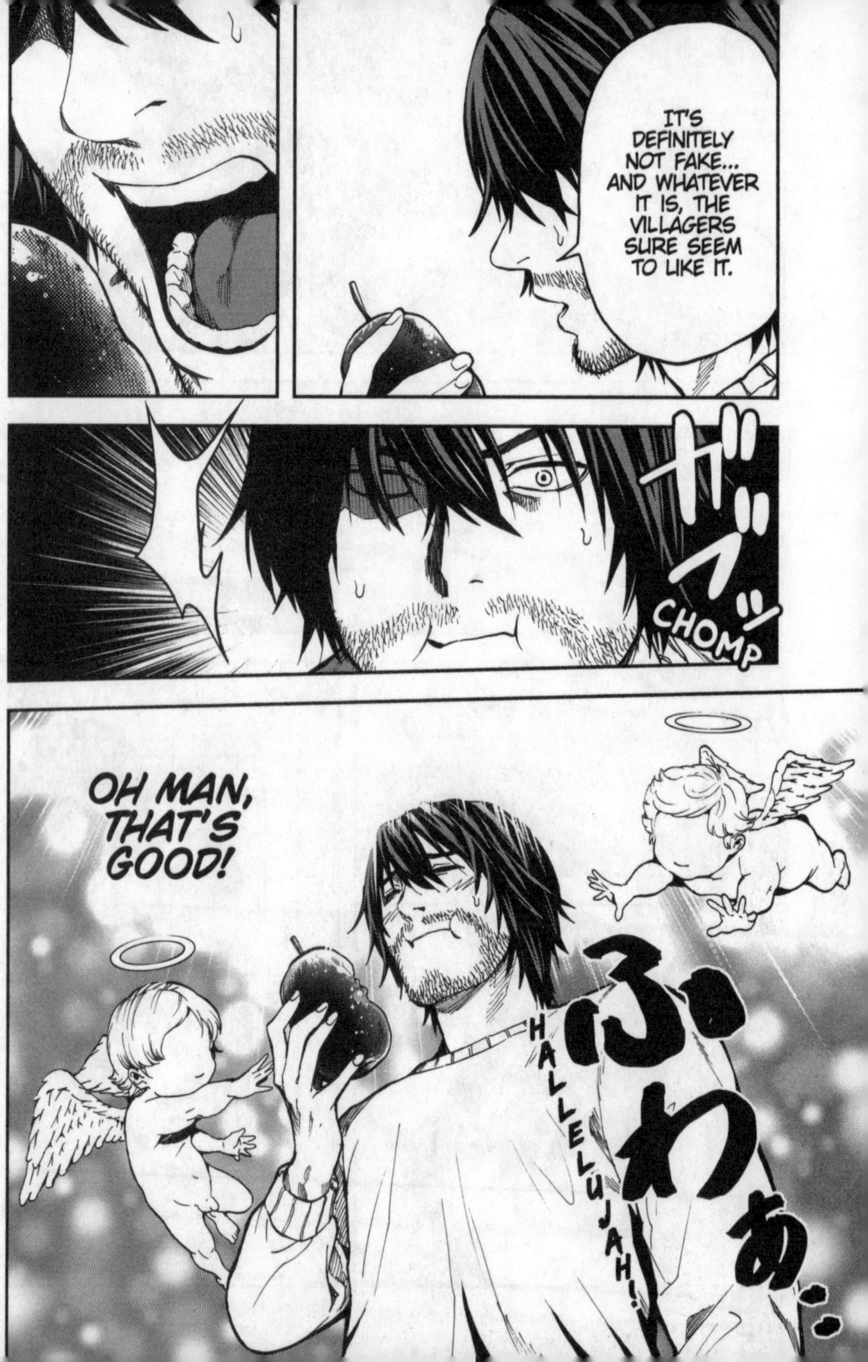
IT'S DEFINITELY NOT FAKE... AND WHATEVER IT IS, THE VILLAGERS SURE SEEM TO LIKE IT.
ガブッ
CHOMP
OH MAN, THAT'S GOOD!
ふわぁ
HALLELUJAH!!

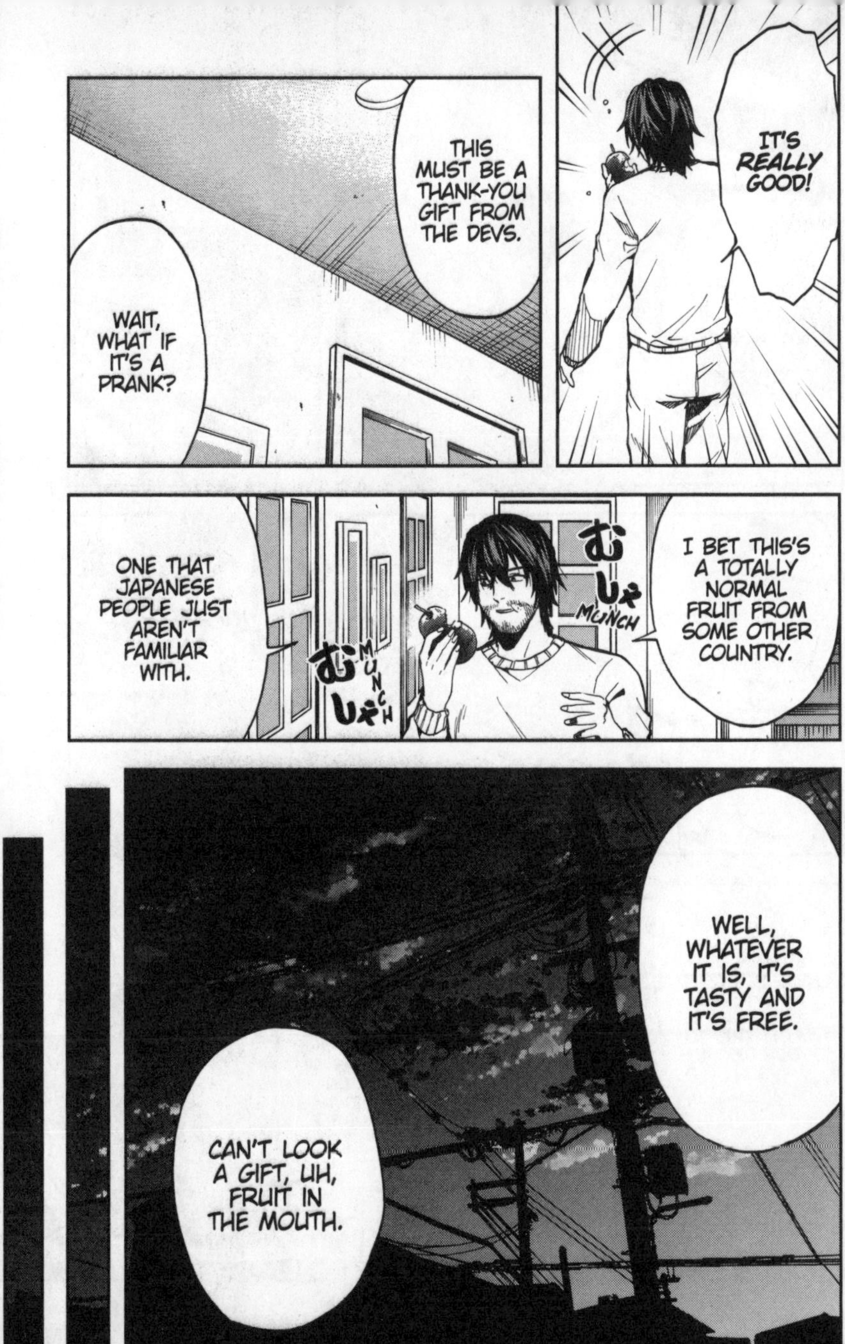
IT'S REALLY GOOD!
THIS MUST BE A THANK-YOU GIFT FROM THE DEVS.
WAIT, WHAT IF IT'S A PRANK?
I BET THIS'S A TOTALLY NORMAL FRUIT FROM SOME OTHER COUNTRY.
むしゃ MUNCH
むしゃ MUNCH
ONE THAT JAPANESE PEOPLE JUST AREN'T FAMILIAR WITH.
WELL, WHATEVER IT IS, IT'S TASTY AND IT'S FREE.
CAN'T LOOK A GIFT, UH, FRUIT IN THE MOUTH.

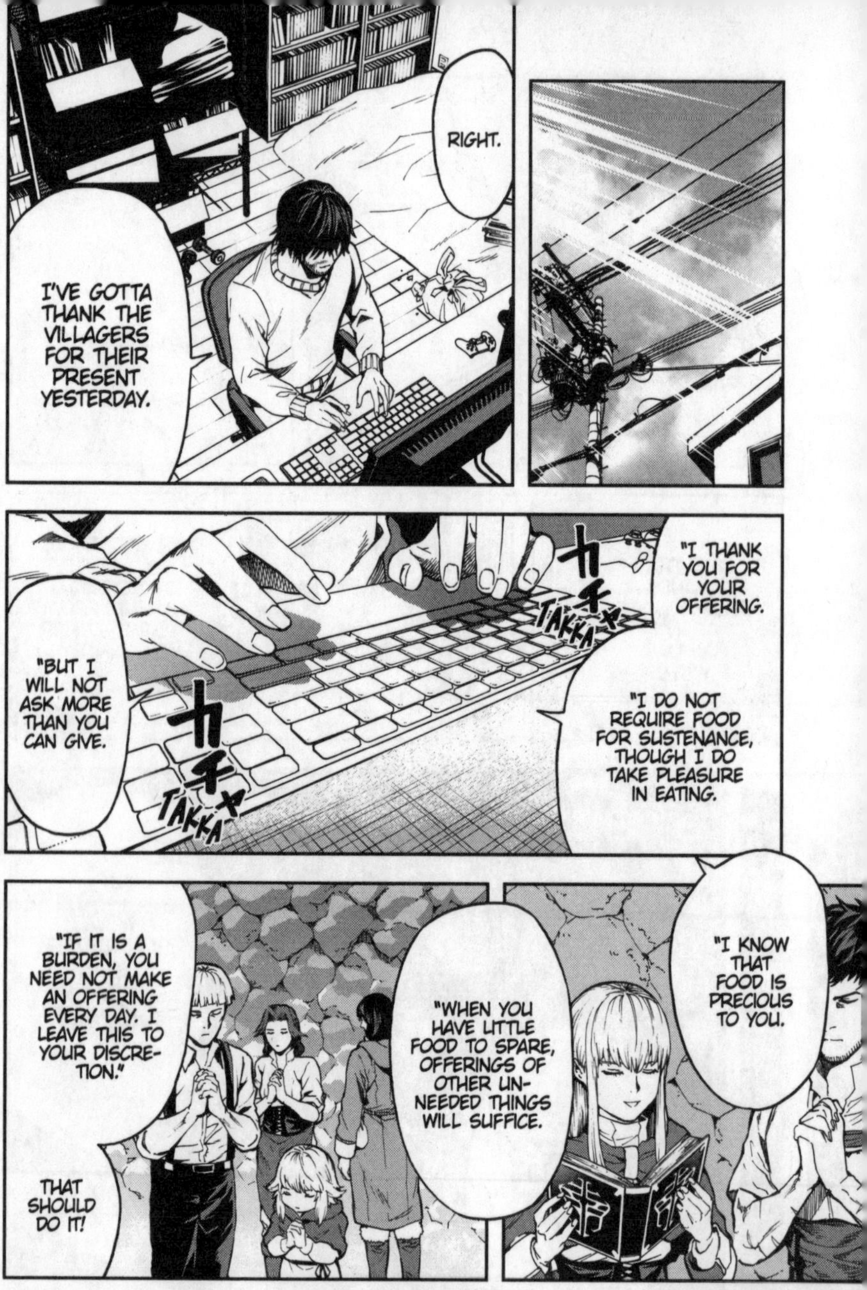
RIGHT.
I'VE GOTTA THANK THE VILLAGERS FOR THEIR PRESENT YESTERDAY.
"I THANK YOU FOR YOUR OFFERING.
カチャ TAKKA
"I DO NOT REQUIRE FOOD FOR SUSTENANCE, THOUGH I DO TAKE PLEASURE IN EATING.
"BUT I WILL NOT ASK MORE THAN YOU CAN GIVE.
カチャ TAKKA
"I KNOW THAT FOOD IS PRECIOUS TO YOU.
"WHEN YOU HAVE LITTLE FOOD TO SPARE, OFFERINGS OF OTHER UN-NEEDED THINGS WILL SUFFICE.
"IF IT IS A BURDEN, YOU NEED NOT MAKE AN OFFERING EVERY DAY. I LEAVE THIS TO YOUR DISCRE-TION."
THAT SHOULD DO IT!

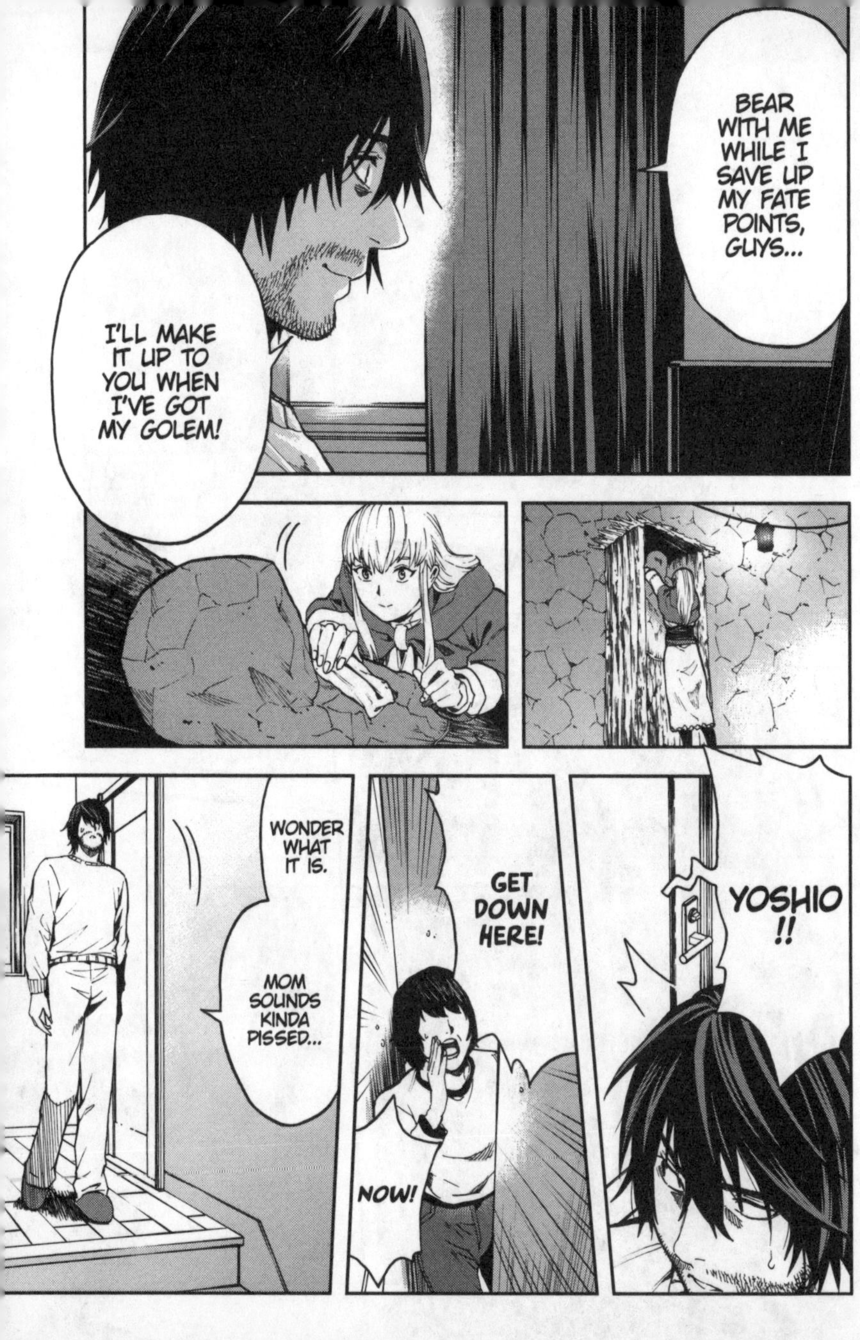
BEAR WITH ME WHILE I SAVE UP MY FATE POINTS, GUYS...
I'LL MAKE IT UP TO YOU WHEN I'VE GOT MY GOLEM!
YOSHIO!!
GET DOWN HERE!
NOW!
WONDER WHAT IT IS.
MOM SOUNDS KINDA PISSED...

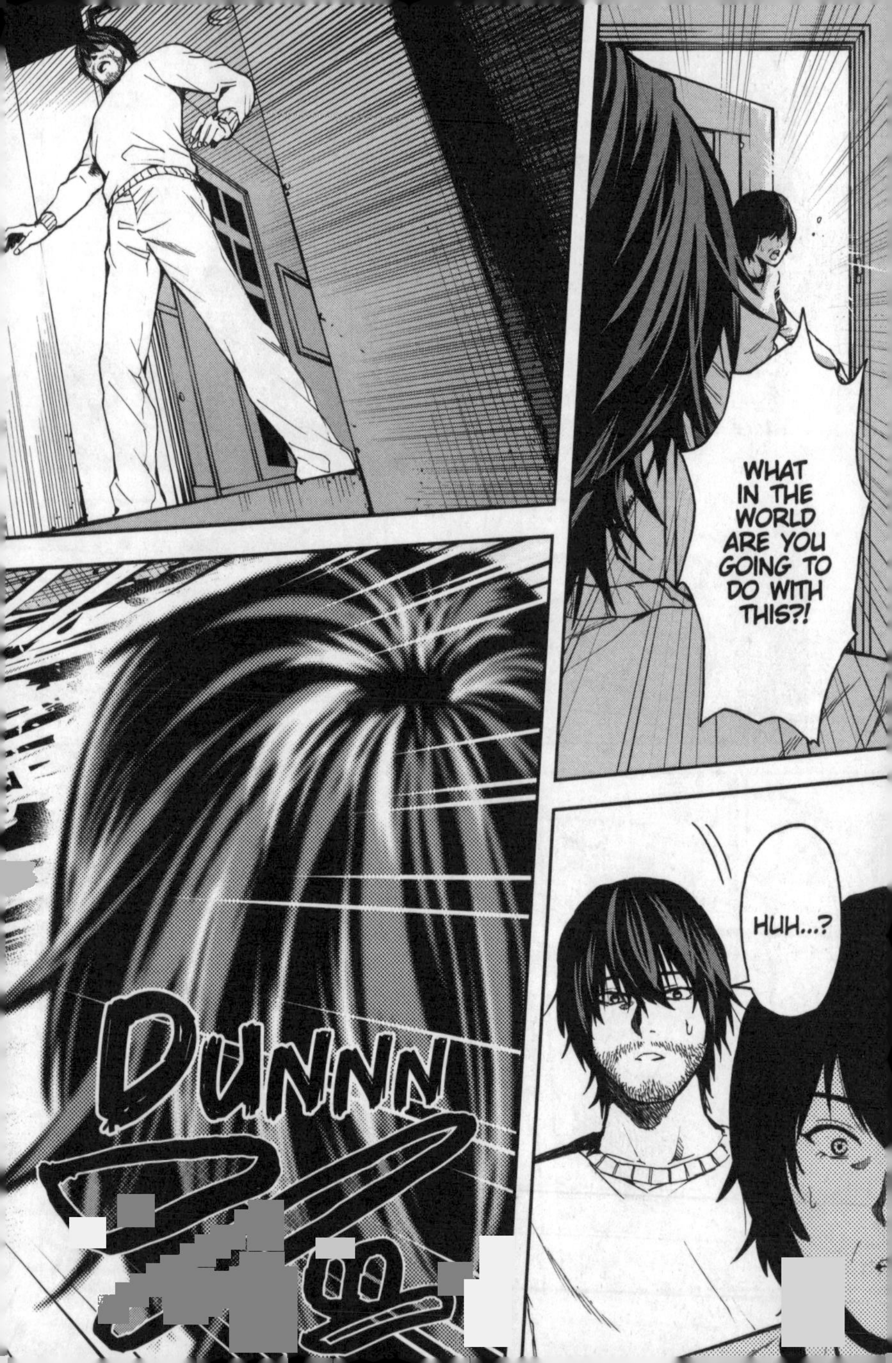
WHAT IN THE WORLD ARE YOU GOING TO DO WITH THIS?!
DUNNN
HUH...?

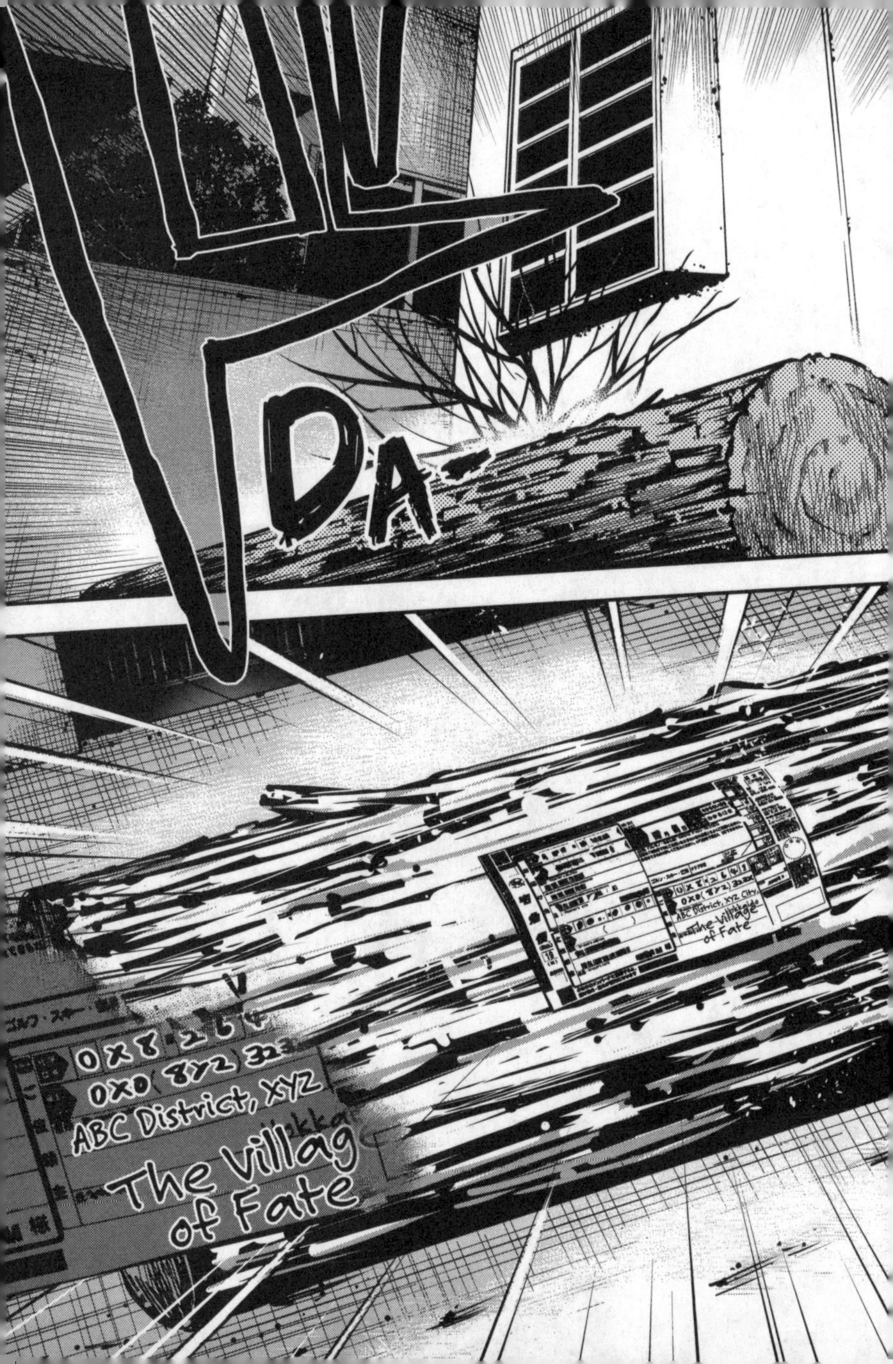
DA
0X0 (8Y2) 32
ABC District, XYZ City,
The Village
of Fate
0X8 2 6 4
0X0 (8Y2) 323
ABC District, XYZ
The Villag
of Fate

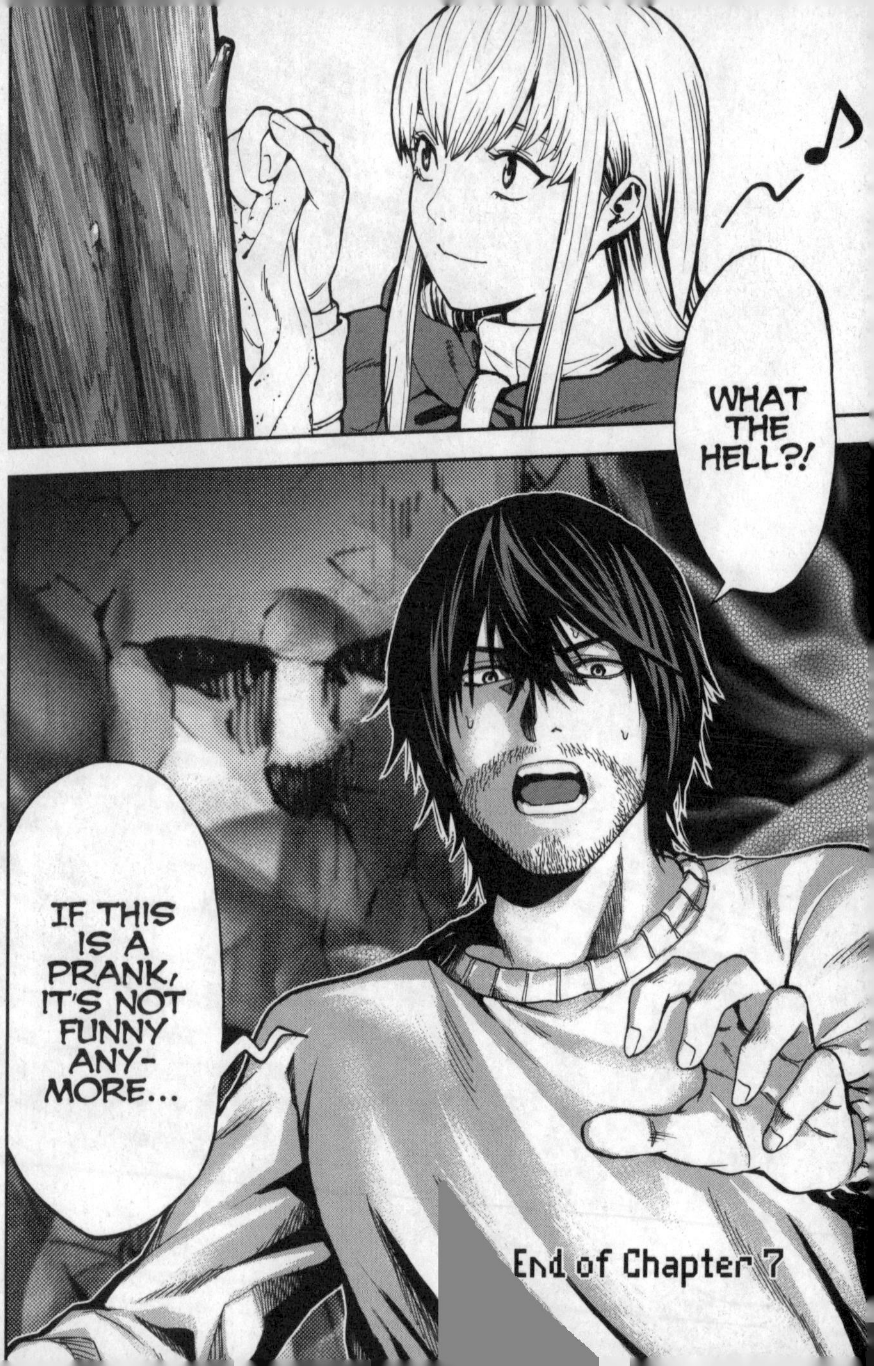
♪
WHAT THE HELL?!
IF THIS IS A PRANK, IT'S NOT FUNNY ANY-MORE...
End of Chapter 7

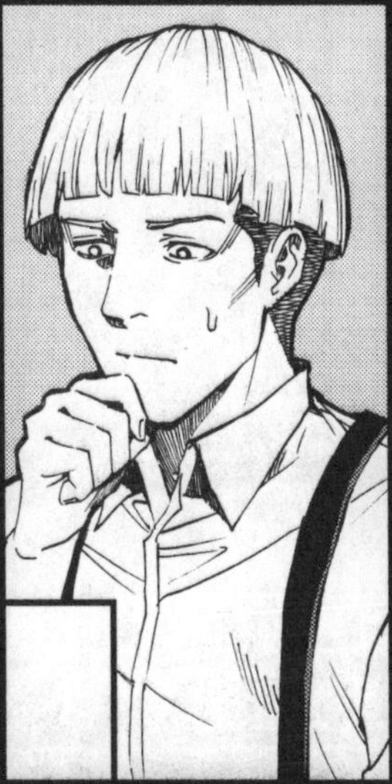

Character

Rodice

▶ Gender: Male

Class: Villager

E : Clothes (cloth)

E : Love for his family

E : Trauma

THE NPCs IN THIS VILLAGE SIM GAME MUST BE REAL!

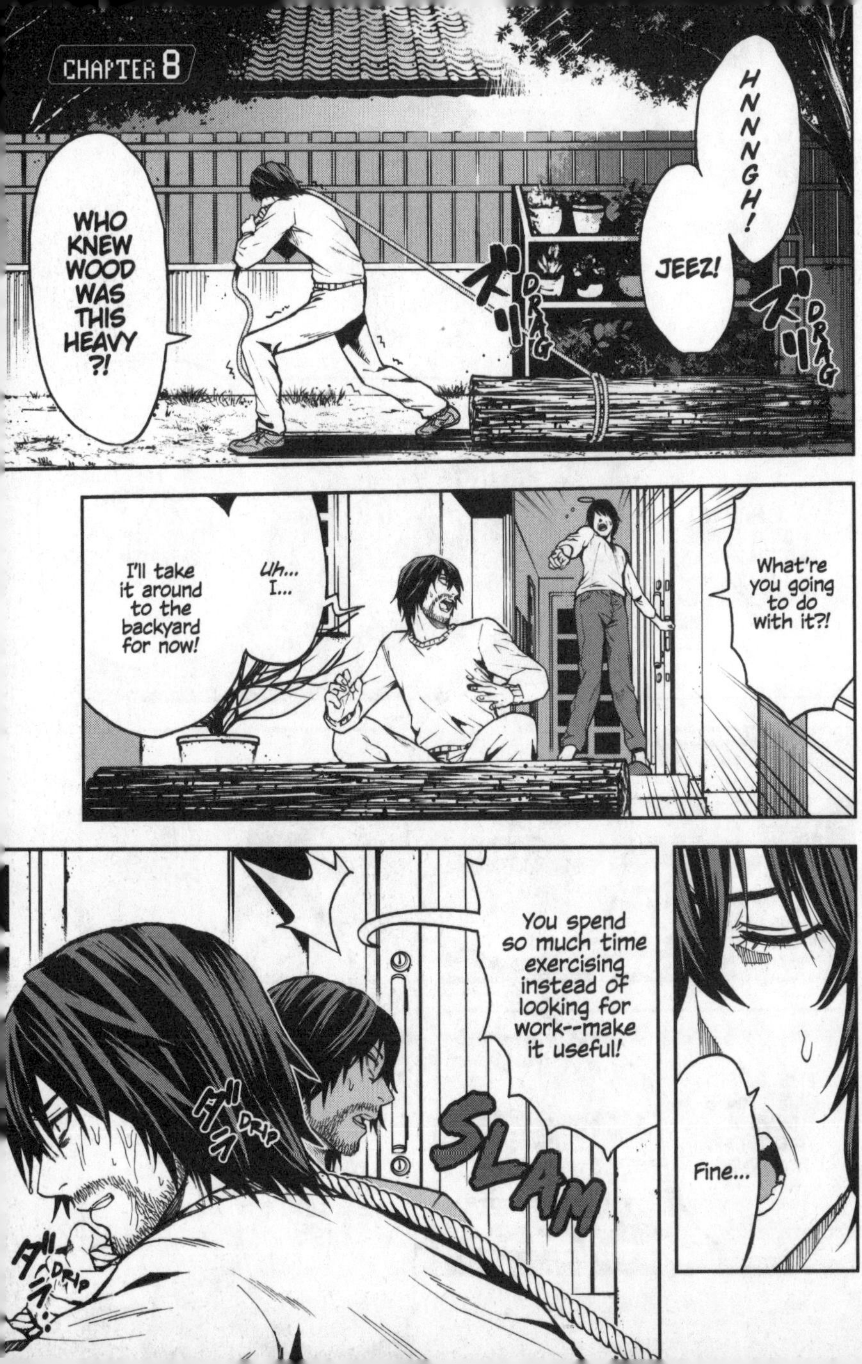
CHAPTER 8
HNNNGH!
JEEZ!
DRAG
DRAG
WHO KNEW WOOD WAS THIS HEAVY?!
What're you going to do with it?!
Uh... I...
I'll take it around to the backyard for now!
Fine...
You spend so much time exercising instead of looking for work--make it useful!
SLAM
DRIP
DRIP

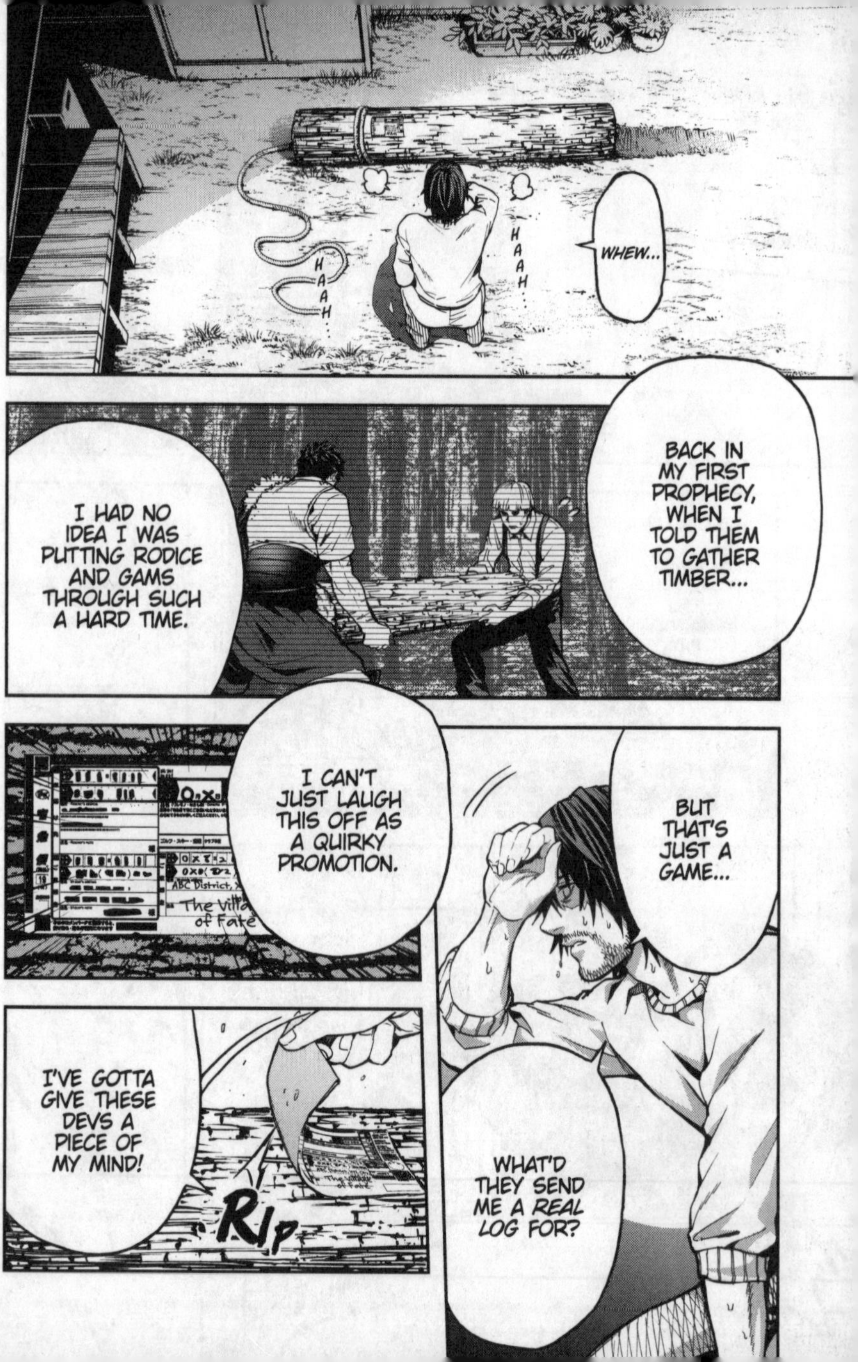
WHEW...
HAAH...
HAAH...
BACK IN MY FIRST PROPHECY, WHEN I TOLD THEM TO GATHER TIMBER...
I HAD NO IDEA I WAS PUTTING RODICE AND GAMS THROUGH SUCH A HARD TIME.
BUT THAT'S JUST A GAME...
WHAT'D THEY SEND ME A *REAL* LOG FOR?
I CAN'T JUST LAUGH THIS OFF AS A QUIRKY PROMOTION.
I'VE GOTTA GIVE THESE DEVS A PIECE OF MY MIND!
RIP

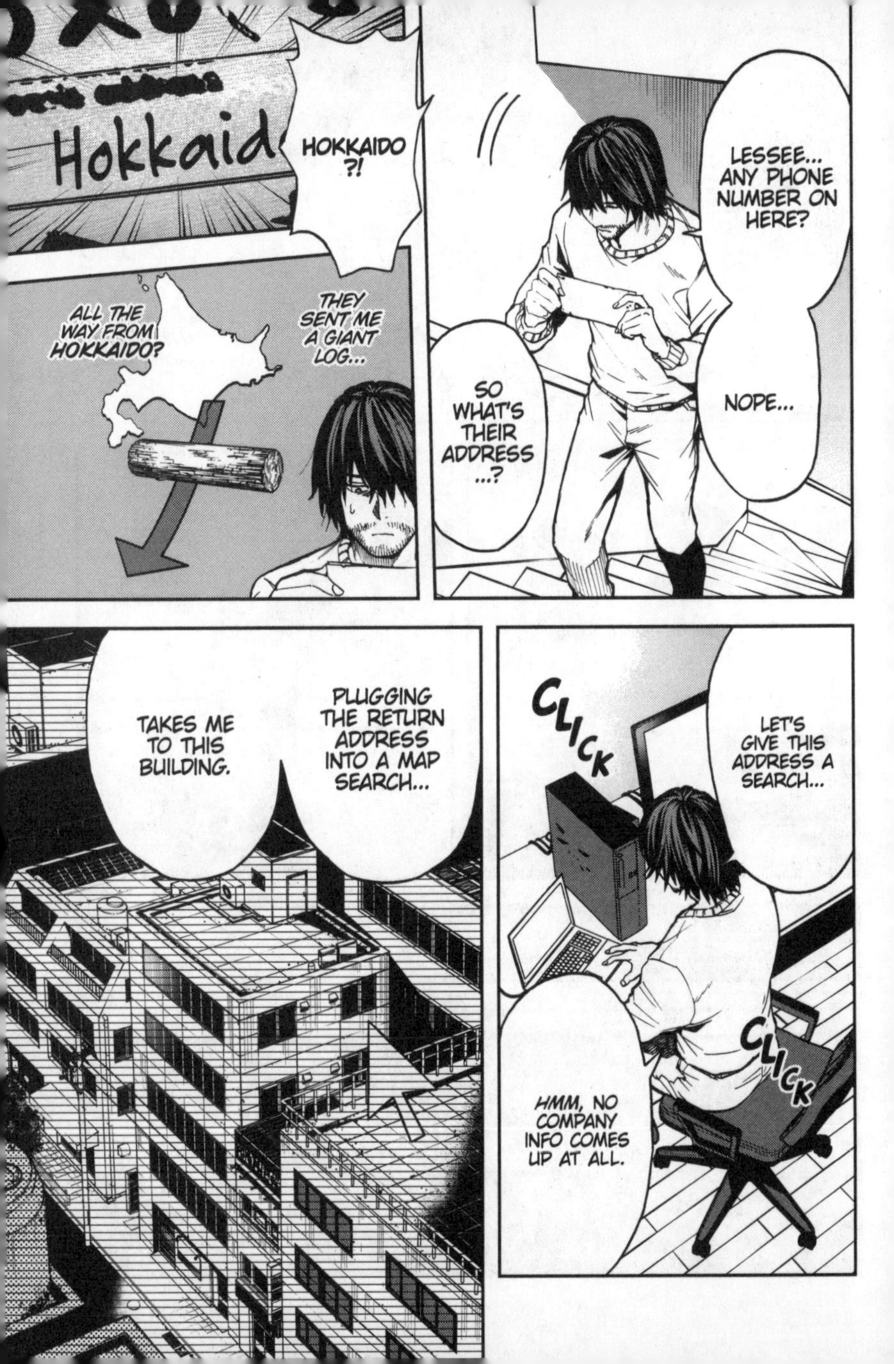
LESSEE... ANY PHONE NUMBER ON HERE?
NOPE...
SO WHAT'S THEIR ADDRESS ...?
Hokkaid
HOKKAIDO ?!
THEY SENT ME A GIANT LOG...
ALL THE WAY FROM HOKKAIDO?
LET'S GIVE THIS ADDRESS A SEARCH...
CLICK
CLICK
HMM, NO COMPANY INFO COMES UP AT ALL.
PLUGGING THE RETURN ADDRESS INTO A MAP SEARCH...
TAKES ME TO THIS BUILDING.

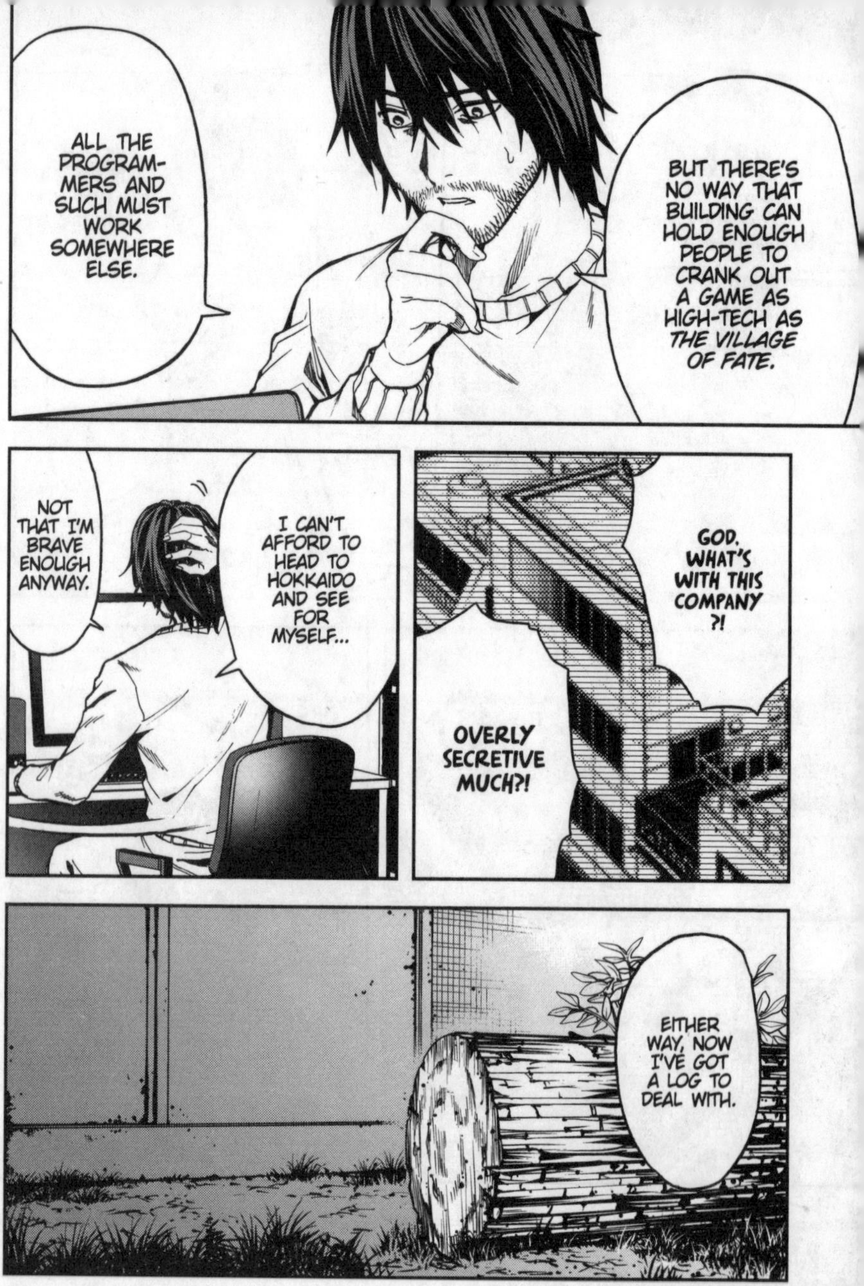
BUT THERE'S NO WAY THAT BUILDING CAN HOLD ENOUGH PEOPLE TO CRANK OUT A GAME AS HIGH-TECH AS *THE VILLAGE OF FATE.*
ALL THE PROGRAMMERS AND SUCH MUST WORK SOMEWHERE ELSE.
GOD. WHAT'S WITH THIS COMPANY?!
OVERLY SECRETIVE MUCH?!
I CAN'T AFFORD TO HEAD TO HOKKAIDO AND SEE FOR MYSELF...
NOT THAT I'M BRAVE ENOUGH ANYWAY.
EITHER WAY, NOW I'VE GOT A LOG TO DEAL WITH.

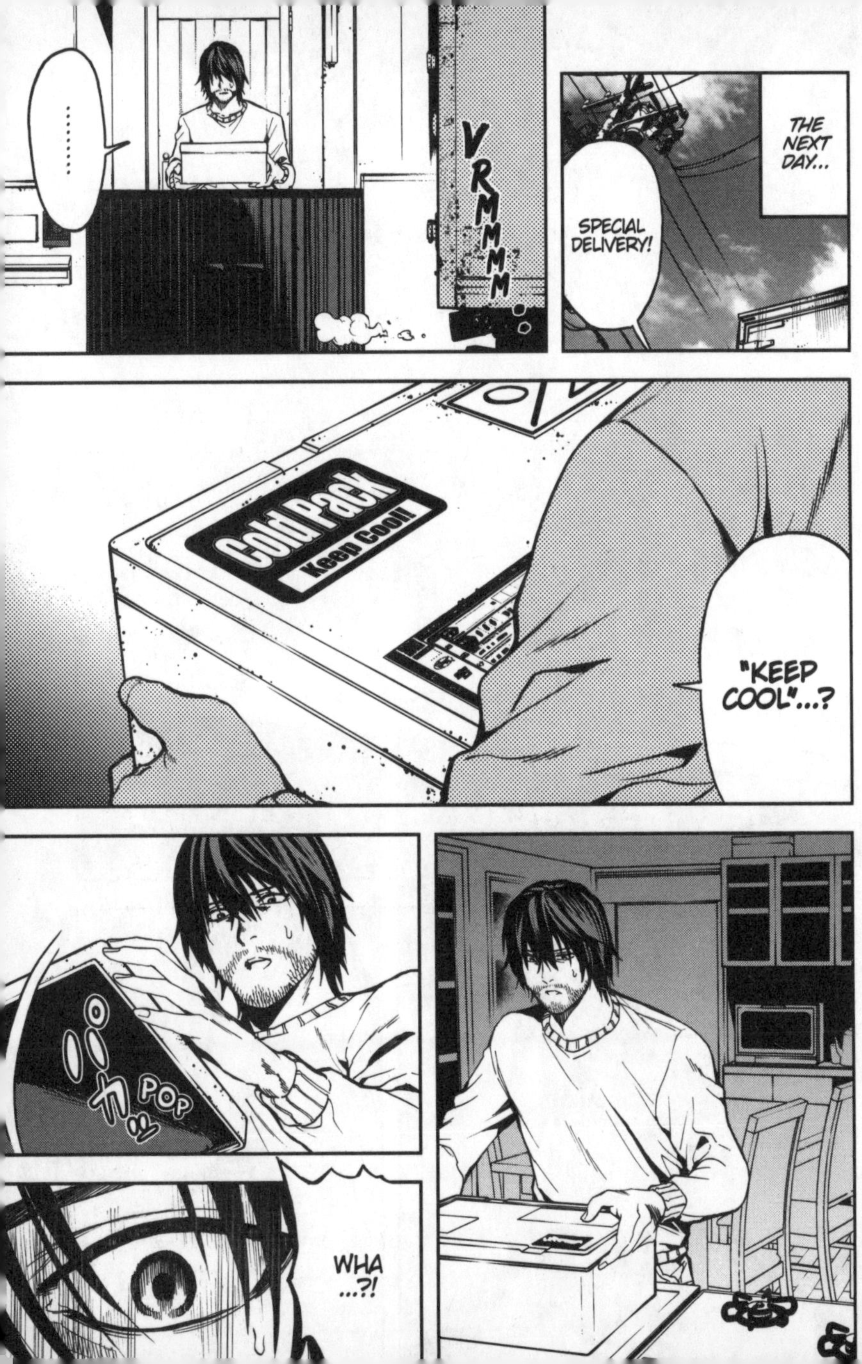
THE NEXT DAY...
SPECIAL DELIVERY!
VRMMMM
......
Cold Pack
Keep Cool!
"KEEP COOL"...?
POP
WHA ...?!

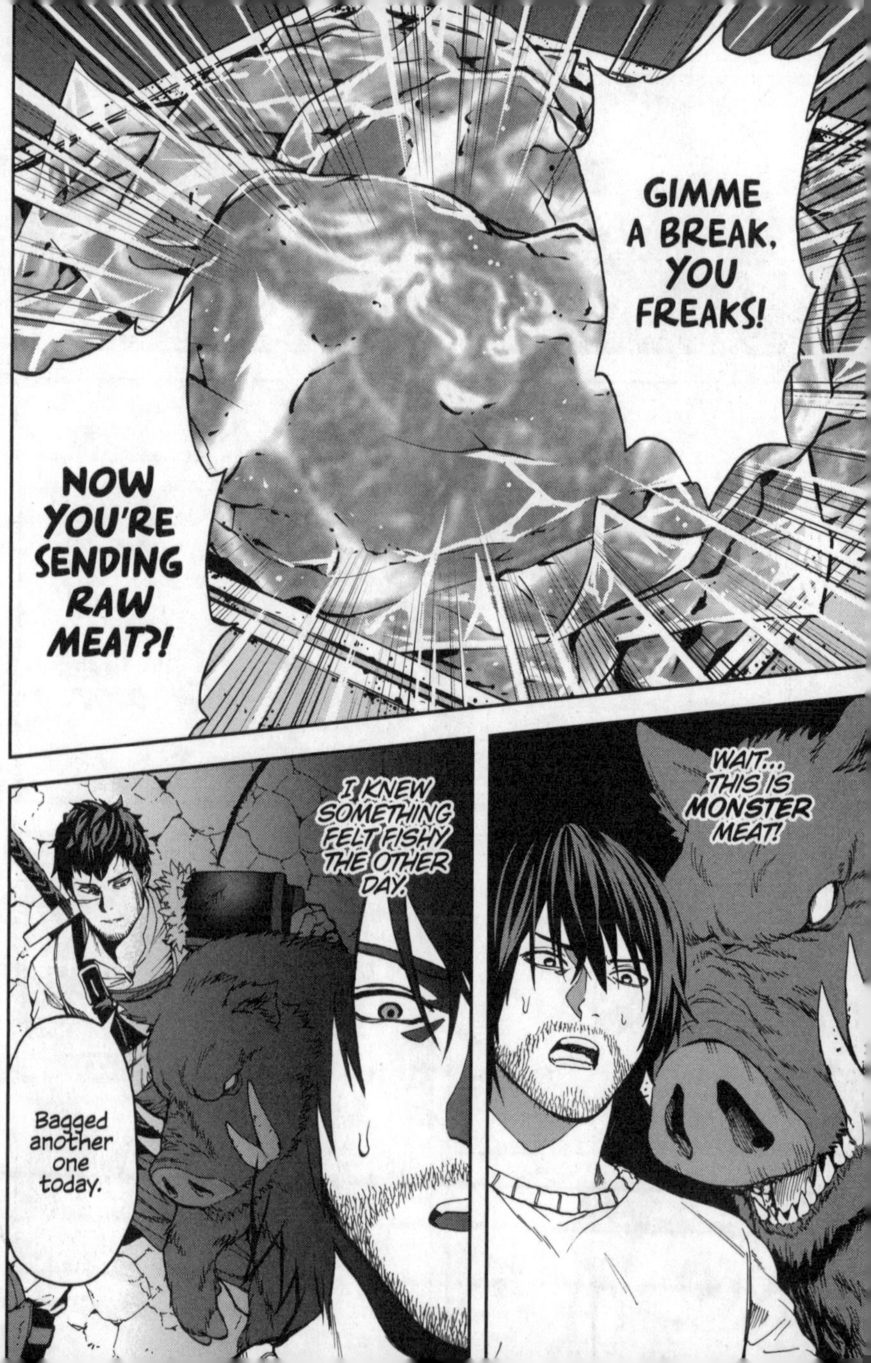
GIMME A BREAK, YOU FREAKS!
NOW YOU'RE SENDING RAW MEAT?!
WAIT... THIS IS MONSTER MEAT!
I KNEW SOMETHING FELT FISHY THE OTHER DAY.
Bagged another one today.

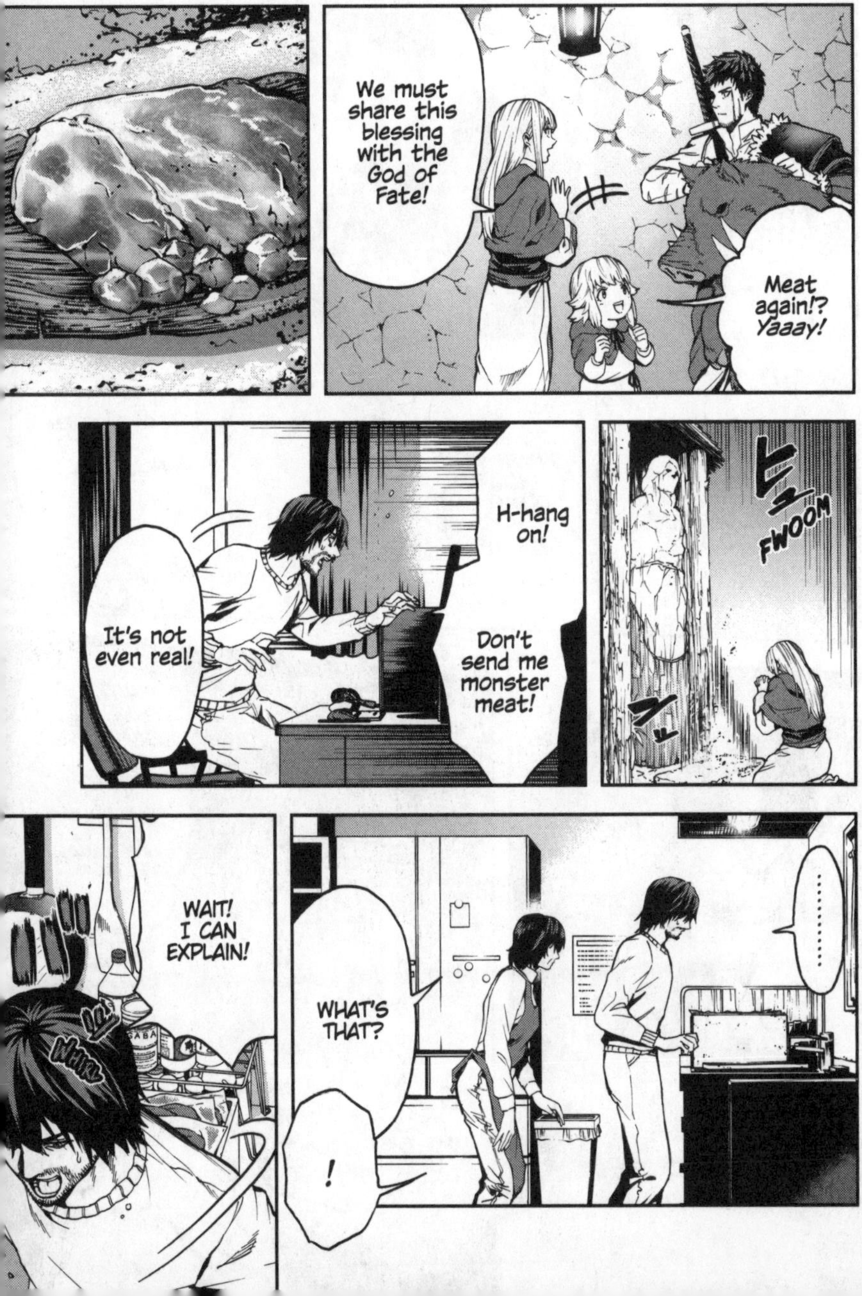
We must share this blessing with the God of Fate!
Meat again!? Yaaay!
FWOOM
H-hang on!
Don't send me monster meat!
It's not even real!
......
WHAT'S THAT?
!
WAIT! I CAN EXPLAIN!

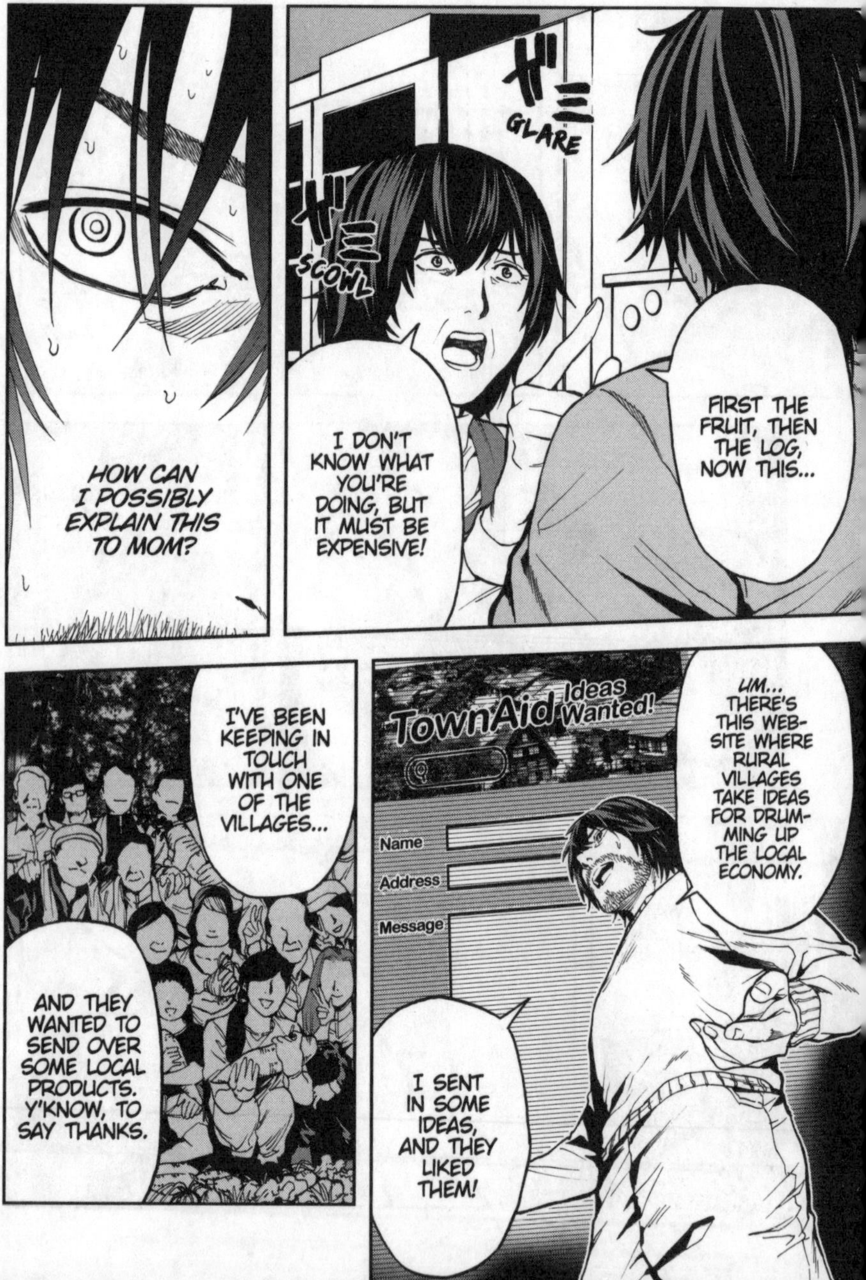
GLARE
FIRST THE FRUIT, THEN THE LOG, NOW THIS...
SCOWL
I DON'T KNOW WHAT YOU'RE DOING, BUT IT MUST BE EXPENSIVE!
HOW CAN I POSSIBLY EXPLAIN THIS TO MOM?
TownAid Ideas Wanted!
Name
Address
Message
UM... THERE'S THIS WEB-SITE WHERE RURAL VILLAGES TAKE IDEAS FOR DRUM-MING UP THE LOCAL ECONOMY.
I SENT IN SOME IDEAS, AND THEY LIKED THEM!
I'VE BEEN KEEPING IN TOUCH WITH ONE OF THE VILLAGES...
AND THEY WANTED TO SEND OVER SOME LOCAL PRODUCTS. Y'KNOW, TO SAY THANKS.

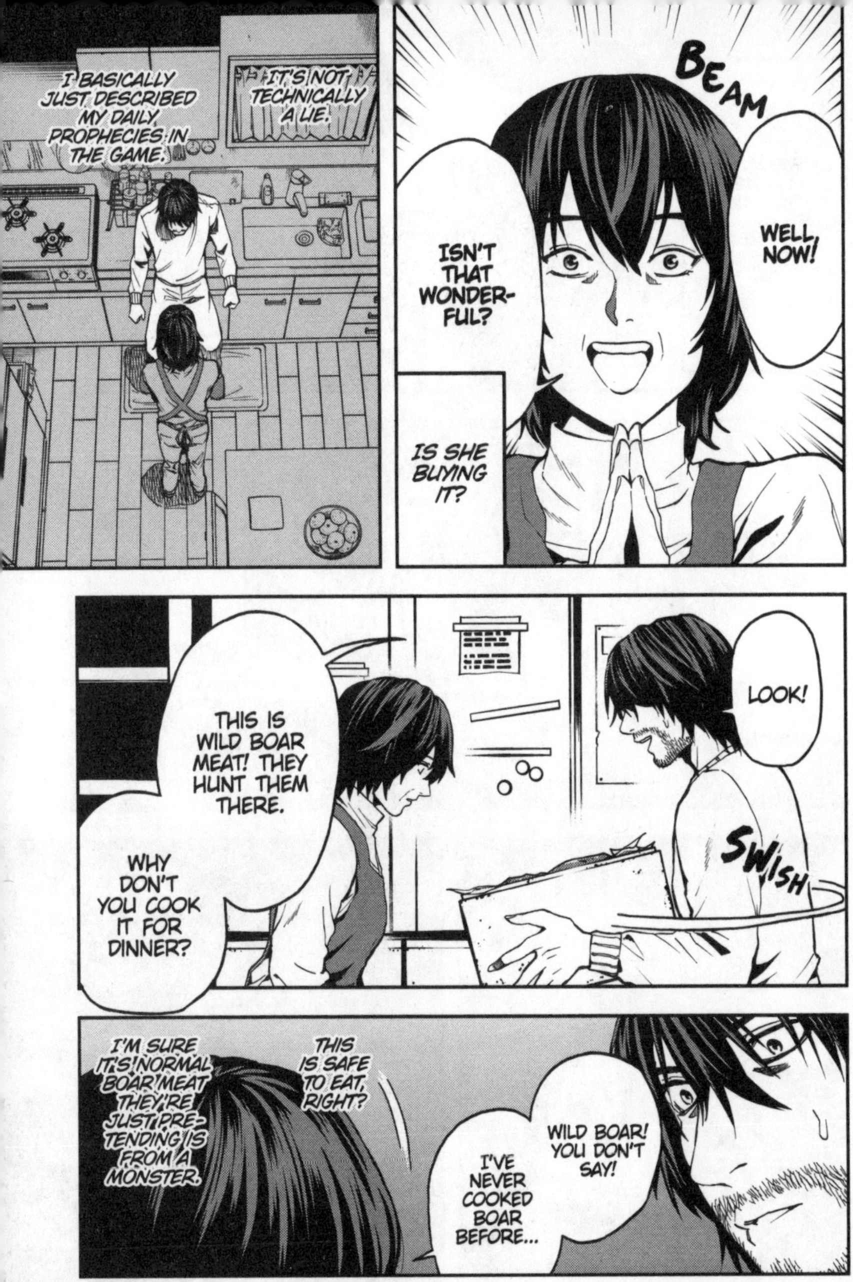
BEAM
WELL NOW!
ISN'T THAT WONDERFUL?
IS SHE BUYING IT?
IT'S NOT TECHNICALLY A LIE.
I BASICALLY JUST DESCRIBED MY DAILY PROPHECIES IN THE GAME.
LOOK!
SWISH
THIS IS WILD BOAR MEAT! THEY HUNT THEM THERE.
WHY DON'T YOU COOK IT FOR DINNER?
WILD BOAR! YOU DON'T SAY!
I'VE NEVER COOKED BOAR BEFORE...
THIS IS SAFE TO EAT, RIGHT?
I'M SURE IT'S NORMAL BOAR MEAT THEY'RE JUST PRETENDING IS FROM A MONSTER.

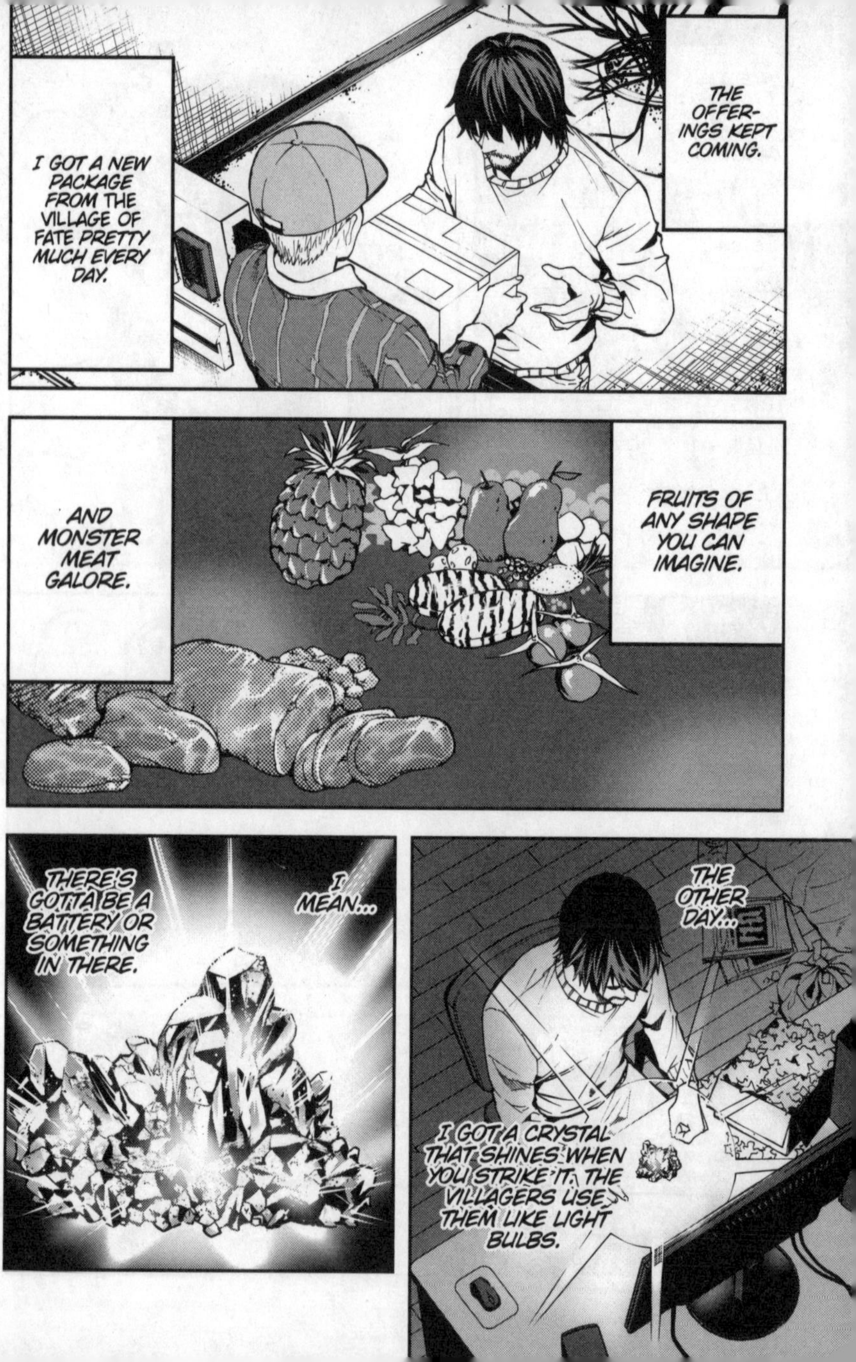
THE OFFER-INGS KEPT COMING.
I GOT A NEW PACKAGE FROM THE VILLAGE OF FATE PRETTY MUCH EVERY DAY.
FRUITS OF ANY SHAPE YOU CAN IMAGINE.
AND MONSTER MEAT GALORE.
THE OTHER DAY...
I GOT A CRYSTAL THAT SHINES WHEN YOU STRIKE IT. THE VILLAGERS USE THEM LIKE LIGHT BULBS.
I MEAN...
THERE'S GOTTA BE A BATTERY OR SOMETHING IN THERE.

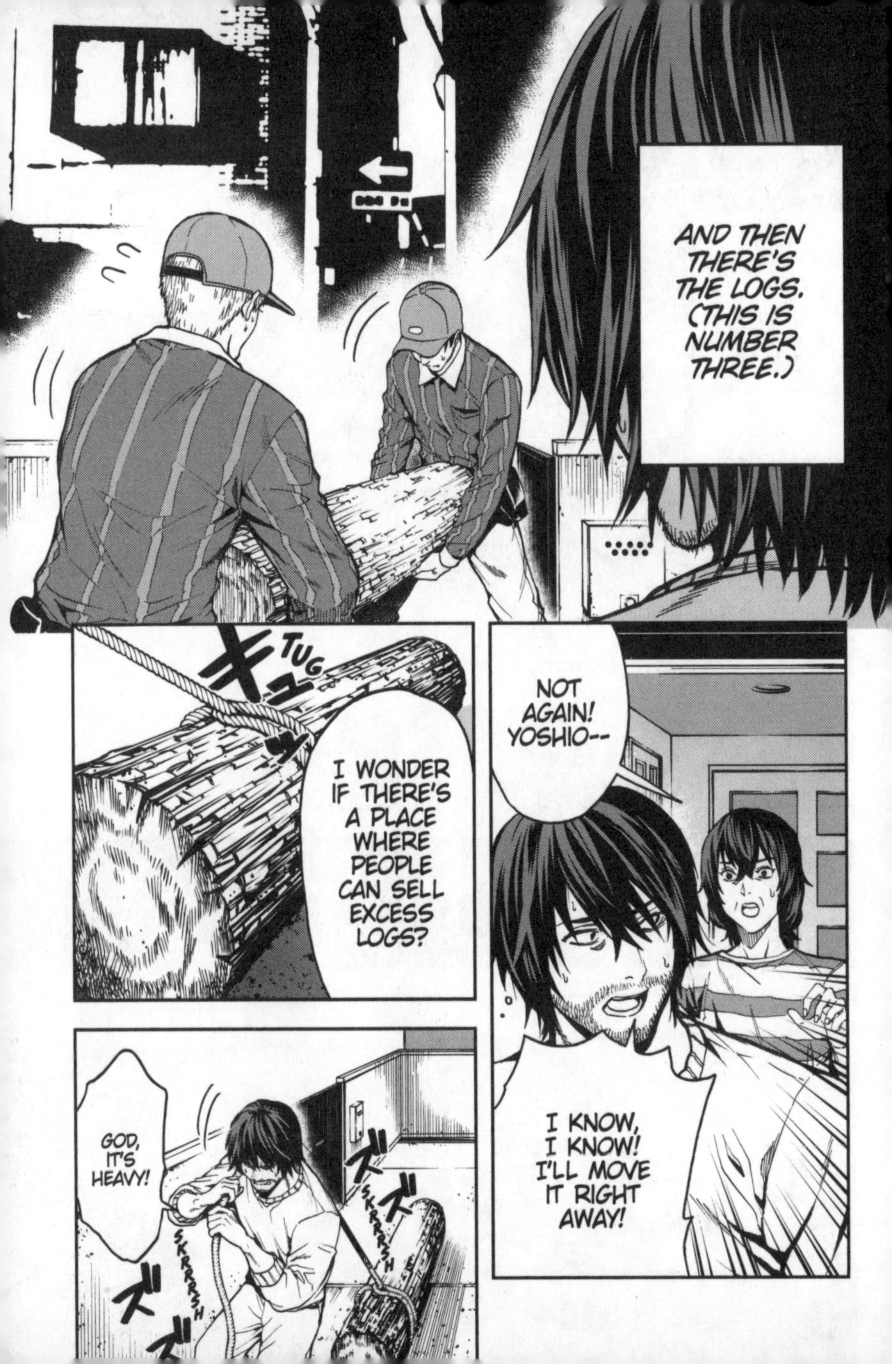
AND THEN THERE'S THE LOGS. (THIS IS NUMBER THREE.)
NOT AGAIN! YOSHIO--
I KNOW, I KNOW! I'LL MOVE IT RIGHT AWAY!
TUG
I WONDER IF THERE'S A PLACE WHERE PEOPLE CAN SELL EXCESS LOGS?
GOD, IT'S HEAVY!
SKRRRSH
SKRRRSH

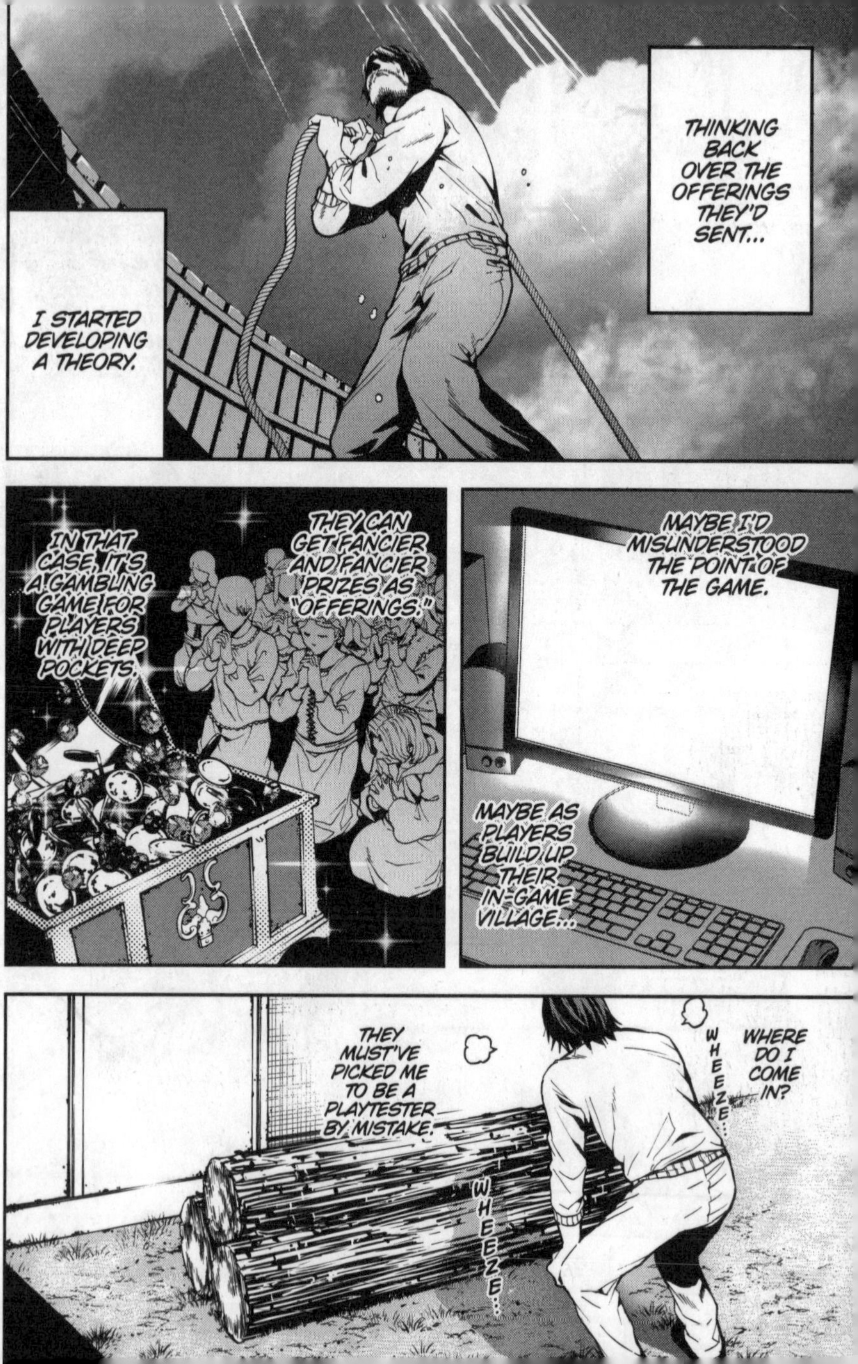
THINKING BACK OVER THE OFFERINGS THEY'D SENT...
I STARTED DEVELOPING A THEORY.
MAYBE I'D MISUNDERSTOOD THE POINT OF THE GAME.
MAYBE AS PLAYERS BUILD UP THEIR IN-GAME VILLAGE...
THEY CAN GET FANCIER AND FANCIER PRIZES AS "OFFERINGS."
IN THAT CASE, IT'S A GAMBLING GAME FOR PLAYERS WITH DEEP POCKETS.
WHERE DO I COME IN?
WHEEZE...
THEY MUST'VE PICKED ME TO BE A PLAYTESTER BY MISTAKE.
WHEEZE...

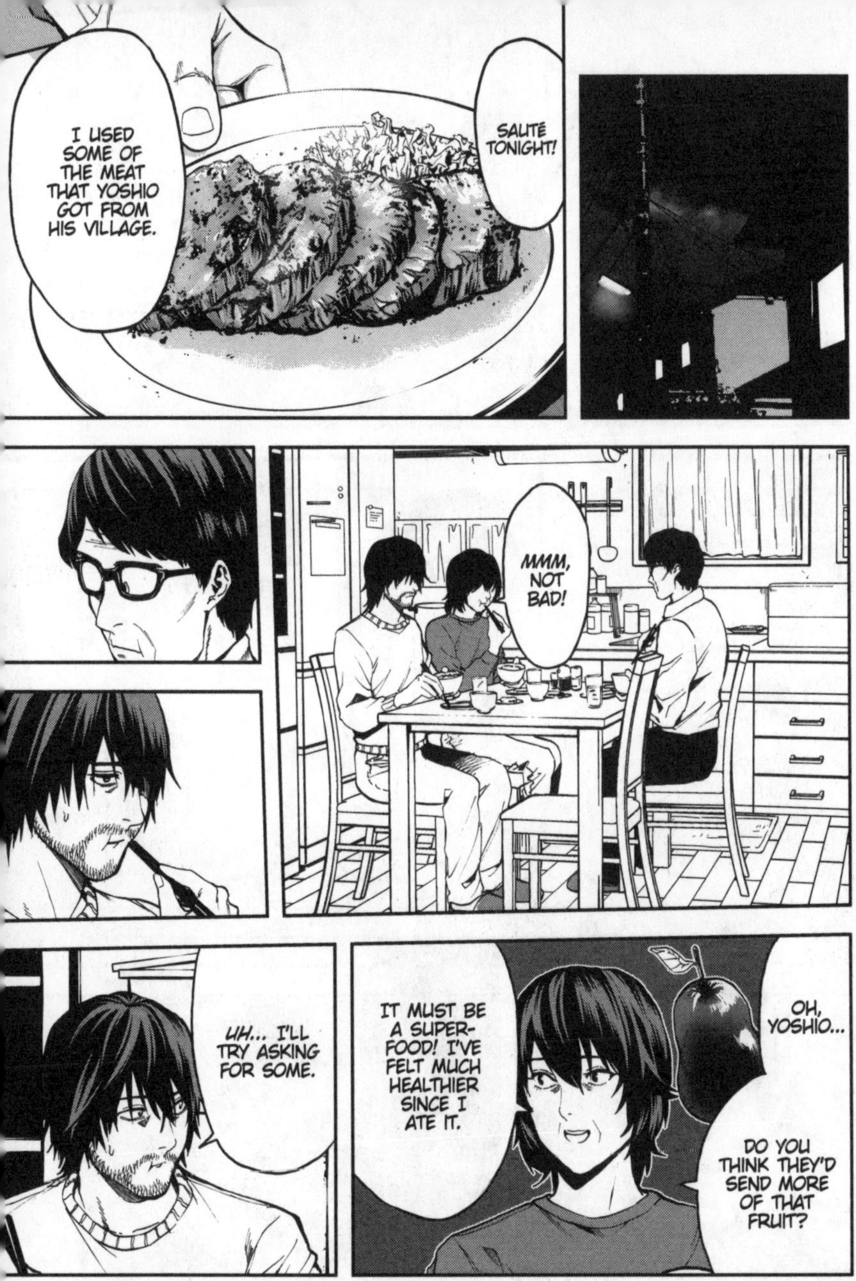
SAUTÉ TONIGHT!
I USED SOME OF THE MEAT THAT YOSHIO GOT FROM HIS VILLAGE.
MMM, NOT BAD!
OH, YOSHIO...
IT MUST BE A SUPER-FOOD! I'VE FELT MUCH HEALTHIER SINCE I ATE IT.
DO YOU THINK THEY'D SEND MORE OF THAT FRUIT?
UH... I'LL TRY ASKING FOR SOME.

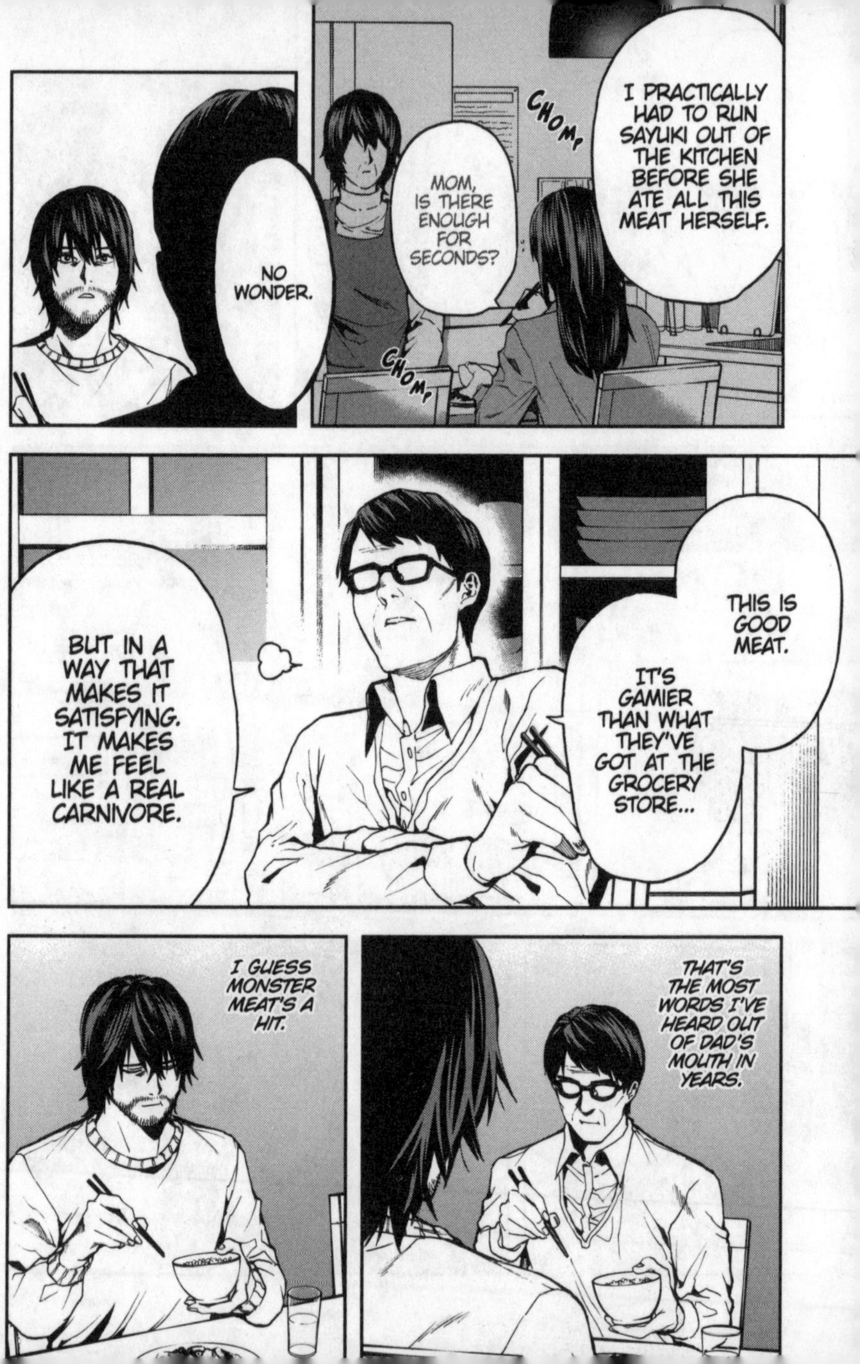
I PRACTICALLY HAD TO RUN SAYUKI OUT OF THE KITCHEN BEFORE SHE ATE ALL THIS MEAT HERSELF.
CHOMP
MOM, IS THERE ENOUGH FOR SECONDS?
CHOMP
NO WONDER.
THIS IS GOOD MEAT.
IT'S GAMIER THAN WHAT THEY'VE GOT AT THE GROCERY STORE...
BUT IN A WAY THAT MAKES IT SATISFYING. IT MAKES ME FEEL LIKE A REAL CARNIVORE.
THAT'S THE MOST WORDS I'VE HEARD OUT OF DAD'S MOUTH IN YEARS.
I GUESS MONSTER MEAT'S A HIT.

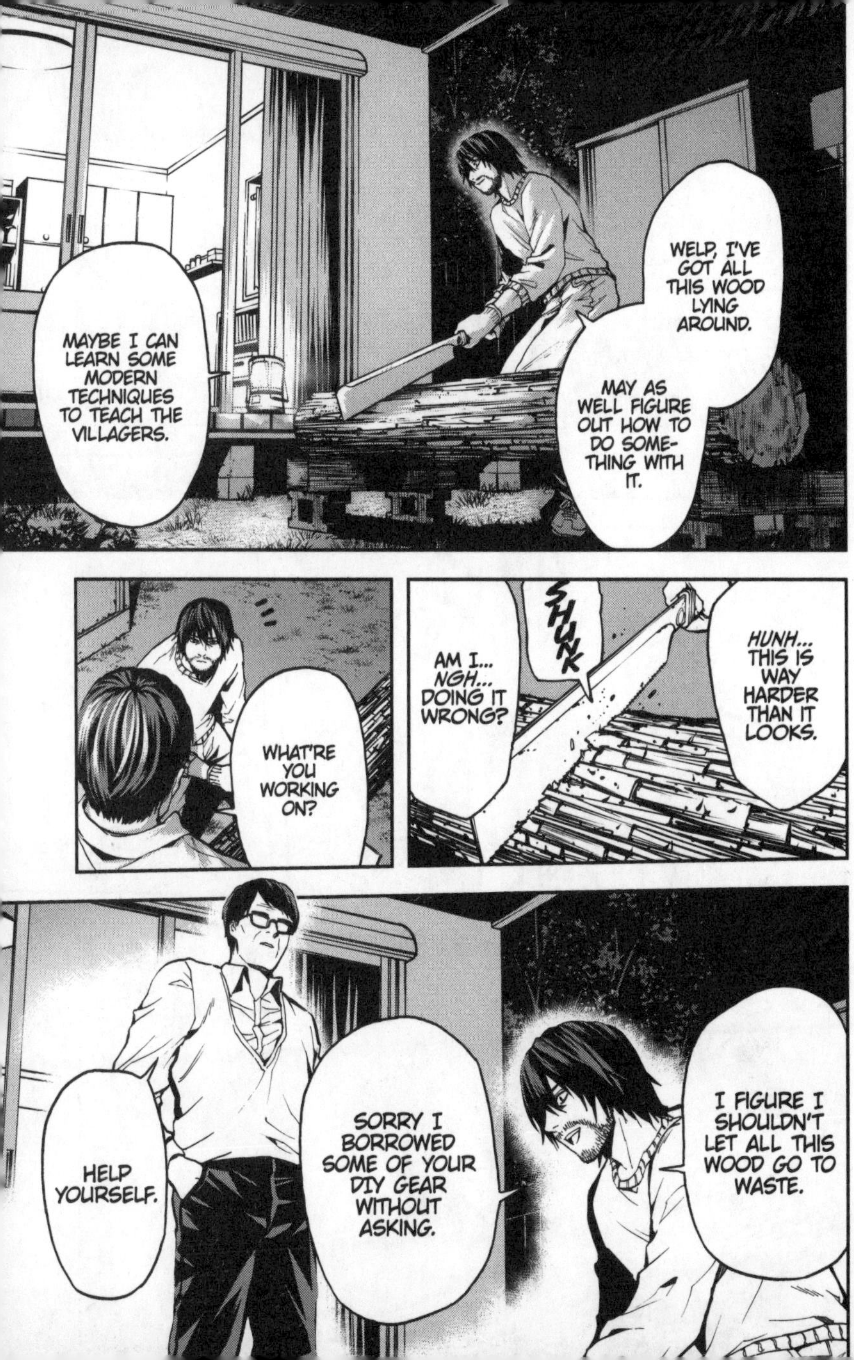
WELP, I'VE GOT ALL THIS WOOD LYING AROUND.
MAY AS WELL FIGURE OUT HOW TO DO SOME-THING WITH IT.
MAYBE I CAN LEARN SOME MODERN TECHNIQUES TO TEACH THE VILLAGERS.
HUNH... THIS IS WAY HARDER THAN IT LOOKS.
SHUNK
AM I... NGH... DOING IT WRONG?
WHAT'RE YOU WORKING ON?
I FIGURE I SHOULDN'T LET ALL THIS WOOD GO TO WASTE.
SORRY I BORROWED SOME OF YOUR DIY GEAR WITHOUT ASKING.
HELP YOURSELF.

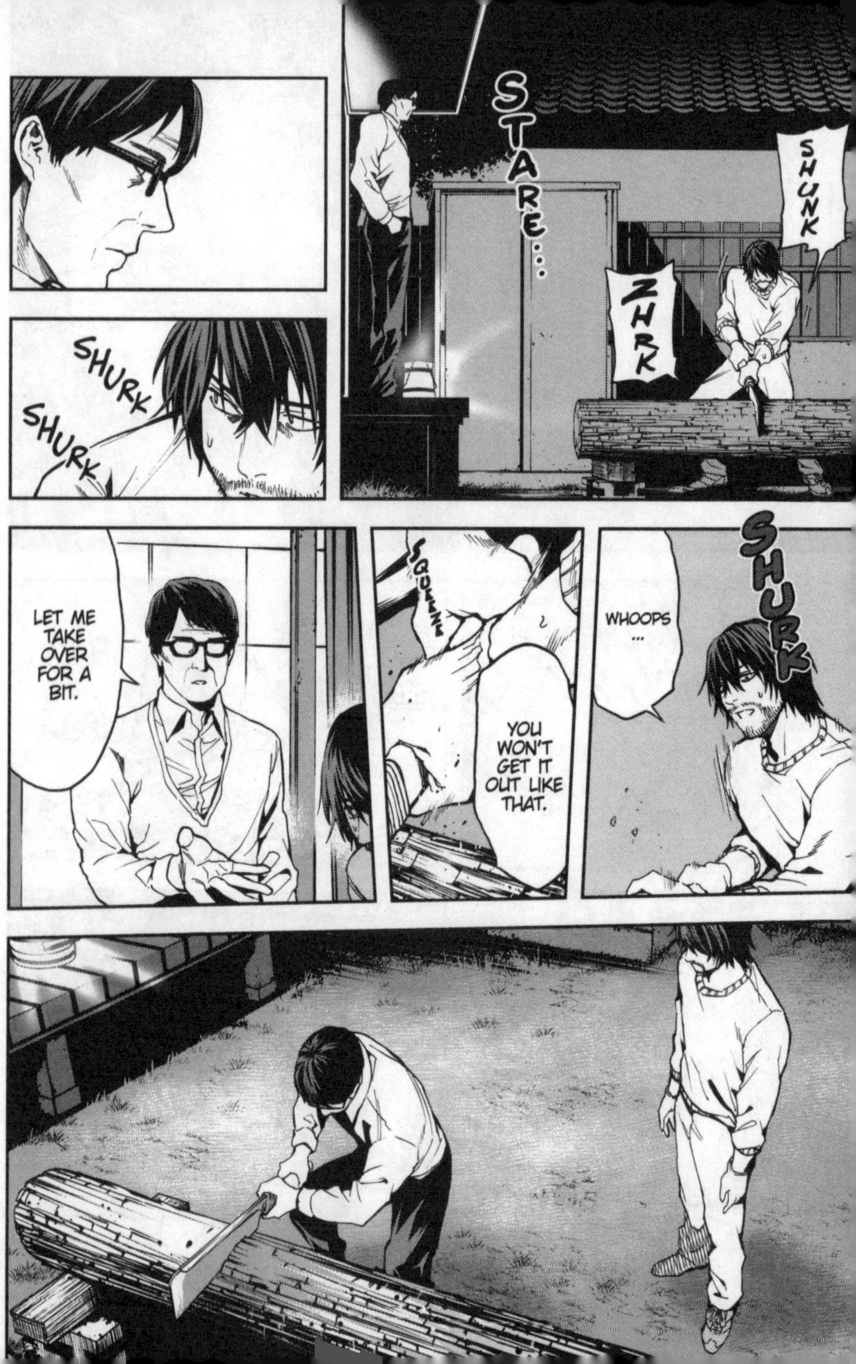
SHUNK
STARE...
ZHRK
SHURK
SHURK
SHURK
WHOOPS...
SQUEEZE
YOU WON'T GET IT OUT LIKE THAT.
LET ME TAKE OVER FOR A BIT.

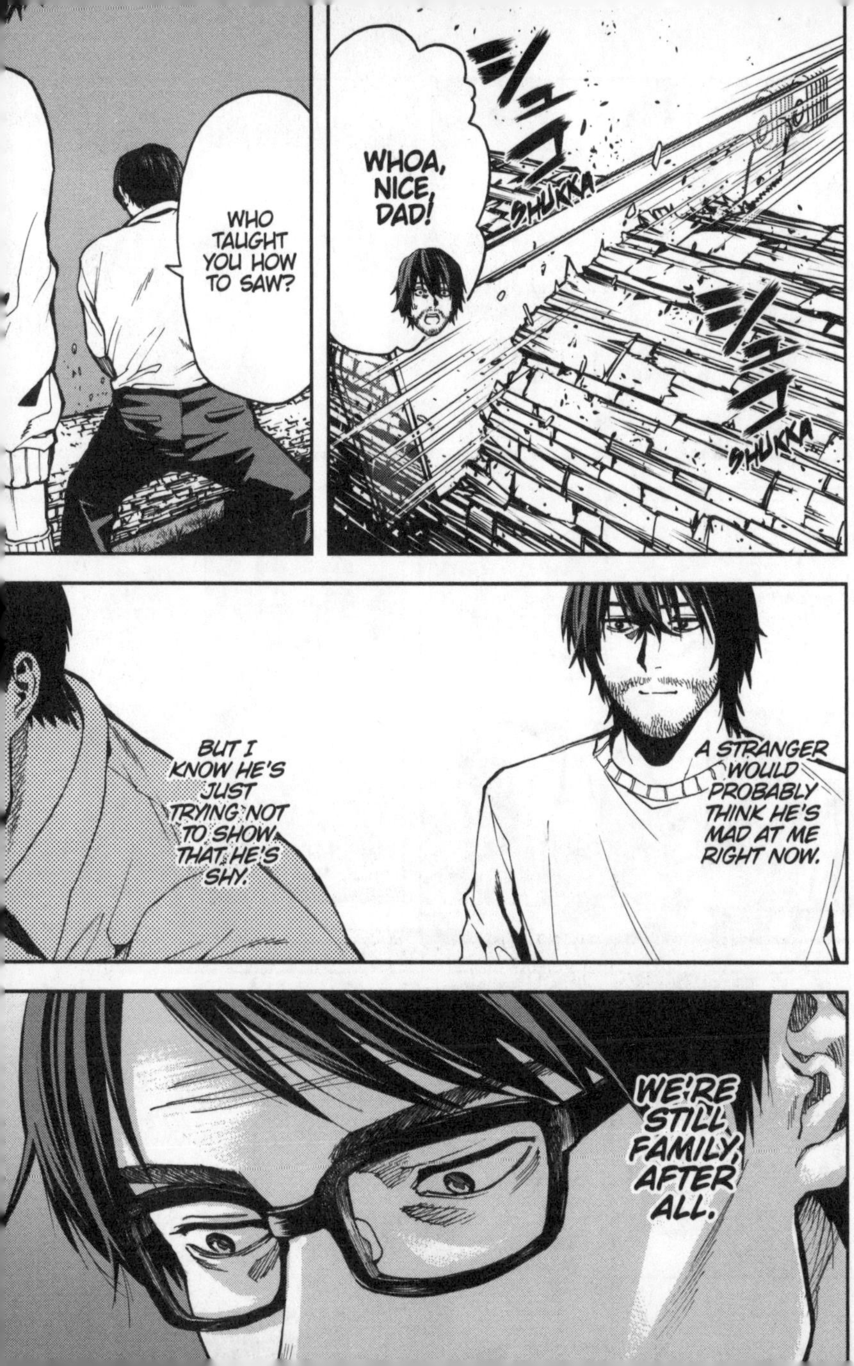
WHOA, NICE, DAD!
SHUKKA
SHUKKA
WHO TAUGHT YOU HOW TO SAW?
A STRANGER WOULD PROBABLY THINK HE'S MAD AT ME RIGHT NOW.
BUT I KNOW HE'S JUST TRYING NOT TO SHOW THAT HE'S SHY.
WE'RE STILL FAMILY, AFTER ALL.

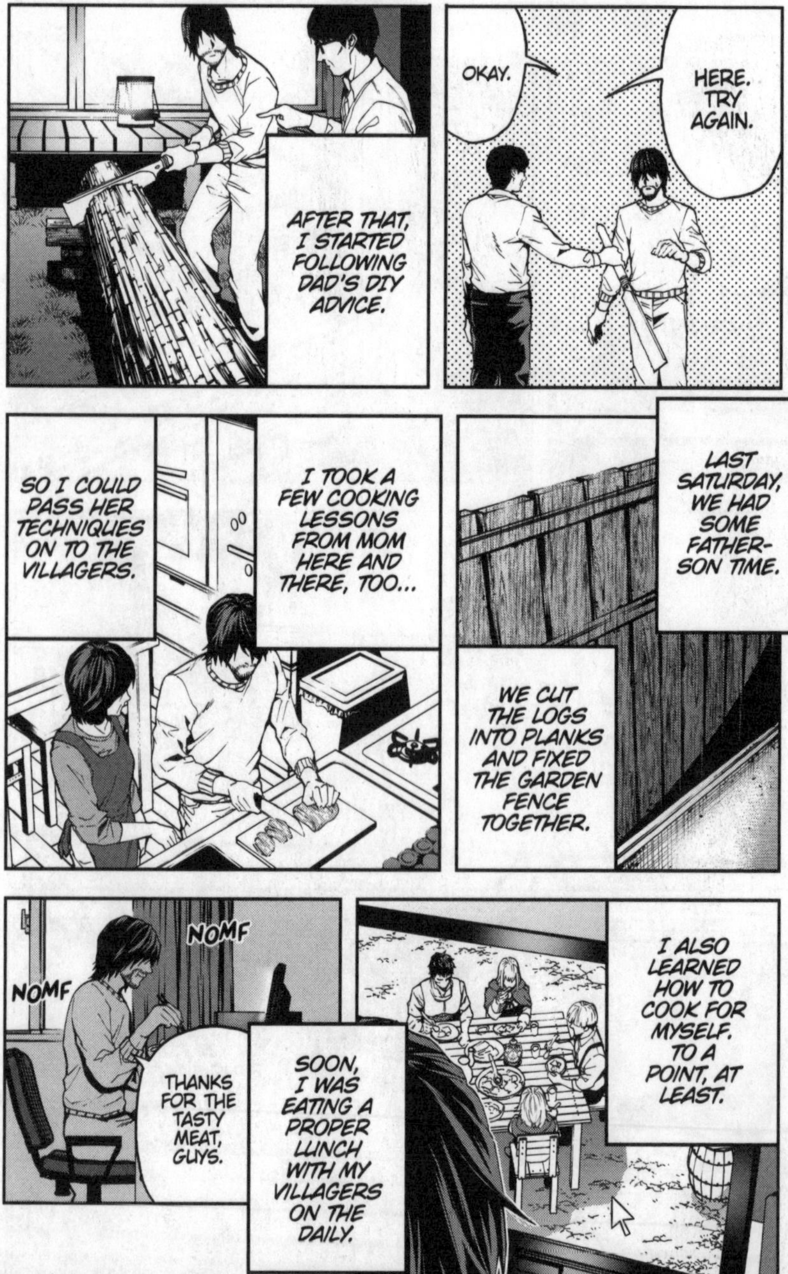
HERE. TRY AGAIN.
OKAY.
AFTER THAT, I STARTED FOLLOWING DAD'S DIY ADVICE.
LAST SATURDAY, WE HAD SOME FATHER-SON TIME.
WE CUT THE LOGS INTO PLANKS AND FIXED THE GARDEN FENCE TOGETHER.
I TOOK A FEW COOKING LESSONS FROM MOM HERE AND THERE, TOO...
SO I COULD PASS HER TECHNIQUES ON TO THE VILLAGERS.
I ALSO LEARNED HOW TO COOK FOR MYSELF. TO A POINT, AT LEAST.
SOON, I WAS EATING A PROPER LUNCH WITH MY VILLAGERS ON THE DAILY.
NOMF
NOMF
THANKS FOR THE TASTY MEAT, GUYS.

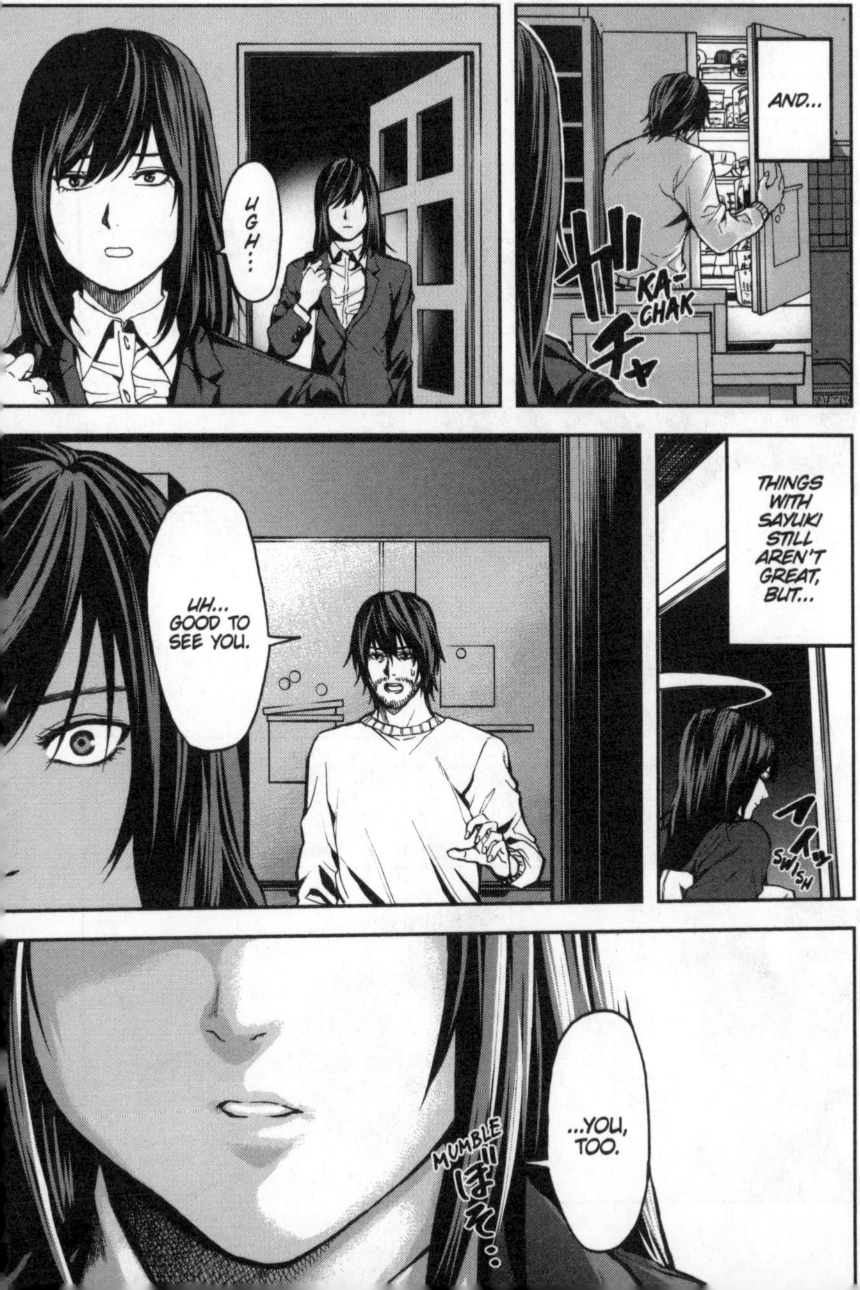
AND...
KA-CHAK
ガチャ
UGH...
THINGS WITH SAYUKI STILL AREN'T GREAT, BUT...
SWISH
スイッ
UH... GOOD TO SEE YOU.
...YOU, TOO.
MUMBLE
ぼそ…

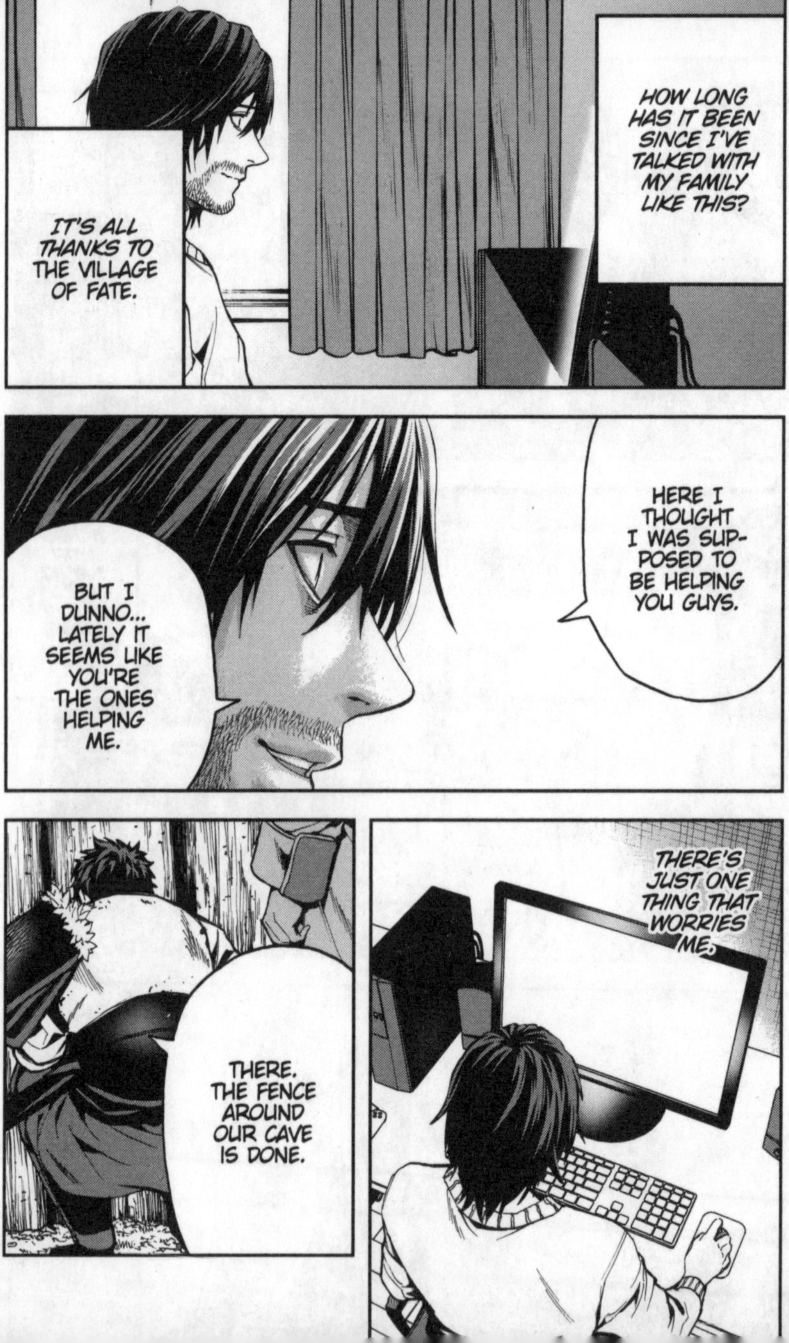
HOW LONG HAS IT BEEN SINCE I'VE TALKED WITH MY FAMILY LIKE THIS?
IT'S ALL THANKS TO THE VILLAGE OF FATE.
HERE I THOUGHT I WAS SUP-POSED TO BE HELPING YOU GUYS.
BUT I DUNNO... LATELY IT SEEMS LIKE YOU'RE THE ONES HELPING ME.
THERE'S JUST ONE THING THAT WORRIES ME.
THERE. THE FENCE AROUND OUR CAVE IS DONE.

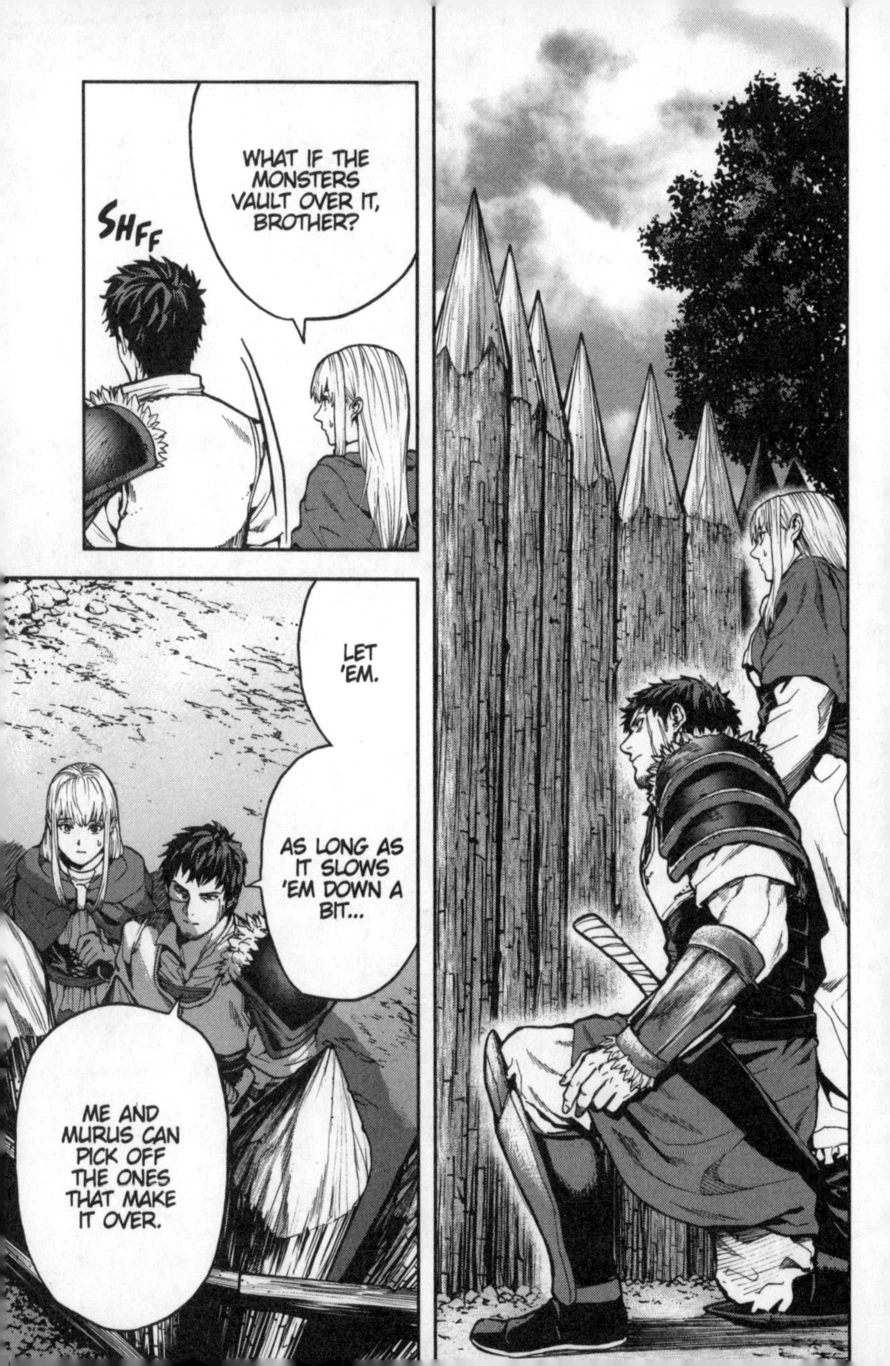
WHAT IF THE MONSTERS VAULT OVER IT, BROTHER?
SHFF
LET 'EM.
AS LONG AS IT SLOWS 'EM DOWN A BIT...
ME AND MURUS CAN PICK OFF THE ONES THAT MAKE IT OVER.

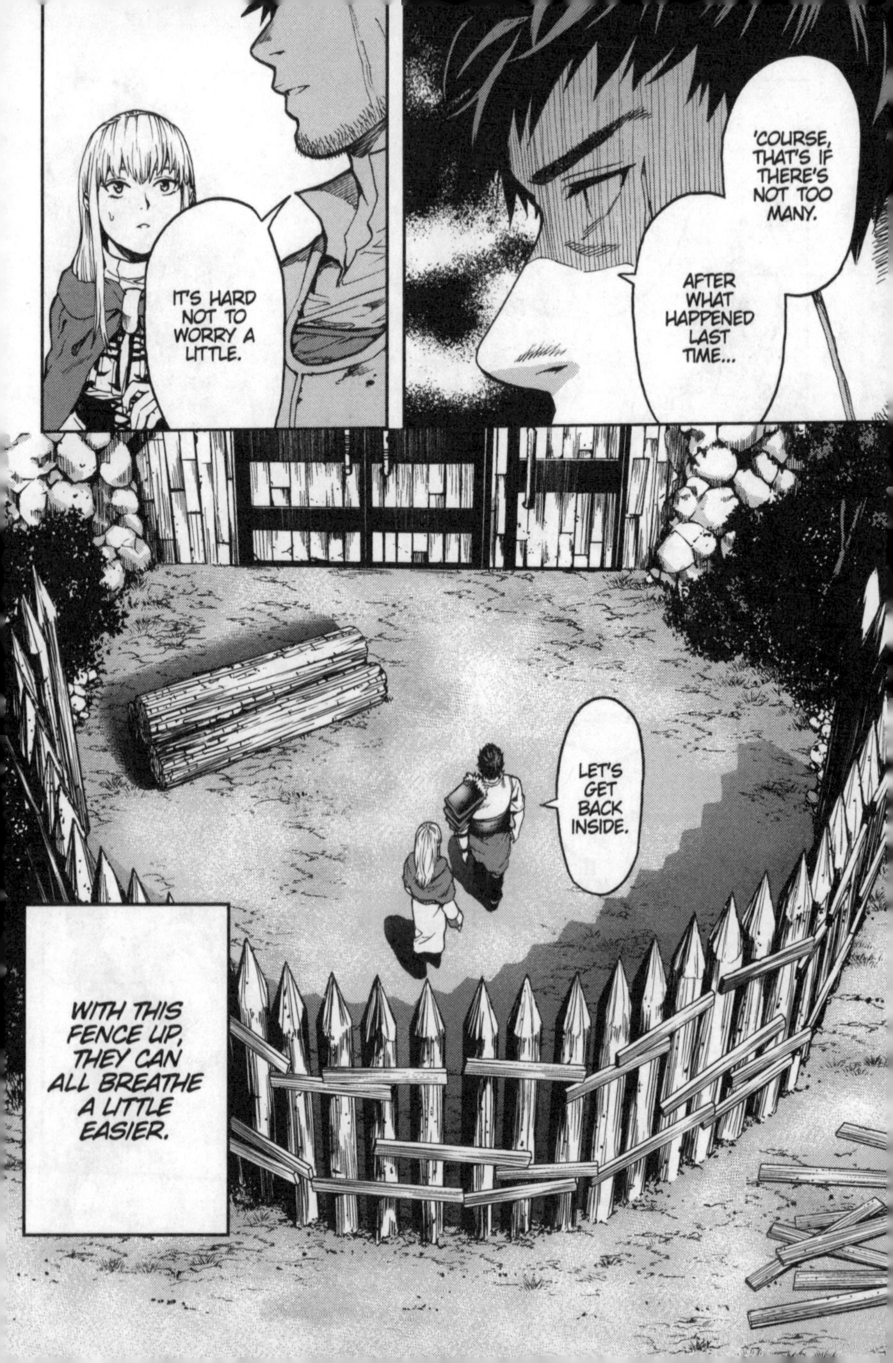
'COURSE, THAT'S IF THERE'S NOT TOO MANY.
AFTER WHAT HAPPENED LAST TIME...
IT'S HARD NOT TO WORRY A LITTLE.
LET'S GET BACK INSIDE.
WITH THIS FENCE UP, THEY CAN ALL BREATHE A LITTLE EASIER.

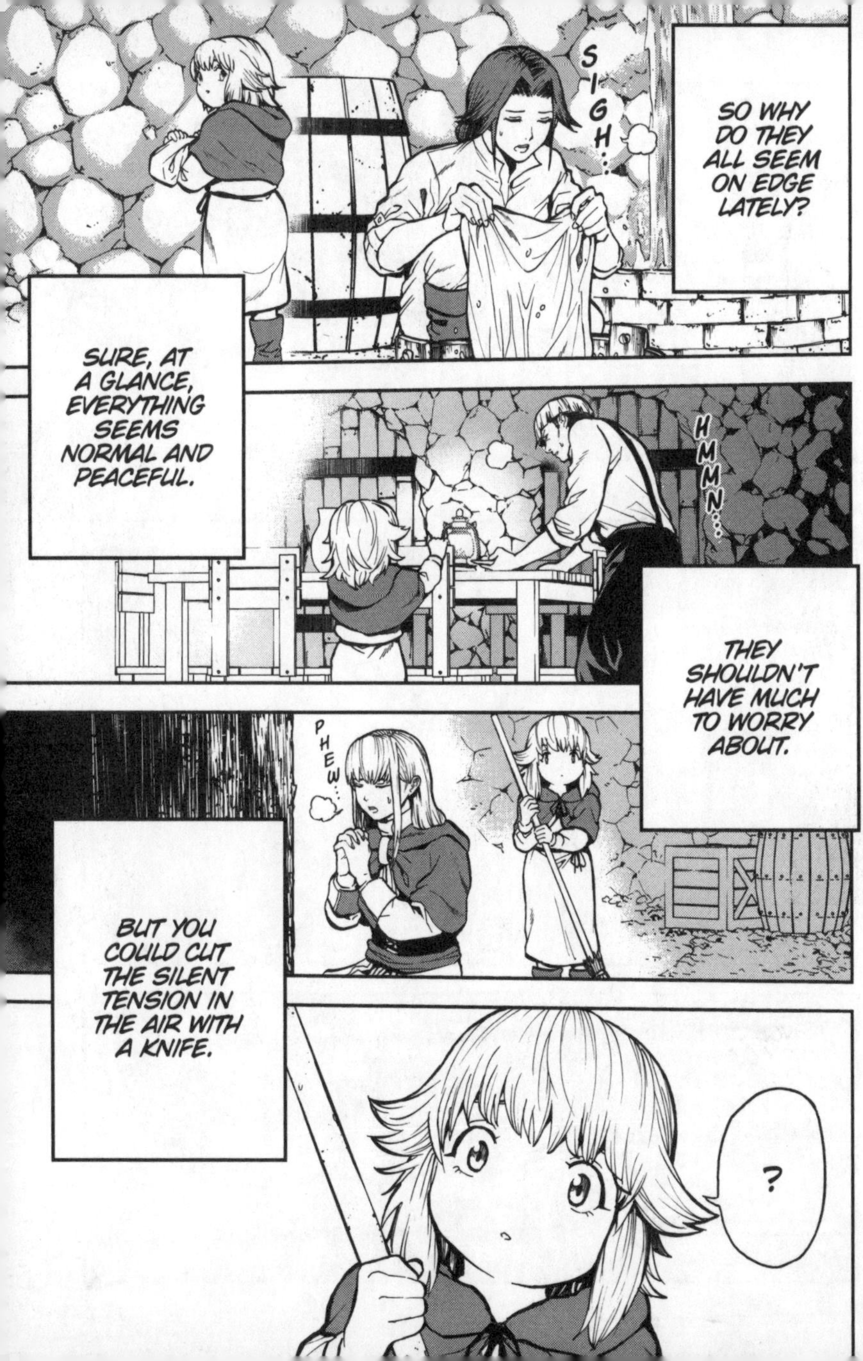
SO WHY DO THEY ALL SEEM ON EDGE LATELY?
SIGH...
SURE, AT A GLANCE, EVERYTHING SEEMS NORMAL AND PEACEFUL.
HMMN...
THEY SHOULDN'T HAVE MUCH TO WORRY ABOUT.
PHEW...
BUT YOU COULD CUT THE SILENT TENSION IN THE AIR WITH A KNIFE.
?

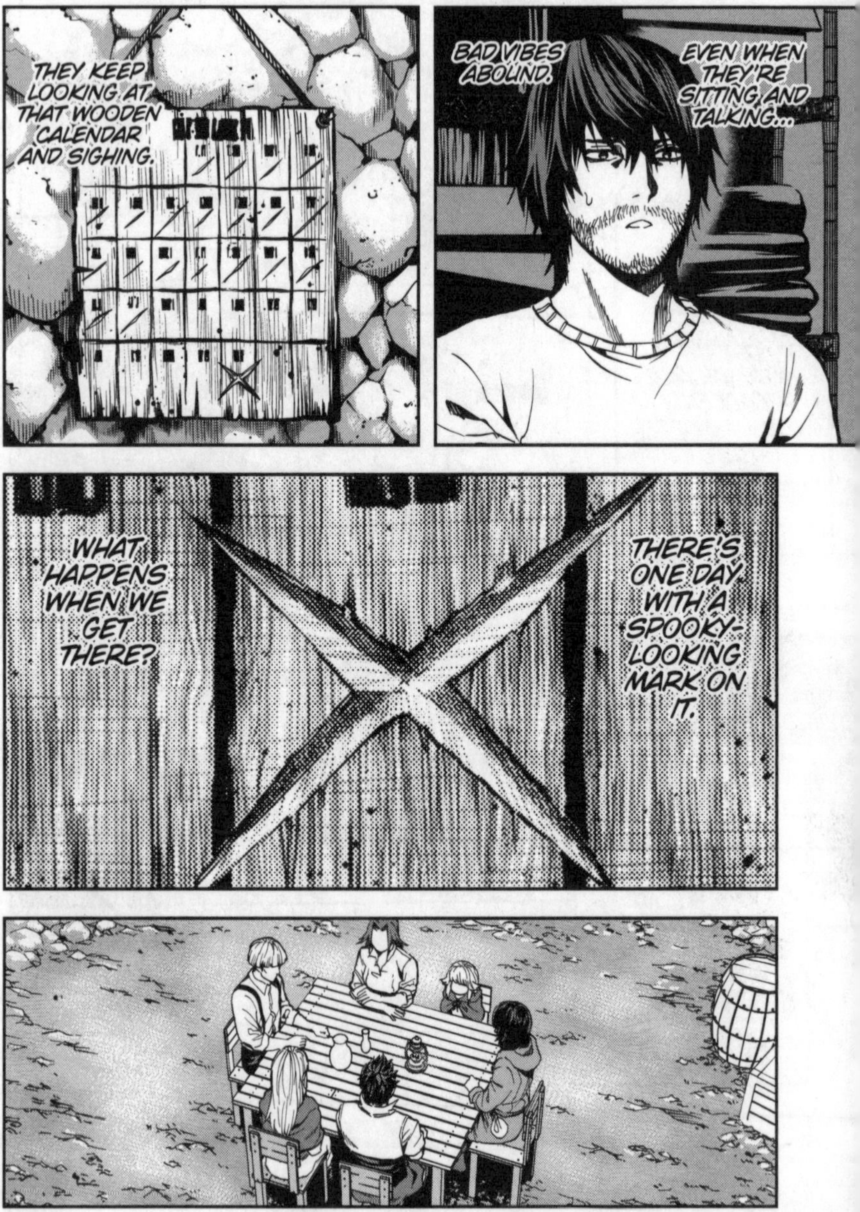
EVEN WHEN THEY'RE SITTING AND TALKING...
BAD VIBES ABOUND.
THEY KEEP LOOKING AT THAT WOODEN CALENDAR AND SIGHING.
THERE'S ONE DAY WITH A SPOOKY-LOOKING MARK ON IT.
WHAT HAPPENS WHEN WE GET THERE?

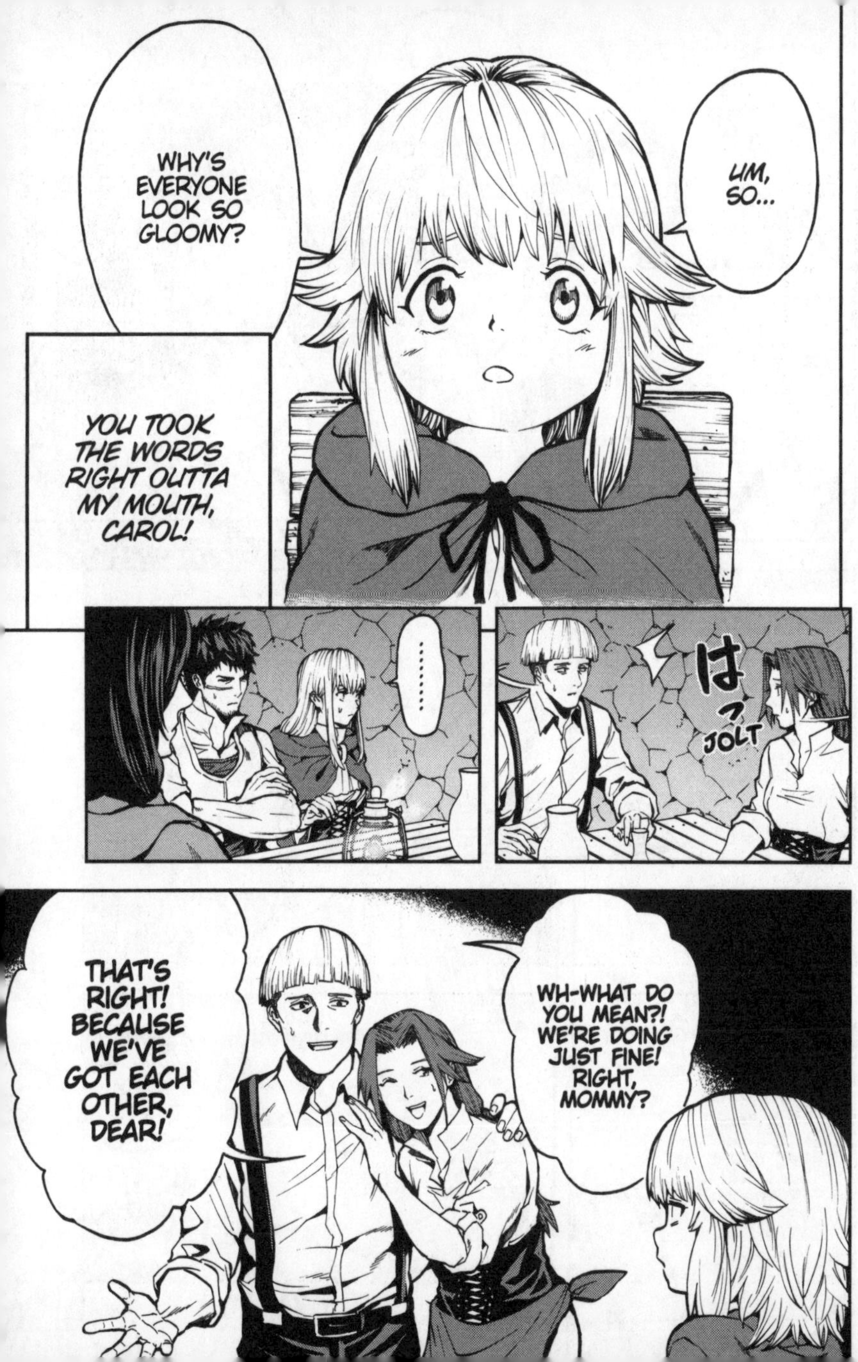
UM, SO...
WHY'S EVERYONE LOOK SO GLOOMY?
YOU TOOK THE WORDS RIGHT OUTTA MY MOUTH, CAROL!
はっ
JOLT
......
WH-WHAT DO YOU MEAN?! WE'RE DOING JUST FINE! RIGHT, MOMMY?
THAT'S RIGHT! BECAUSE WE'VE GOT EACH OTHER, DEAR!

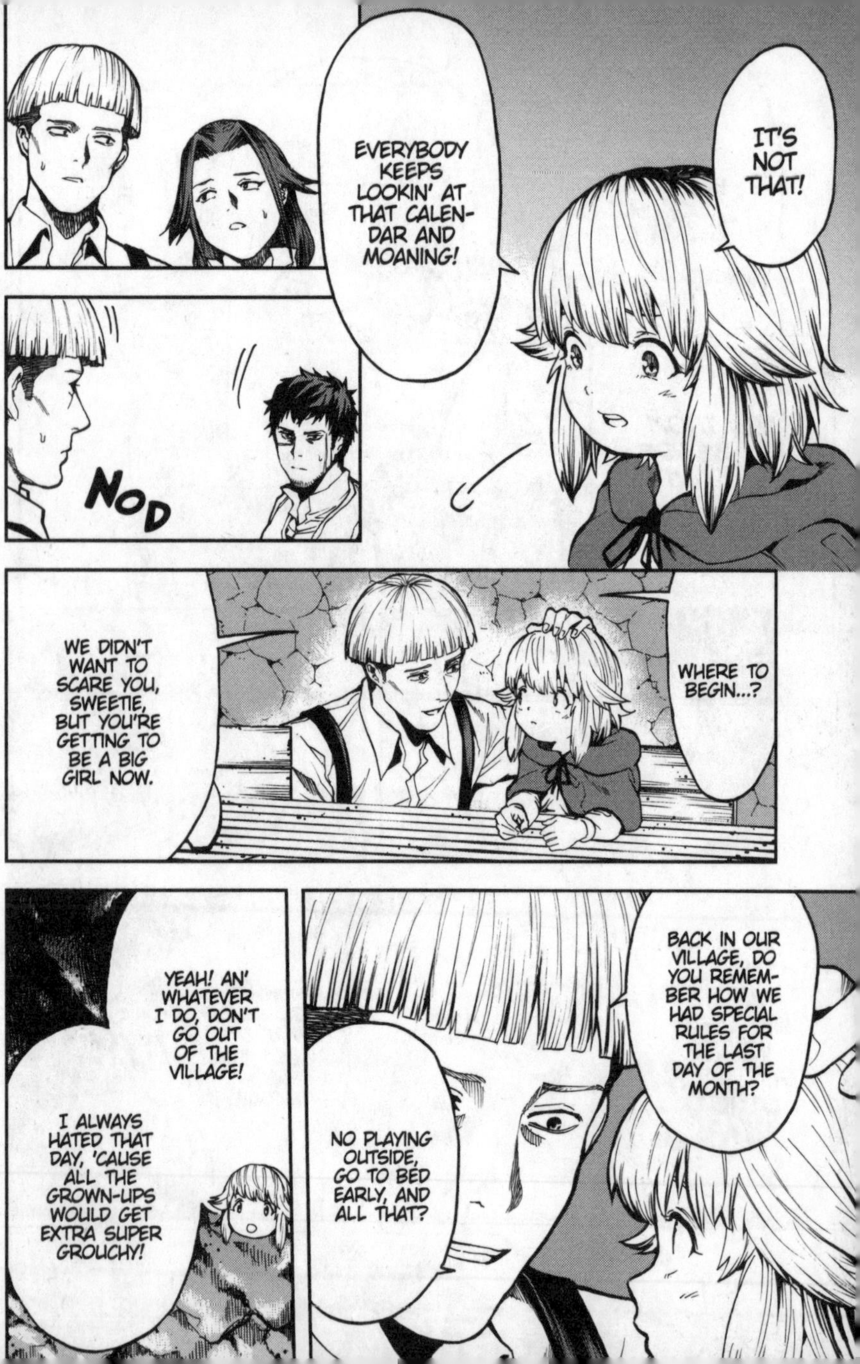
IT'S NOT THAT!
EVERYBODY KEEPS LOOKIN' AT THAT CALEN-DAR AND MOANING!
NOD
WHERE TO BEGIN...?
WE DIDN'T WANT TO SCARE YOU, SWEETIE, BUT YOU'RE GETTING TO BE A BIG GIRL NOW.
BACK IN OUR VILLAGE, DO YOU REMEM-BER HOW WE HAD SPECIAL RULES FOR THE LAST DAY OF THE MONTH?
NO PLAYING OUTSIDE, GO TO BED EARLY, AND ALL THAT?
YEAH! AN' WHATEVER I DO, DON'T GO OUT OF THE VILLAGE!
I ALWAYS HATED THAT DAY, 'CAUSE ALL THE GROWN-UPS WOULD GET EXTRA SUPER GROUCHY!

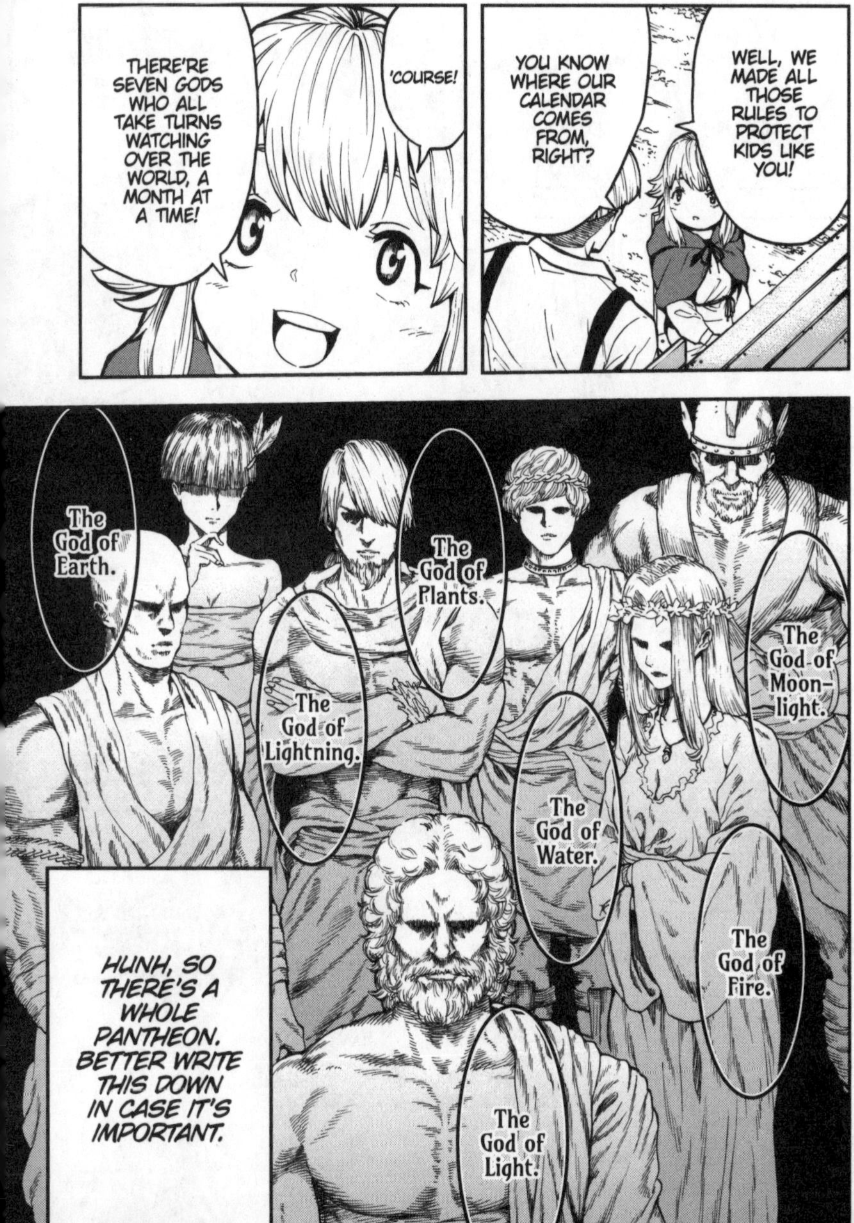

WELL, WE MADE ALL THOSE RULES TO PROTECT KIDS LIKE YOU!
YOU KNOW WHERE OUR CALENDAR COMES FROM, RIGHT?
'COURSE!
THERE'RE SEVEN GODS WHO ALL TAKE TURNS WATCHING OVER THE WORLD, A MONTH AT A TIME!
The God of Moonlight.
The God of Fire.
The God of Plants.
The God of Water.
The God of Light.
The God of Lightning.
The God of Earth.
HUNH, SO THERE'S A WHOLE PANTHEON. BETTER WRITE THIS DOWN IN CASE IT'S IMPORTANT.

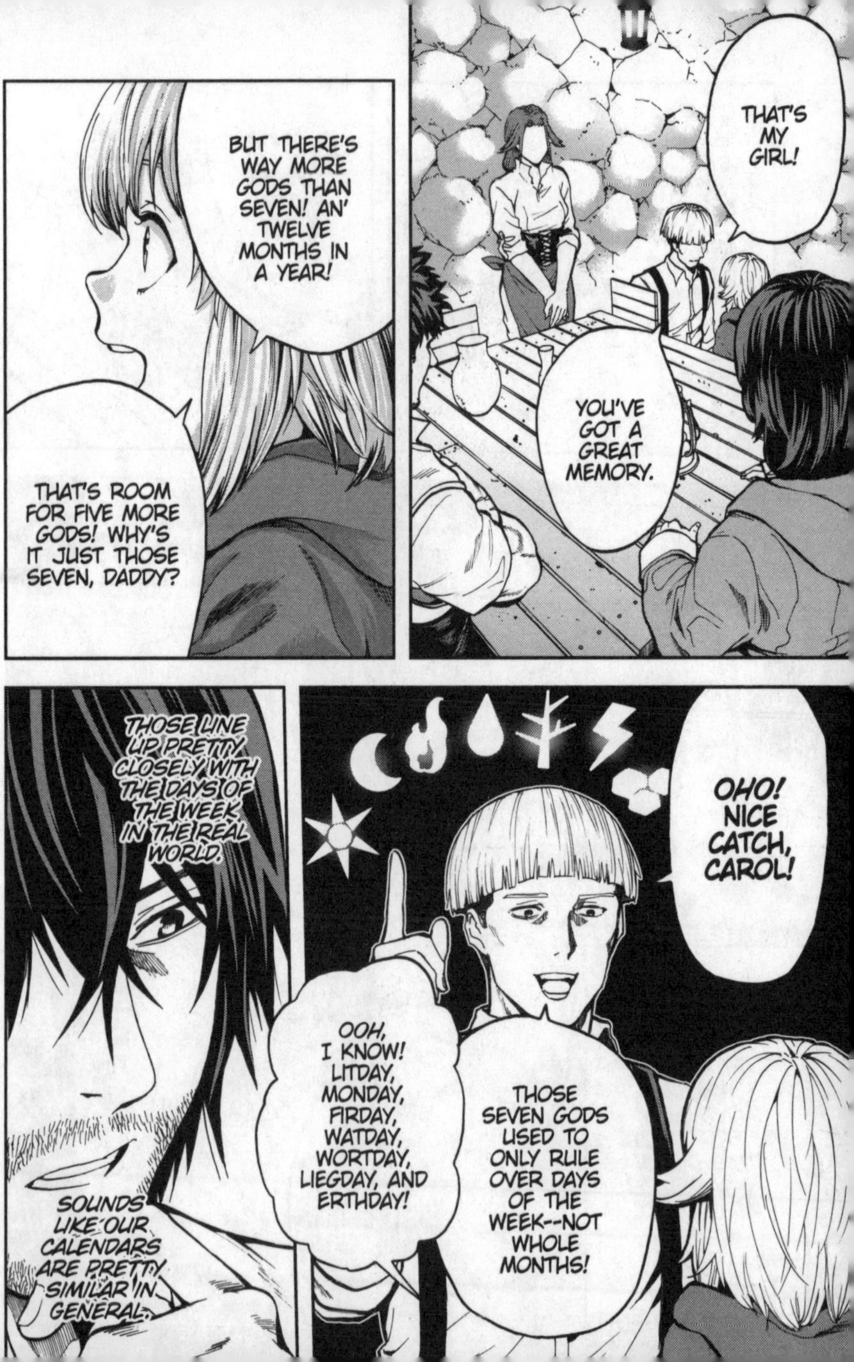
THAT'S MY GIRL!
YOU'VE GOT A GREAT MEMORY.
BUT THERE'S WAY MORE GODS THAN SEVEN! AN' TWELVE MONTHS IN A YEAR!
THAT'S ROOM FOR FIVE MORE GODS! WHY'S IT JUST THOSE SEVEN, DADDY?
OHO! NICE CATCH, CAROL!
THOSE SEVEN GODS USED TO ONLY RULE OVER DAYS OF THE WEEK--NOT WHOLE MONTHS!
OOH, I KNOW! LITDAY, MONDAY, FIRDAY, WATDAY, WORTDAY, LIEGDAY, AND ERTHDAY!
THOSE LINE UP PRETTY CLOSELY WITH THE DAYS OF THE WEEK IN THE REAL WORLD.
SOUNDS LIKE OUR CALENDARS ARE PRETTY SIMILAR IN GENERAL.

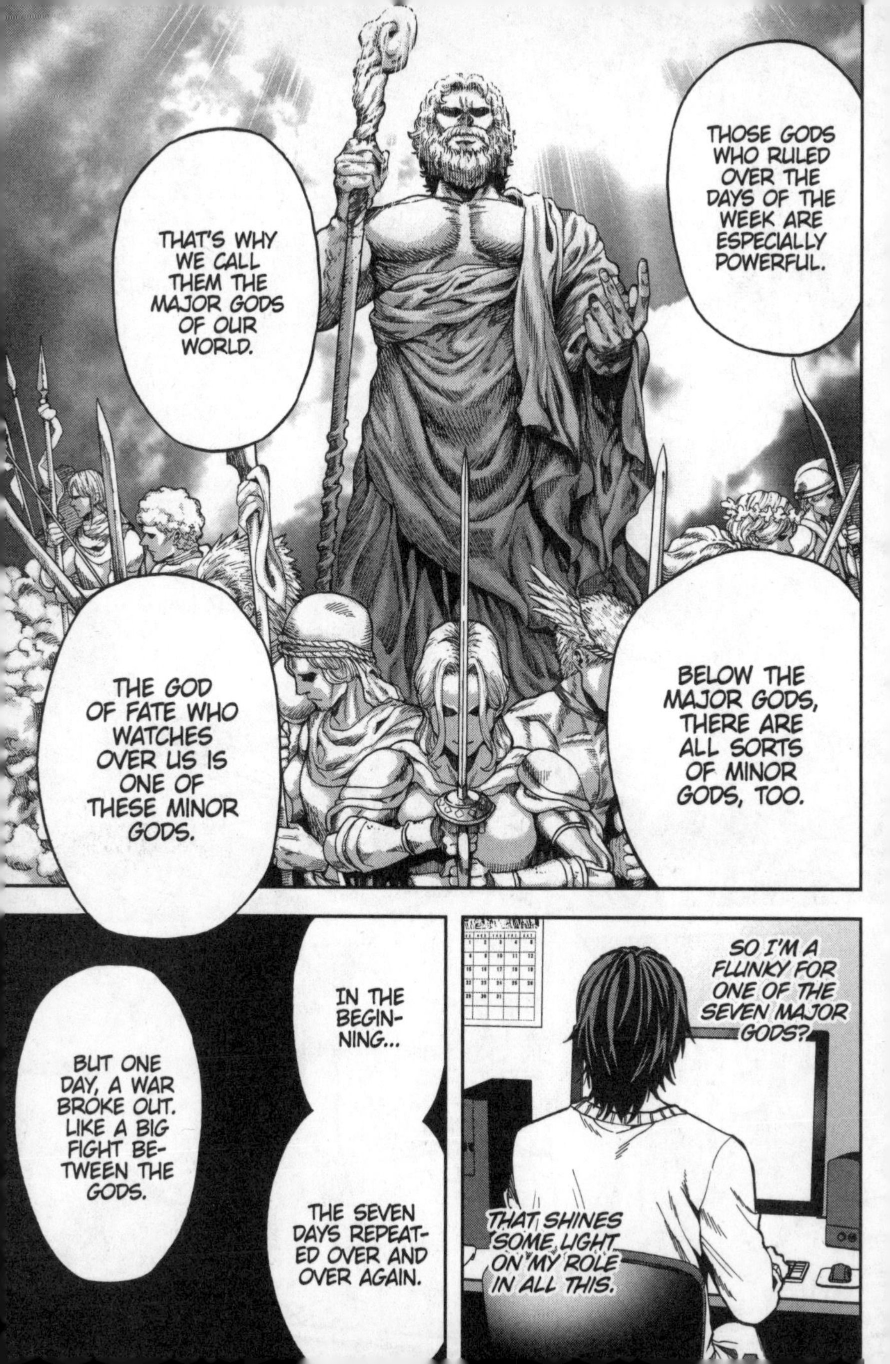
THOSE GODS WHO RULED OVER THE DAYS OF THE WEEK ARE ESPECIALLY POWERFUL.
THAT'S WHY WE CALL THEM THE MAJOR GODS OF OUR WORLD.
BELOW THE MAJOR GODS, THERE ARE ALL SORTS OF MINOR GODS, TOO.
THE GOD OF FATE WHO WATCHES OVER US IS ONE OF THESE MINOR GODS.
SO I'M A FLUNKY FOR ONE OF THE SEVEN MAJOR GODS?
THAT SHINES SOME LIGHT ON MY ROLE IN ALL THIS.
IN THE BEGIN-NING...
THE SEVEN DAYS REPEAT-ED OVER AND OVER AGAIN.
BUT ONE DAY, A WAR BROKE OUT. LIKE A BIG FIGHT BE-TWEEN THE GODS.

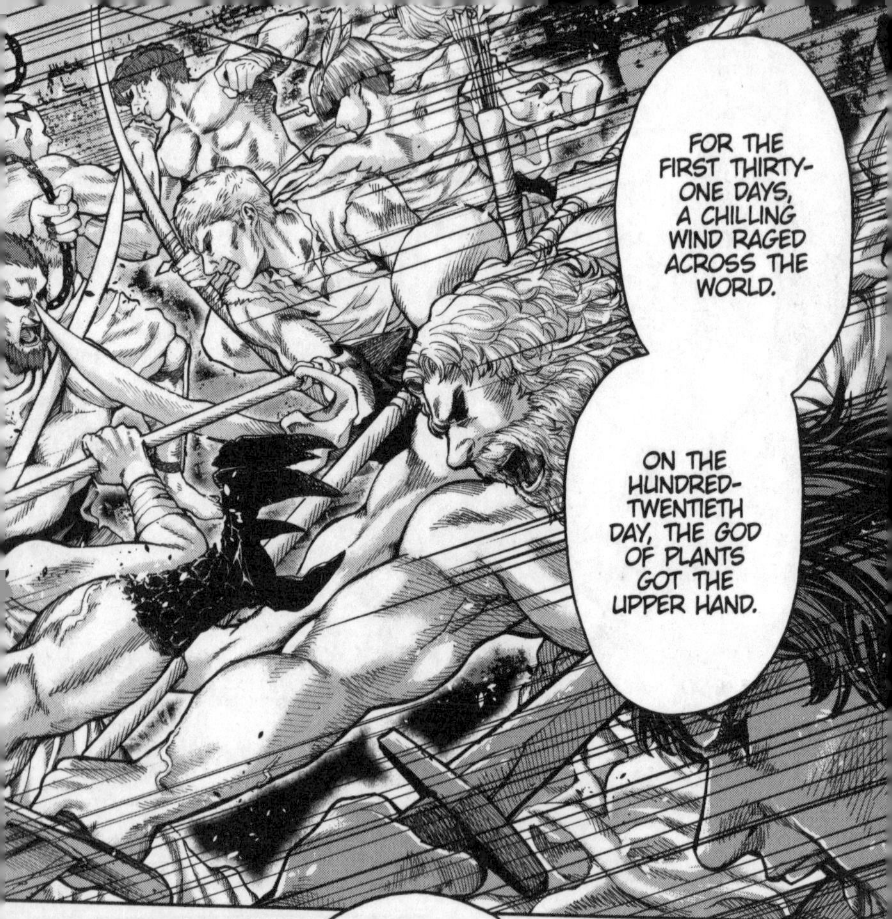
FOR THE FIRST THIRTY-ONE DAYS, A CHILLING WIND RAGED ACROSS THE WORLD.
ON THE HUNDRED-TWENTIETH DAY, THE GOD OF PLANTS GOT THE UPPER HAND.
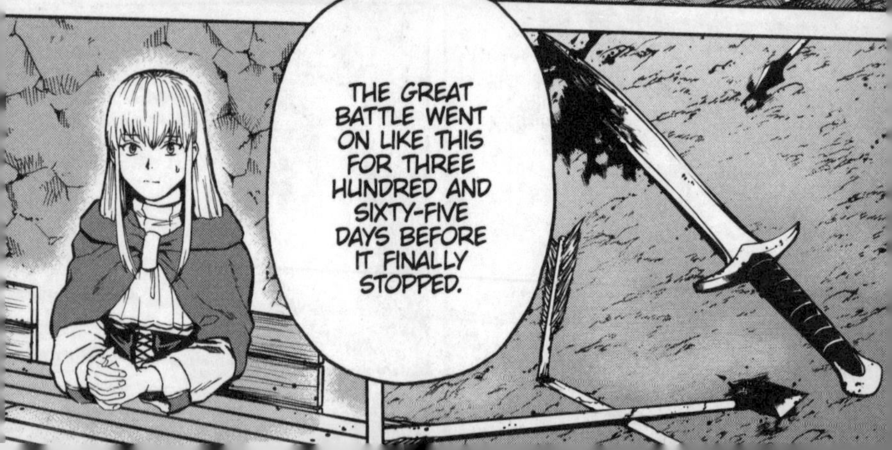
THE GREAT BATTLE WENT ON LIKE THIS FOR THREE HUNDRED AND SIXTY-FIVE DAYS BEFORE IT FINALLY STOPPED.

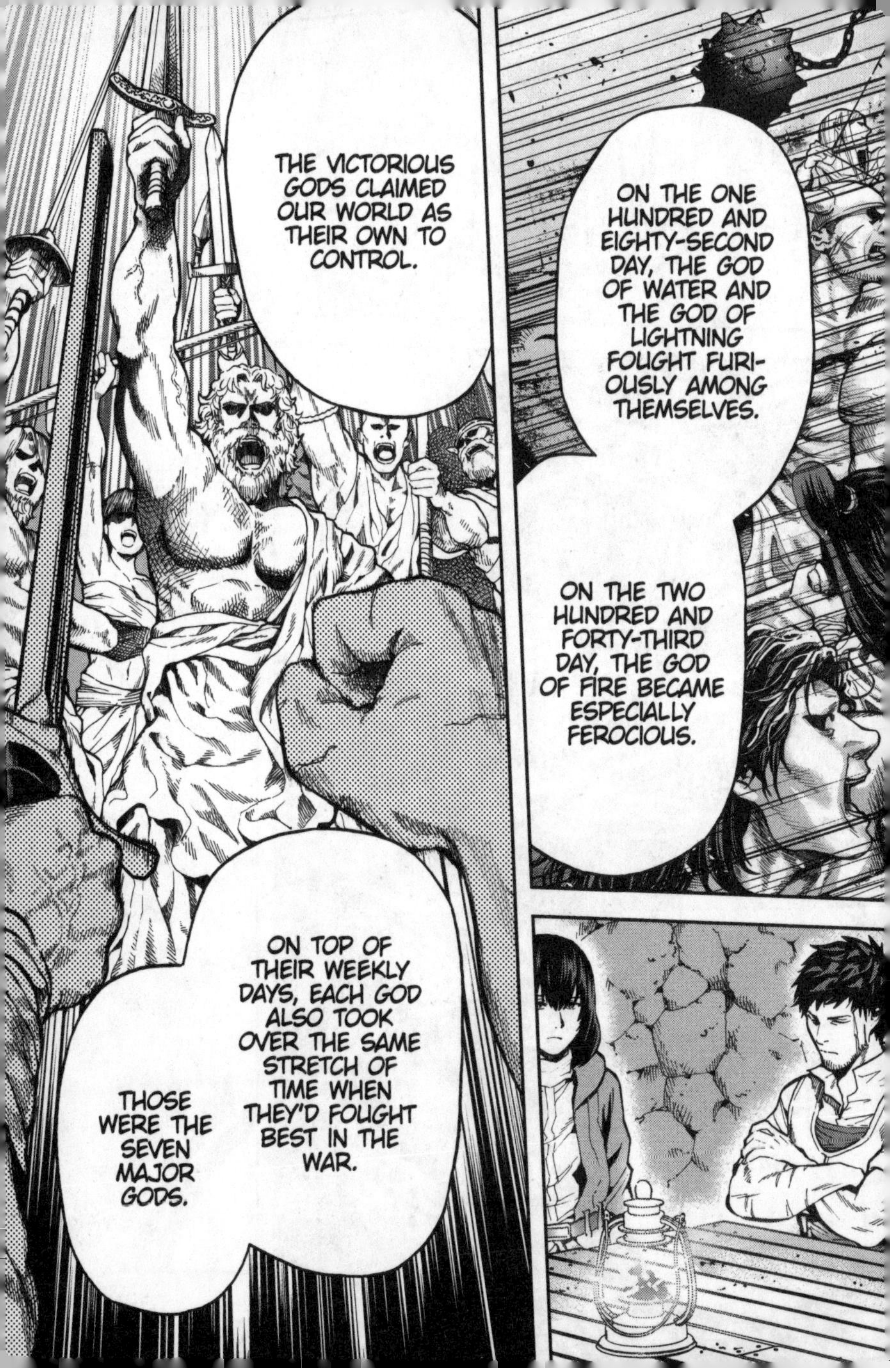
ON THE ONE HUNDRED AND EIGHTY-SECOND DAY, THE GOD OF WATER AND THE GOD OF LIGHTNING FOUGHT FURI-OUSLY AMONG THEMSELVES.
ON THE TWO HUNDRED AND FORTY-THIRD DAY, THE GOD OF FIRE BECAME ESPECIALLY FEROCIOUS.
THE VICTORIOUS GODS CLAIMED OUR WORLD AS THEIR OWN TO CONTROL.
ON TOP OF THEIR WEEKLY DAYS, EACH GOD ALSO TOOK OVER THE SAME STRETCH OF TIME WHEN THEY'D FOUGHT BEST IN THE WAR.
THOSE WERE THE SEVEN MAJOR GODS.

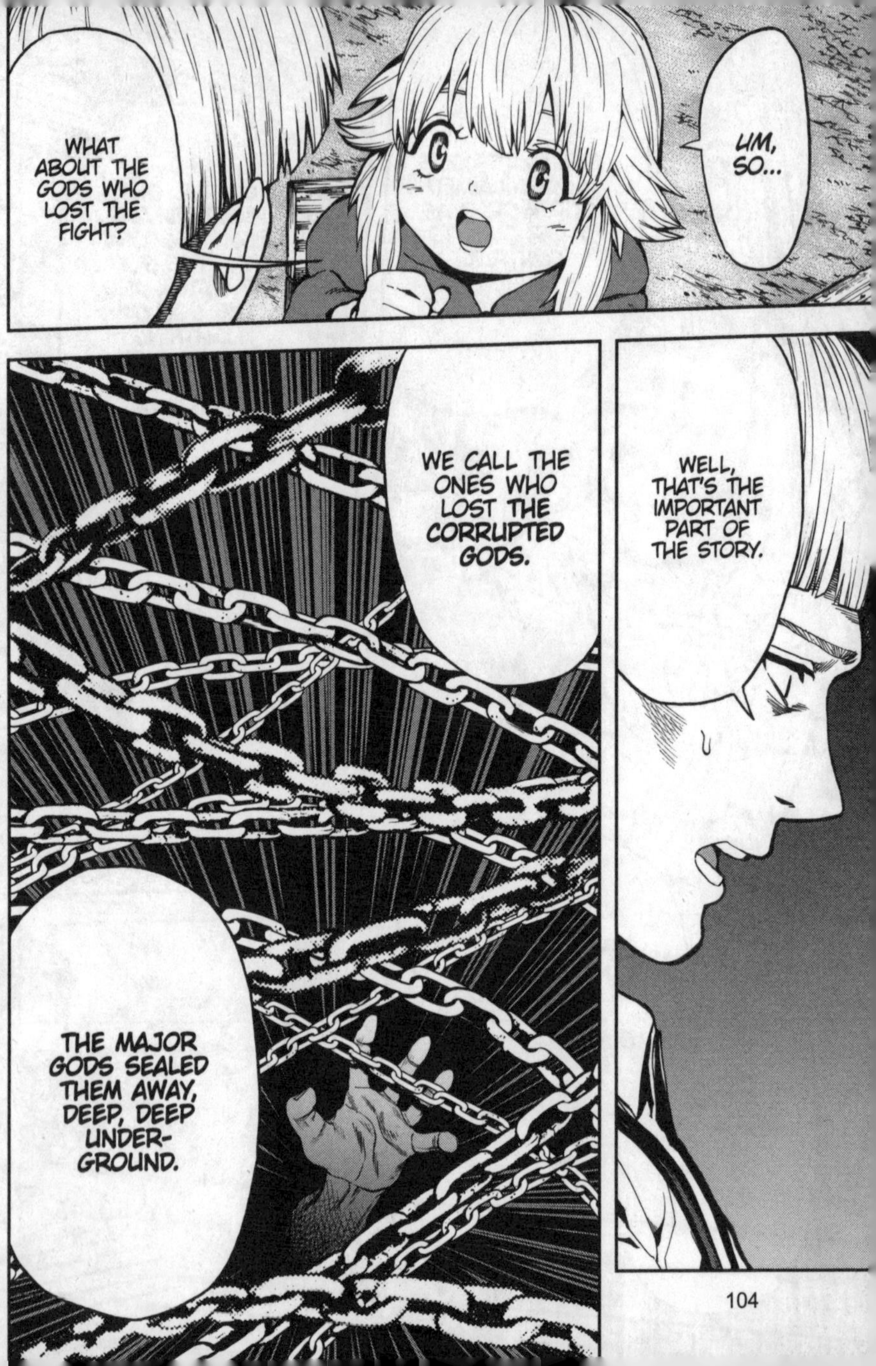
UM, SO...
WHAT ABOUT THE GODS WHO LOST THE FIGHT?
WELL, THAT'S THE IMPORTANT PART OF THE STORY.
WE CALL THE ONES WHO LOST THE CORRUPTED GODS.
THE MAJOR GODS SEALED THEM AWAY, DEEP, DEEP UNDER-GROUND.

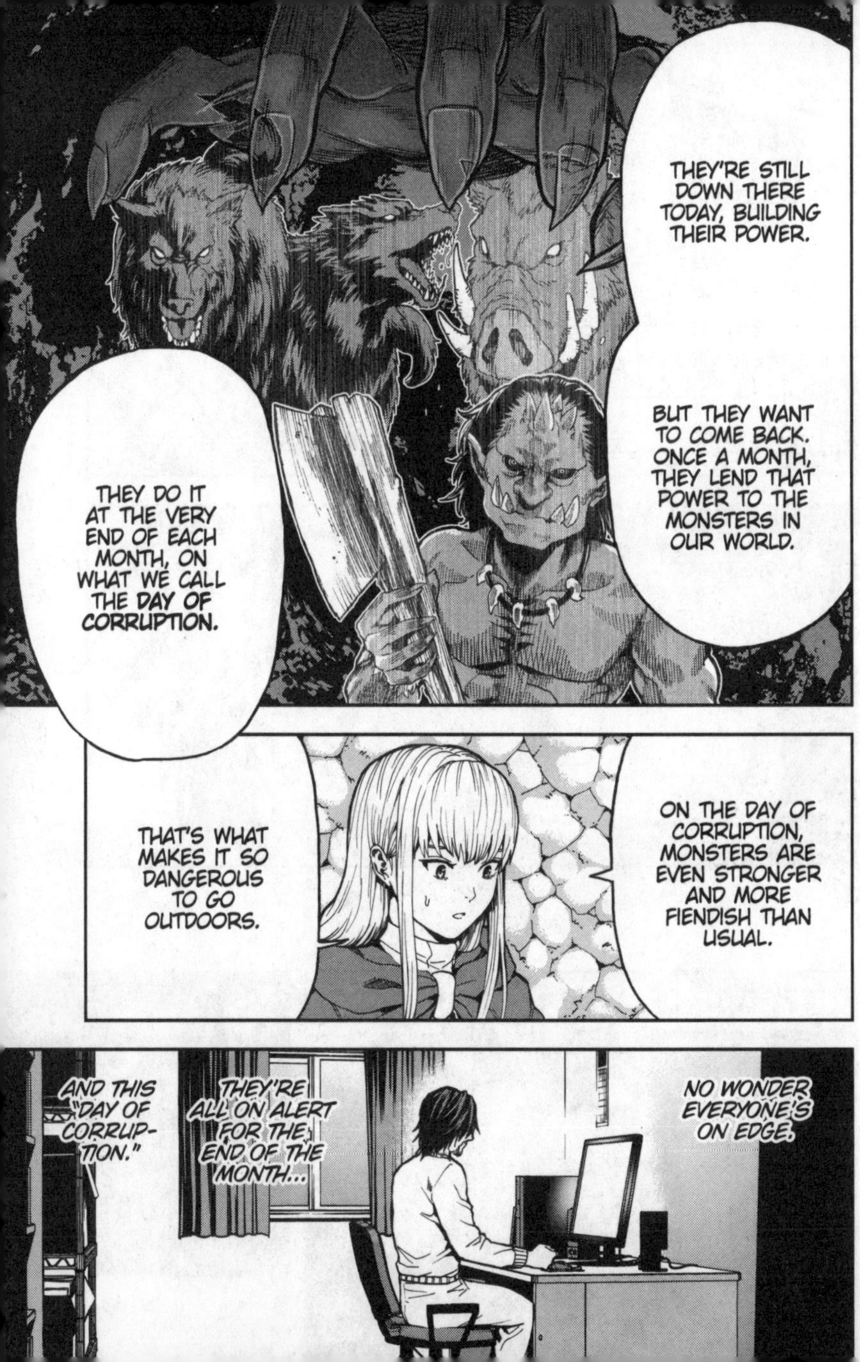
THEY'RE STILL DOWN THERE TODAY, BUILDING THEIR POWER.
BUT THEY WANT TO COME BACK. ONCE A MONTH, THEY LEND THAT POWER TO THE MONSTERS IN OUR WORLD.
THEY DO IT AT THE VERY END OF EACH MONTH, ON WHAT WE CALL THE DAY OF CORRUPTION.
ON THE DAY OF CORRUPTION, MONSTERS ARE EVEN STRONGER AND MORE FIENDISH THAN USUAL.
THAT'S WHAT MAKES IT SO DANGEROUS TO GO OUTDOORS.
NO WONDER EVERYONE'S ON EDGE.
THEY'RE ALL ON ALERT FOR THE END OF THE MONTH...
AND THIS "DAY OF CORRUP-TION."

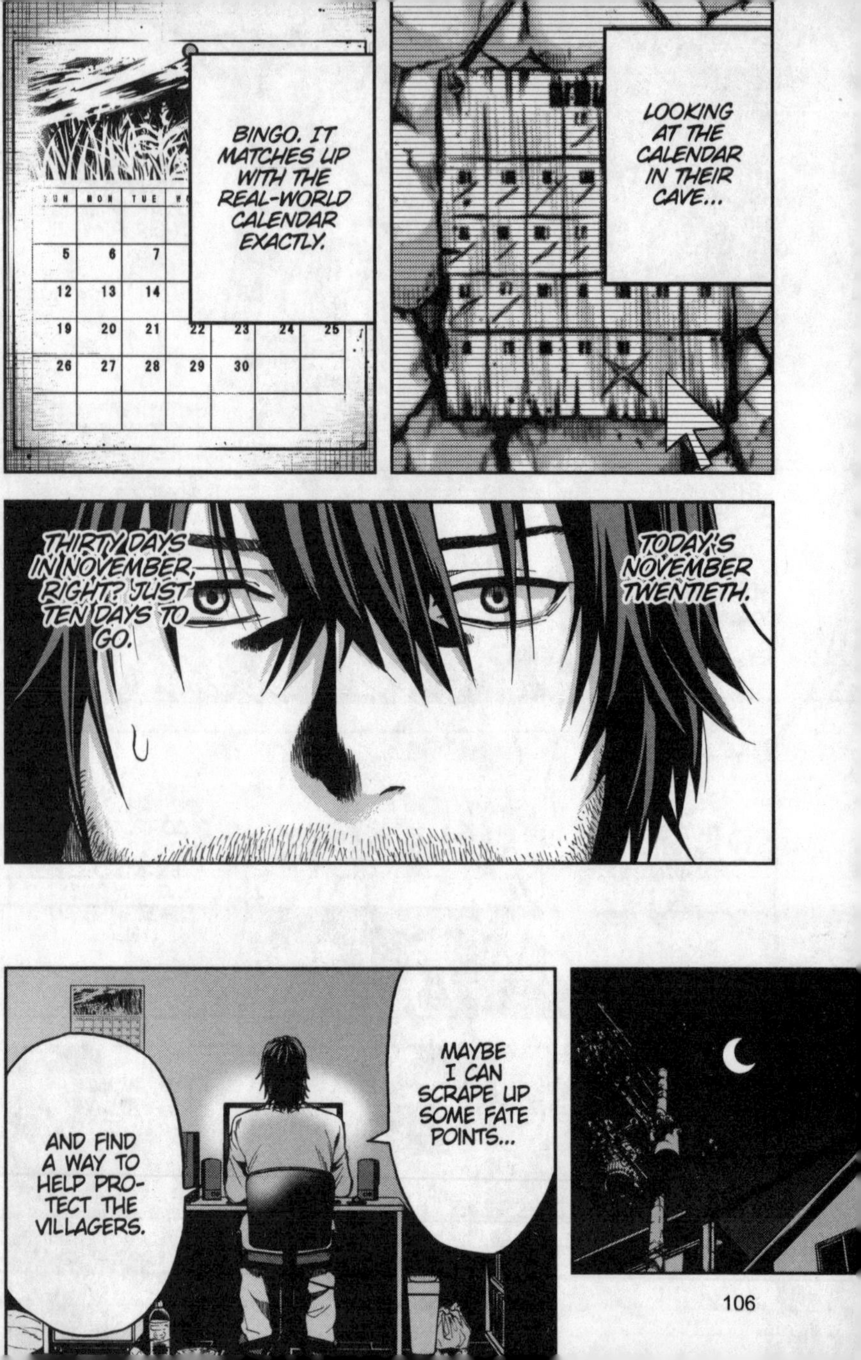
LOOKING AT THE CALENDAR IN THEIR CAVE...
BINGO. IT MATCHES UP WITH THE REAL-WORLD CALENDAR EXACTLY.
TODAY'S NOVEMBER TWENTIETH.
THIRTY DAYS IN NOVEMBER, RIGHT? JUST TEN DAYS TO GO.
MAYBE I CAN SCRAPE UP SOME FATE POINTS...
AND FIND A WAY TO HELP PROTECT THE VILLAGERS.

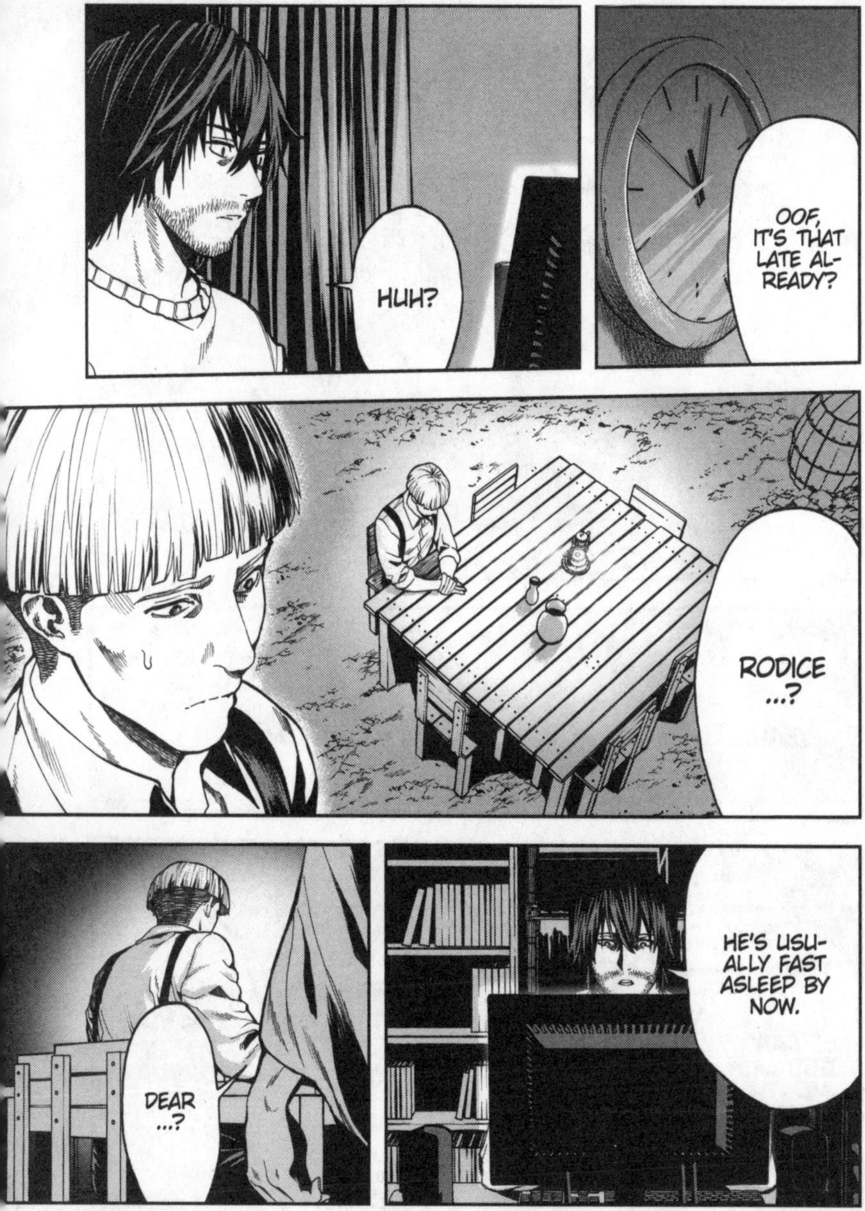
OOF, IT'S THAT LATE AL-READY?
HUH?
RODICE ...?
HE'S USU-ALLY FAST ASLEEP BY NOW.
DEAR ...?

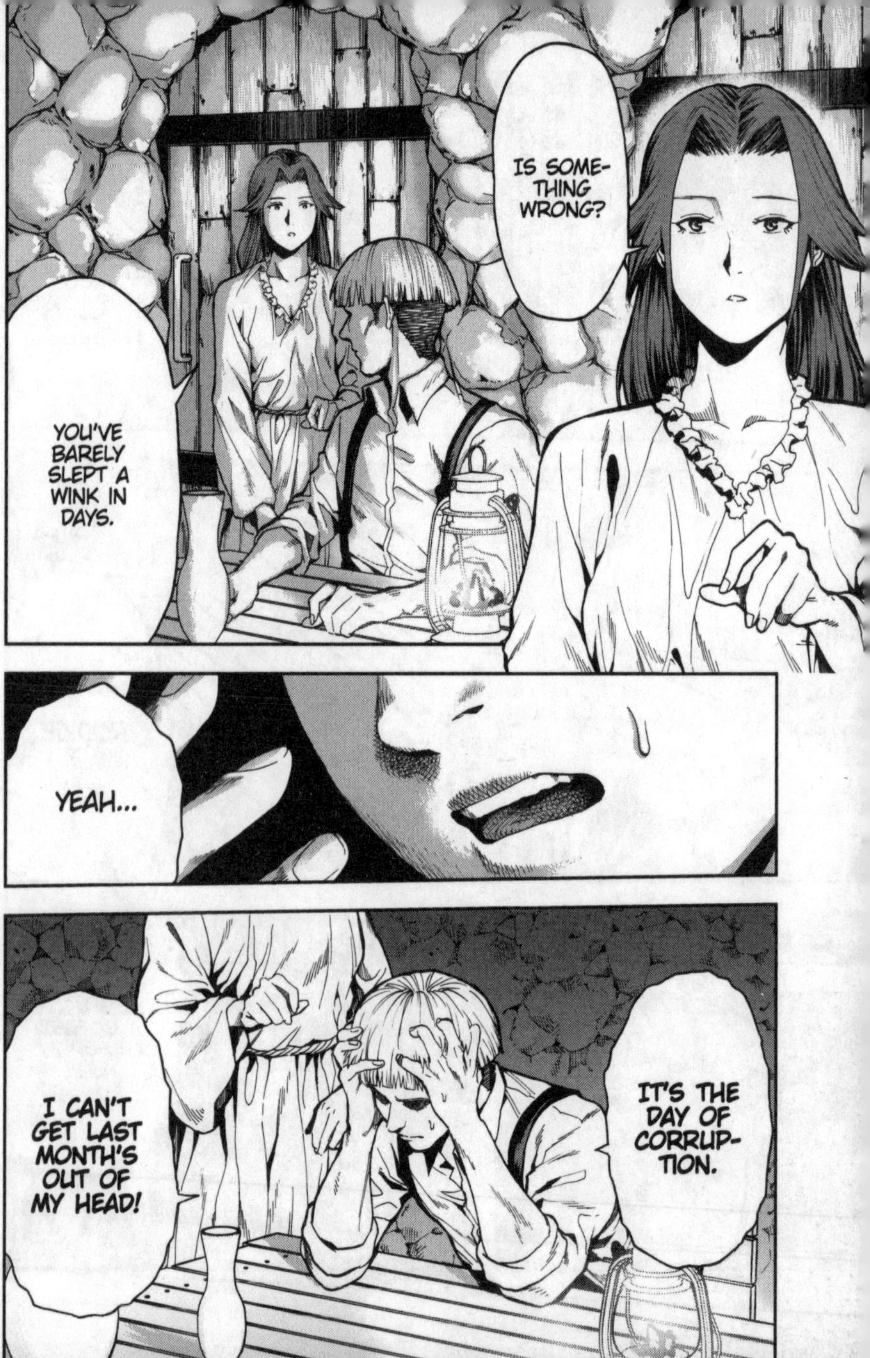
IS SOME-THING WRONG?
YOU'VE BARELY SLEPT A WINK IN DAYS.
YEAH...
IT'S THE DAY OF CORRUP-TION.
I CAN'T GET LAST MONTH'S OUT OF MY HEAD!

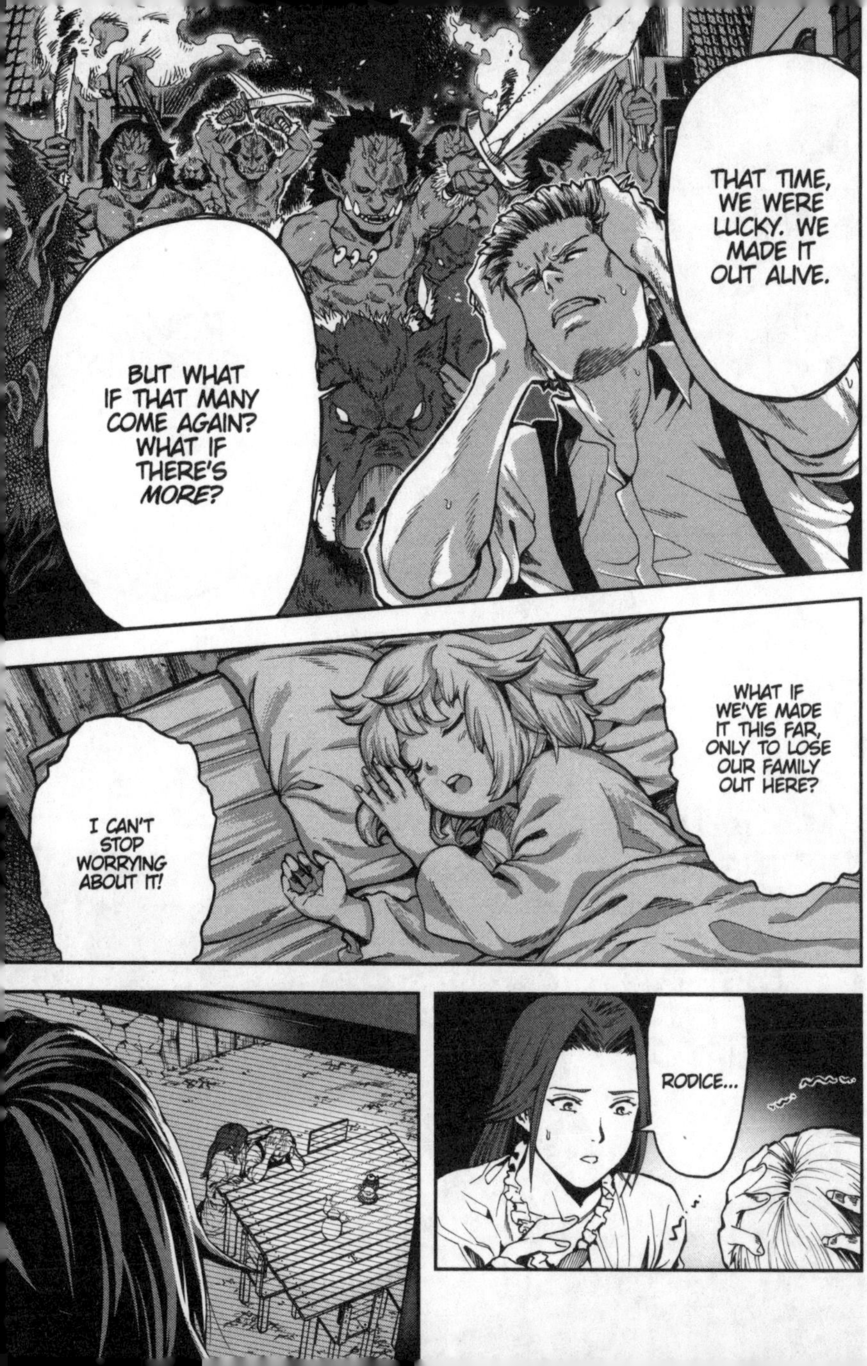
THAT TIME, WE WERE LUCKY. WE MADE IT OUT ALIVE.
BUT WHAT IF THAT MANY COME AGAIN? WHAT IF THERE'S *MORE?*
WHAT IF WE'VE MADE IT THIS FAR, ONLY TO LOSE OUR FAMILY OUT HERE?
I CAN'T STOP WORRYING ABOUT IT!
RODICE...

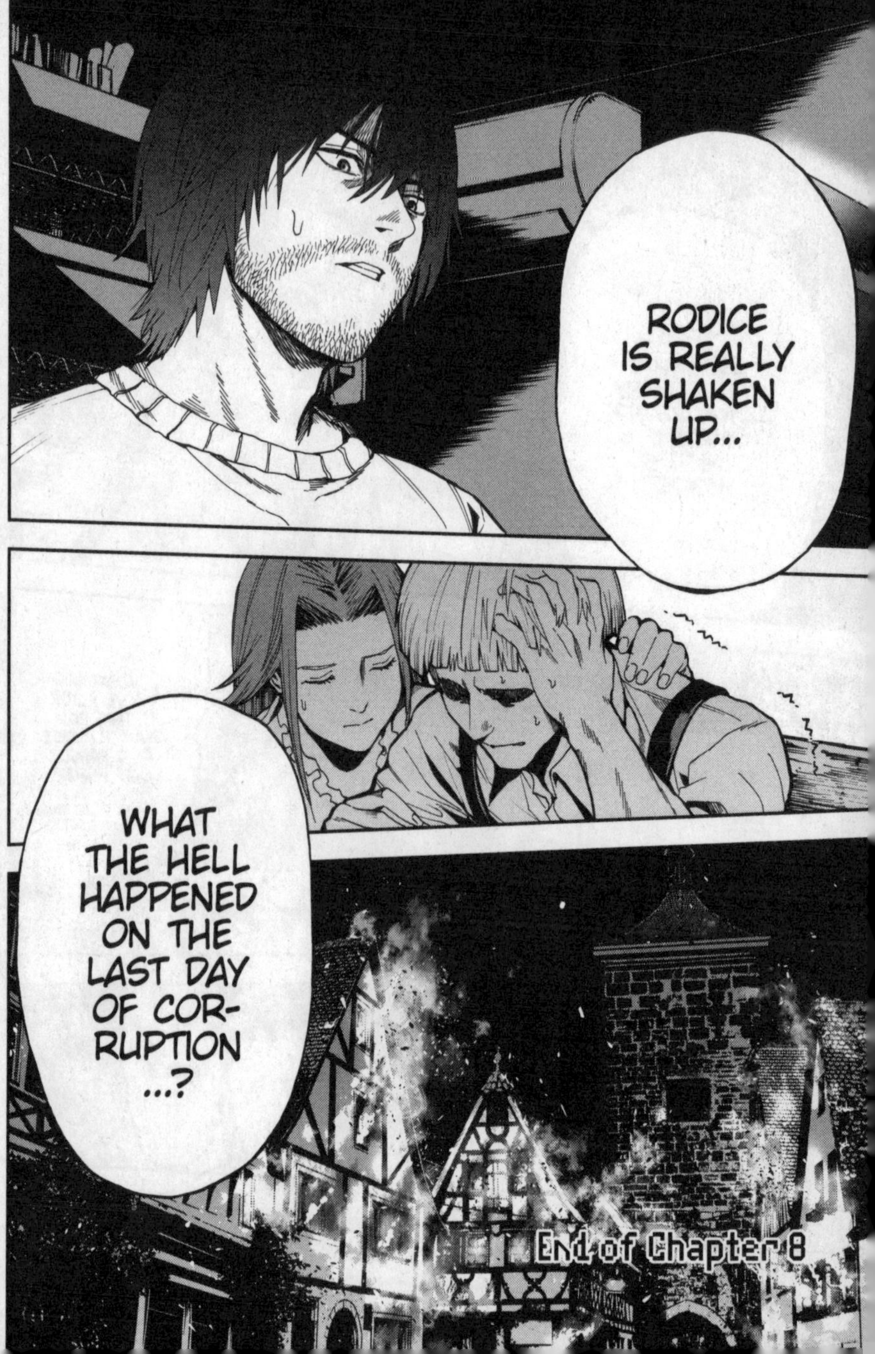
RODICE IS REALLY SHAKEN UP...
WHAT THE HELL HAPPENED ON THE LAST DAY OF COR-RUPTION ...?
End of Chapter 8

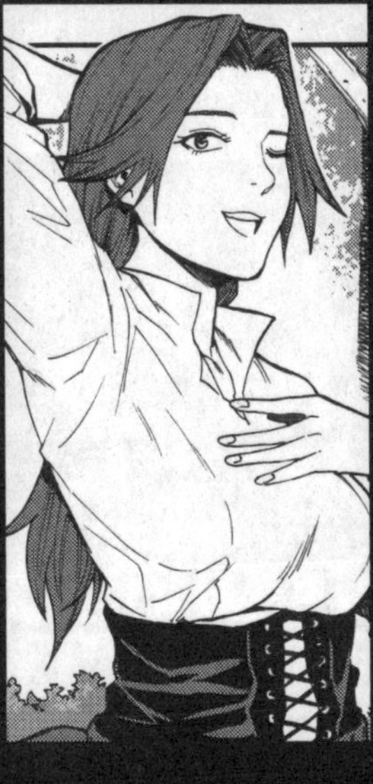

Character

Lyra

▶ Gender: Female

Class: Villager

E : Clothes (cloth)

E : Love for her family

E : Spunk

THE NPCs IN THIS
VILLAGE SIM GAME
MUST BE REAL!

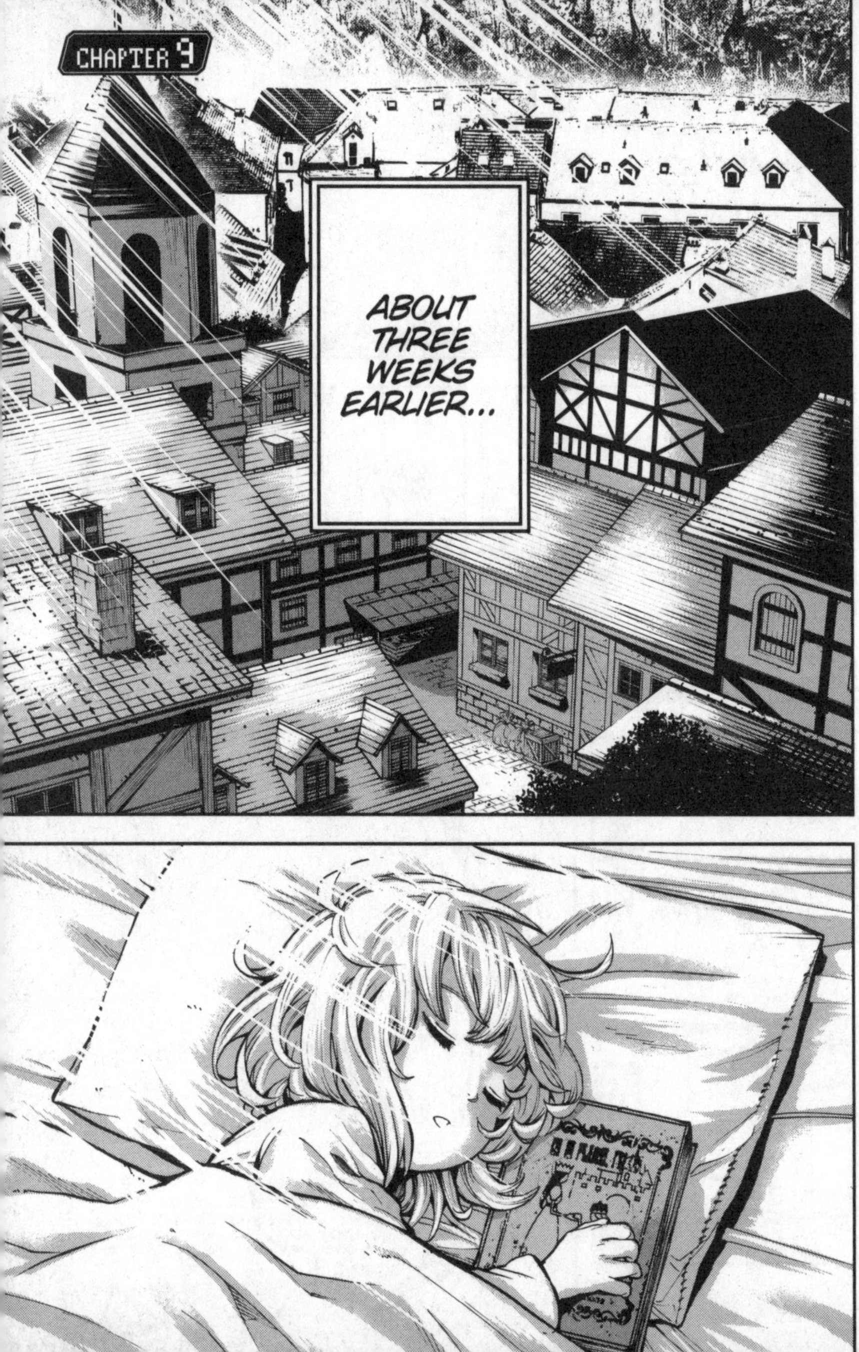
CHAPTER 9
ABOUT THREE WEEKS EARLIER...

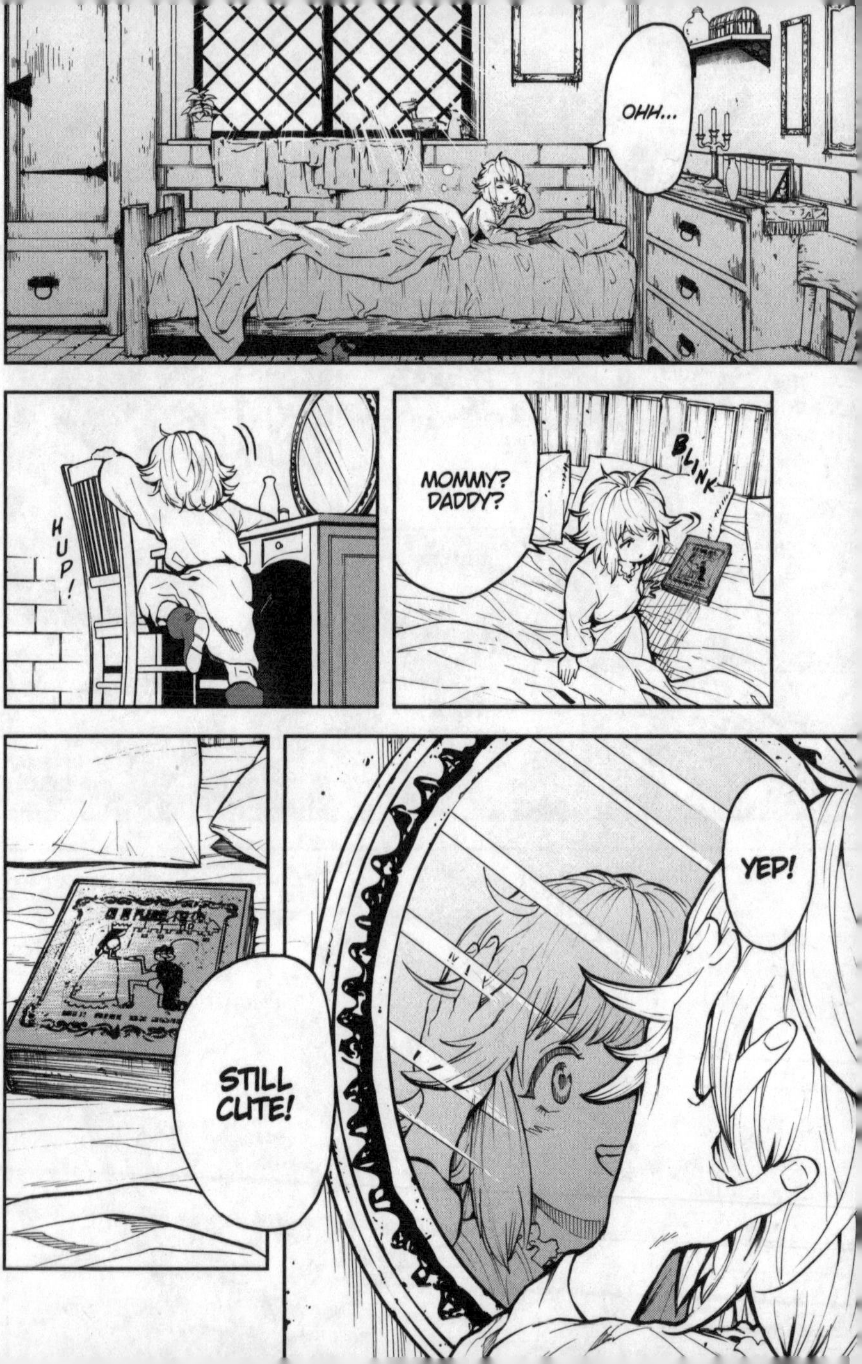
OHH...
MOMMY? DADDY?
BLINK
HUP!
YEP!
STILL CUTE!

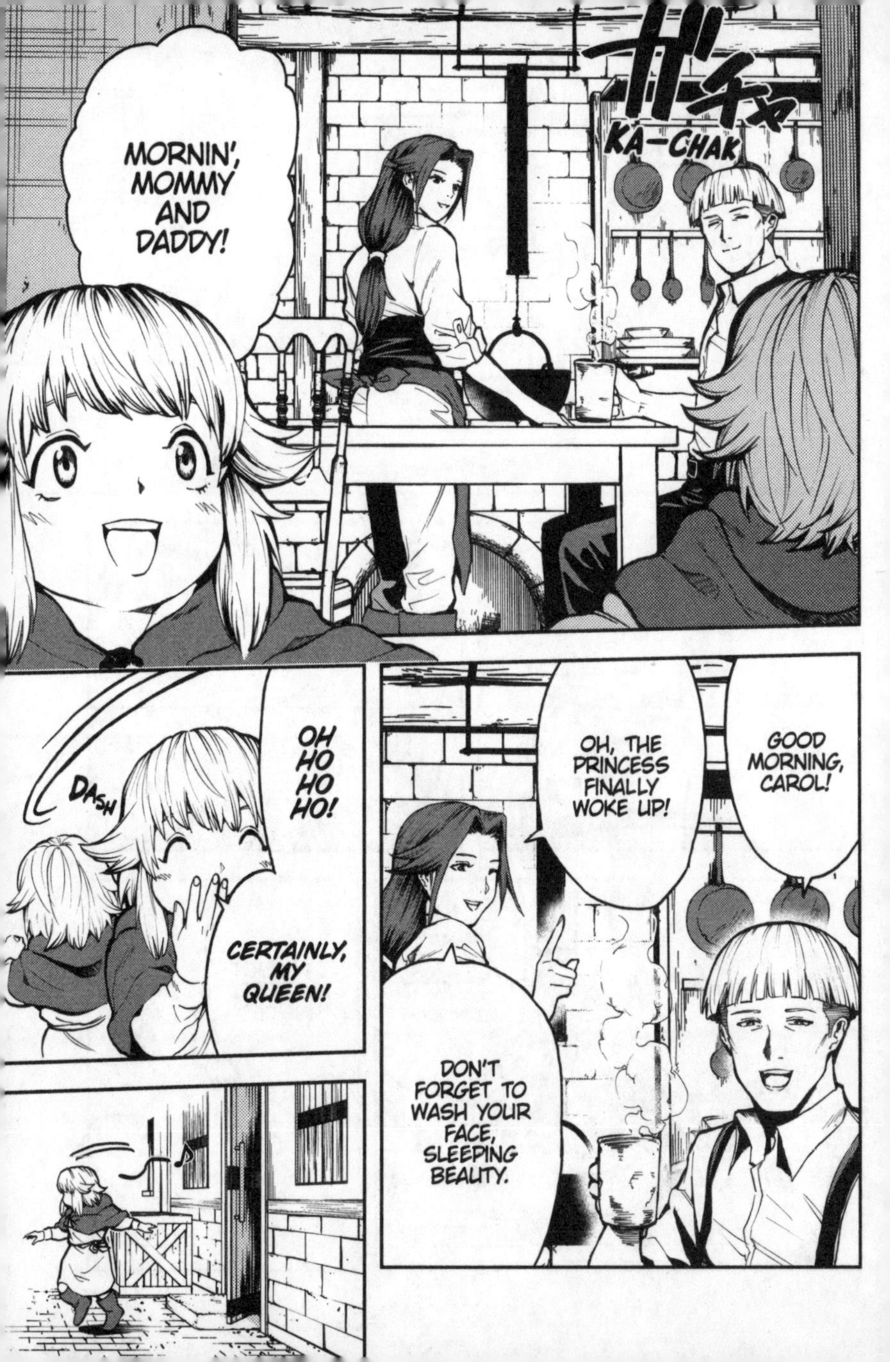
ガチャ
KA-CHAK
MORNIN', MOMMY AND DADDY!
GOOD MORNING, CAROL!
OH, THE PRINCESS FINALLY WOKE UP!
DON'T FORGET TO WASH YOUR FACE, SLEEPING BEAUTY.
OH HO HO HO!
CERTAINLY, MY QUEEN!
DASH

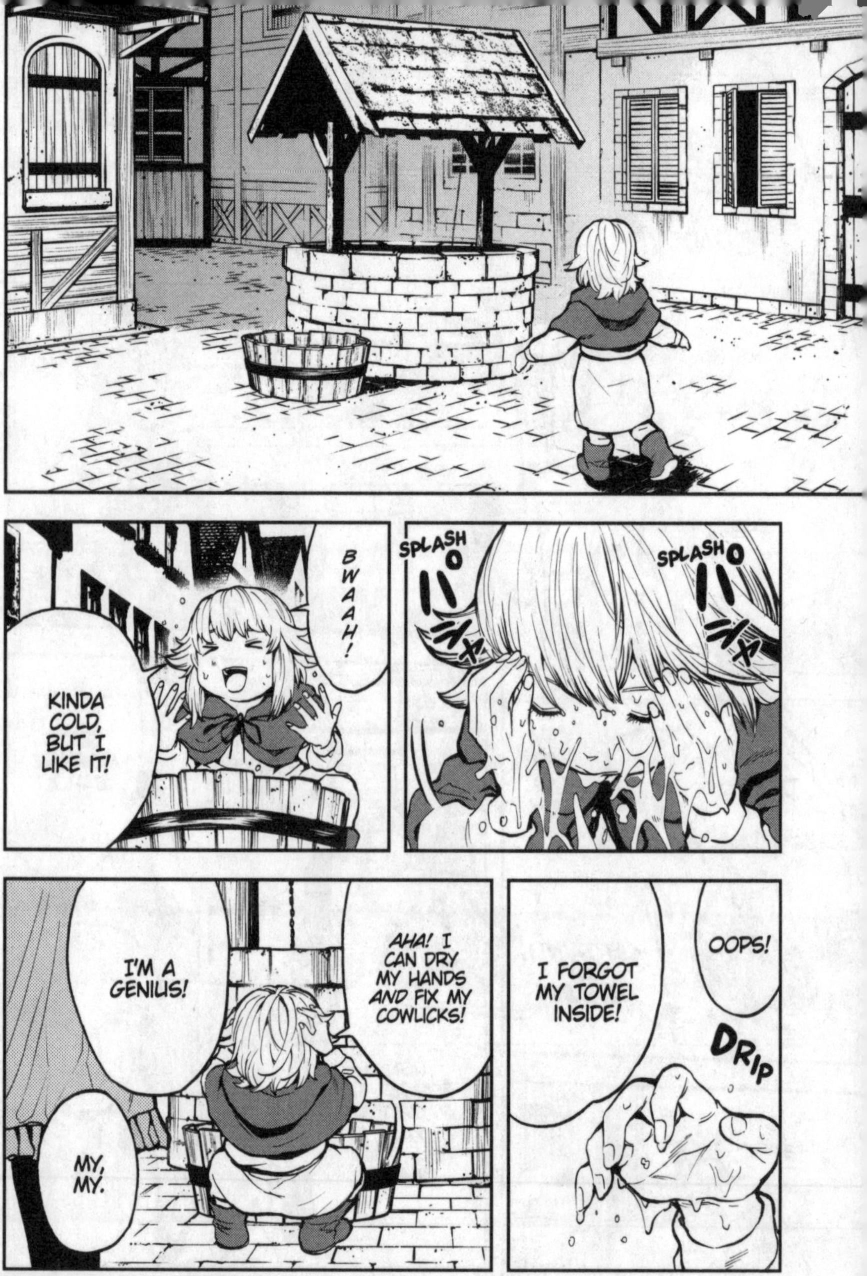
SPLASH
SPLASH
BWAAAH!
KINDA COLD, BUT I LIKE IT!
OOPS!
I FORGOT MY TOWEL INSIDE!
DRIP
AHA! I CAN DRY MY HANDS AND FIX MY COWLICKS!
I'M A GENIUS!
MY, MY.

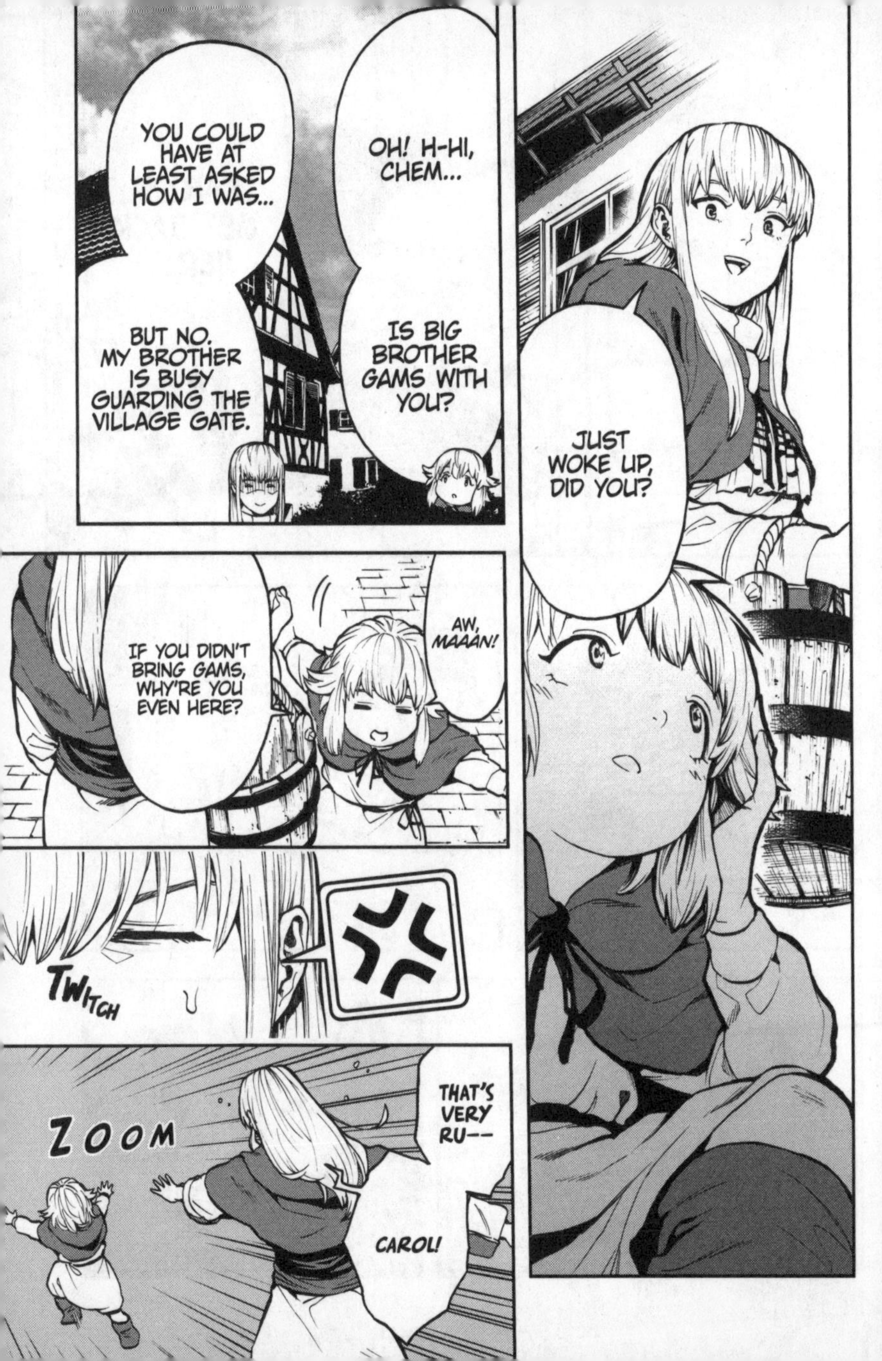
JUST WOKE UP, DID YOU?
OH! H-HI, CHEM...
IS BIG BROTHER GAMS WITH YOU?
YOU COULD HAVE AT LEAST ASKED HOW I WAS...
BUT NO. MY BROTHER IS BUSY GUARDING THE VILLAGE GATE.
AW, MAAAN!
IF YOU DIDN'T BRING GAMS, WHY'RE YOU EVEN HERE?
TWITCH
THAT'S VERY RU--
ZOOM
CAROL!

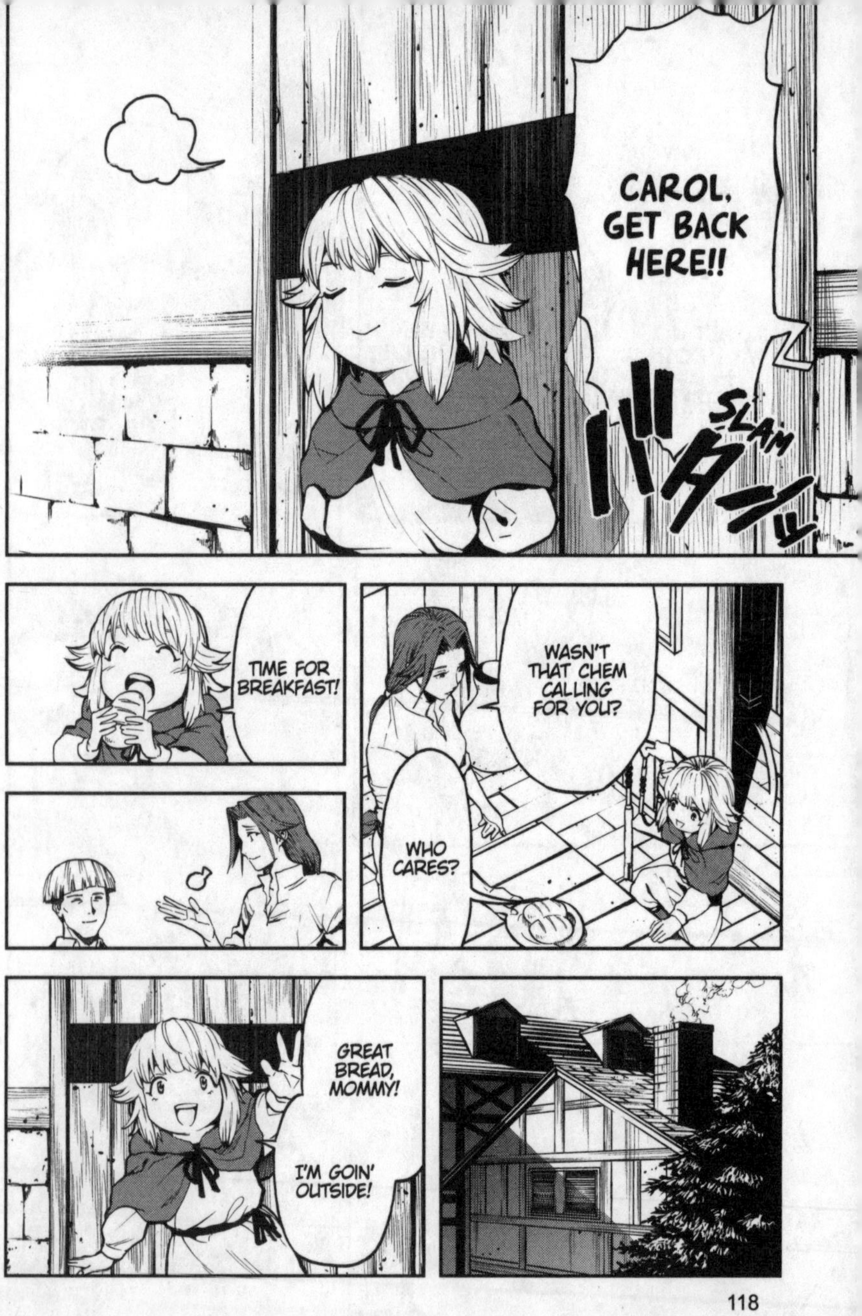
CAROL, GET BACK HERE!!
SLAM
WASN'T THAT CHEM CALLING FOR YOU?
WHO CARES?
TIME FOR BREAKFAST!
GREAT BREAD, MOMMY!
I'M GOIN' OUTSIDE!

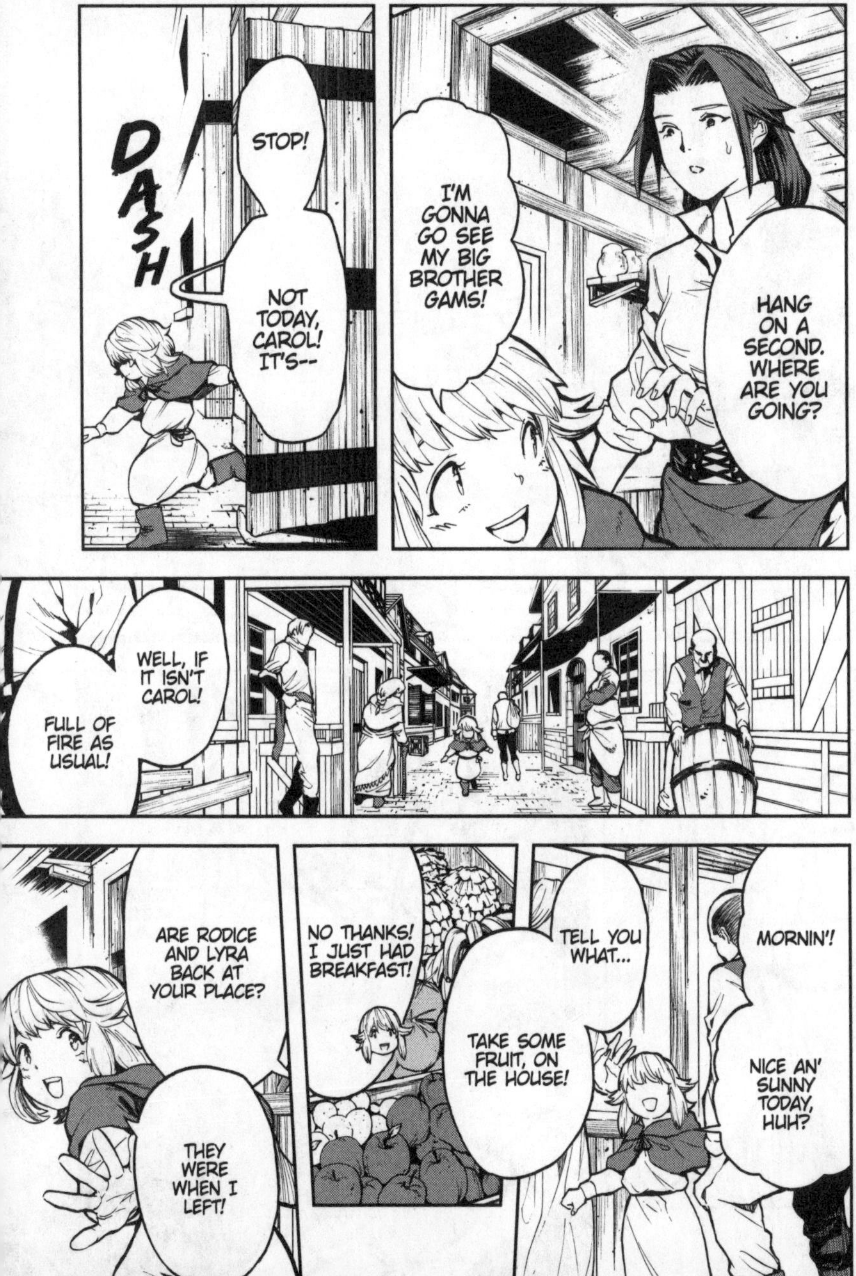
HANG ON A SECOND. WHERE ARE YOU GOING?
I'M GONNA GO SEE MY BIG BROTHER GAMS!
STOP!
NOT TODAY, CAROL! IT'S--
DASH
WELL, IF IT ISN'T CAROL!
FULL OF FIRE AS USUAL!
MORNIN'!
NICE AN' SUNNY TODAY, HUH?
TELL YOU WHAT...
TAKE SOME FRUIT, ON THE HOUSE!
NO THANKS! I JUST HAD BREAKFAST!
ARE RODICE AND LYRA BACK AT YOUR PLACE?
THEY WERE WHEN I LEFT!

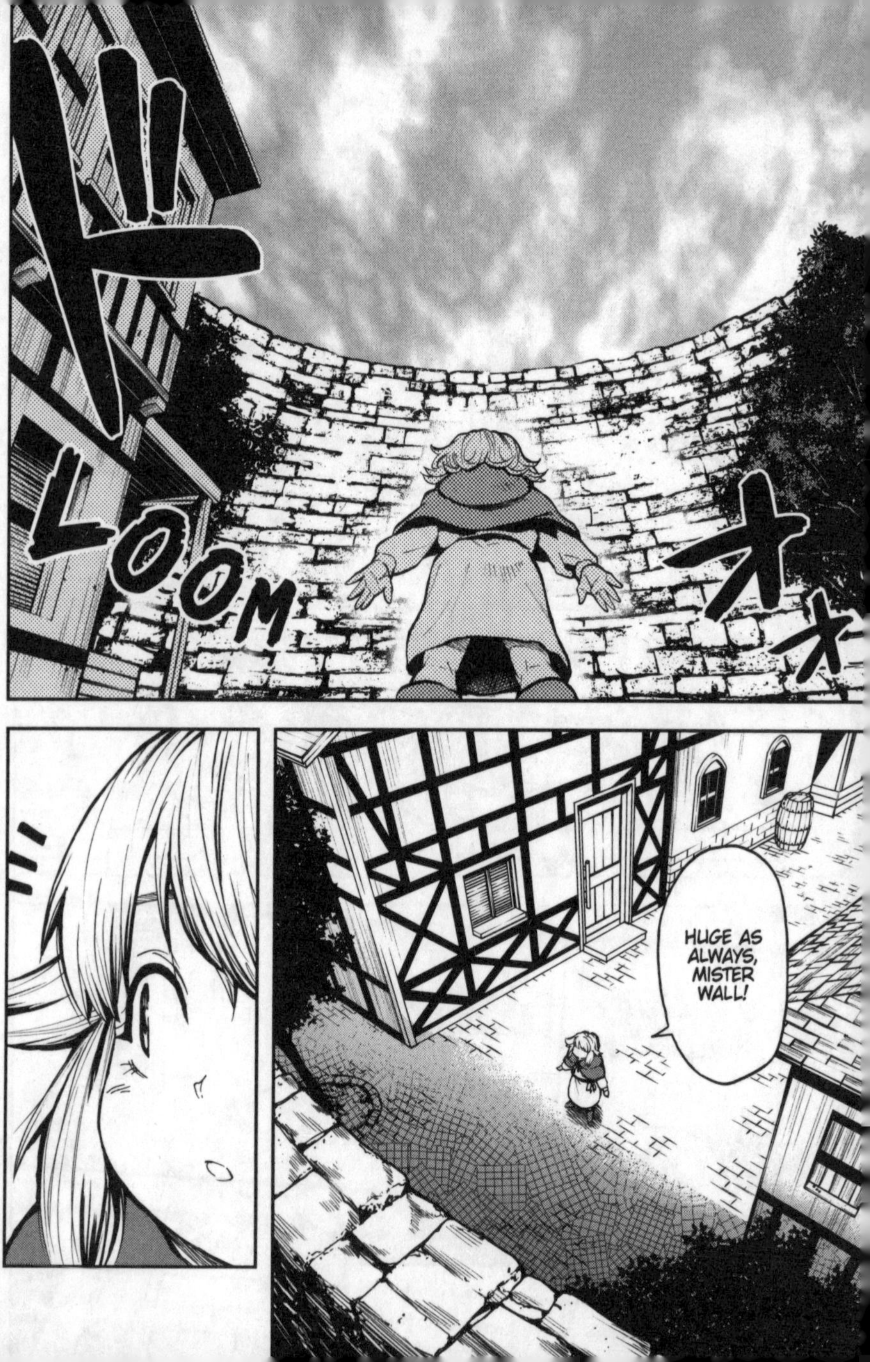
LOOM
HUGE AS ALWAYS, MISTER WALL!

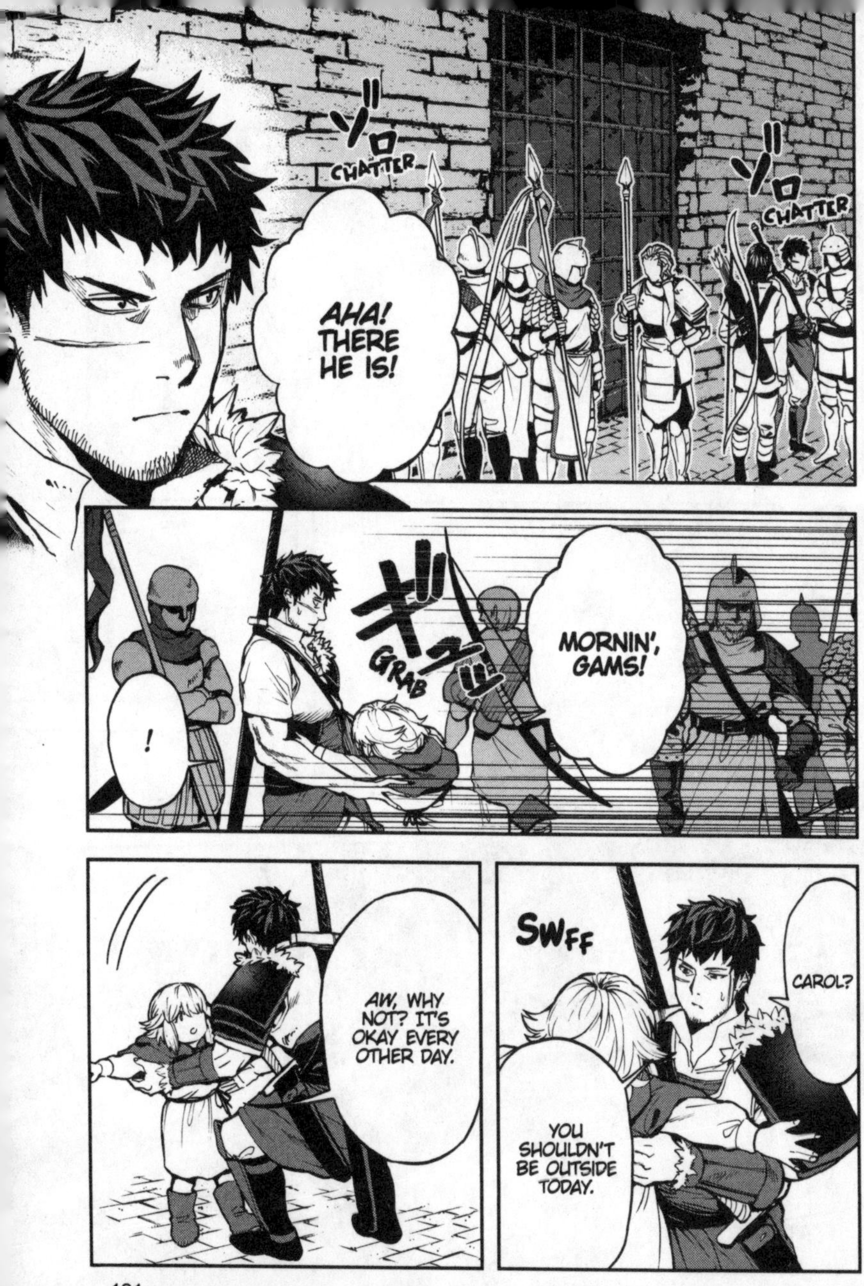
ゾロ
CHATTER
AHA! THERE HE IS!
ゾロ
CHATTER
MORNIN', GAMS!
ギュッ
GRAB
!
CAROL?
SWFF
YOU SHOULDN'T BE OUTSIDE TODAY.
AW, WHY NOT? IT'S OKAY EVERY OTHER DAY.

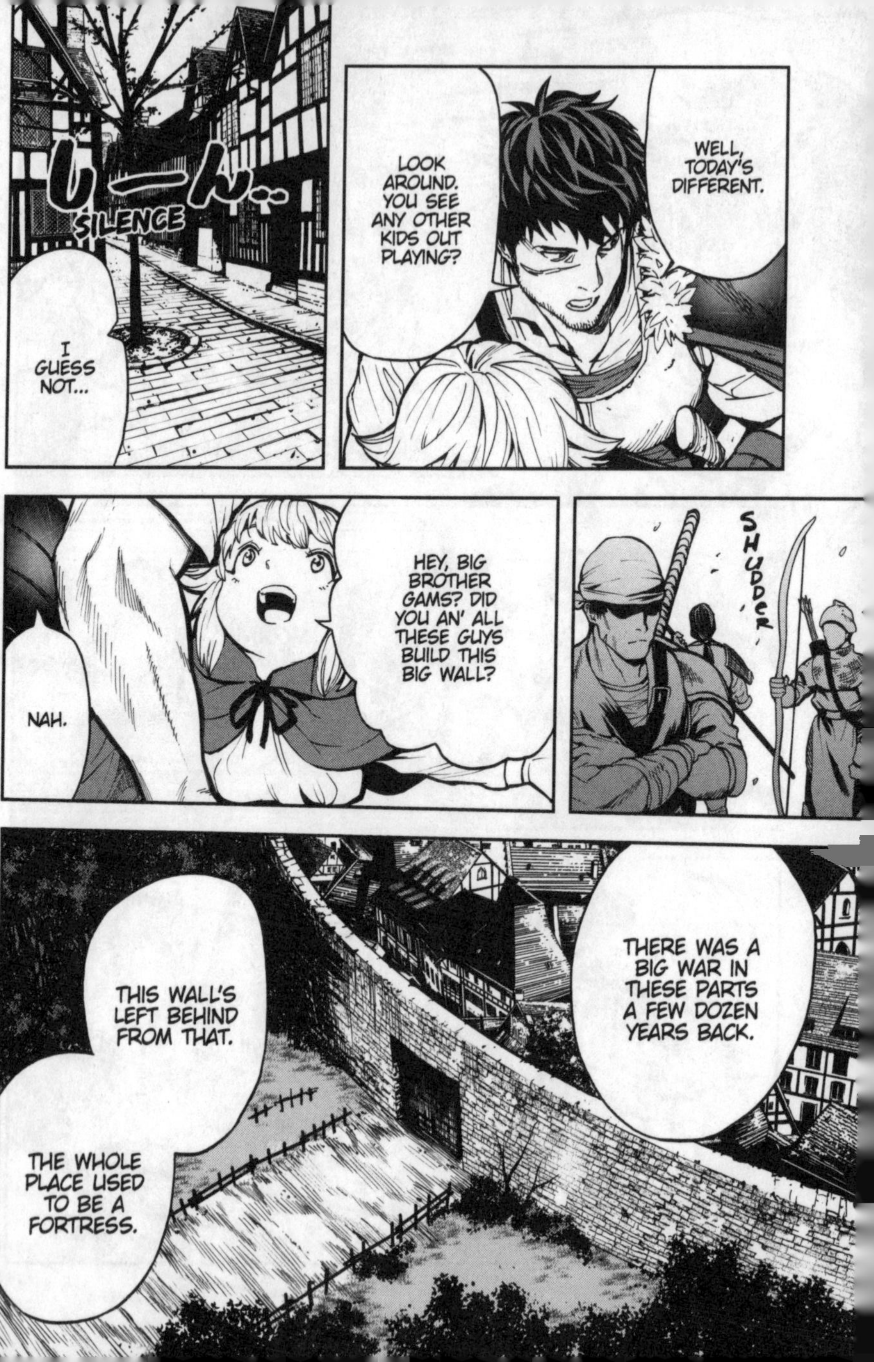
WELL, TODAY'S DIFFERENT.
LOOK AROUND. YOU SEE ANY OTHER KIDS OUT PLAYING?
しーん…
SILENCE
I GUESS NOT...
SHUDDER
HEY, BIG BROTHER GAMS? DID YOU AN' ALL THESE GUYS BUILD THIS BIG WALL?
NAH.
THERE WAS A BIG WAR IN THESE PARTS A FEW DOZEN YEARS BACK.
THIS WALL'S LEFT BEHIND FROM THAT.
THE WHOLE PLACE USED TO BE A FORTRESS.

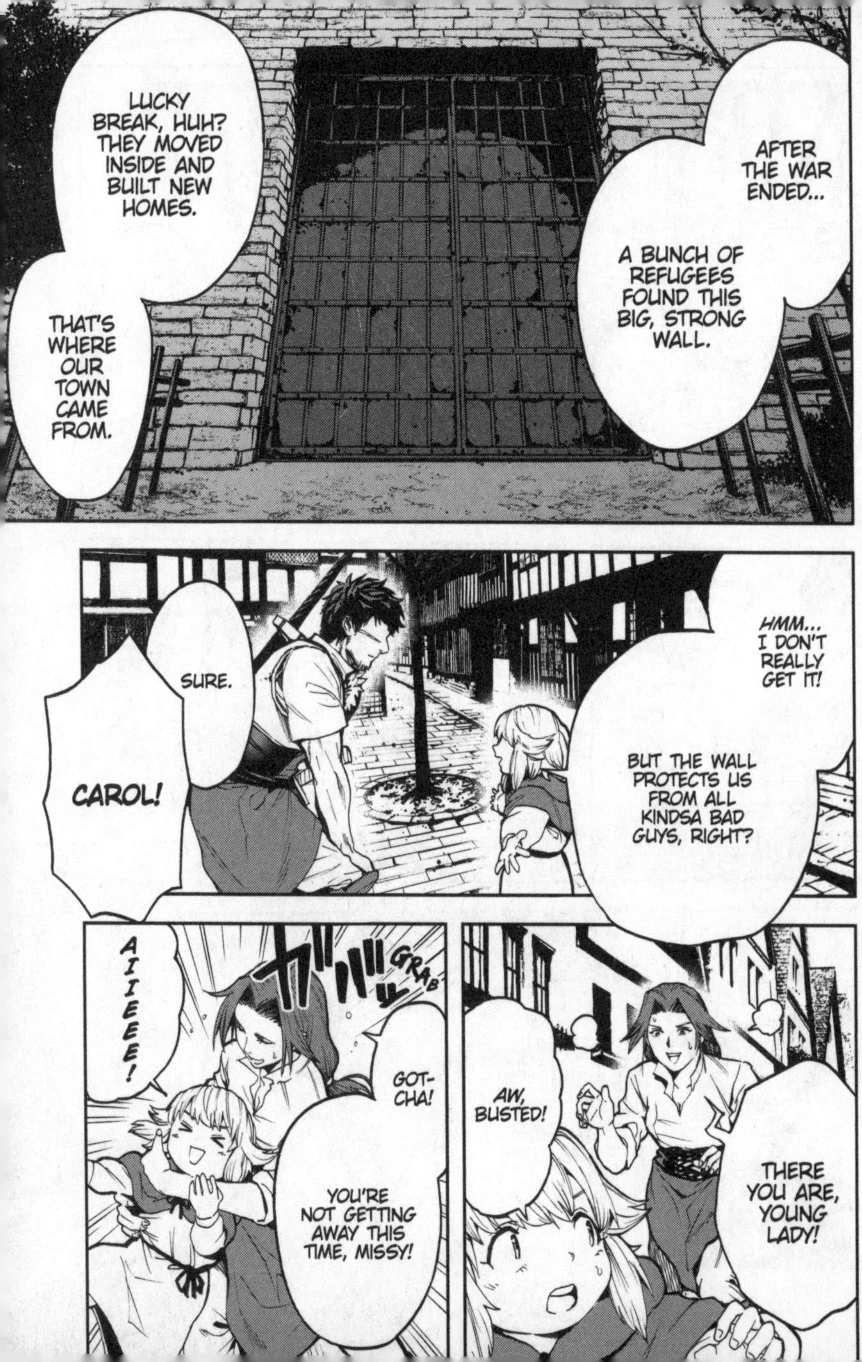
AFTER THE WAR ENDED...
A BUNCH OF REFUGEES FOUND THIS BIG, STRONG WALL.
LUCKY BREAK, HUH? THEY MOVED INSIDE AND BUILT NEW HOMES.
THAT'S WHERE OUR TOWN CAME FROM.
HMM... I DON'T REALLY GET IT!
BUT THE WALL PROTECTS US FROM ALL KINDSA BAD GUYS, RIGHT?
SURE.
CAROL!
THERE YOU ARE, YOUNG LADY!
AW, BUSTED!
GRAB
GOT-CHA!
AIIEEEE!
YOU'RE NOT GETTING AWAY THIS TIME, MISSY!

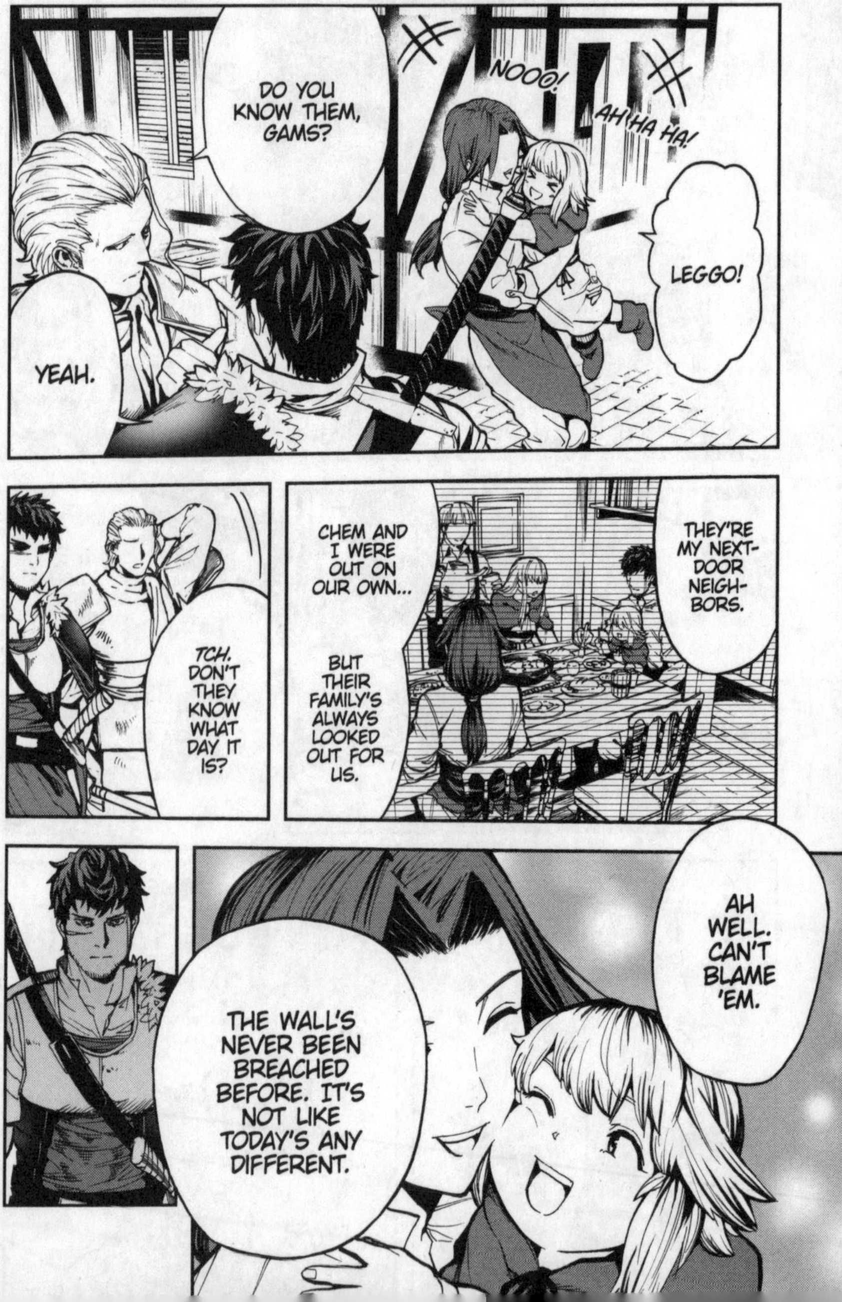
NOOO!
AH HA HA!
LEGGO!
DO YOU KNOW THEM, GAMS?
YEAH.
THEY'RE MY NEXT-DOOR NEIGHBORS.
CHEM AND I WERE OUT ON OUR OWN...
BUT THEIR FAMILY'S ALWAYS LOOKED OUT FOR US.
TCH. DON'T THEY KNOW WHAT DAY IT IS?
AH WELL. CAN'T BLAME 'EM.
THE WALL'S NEVER BEEN BREACHED BEFORE. IT'S NOT LIKE TODAY'S ANY DIFFERENT.

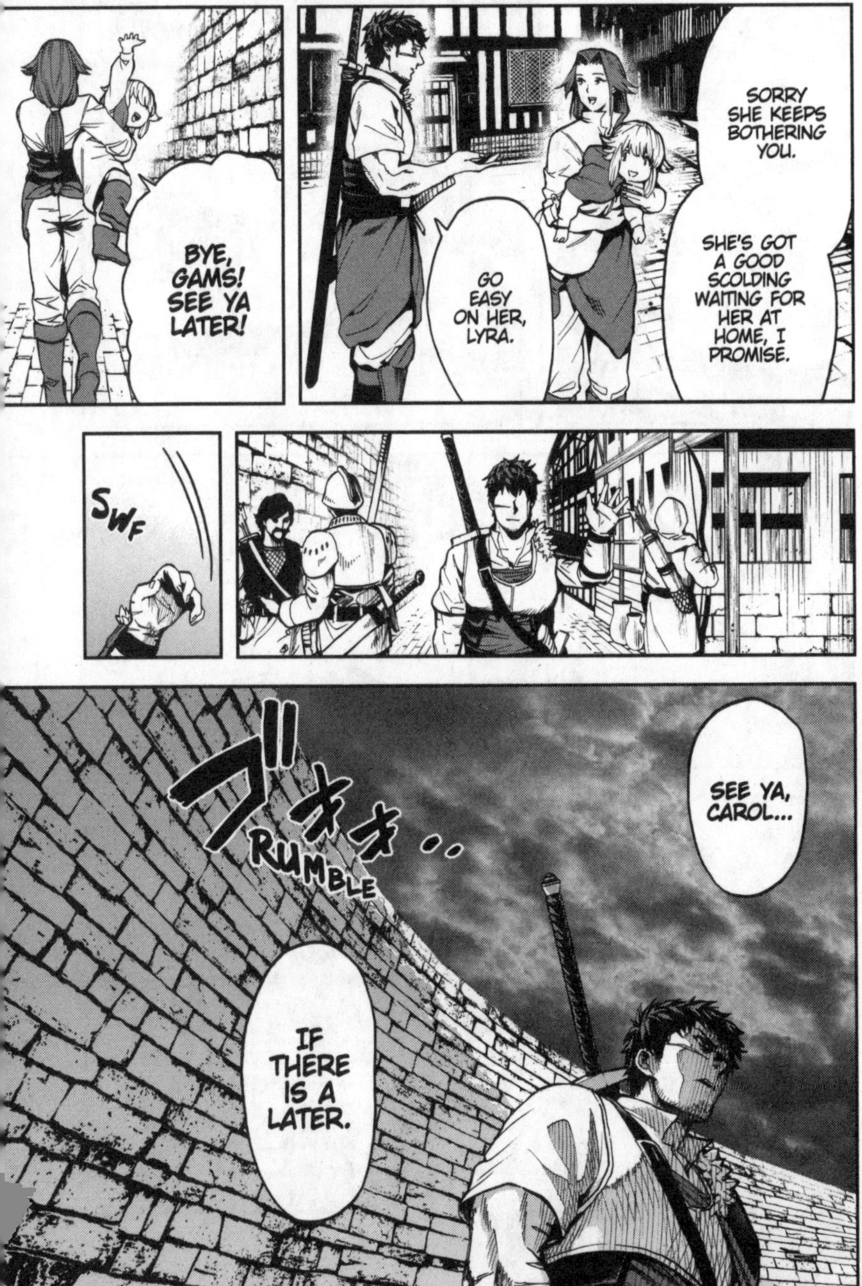
SORRY SHE KEEPS BOTHERING YOU.
SHE'S GOT A GOOD SCOLDING WAITING FOR HER AT HOME, I PROMISE.
GO EASY ON HER, LYRA.
BYE, GAMS! SEE YA LATER!
SWF
SEE YA, CAROL...
ゴォォ..
RUMBLE
IF THERE IS A LATER.

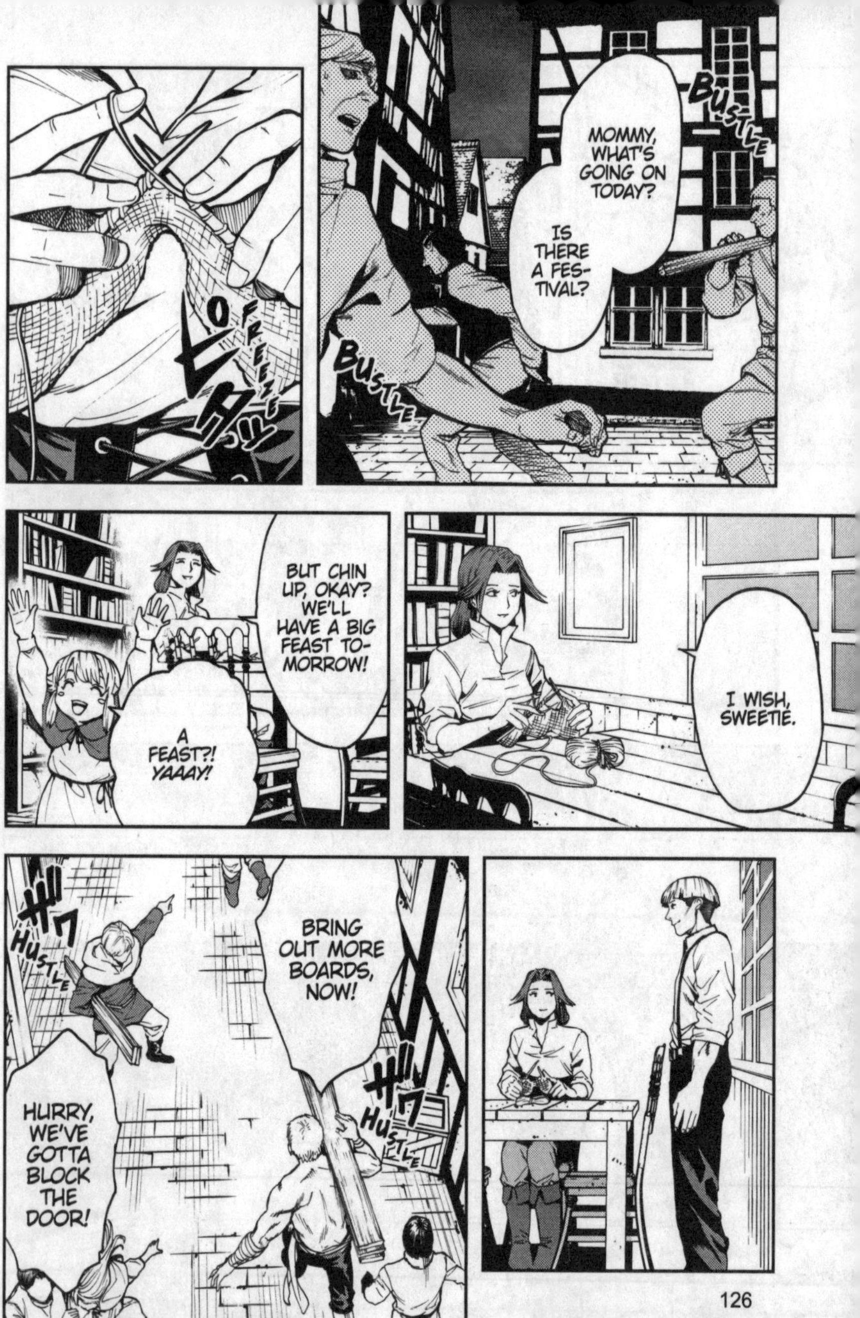
BUSTLE
MOMMY, WHAT'S GOING ON TODAY?
IS THERE A FES-TIVAL?
BUSTLE
FREEZE
I WISH, SWEETIE.
BUT CHIN UP, OKAY? WE'LL HAVE A BIG FEAST TO-MORROW!
A FEAST?! YAAAY!
BRING OUT MORE BOARDS, NOW!
HUSTLE
HUSTLE
HURRY, WE'VE GOTTA BLOCK THE DOOR!

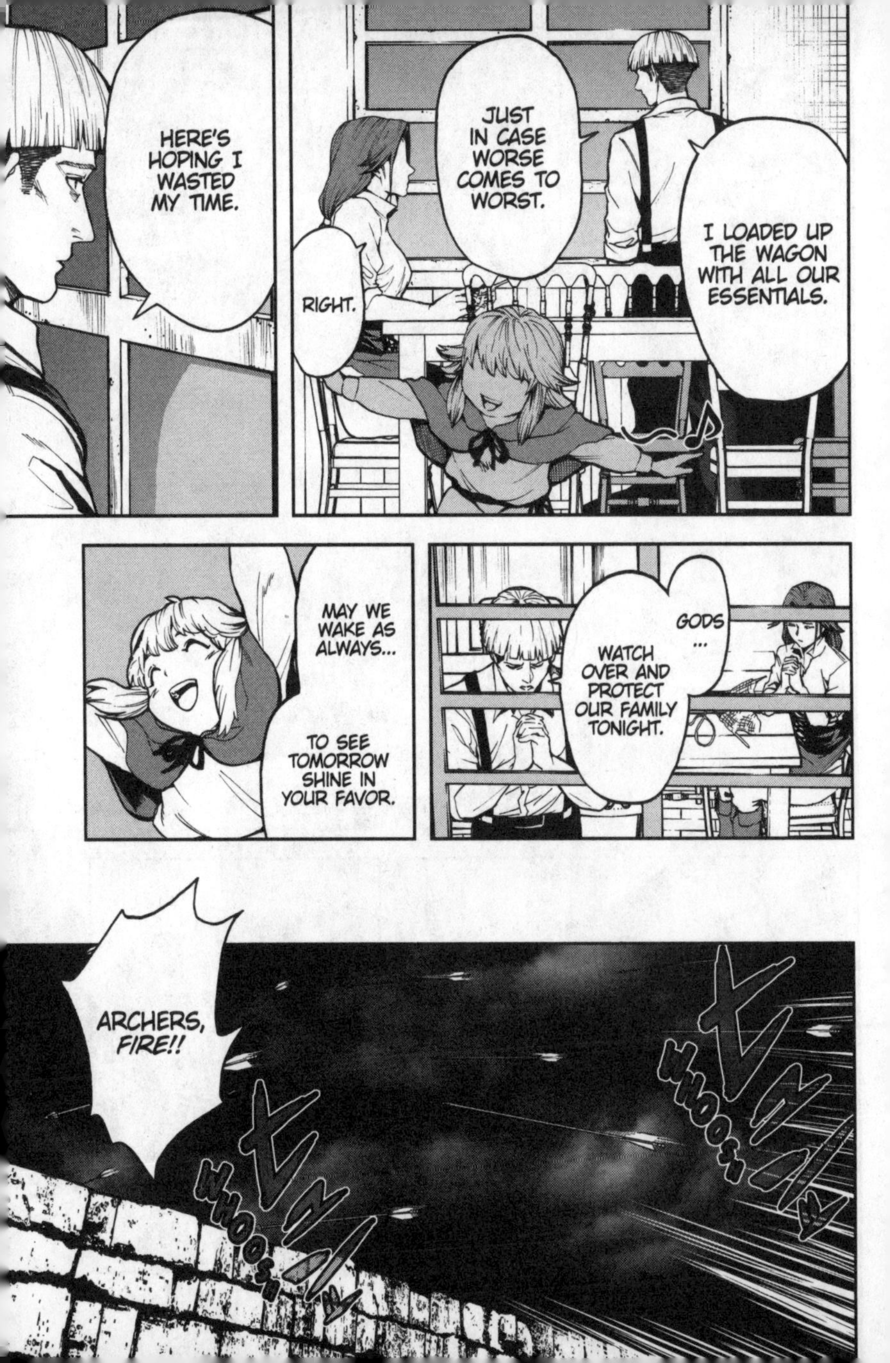
I LOADED UP THE WAGON WITH ALL OUR ESSENTIALS.
JUST IN CASE WORSE COMES TO WORST.
RIGHT.
HERE'S HOPING I WASTED MY TIME.
GODS ...
WATCH OVER AND PROTECT OUR FAMILY TONIGHT.
MAY WE WAKE AS ALWAYS...
TO SEE TOMORROW SHINE IN YOUR FAVOR.
ARCHERS, FIRE!!
WHOOSH
WHOOSH

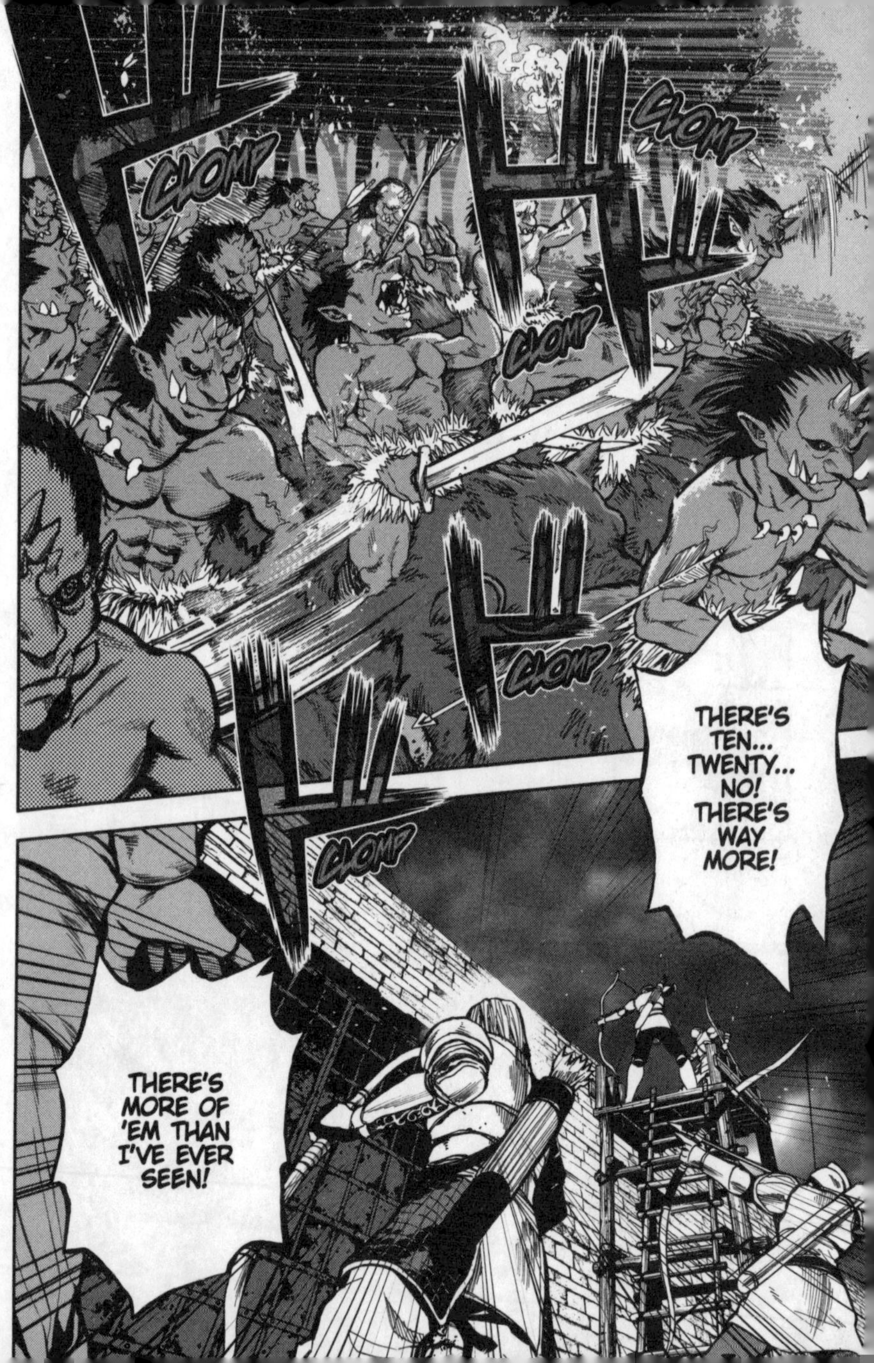
CLOMP
CLOMP
CLOMP
CLOMP
THERE'S TEN... TWENTY... NO! THERE'S WAY MORE!
CLOMP
THERE'S MORE OF 'EM THAN I'VE EVER SEEN!

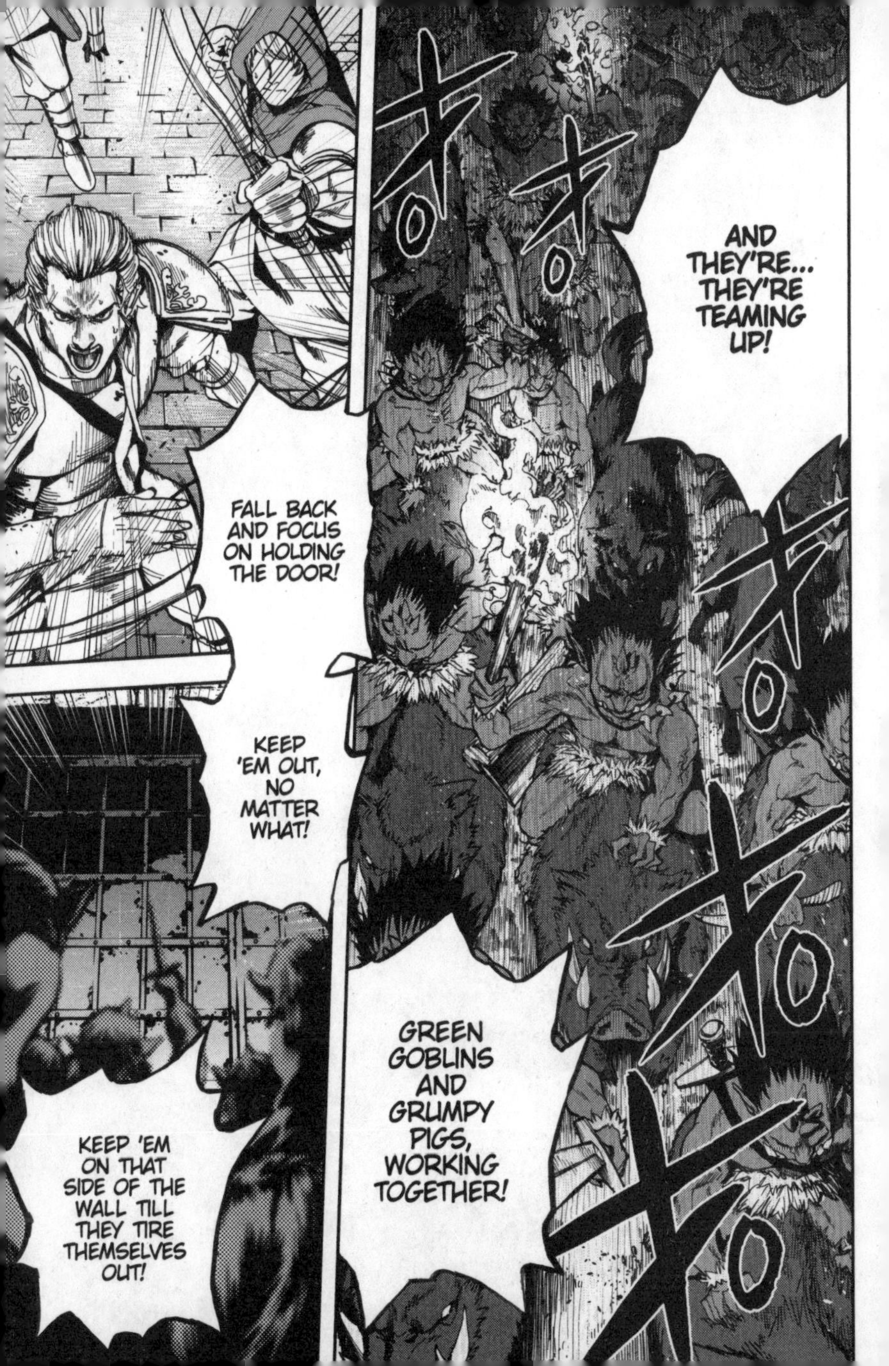
AND THEY'RE... THEY'RE TEAMING UP!
GREEN GOBLINS AND GRUMPY PIGS, WORKING TOGETHER!
FALL BACK AND FOCUS ON HOLDING THE DOOR!
KEEP 'EM OUT, NO MATTER WHAT!
KEEP 'EM ON THAT SIDE OF THE WALL TILL THEY TIRE THEMSELVES OUT!

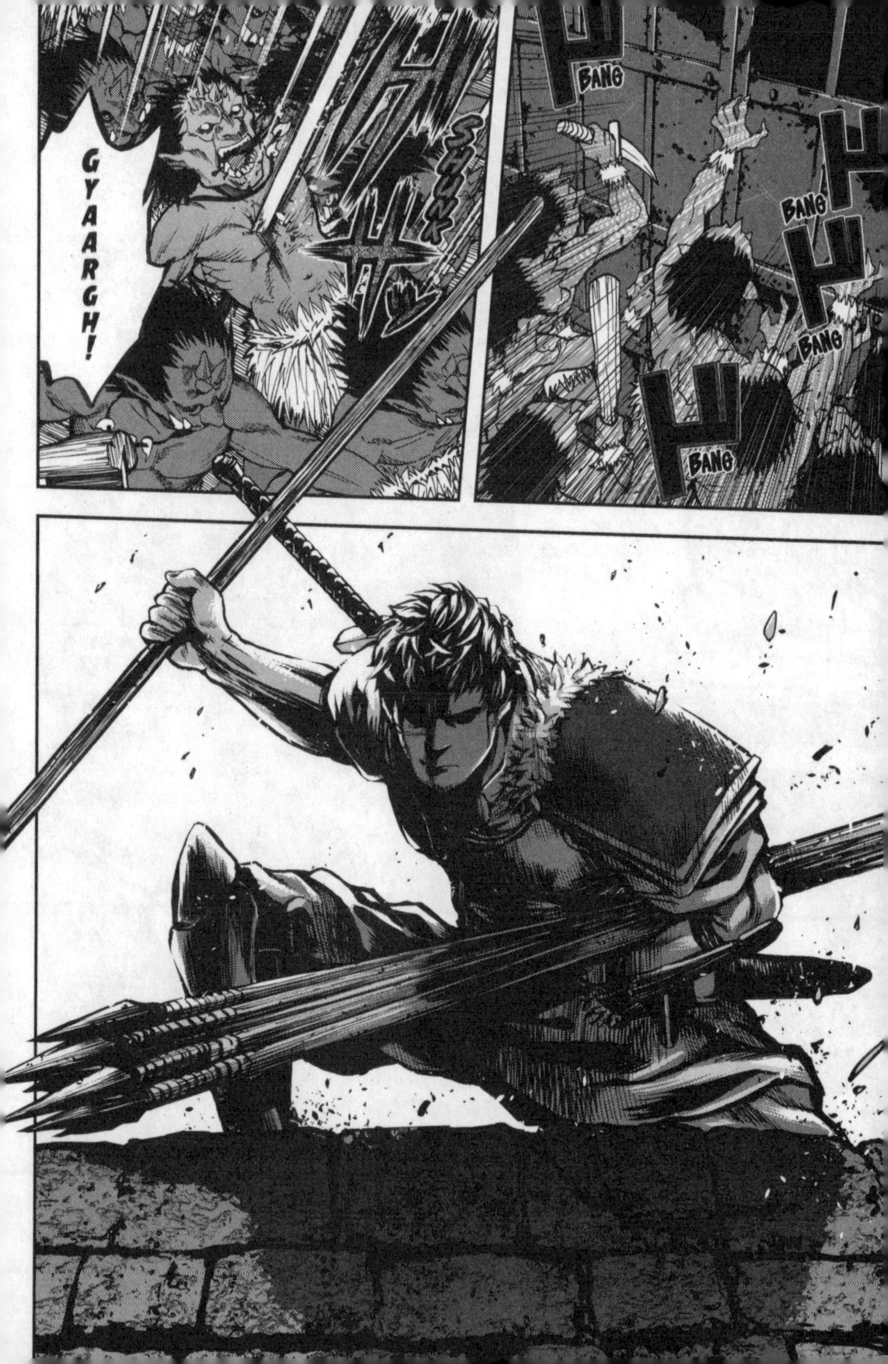
BANG
BANG
BANG
BANG
SHUNK
GYAARGH!

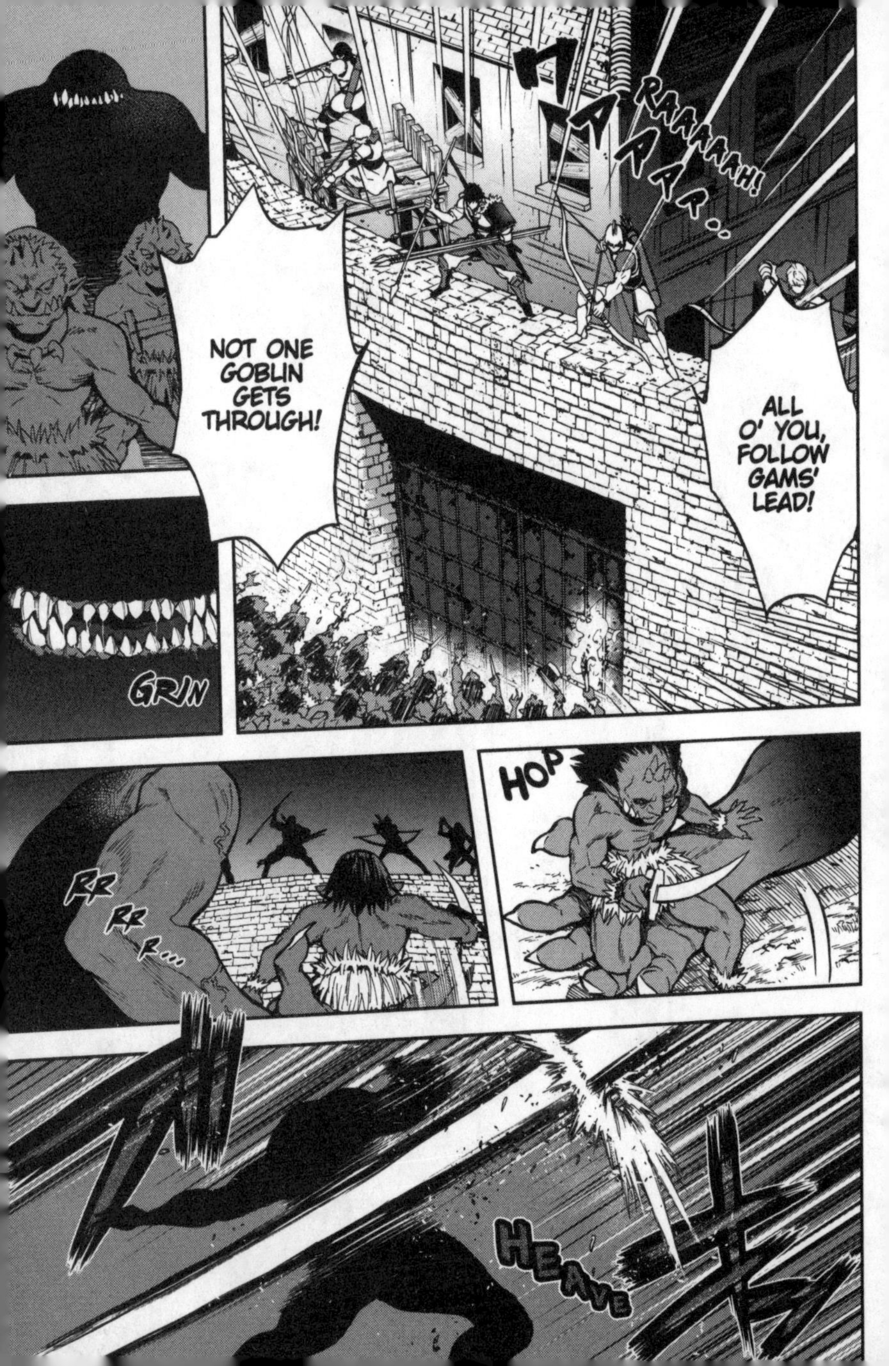
RAAAAAAH!
ALL O' YOU, FOLLOW GAMS' LEAD!
NOT ONE GOBLIN GETS THROUGH!
GRIN
HOP
RR RR R...
HEAVE

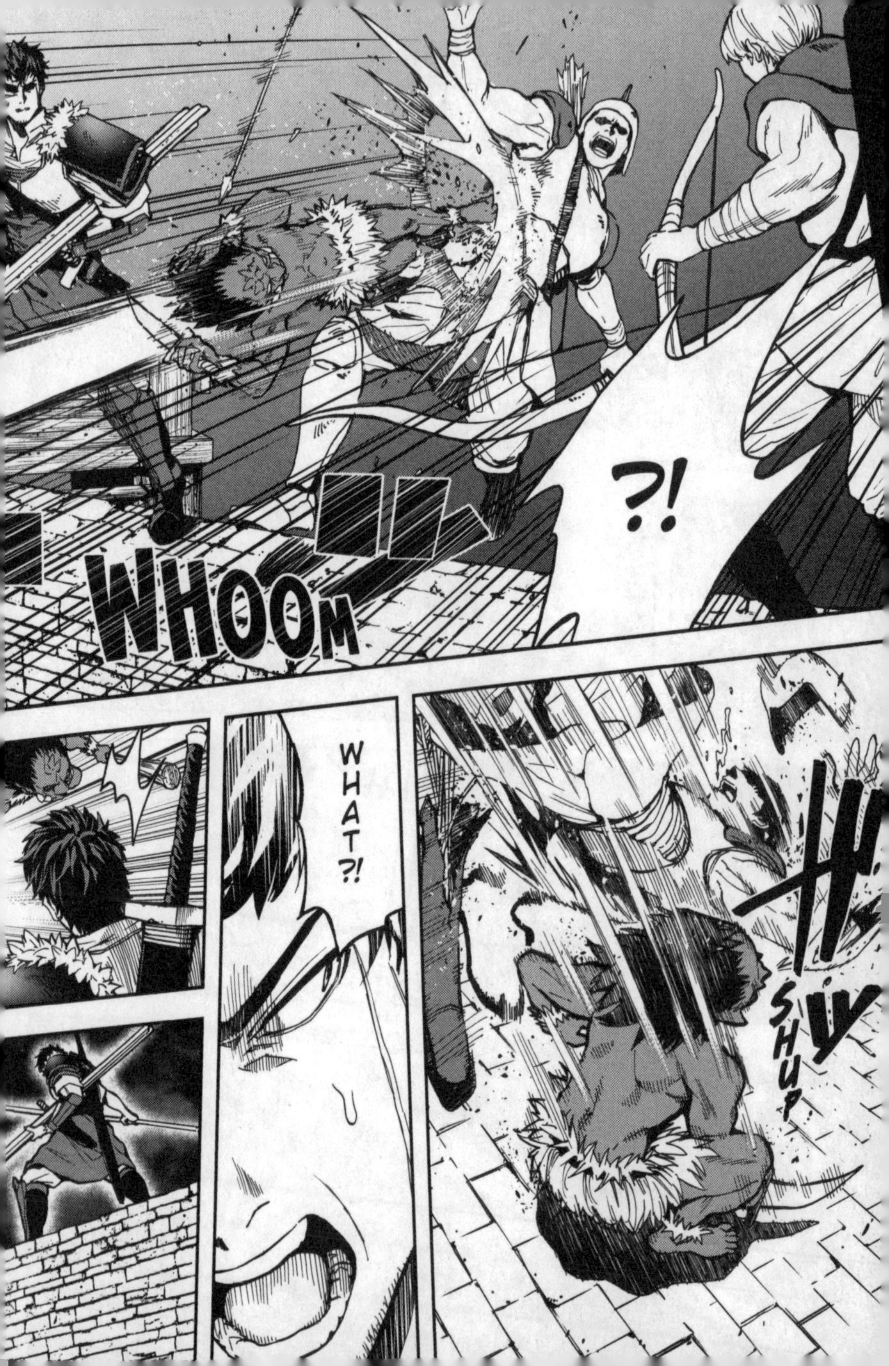
?!
WHOOM
SHUP
WHAT?!

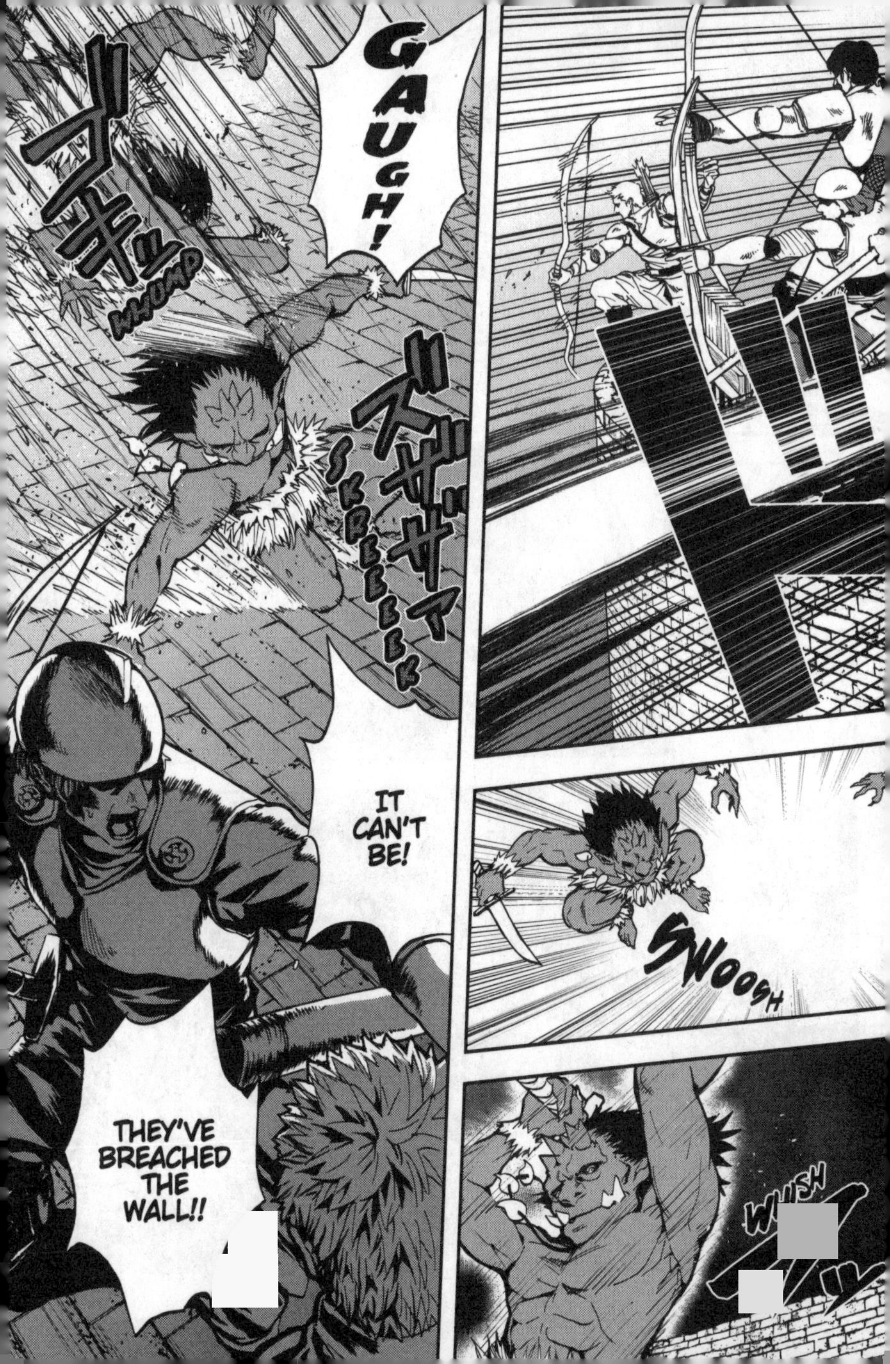
SWOOSH
WHUSH
GAUGH!
WHUMP
SKREEEEEK
IT CAN'T BE!
THEY'VE BREACHED THE WALL!!

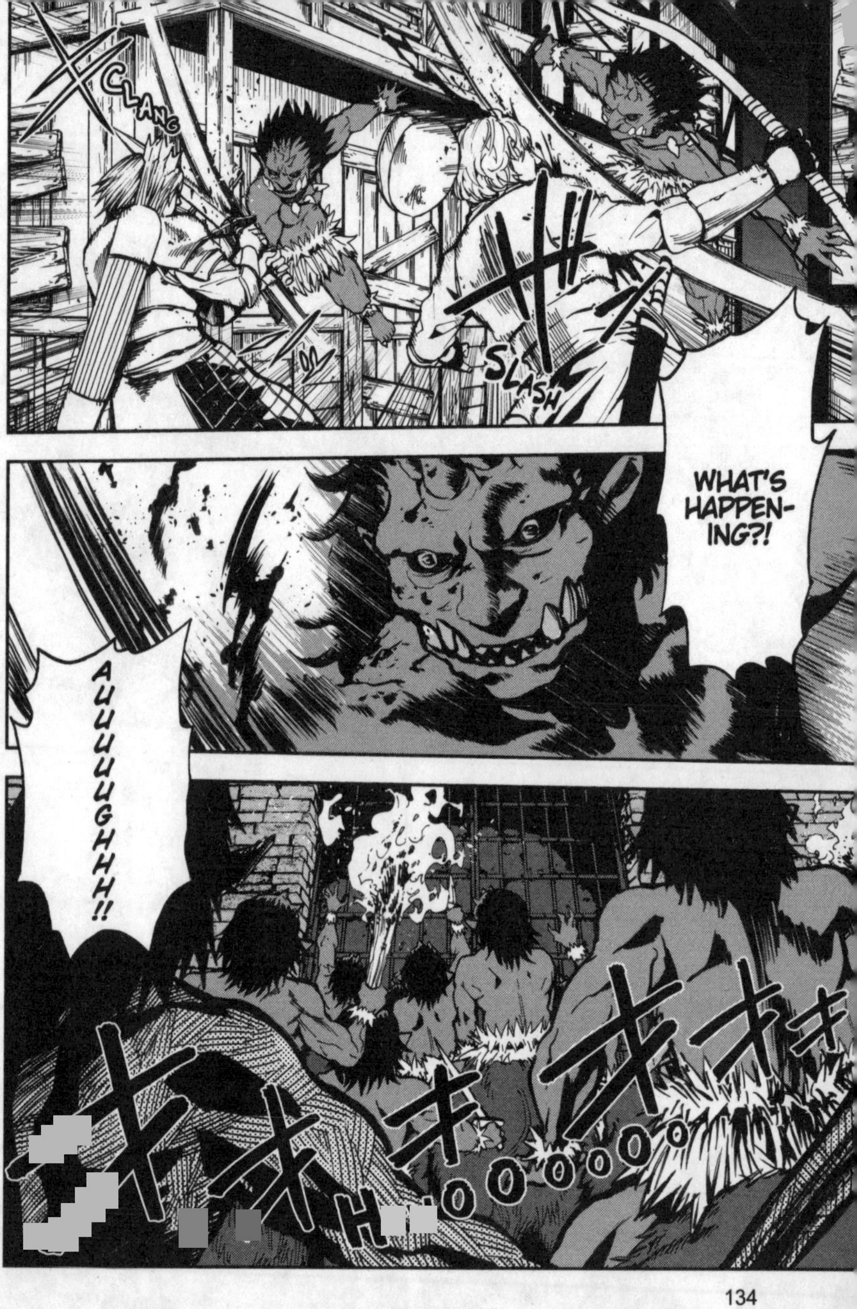
CLANG
SLASH
WHAT'S HAPPENING?!
AUUUUUGHHHH!!
H..OOOOOOO

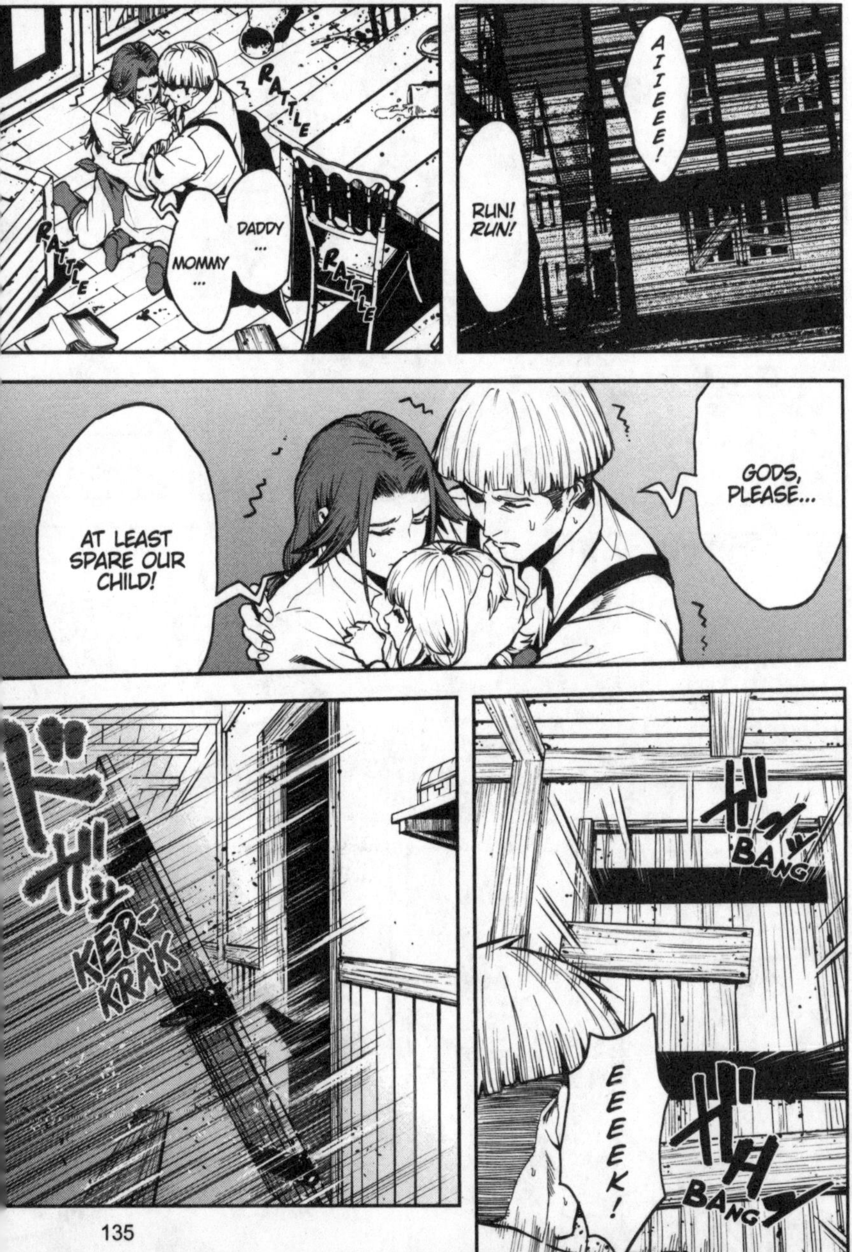
AIIEEE!
RUN! RUN!
RATTLE
DADDY ...
MOMMY ...
RATTLE
RATTLE
GODS, PLEASE...
AT LEAST SPARE OUR CHILD!
BANG
EEEEK!
BANG
KER-KRAK

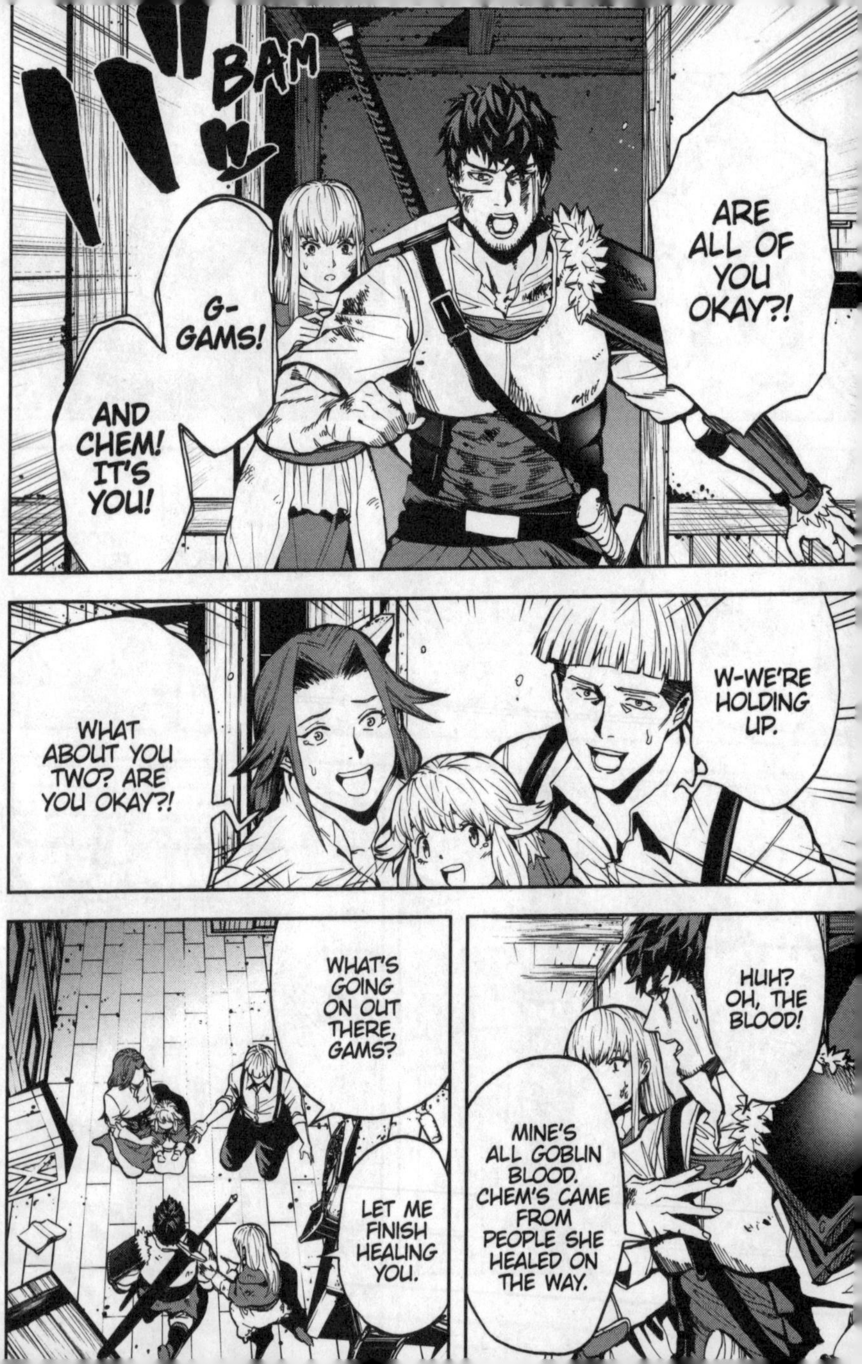
ARE ALL OF YOU OKAY?!
BAM
G-GAMS!
AND CHEM! IT'S YOU!
W-WE'RE HOLDING UP.
WHAT ABOUT YOU TWO? ARE YOU OKAY?!
HUH? OH, THE BLOOD!
MINE'S ALL GOBLIN BLOOD. CHEM'S CAME FROM PEOPLE SHE HEALED ON THE WAY.
WHAT'S GOING ON OUT THERE, GAMS?
LET ME FINISH HEALING YOU.

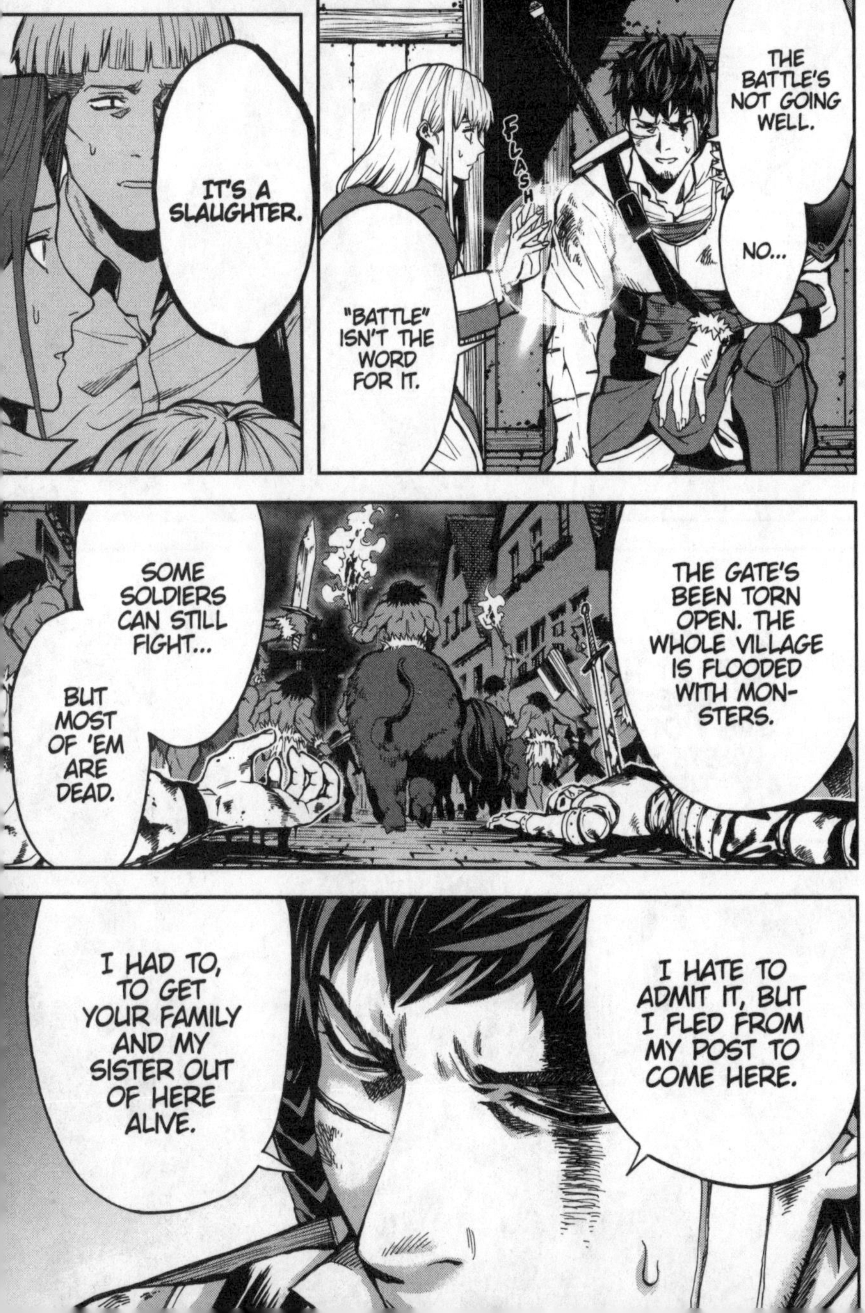
THE BATTLE'S NOT GOING WELL.
NO...
FLASH
"BATTLE" ISN'T THE WORD FOR IT.
IT'S A SLAUGHTER.
THE GATE'S BEEN TORN OPEN. THE WHOLE VILLAGE IS FLOODED WITH MON-STERS.
SOME SOLDIERS CAN STILL FIGHT...
BUT MOST OF 'EM ARE DEAD.
I HATE TO ADMIT IT, BUT I FLED FROM MY POST TO COME HERE.
I HAD TO, TO GET YOUR FAMILY AND MY SISTER OUT OF HERE ALIVE.

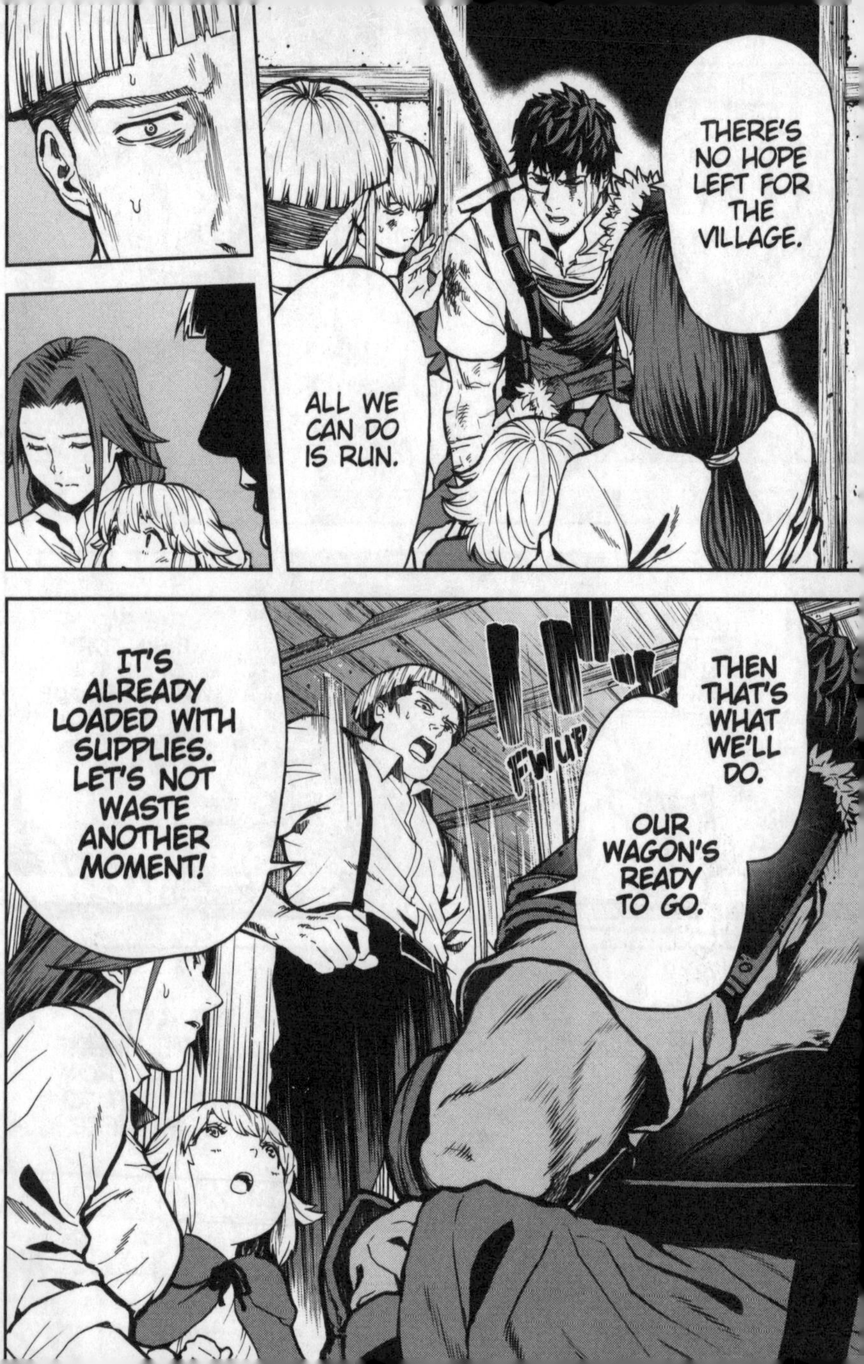
THERE'S NO HOPE LEFT FOR THE VILLAGE.
ALL WE CAN DO IS RUN.
THEN THAT'S WHAT WE'LL DO.
OUR WAGON'S READY TO GO.
FWUP
IT'S ALREADY LOADED WITH SUPPLIES. LET'S NOT WASTE ANOTHER MOMENT!

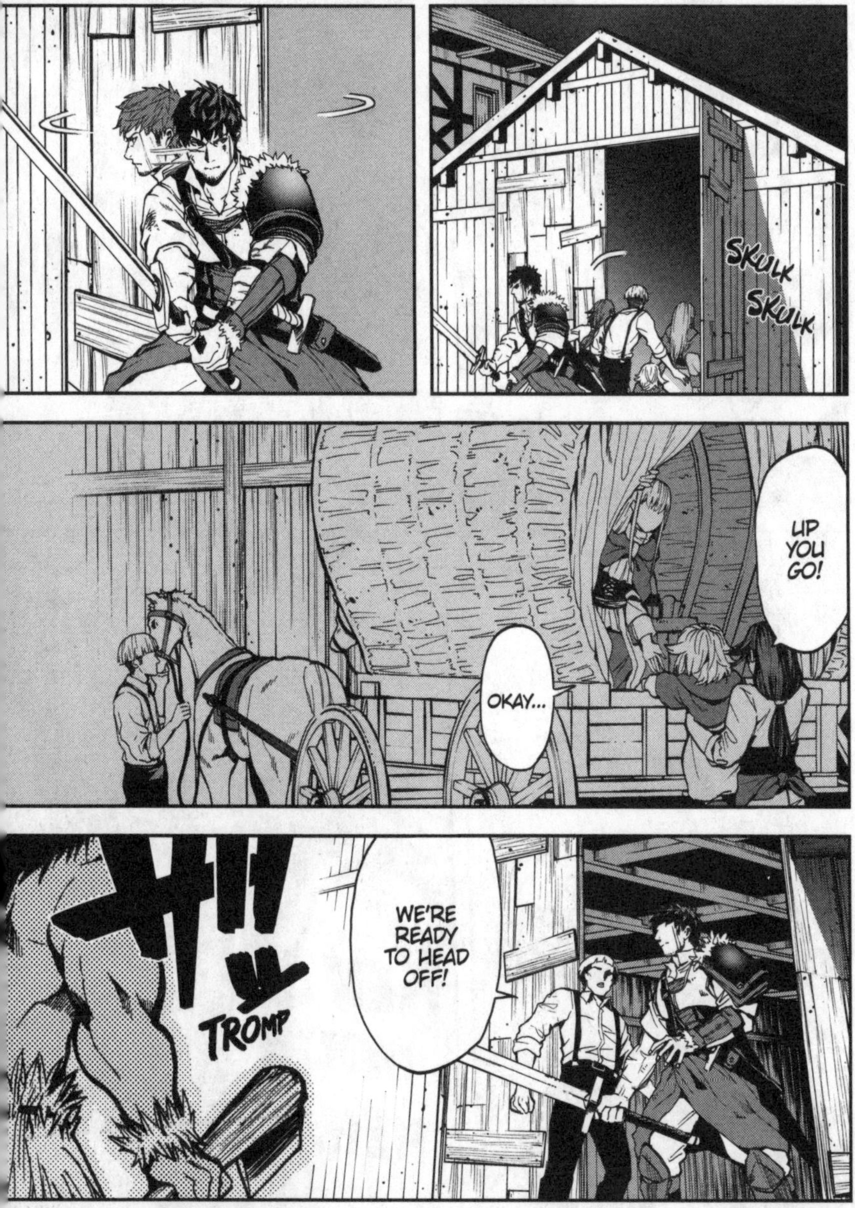
SKULK SKULK
UP YOU GO!
OKAY...
WE'RE READY TO HEAD OFF!
TROMP

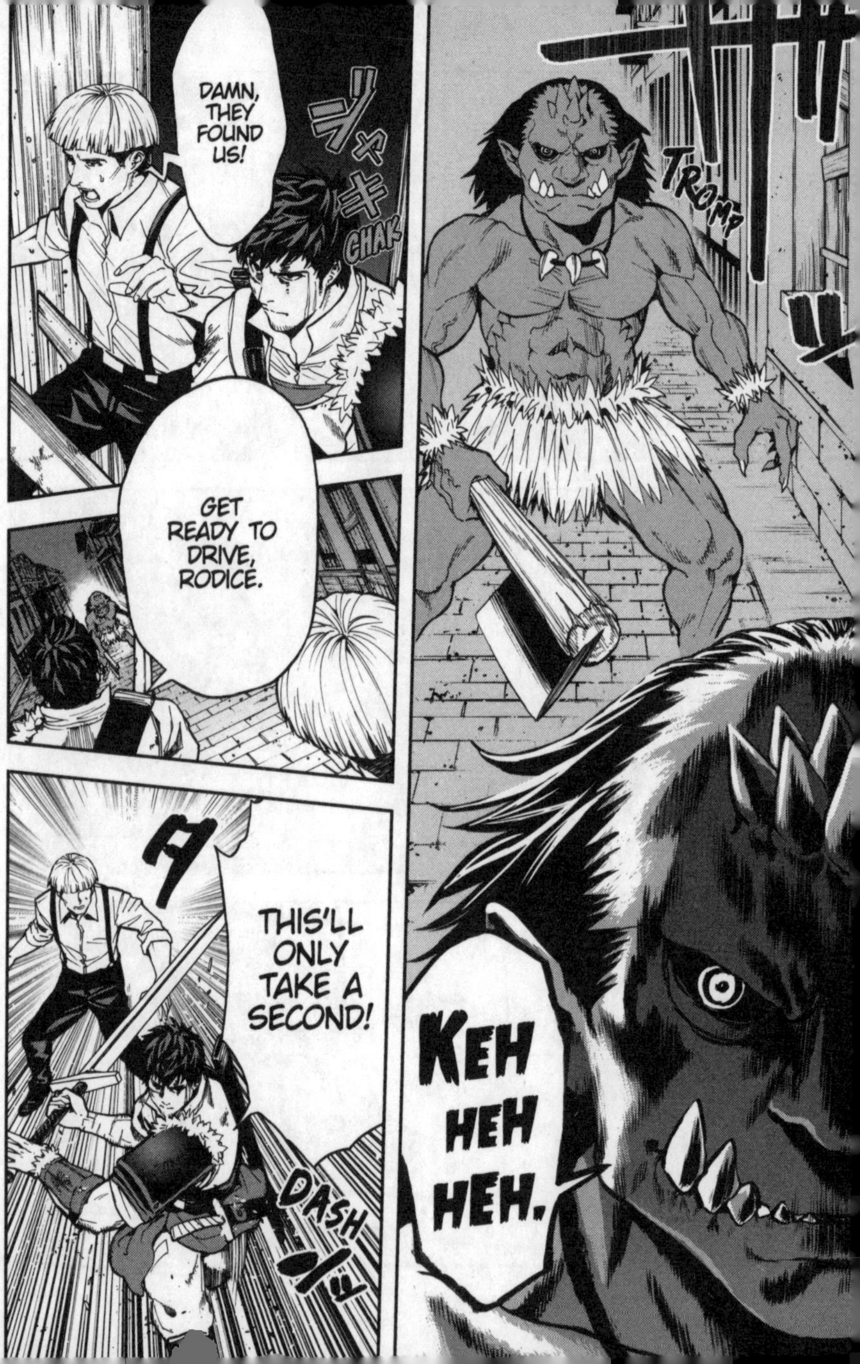
TROMP
KEH HEH HEH.
DAMN, THEY FOUND US!
CHAK
GET READY TO DRIVE, RODICE.
THIS'LL ONLY TAKE A SECOND!
DASH

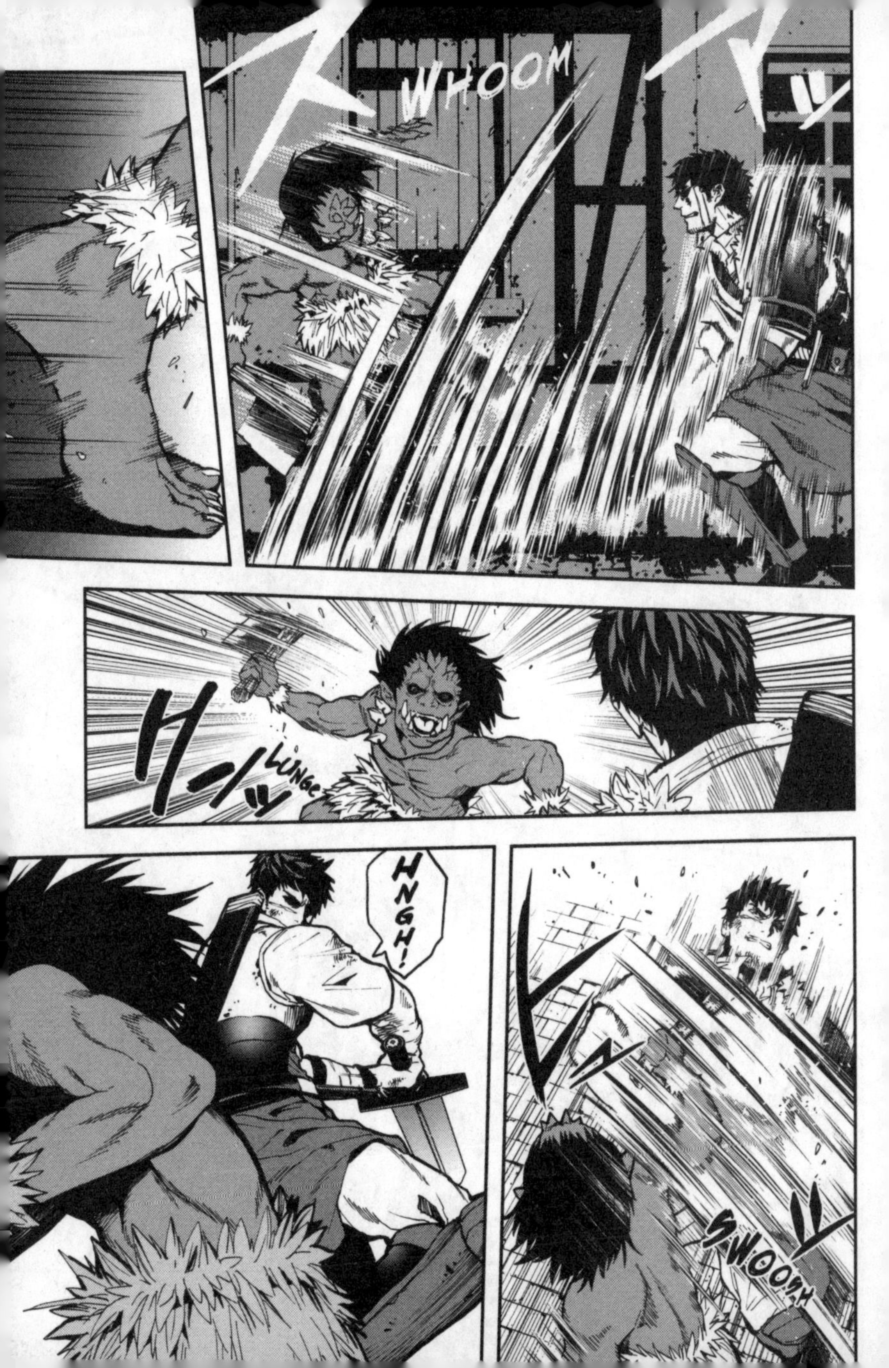
WHOOM
LUNGE
HNGH!
SWOOSH

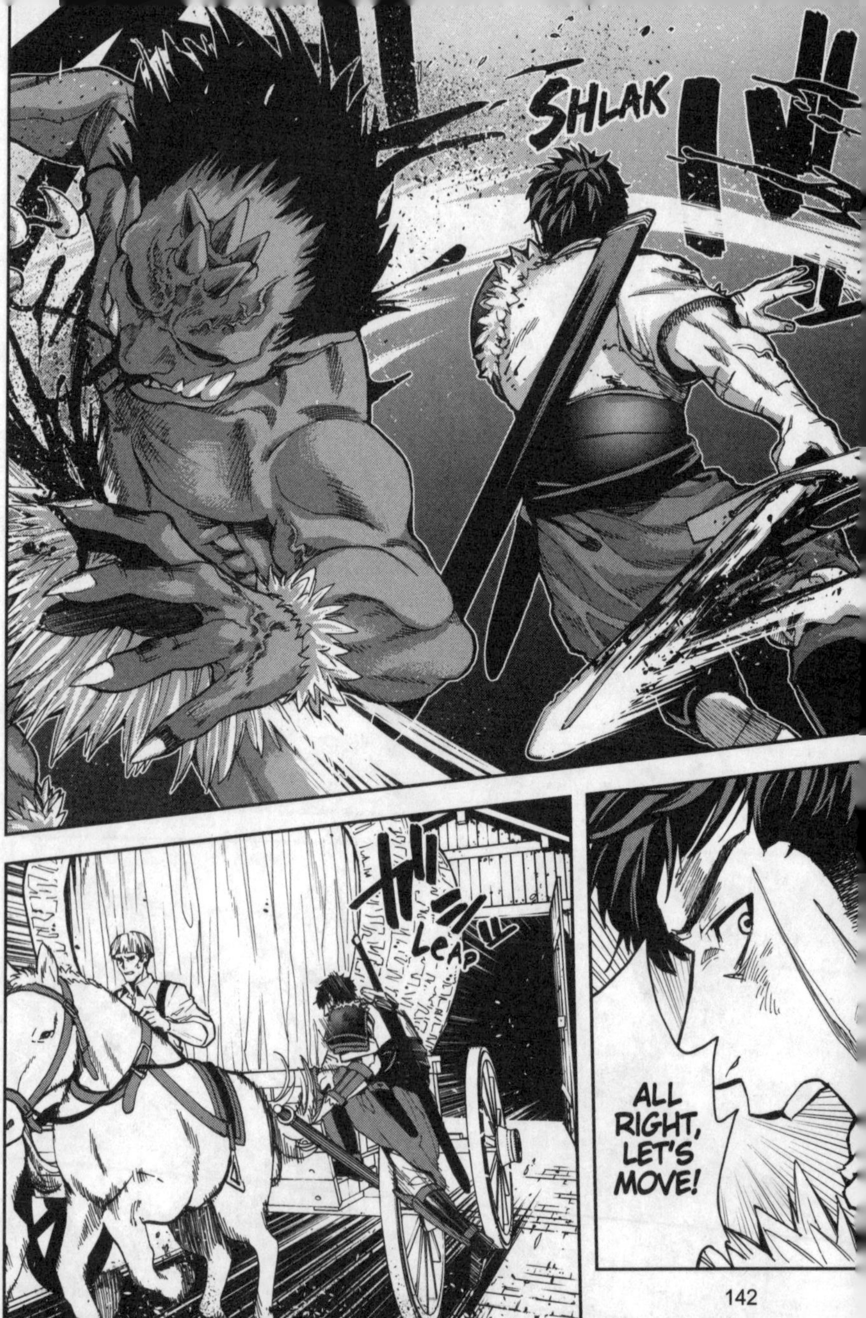
SHLAK
ALL RIGHT, LET'S MOVE!
LEAP

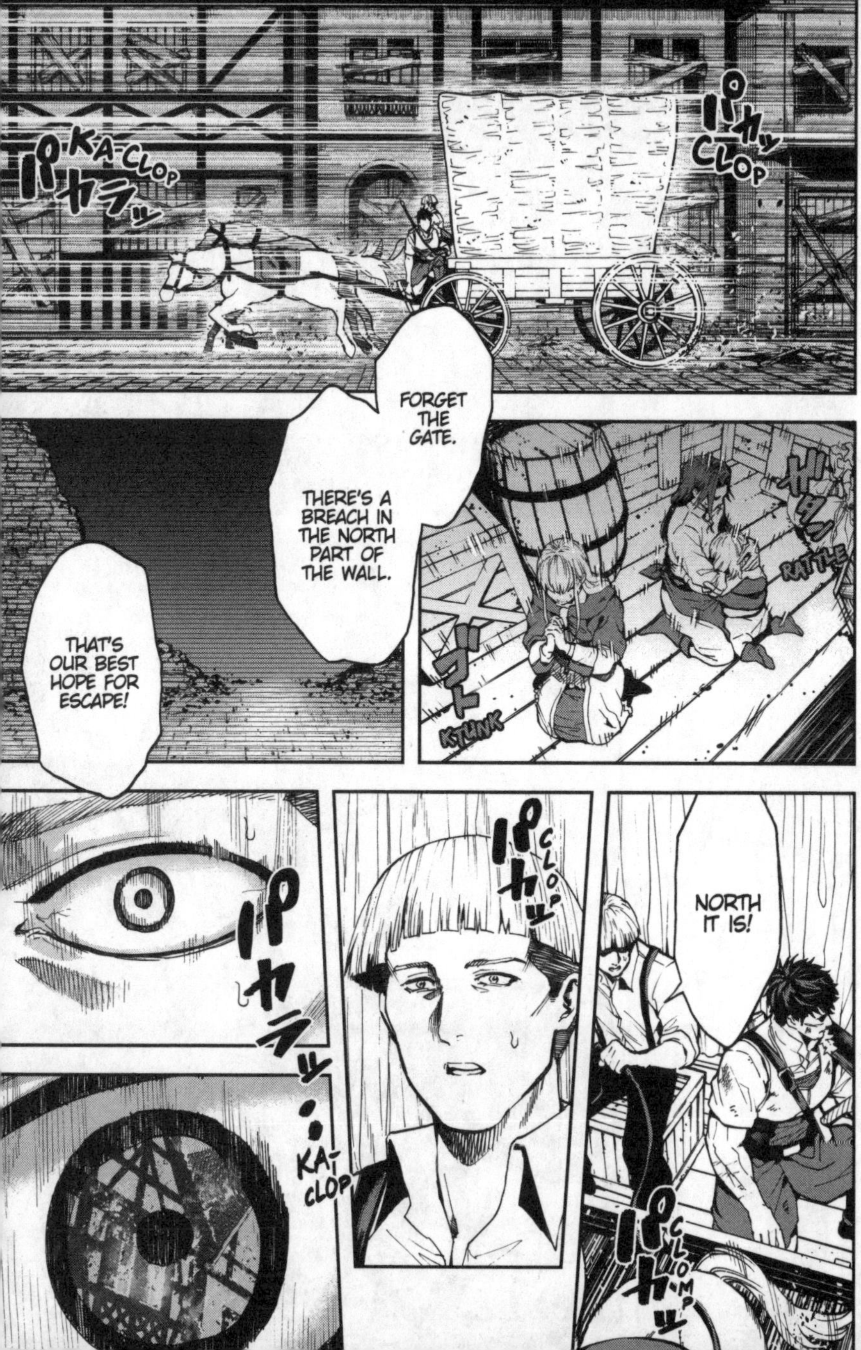

パカッ
CLOP
パカラッ
KA-CLOP
FORGET THE GATE.
THERE'S A BREACH IN THE NORTH PART OF THE WALL.
RATTLE
KTUNK
THAT'S OUR BEST HOPE FOR ESCAPE!
NORTH IT IS!
パカッ
CLOMP
パカッ
CLOP
パカラッ
KA-CLOP

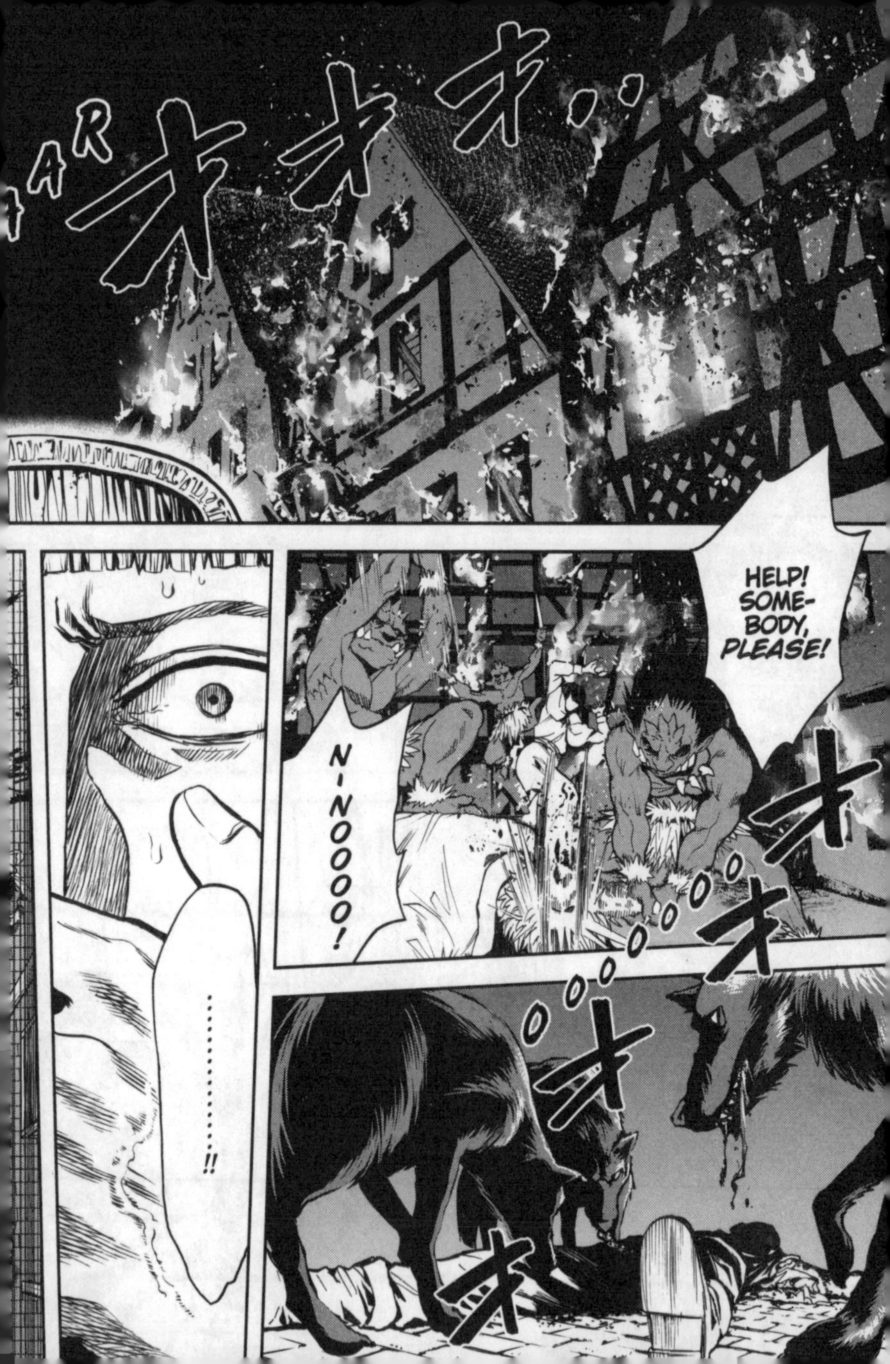
AR オオオ
HELP! SOMEBODY, PLEASE!
N-NOOOOO!
オオ OOOO
OOOO オオ
……!!

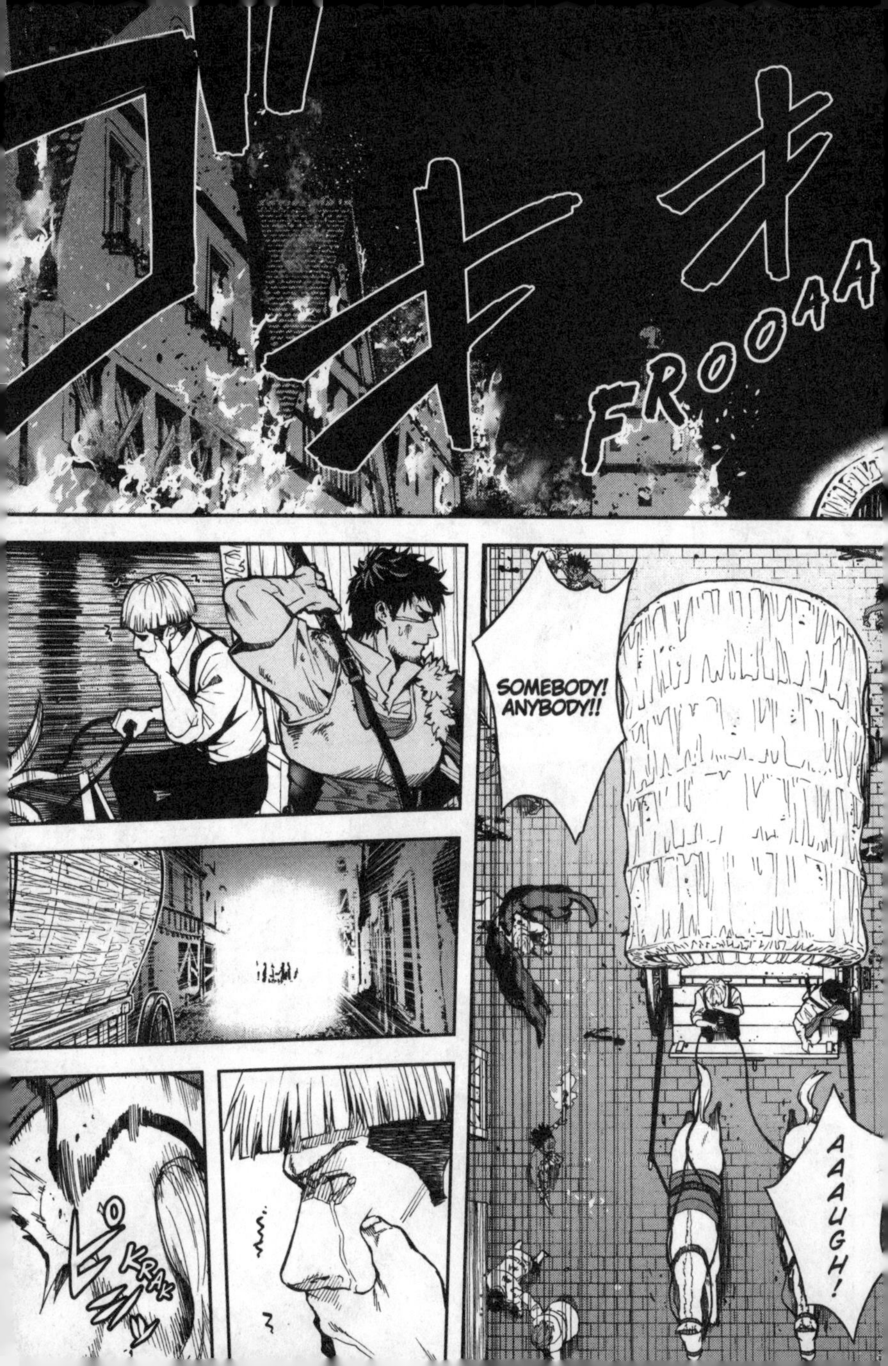
ゴオオ
FROOAA
SOMEBODY! ANYBODY!!
AAAUGH!
KRAK

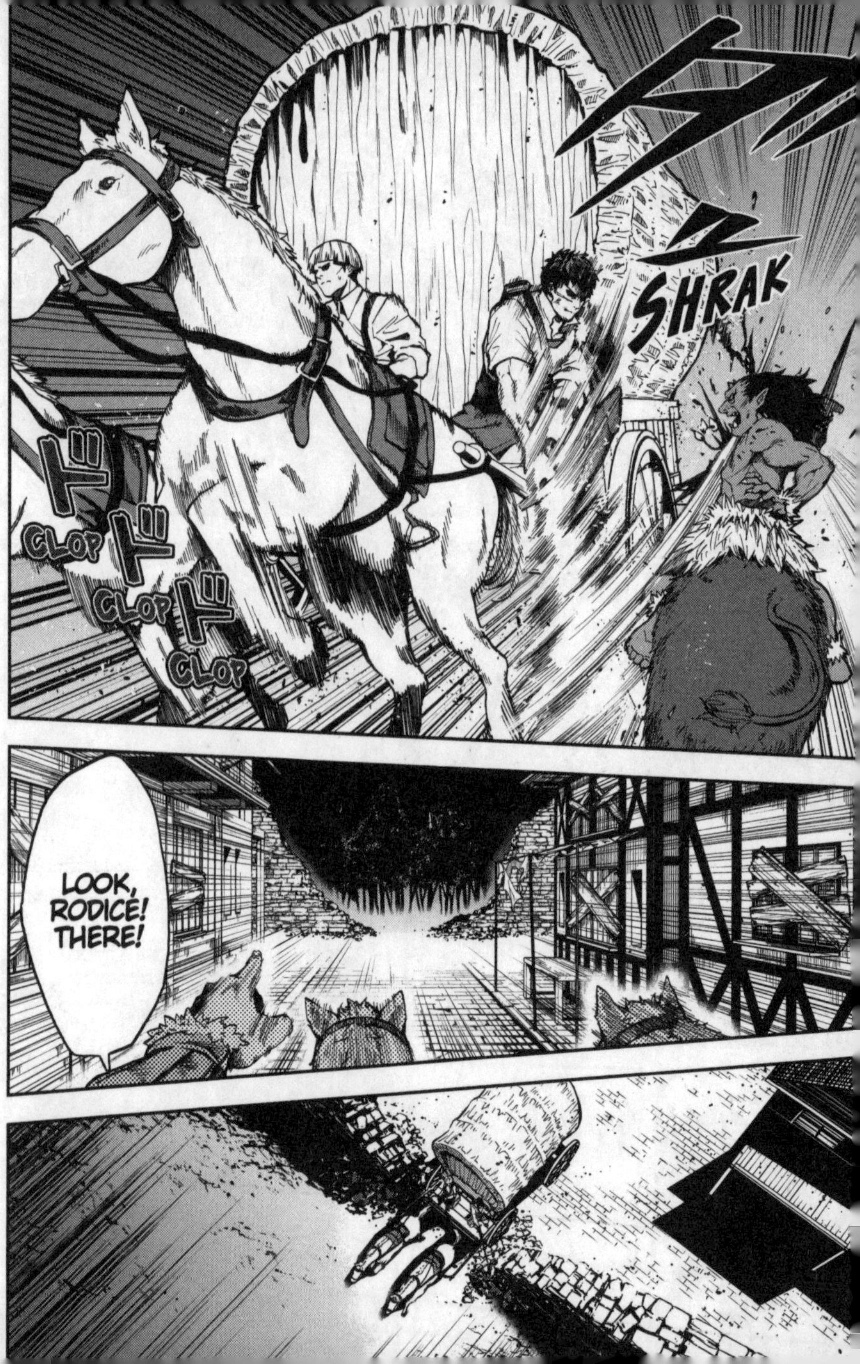
SHRAK
CLOP
CLOP
CLOP
LOOK, RODICE! THERE!

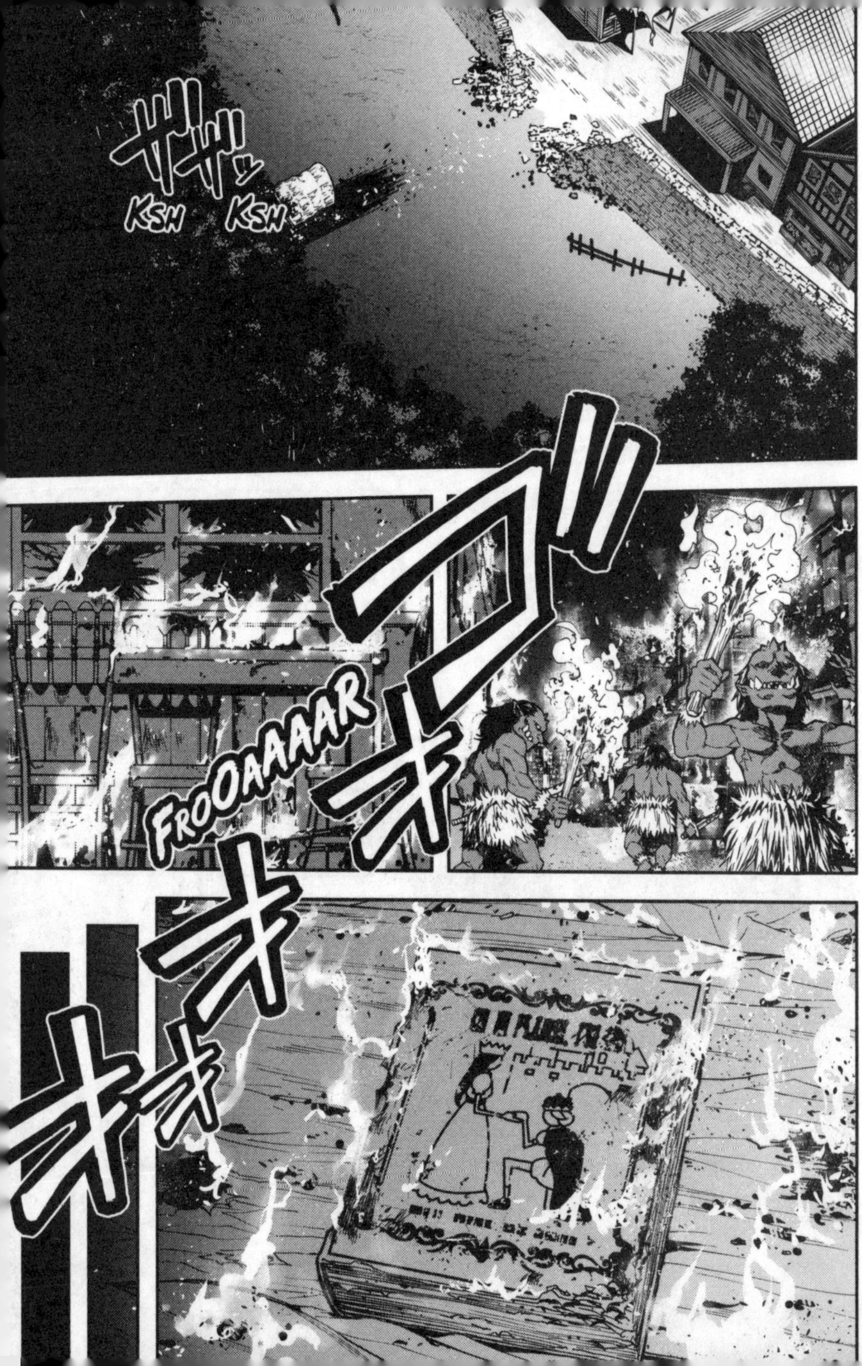
ザザッ
KSH KSH
FROOAAAAR

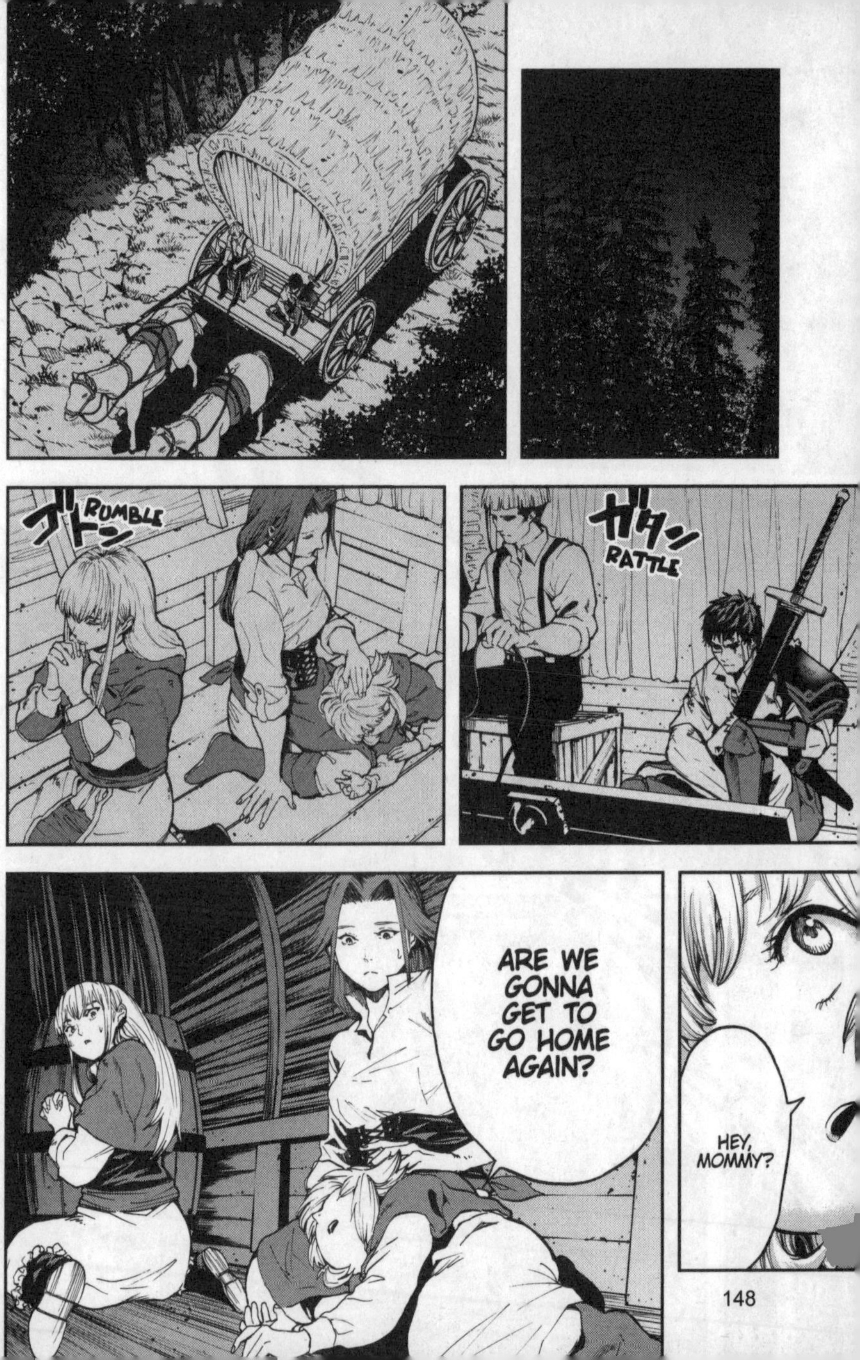
ガタン
RATTLE
ゴトン
RUMBLE
HEY, MOMMY?
ARE WE GONNA GET TO GO HOME AGAIN?

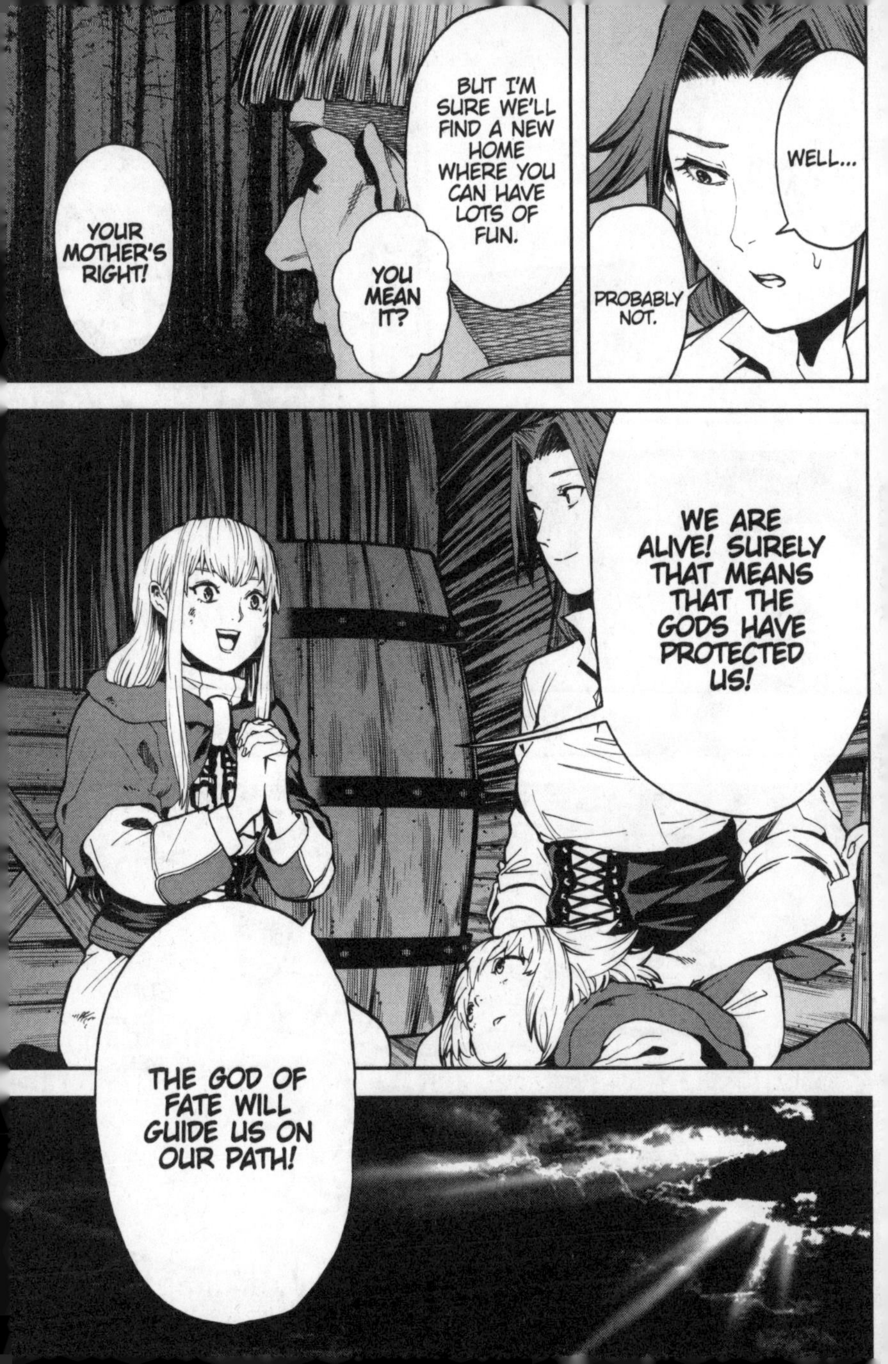
WELL...
PROBABLY NOT.
BUT I'M SURE WE'LL FIND A NEW HOME WHERE YOU CAN HAVE LOTS OF FUN.
YOU MEAN IT?
YOUR MOTHER'S RIGHT!
WE ARE ALIVE! SURELY THAT MEANS THAT THE GODS HAVE PROTECTED US!
THE GOD OF FATE WILL GUIDE US ON OUR PATH!

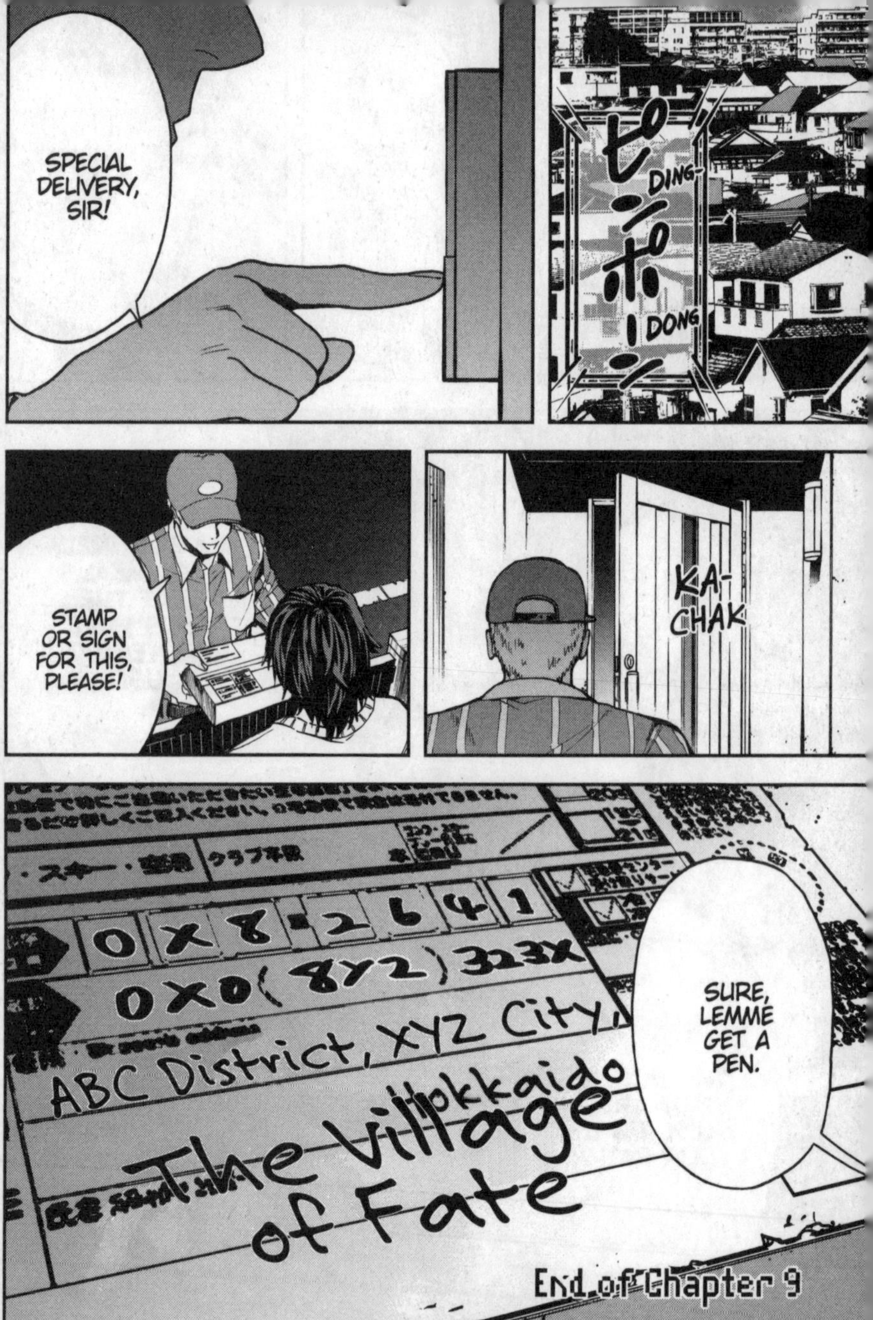
DING-
DONG
SPECIAL DELIVERY, SIR!
KA-CHAK
STAMP OR SIGN FOR THIS, PLEASE!
SURE, LEMME GET A PEN.
0X8-2641
0X0(8Y2)323X
ABC District, XYZ City, Hokkaido
The Village of Fate
End of Chapter 9

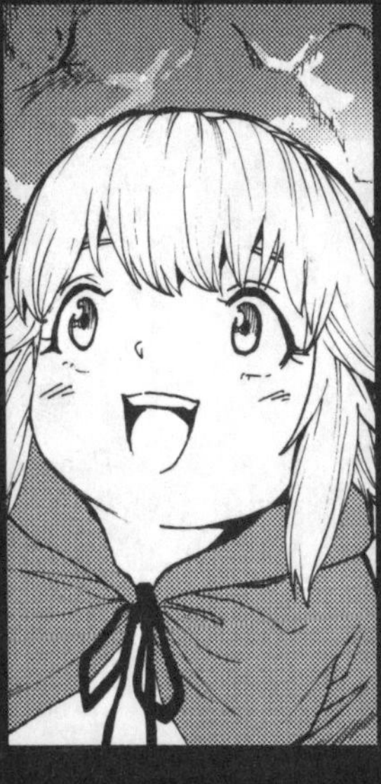

Character

Carol

▶ Gender: Female

Class: Villager

E : Clothes (cloth)

E : Curiosity

E : Puppy Love (?)

THE NPCs IN THIS
VILLAGE SIM GAME
MUST BE REAL! ↵

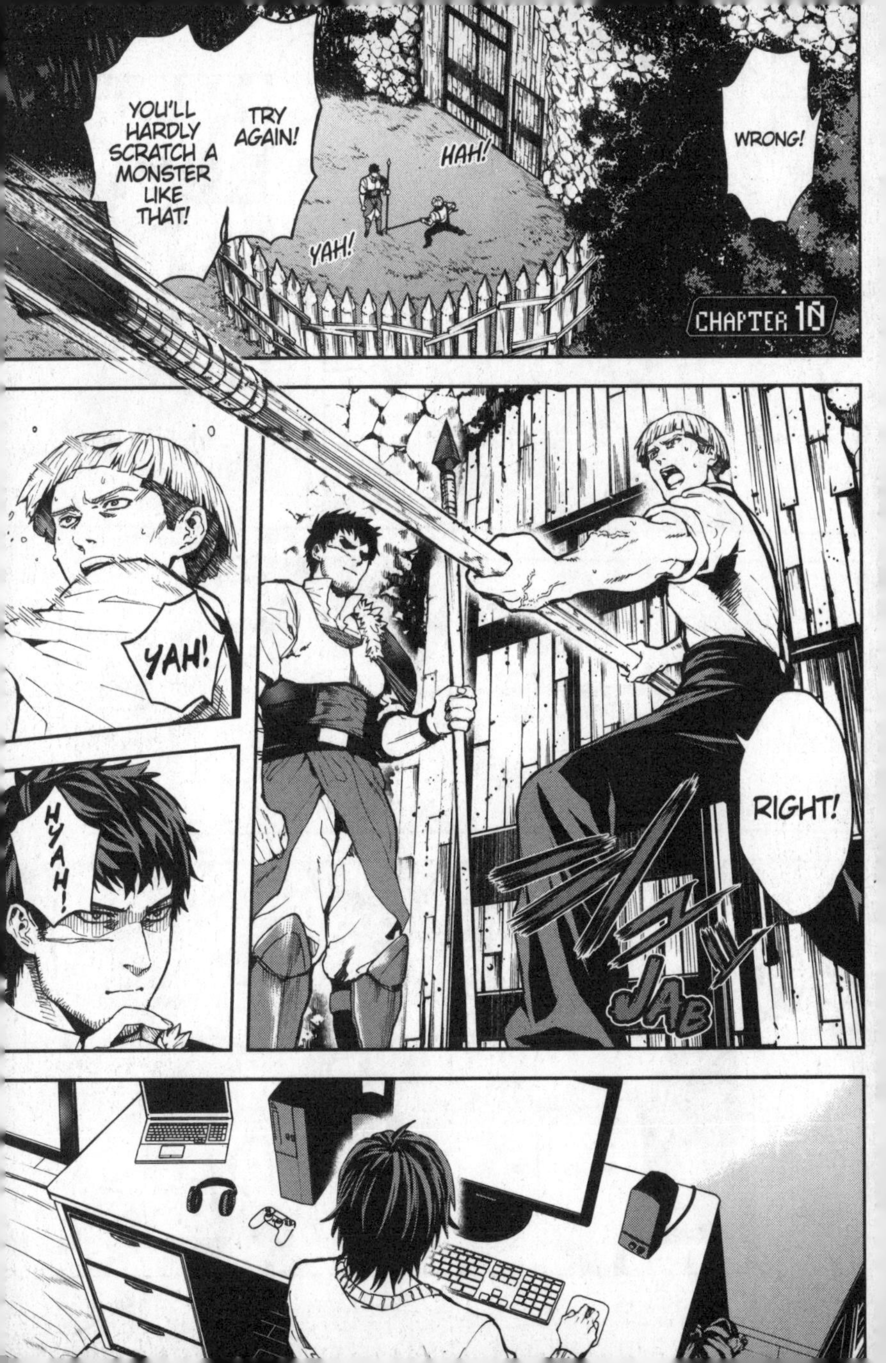
WRONG!
HAH!
TRY AGAIN!
YOU'LL HARDLY SCRATCH A MONSTER LIKE THAT!
YAH!
CHAPTER 10
RIGHT!
JAB
YAH!
HYAH!

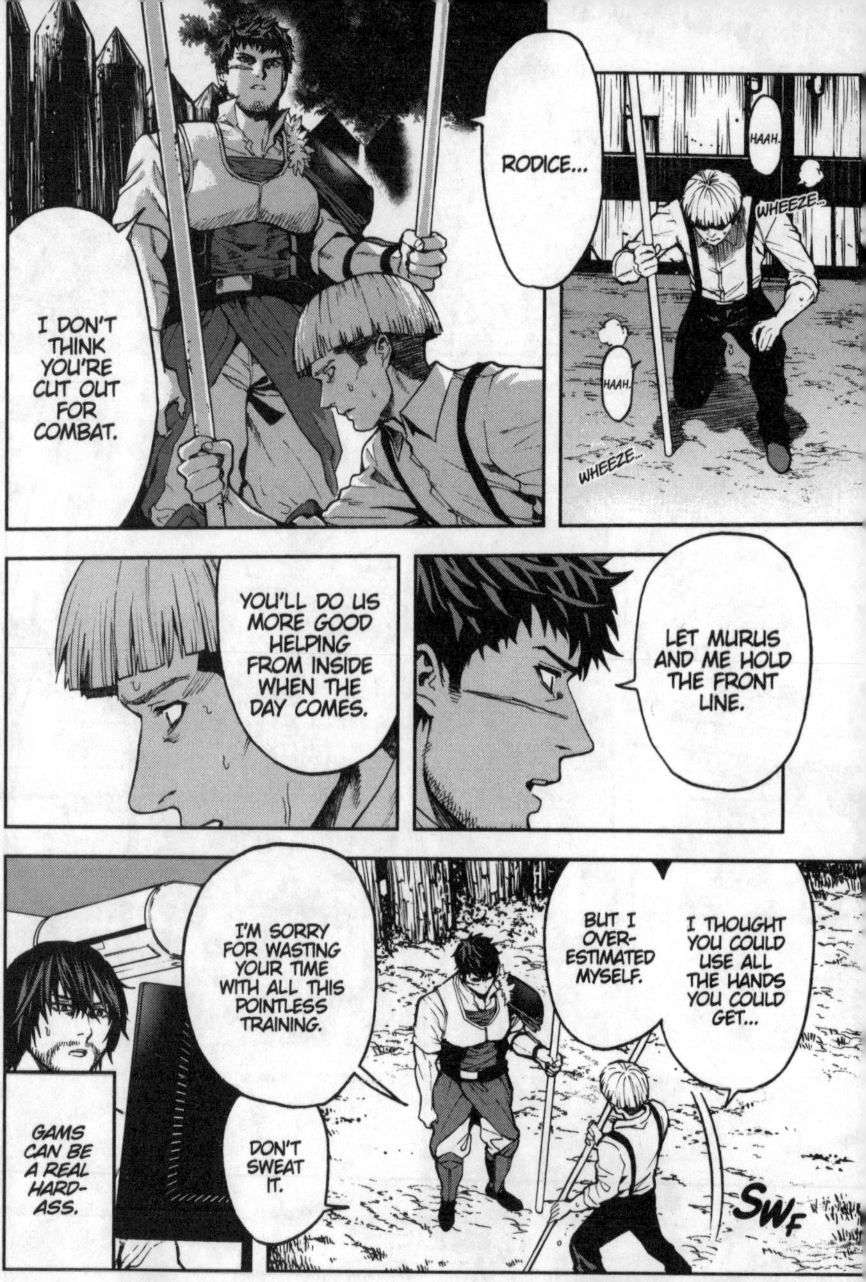
HAAH.
WHEEZE...
HAAH.
WHEEZE...
RODICE...
I DON'T THINK YOU'RE CUT OUT FOR COMBAT.
LET MURUS AND ME HOLD THE FRONT LINE.
YOU'LL DO US MORE GOOD HELPING FROM INSIDE WHEN THE DAY COMES.
I THOUGHT YOU COULD USE ALL THE HANDS YOU COULD GET...
BUT I OVERESTIMATED MYSELF.
I'M SORRY FOR WASTING YOUR TIME WITH ALL THIS POINTLESS TRAINING.
SWF
DON'T SWEAT IT.
GAMS CAN BE A REAL HARD-ASS.

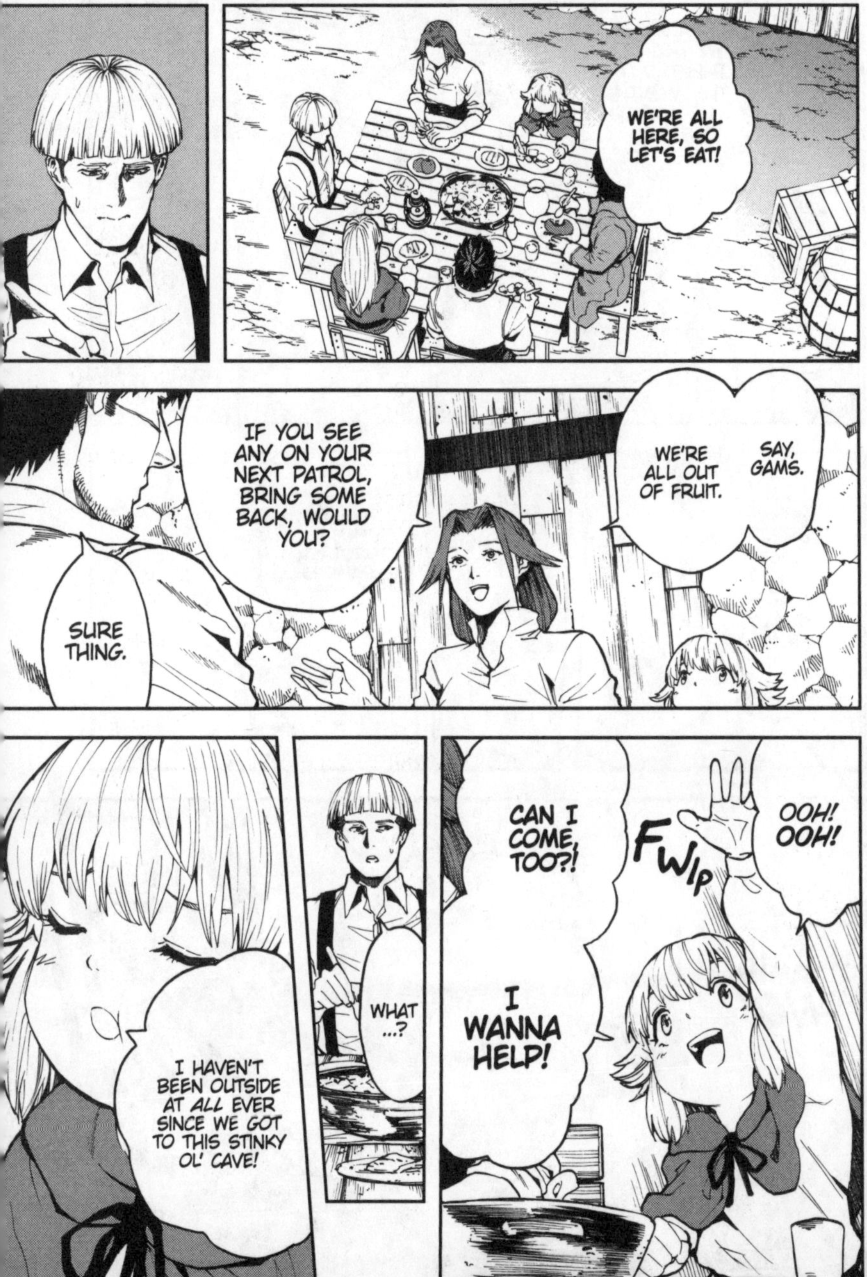
WE'RE ALL HERE, SO LET'S EAT!
SAY, GAMS.
WE'RE ALL OUT OF FRUIT.
IF YOU SEE ANY ON YOUR NEXT PATROL, BRING SOME BACK, WOULD YOU?
SURE THING.
OOH! OOH!
FWIP
CAN I COME, TOO?!
I WANNA HELP!
WHAT ...?
I HAVEN'T BEEN OUTSIDE AT *ALL* EVER SINCE WE GOT TO THIS STINKY OL' CAVE!

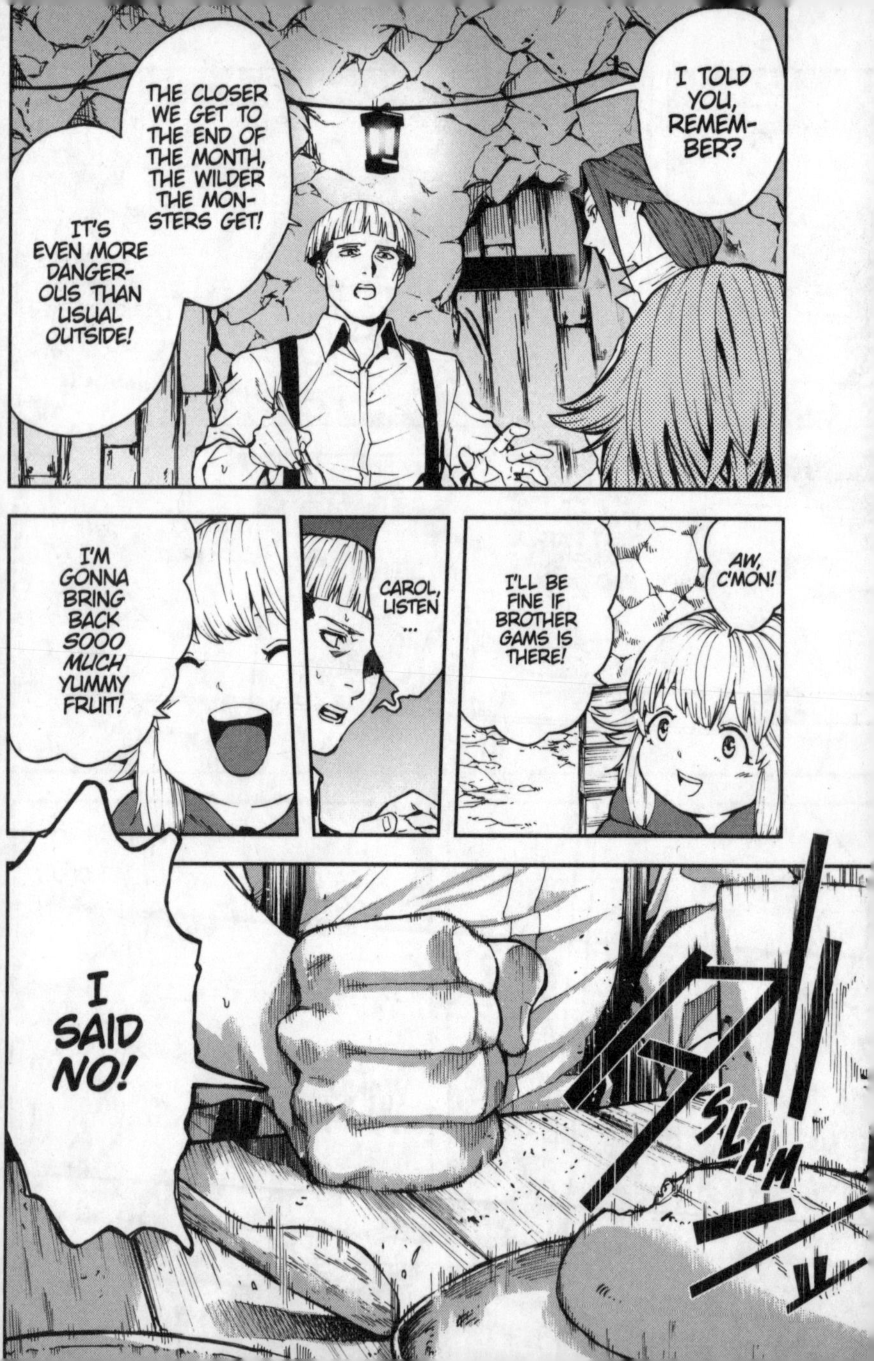
I TOLD YOU, REMEMBER?
THE CLOSER WE GET TO THE END OF THE MONTH, THE WILDER THE MONSTERS GET!
IT'S EVEN MORE DANGEROUS THAN USUAL OUTSIDE!
AW, C'MON!
I'LL BE FINE IF BROTHER GAMS IS THERE!
CAROL, LISTEN ...
I'M GONNA BRING BACK SOOO *MUCH* YUMMY FRUIT!
I SAID NO!
SLAM

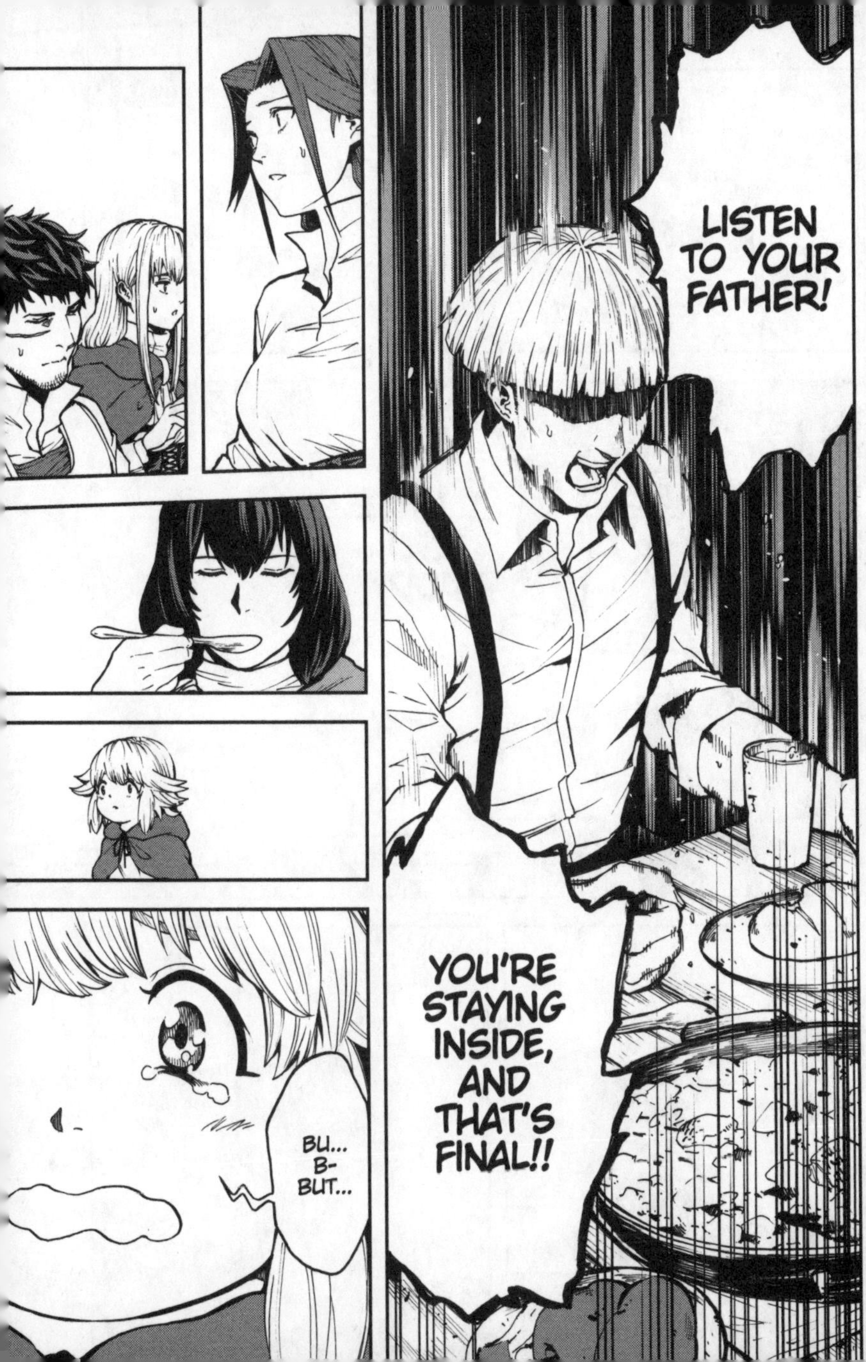
LISTEN TO YOUR FATHER!
YOU'RE STAYING INSIDE, AND THAT'S FINAL!!
BU... B- BUT...

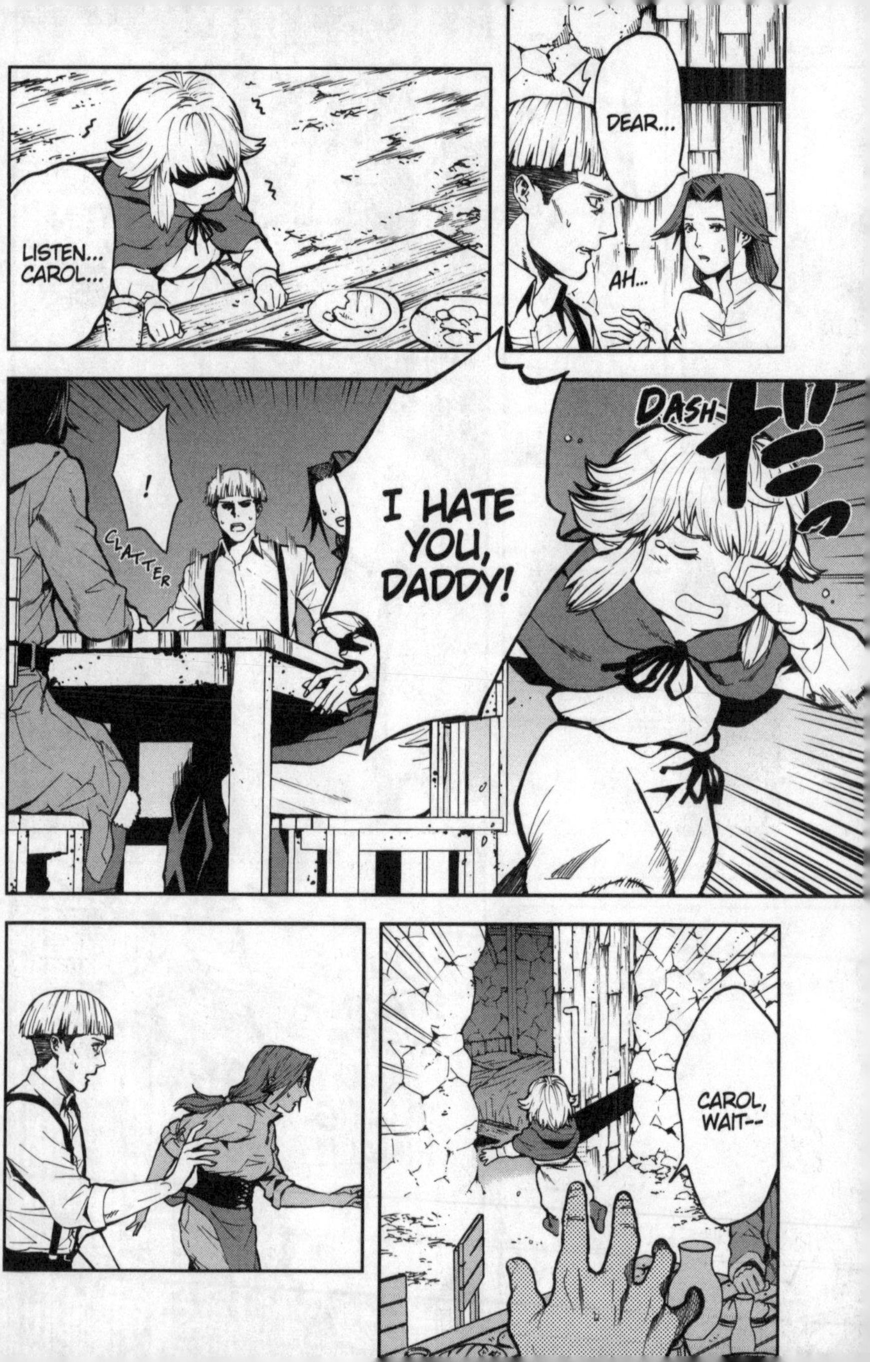
DEAR...
AH...
LISTEN... CAROL...
DASH-
I HATE YOU, DADDY!
!
CLATTER
CAROL, WAIT--

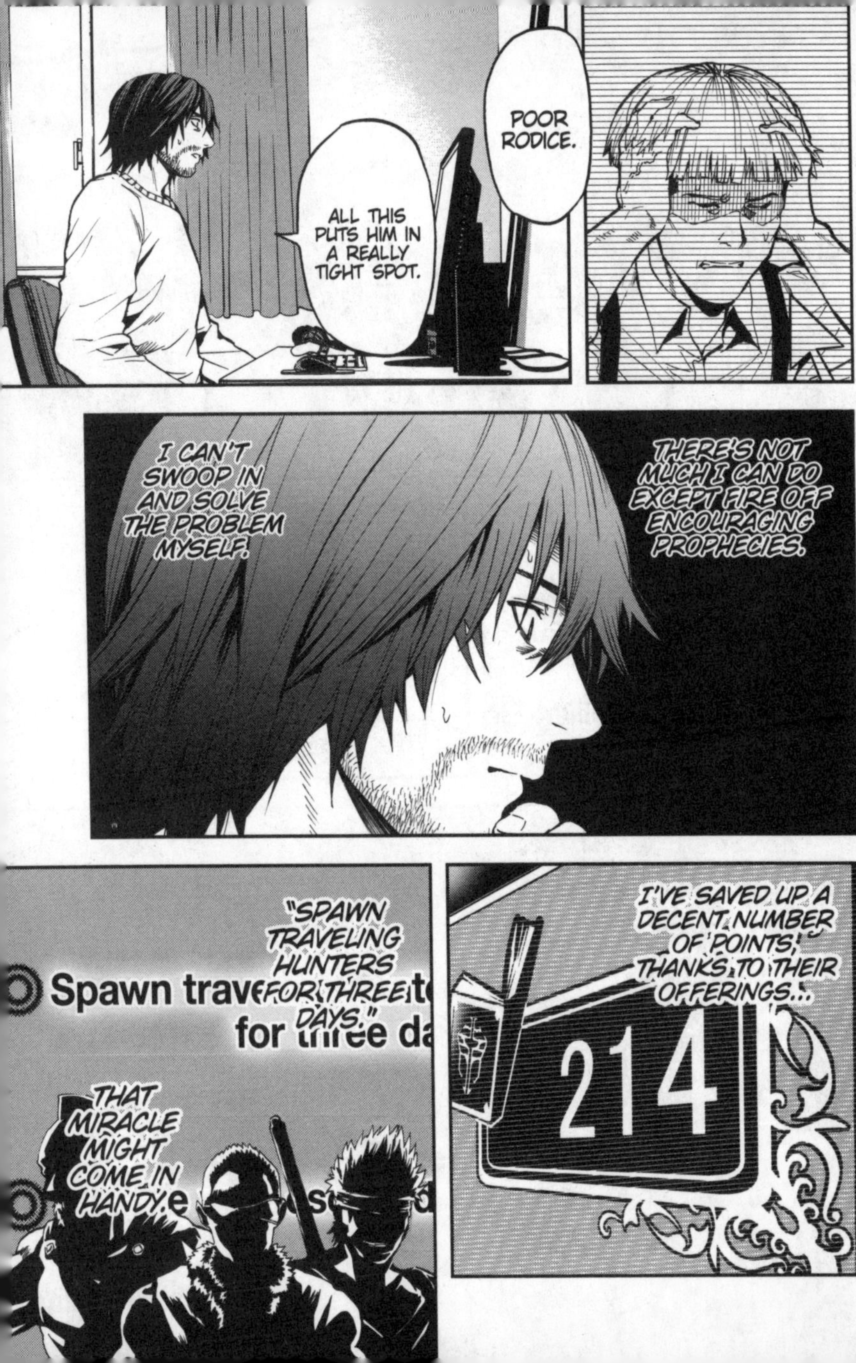

POOR RODICE.
ALL THIS PUTS HIM IN A REALLY TIGHT SPOT.
THERE'S NOT MUCH I CAN DO EXCEPT FIRE OFF ENCOURAGING PROPHECIES.
I CAN'T SWOOP IN AND SOLVE THE PROBLEM MYSELF.
I'VE SAVED UP A DECENT NUMBER OF POINTS, THANKS TO THEIR OFFERINGS...
214
"SPAWN TRAVELING HUNTERS FOR THREE DAYS."
THAT MIRACLE MIGHT COME IN HANDY.

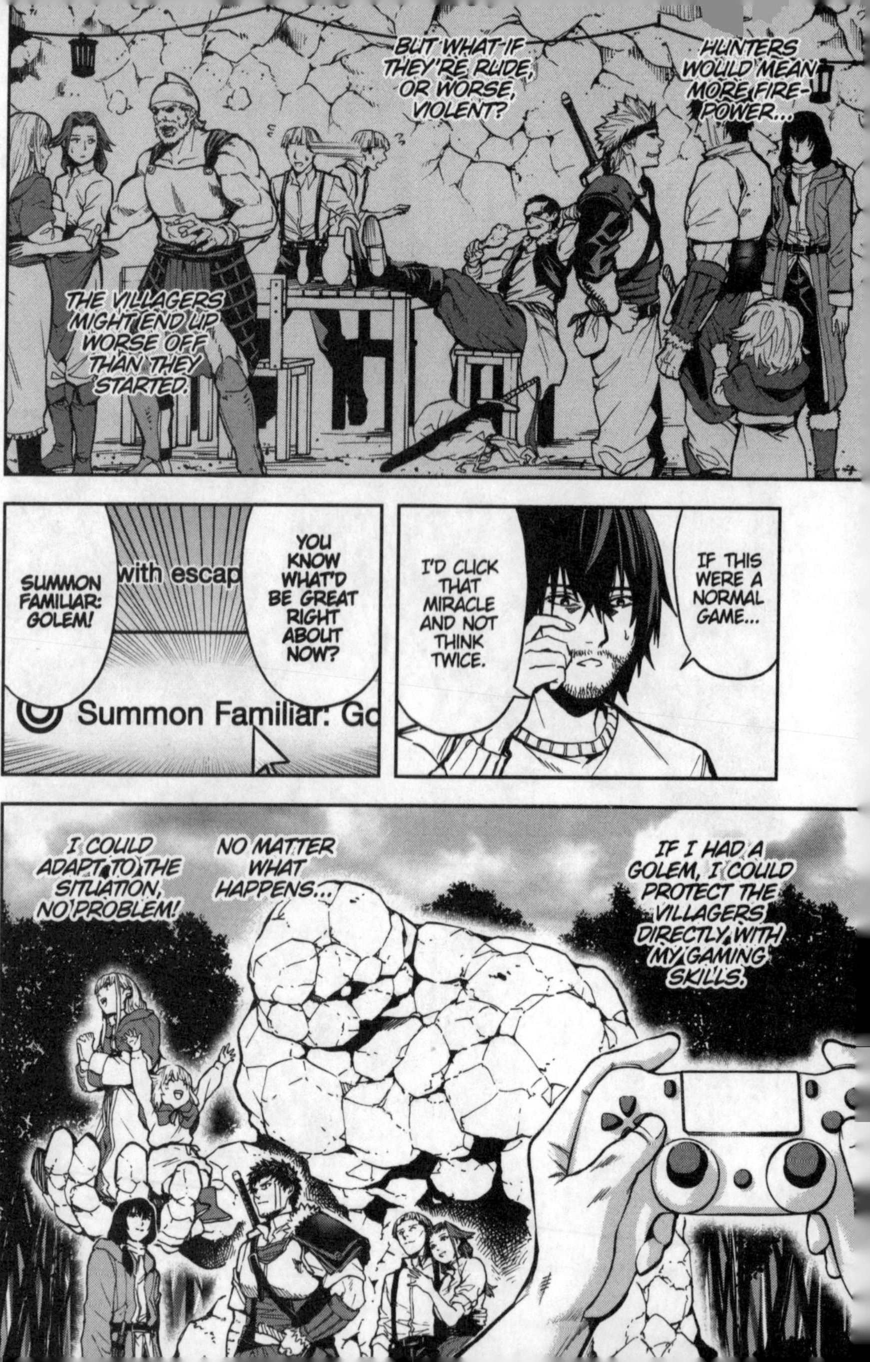
HUNTERS WOULD MEAN MORE FIRE-POWER...
BUT WHAT IF THEY'RE RUDE, OR WORSE, VIOLENT?
THE VILLAGERS MIGHT END UP WORSE OFF THAN THEY STARTED.
IF THIS WERE A NORMAL GAME...
I'D CLICK THAT MIRACLE AND NOT THINK TWICE.
YOU KNOW WHAT'D BE GREAT RIGHT ABOUT NOW?
with escap
SUMMON FAMILIAR: GOLEM!
Summon Familiar: Go
IF I HAD A GOLEM, I COULD PROTECT THE VILLAGERS DIRECTLY WITH MY GAMING SKILLS.
NO MATTER WHAT HAPPENS...
I COULD ADAPT TO THE SITUATION, NO PROBLEM!

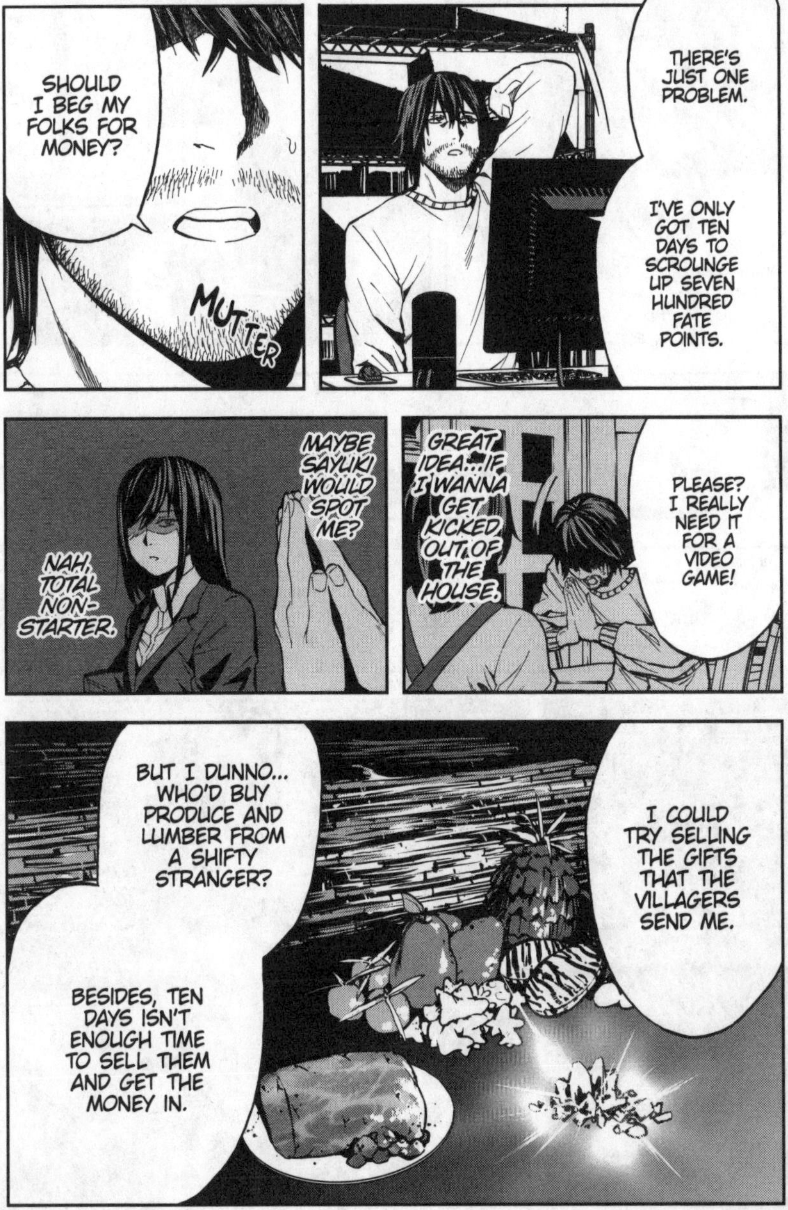
THERE'S JUST ONE PROBLEM.
I'VE ONLY GOT TEN DAYS TO SCROUNGE UP SEVEN HUNDRED FATE POINTS.
SHOULD I BEG MY FOLKS FOR MONEY?
MUTTER
PLEASE? I REALLY NEED IT FOR A VIDEO GAME!
GREAT IDEA...IF I WANNA GET KICKED OUT OF THE HOUSE.
MAYBE SAYUKI WOULD SPOT ME?
NAH, TOTAL NON-STARTER.
I COULD TRY SELLING THE GIFTS THAT THE VILLAGERS SEND ME.
BUT I DUNNO... WHO'D BUY PRODUCE AND LUMBER FROM A SHIFTY STRANGER?
BESIDES, TEN DAYS ISN'T ENOUGH TIME TO SELL THEM AND GET THE MONEY IN.

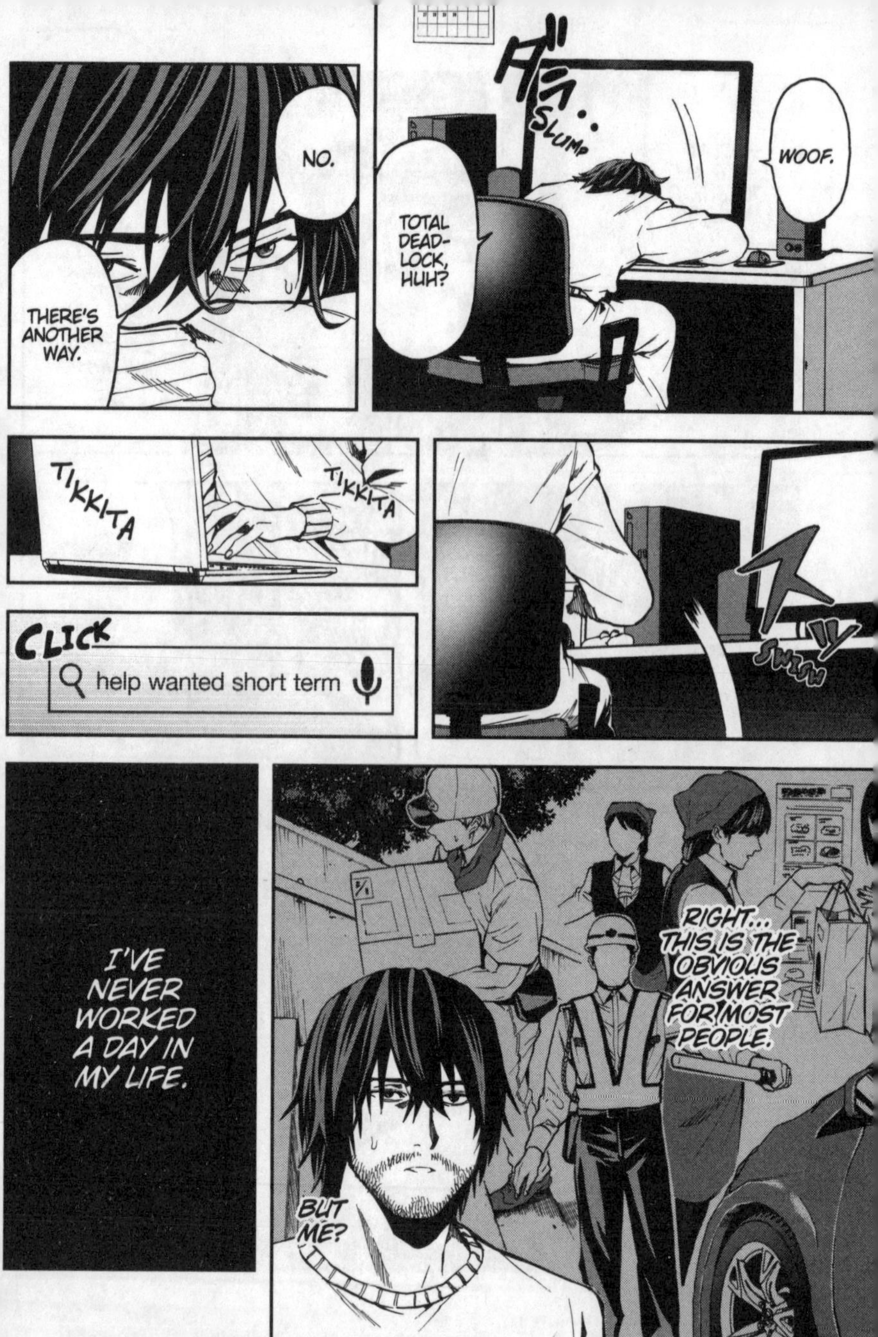

WOOF.
SLUMP
TOTAL DEAD-LOCK, HUH?
NO.
THERE'S ANOTHER WAY.
SWISH
TIKKITA
TIKKITA
CLICK
help wanted short term
RIGHT... THIS IS THE OBVIOUS ANSWER FOR MOST PEOPLE.
BUT ME?
I'VE NEVER WORKED A DAY IN MY LIFE.

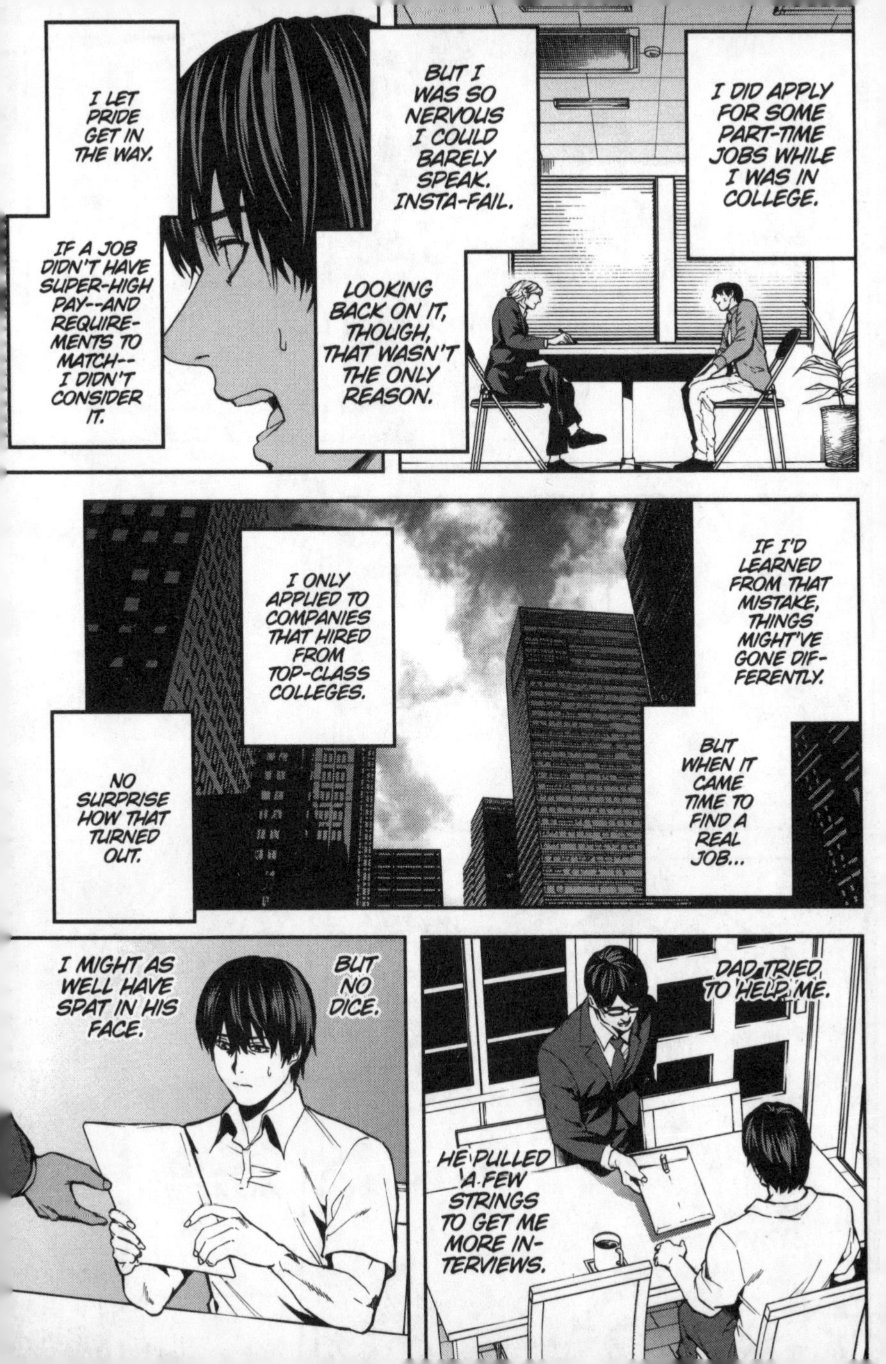
I DID APPLY FOR SOME PART-TIME JOBS WHILE I WAS IN COLLEGE.
BUT I WAS SO NERVOUS I COULD BARELY SPEAK. INSTA-FAIL.
LOOKING BACK ON IT, THOUGH, THAT WASN'T THE ONLY REASON.
I LET PRIDE GET IN THE WAY.
IF A JOB DIDN'T HAVE SUPER-HIGH PAY--AND REQUIRE-MENTS TO MATCH--I DIDN'T CONSIDER IT.
IF I'D LEARNED FROM THAT MISTAKE, THINGS MIGHT'VE GONE DIF-FERENTLY.
BUT WHEN IT CAME TIME TO FIND A REAL JOB...
I ONLY APPLIED TO COMPANIES THAT HIRED FROM TOP-CLASS COLLEGES.
NO SURPRISE HOW THAT TURNED OUT.
DAD TRIED TO HELP ME.
HE PULLED A FEW STRINGS TO GET ME MORE IN-TERVIEWS.
BUT NO DICE.
I MIGHT AS WELL HAVE SPAT IN HIS FACE.

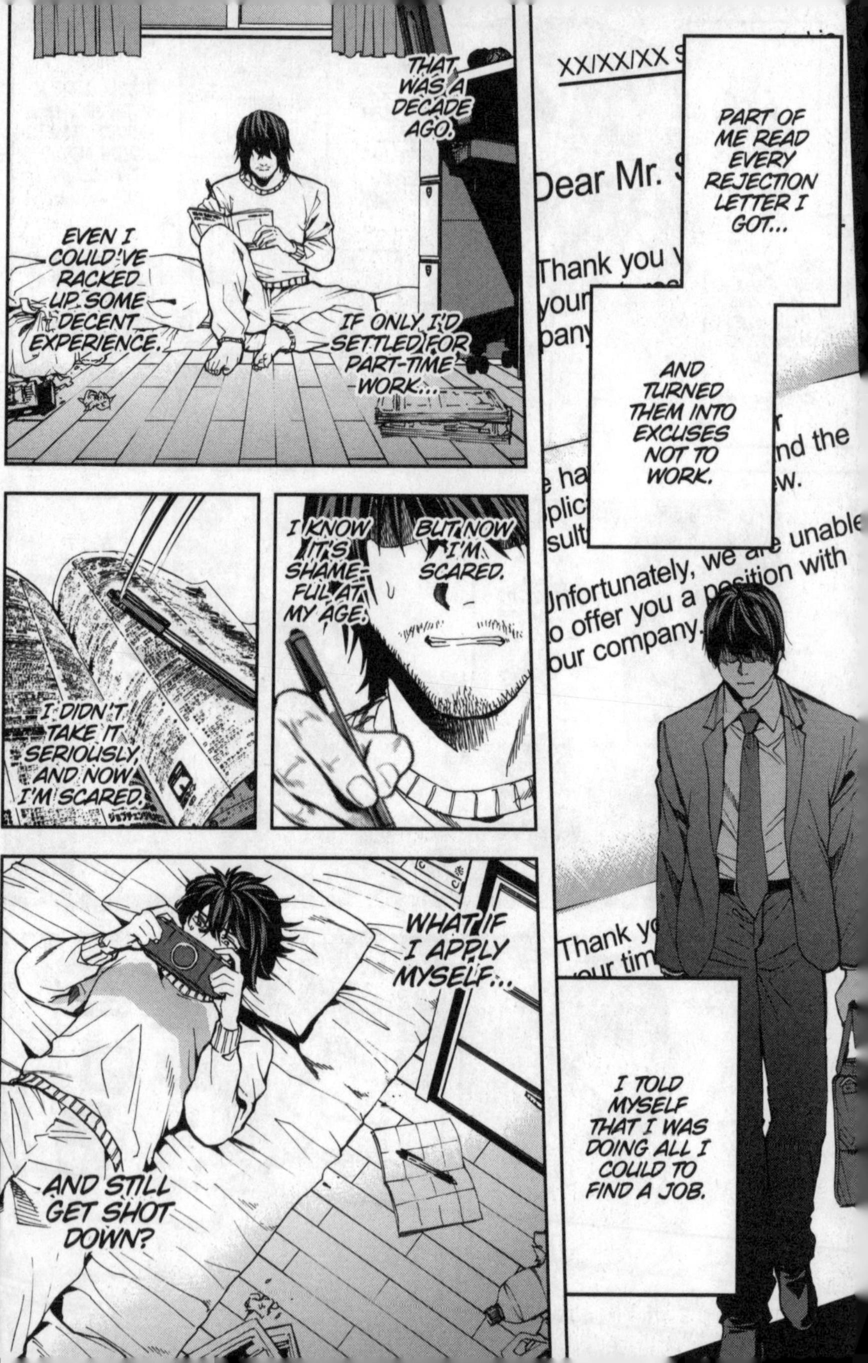
XX/XX/XX S
PART OF ME READ EVERY REJECTION LETTER I GOT...
Dear Mr. S
AND TURNED THEM INTO EXCUSES NOT TO WORK.
Unfortunately, we are unable to offer you a position with our company.
I TOLD MYSELF THAT I WAS DOING ALL I COULD TO FIND A JOB.
THAT WAS A DECADE AGO.
IF ONLY I'D SETTLED FOR PART-TIME WORK...
EVEN I COULD'VE RACKED UP SOME DECENT EXPERIENCE.
BUT NOW I'M SCARED.
I KNOW IT'S SHAMEFUL AT MY AGE.
I DIDN'T TAKE IT SERIOUSLY, AND NOW I'M SCARED.
WHAT IF I APPLY MYSELF...
AND STILL GET SHOT DOWN?

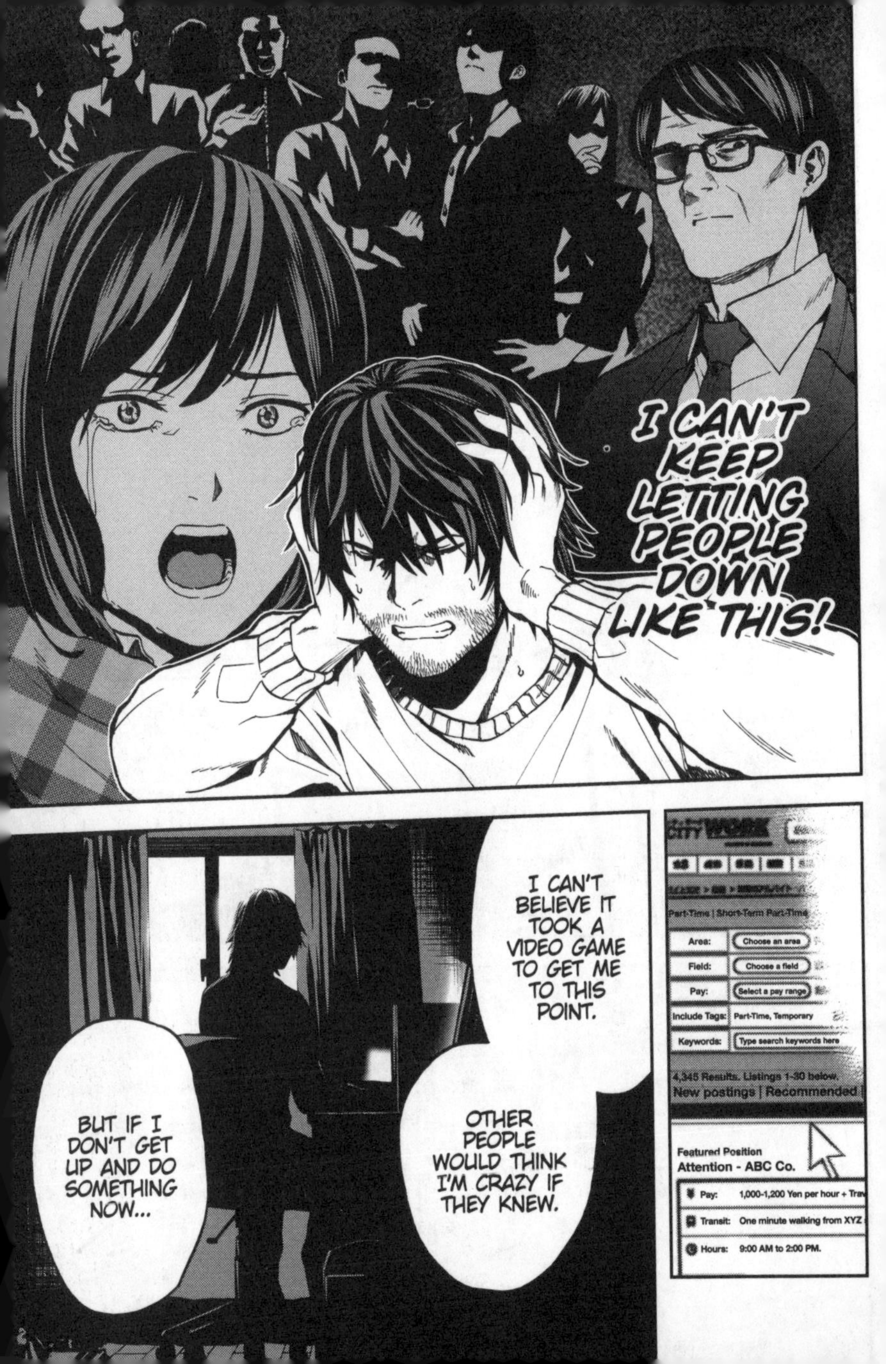
I CAN'T KEEP LETTING PEOPLE DOWN LIKE THIS!
Part-Time | Short-Term Part-Time
Area:
Choose an area
Field:
Choose a field
Pay:
Select a pay range
Include Tags:
Part-Time, Temporary
Keywords:
Type search keywords here
4,345 Results. Listings 1-30 below.
New postings | Recommended
Featured Position
Attention - ABC Co.
Pay:
1,000-1,200 Yen per hour + Trav
Transit:
One minute walking from XYZ
Hours:
9:00 AM to 2:00 PM.
I CAN'T BELIEVE IT TOOK A VIDEO GAME TO GET ME TO THIS POINT.
OTHER PEOPLE WOULD THINK I'M CRAZY IF THEY KNEW.
BUT IF I DON'T GET UP AND DO SOMETHING NOW...

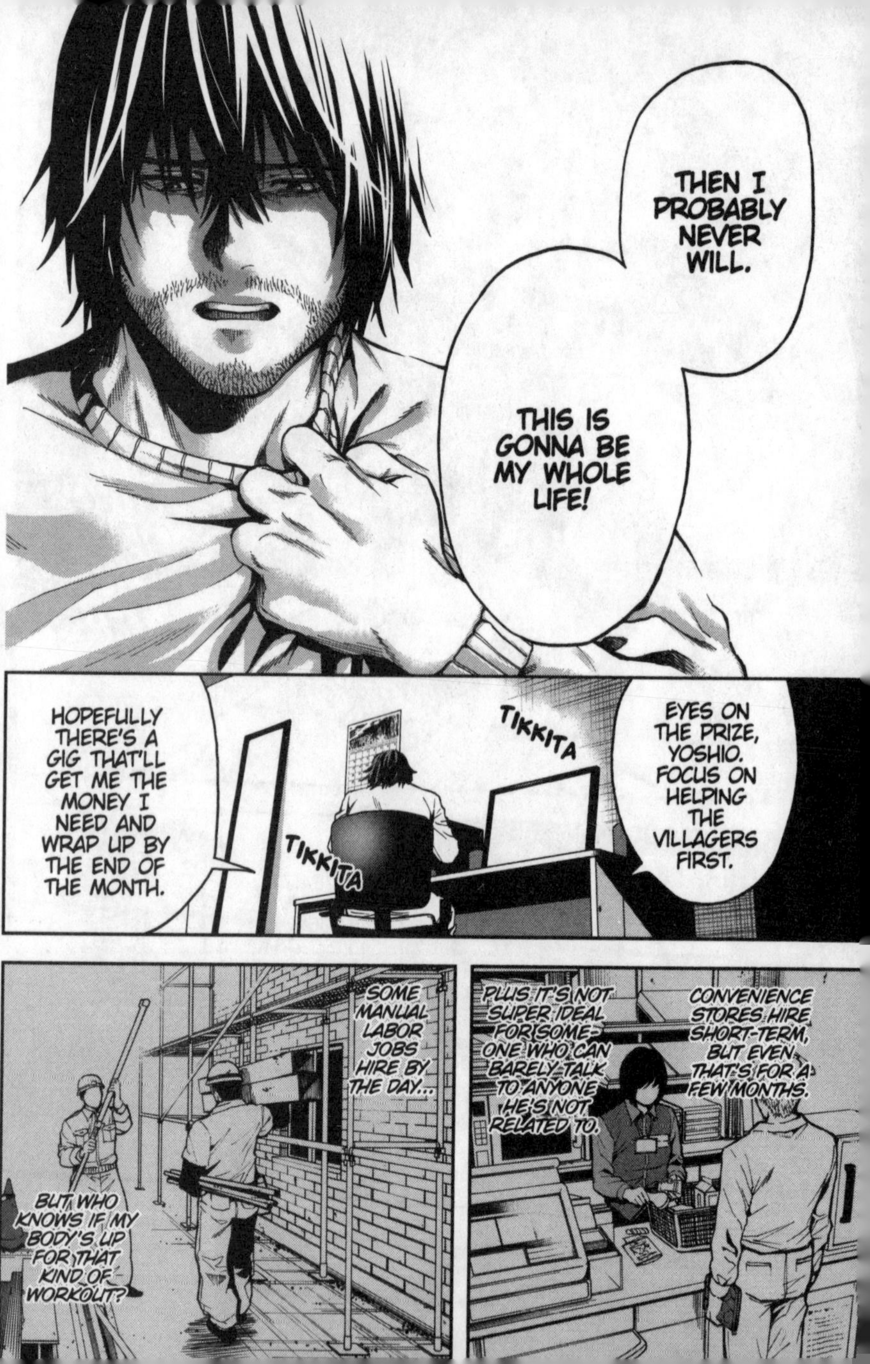
THEN I PROBABLY NEVER WILL.
THIS IS GONNA BE MY WHOLE LIFE!
EYES ON THE PRIZE, YOSHIO. FOCUS ON HELPING THE VILLAGERS FIRST.
TIKKITA
TIKKITA
HOPEFULLY THERE'S A GIG THAT'LL GET ME THE MONEY I NEED AND WRAP UP BY THE END OF THE MONTH.
CONVENIENCE STORES HIRE SHORT-TERM, BUT EVEN THAT'S FOR A FEW MONTHS.
PLUS IT'S NOT SUPER IDEAL FOR SOME-ONE WHO CAN BARELY TALK TO ANYONE HE'S NOT RELATED TO.
SOME MANUAL LABOR JOBS HIRE BY THE DAY...
BUT WHO KNOWS IF MY BODY'S UP FOR THAT KIND OF WORKOUT?

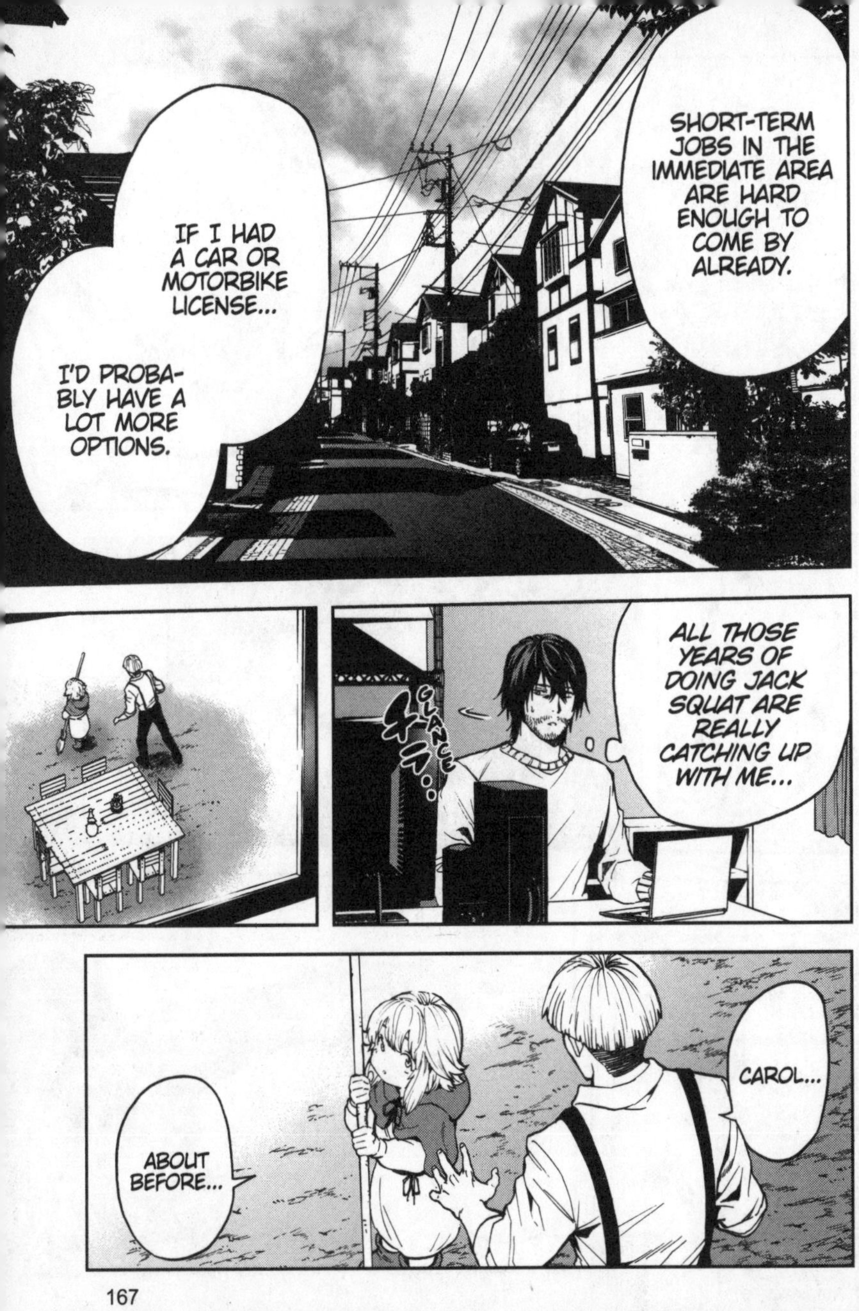
SHORT-TERM JOBS IN THE IMMEDIATE AREA ARE HARD ENOUGH TO COME BY ALREADY.
IF I HAD A CAR OR MOTORBIKE LICENSE...
I'D PROBA-BLY HAVE A LOT MORE OPTIONS.
ALL THOSE YEARS OF DOING JACK SQUAT ARE REALLY CATCHING UP WITH ME...
GLANCE
CAROL...
ABOUT BEFORE...

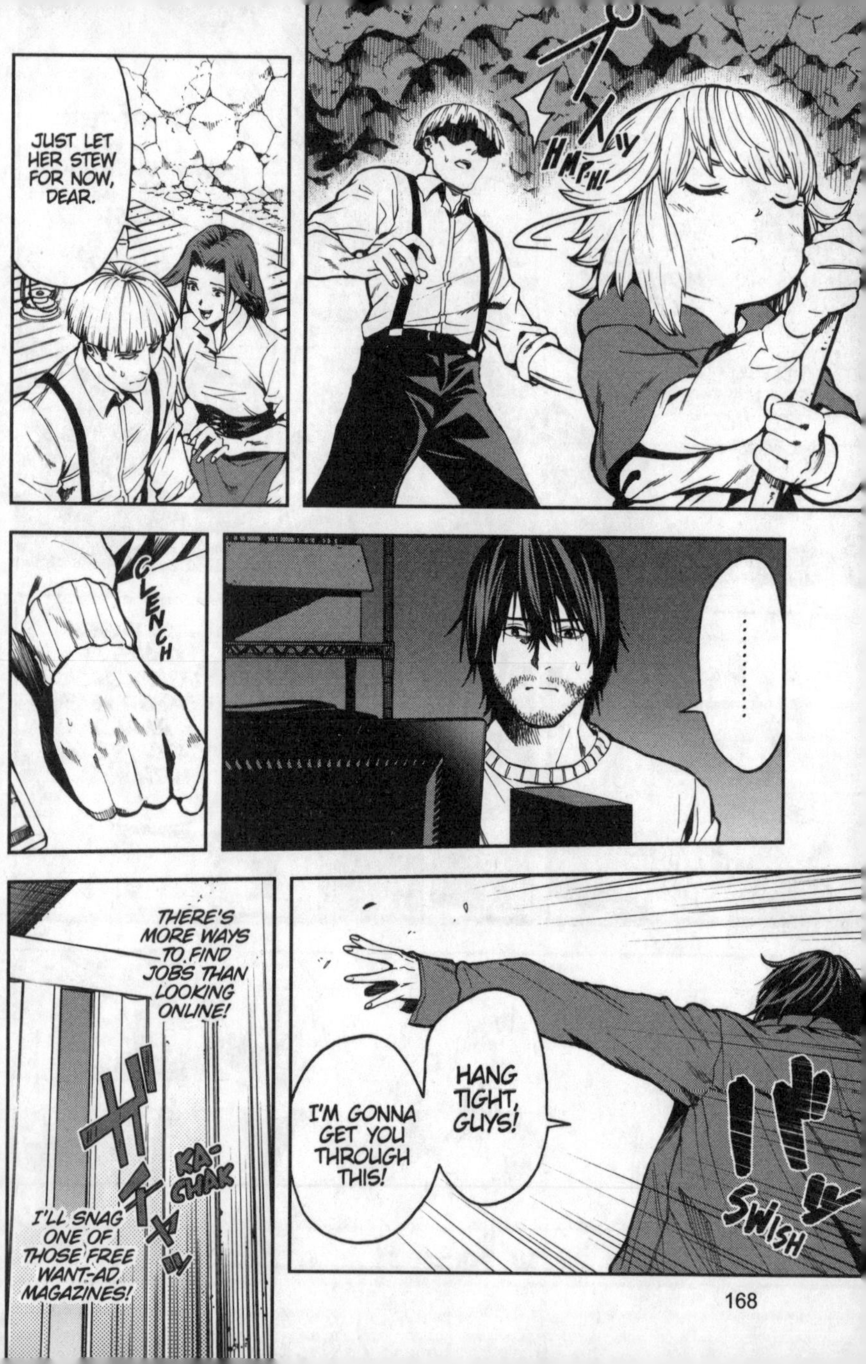
HMPH!
JUST LET HER STEW FOR NOW, DEAR.
......
CLENCH
HANG TIGHT, GUYS!
I'M GONNA GET YOU THROUGH THIS!
SWISH
THERE'S MORE WAYS TO FIND JOBS THAN LOOKING ONLINE!
KA-CHAK
I'LL SNAG ONE OF THOSE FREE WANT-AD MAGAZINES!

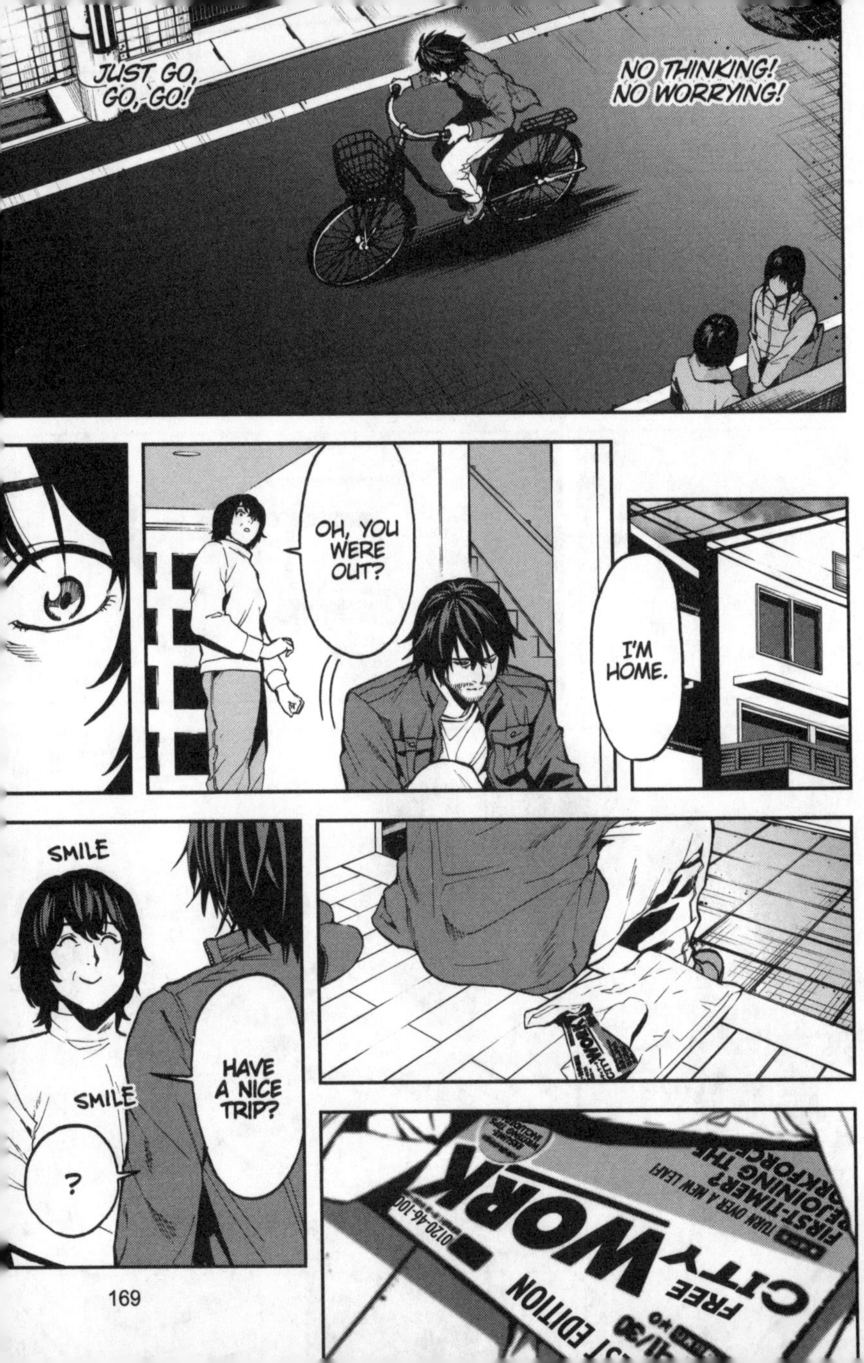
NO THINKING! NO WORRYING!
JUST GO, GO, GO!
I'M HOME.
OH, YOU WERE OUT?
CITY WORK
FREE
FIRST-TIMER? REJOINING THE WORKFORCE?
TURN OVER A NEW LEAF
0120-46-100
SMILE
HAVE A NICE TRIP?
SMILE
?

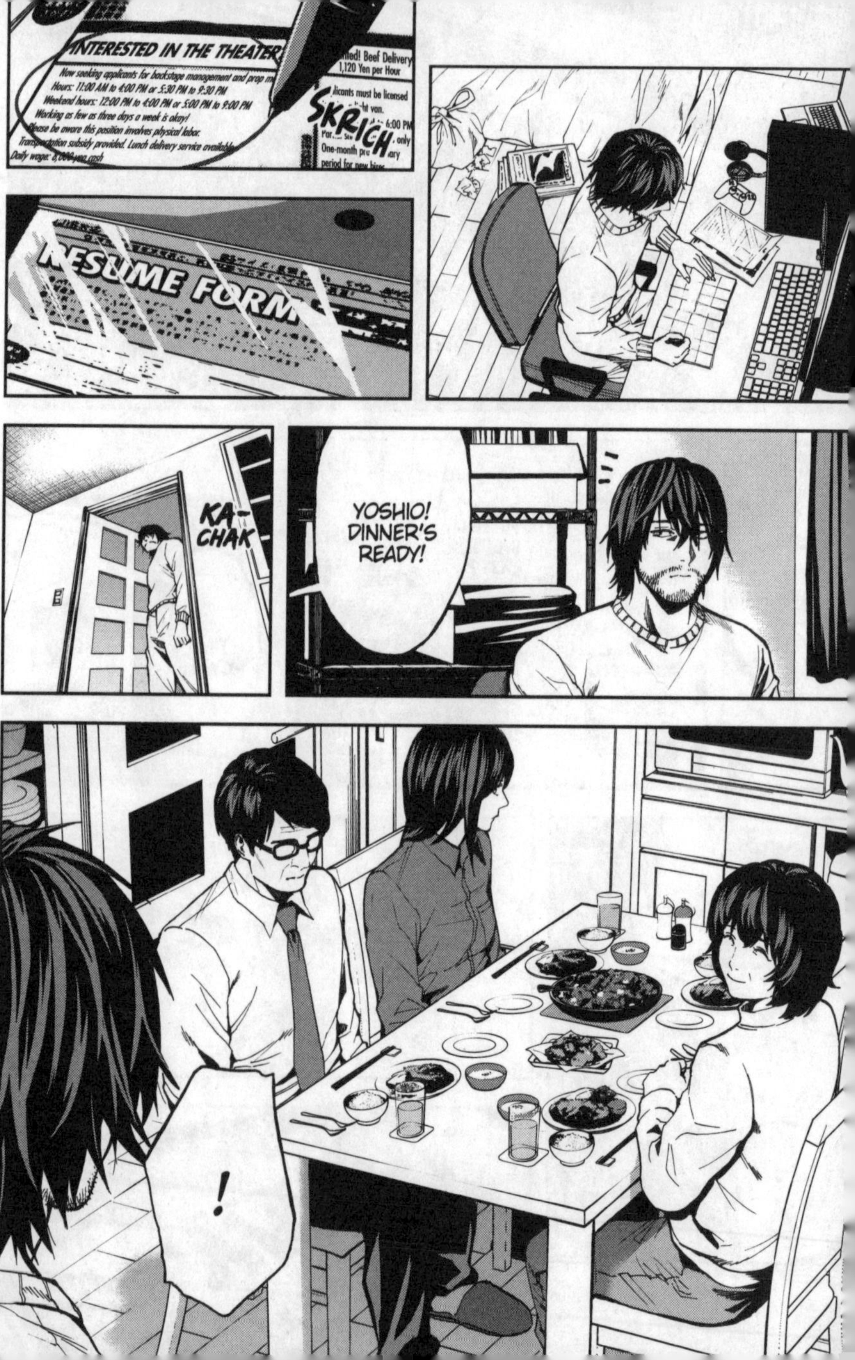

ted! Beef Delivery
1,120 Yen per Hour
licants must be licensed
ht van.
6:00 PM
only
One-month pr ary
period for new hires
SKRICH
INTERESTED IN THE THEATER
Now seeking applicants for backstage management and prop m
Hours: 11:00 AM to 4:00 PM or 5:30 PM to 9:30 PM
Weekend hours: 12:00 PM to 4:00 PM or 5:00 PM to 9:00 PM
Working as few as three days a week is okay!
Please be aware this position involves physical labor.
Transportation subsidy provided. Lunch delivery service available.
Daily wage: 8,000 yen cash
RESUME FORM
YOSHIO! DINNER'S READY!
KA-CHAK
!

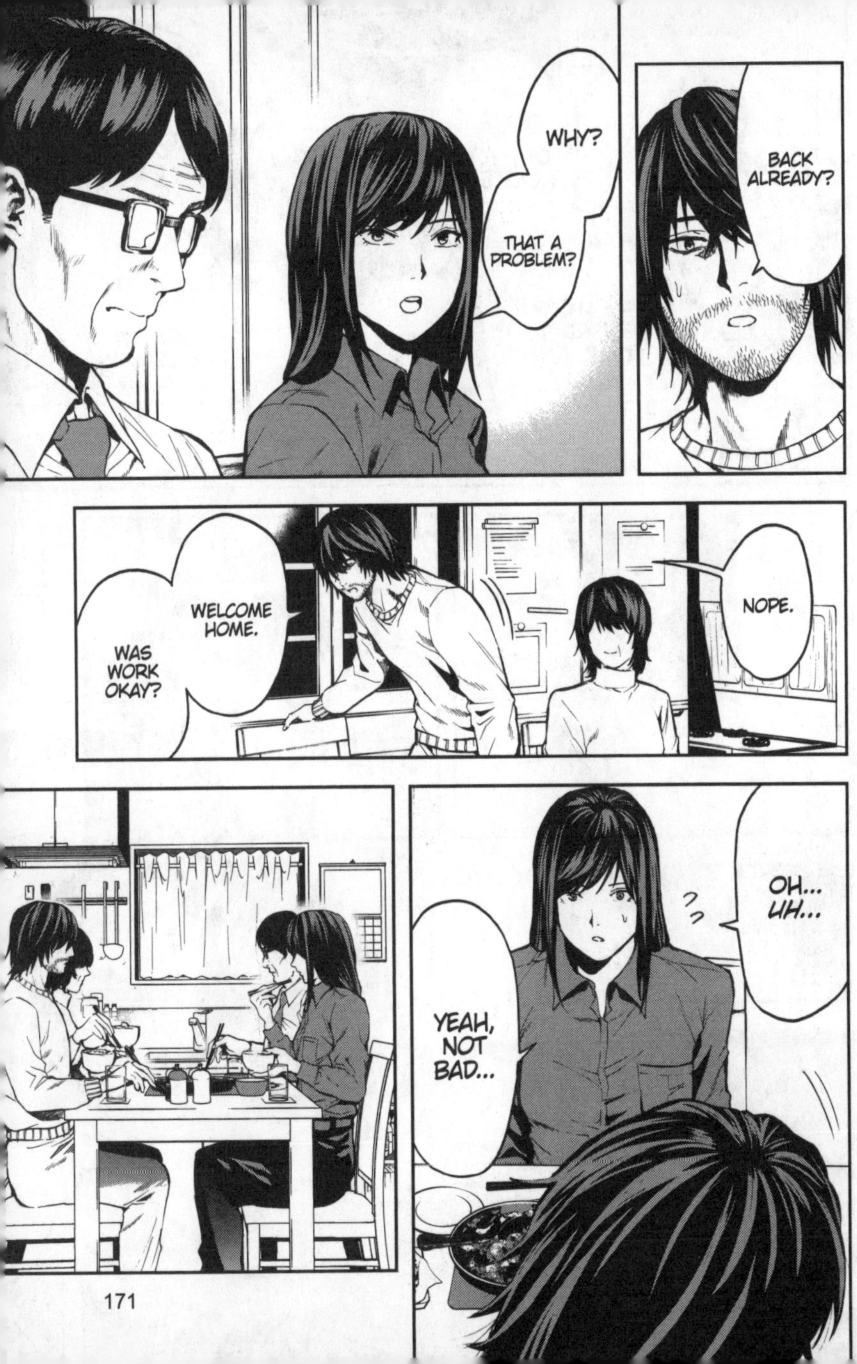
BACK ALREADY?
WHY?
THAT A PROBLEM?
NOPE.
WELCOME HOME.
WAS WORK OKAY?
OH... UH...
YEAH, NOT BAD...

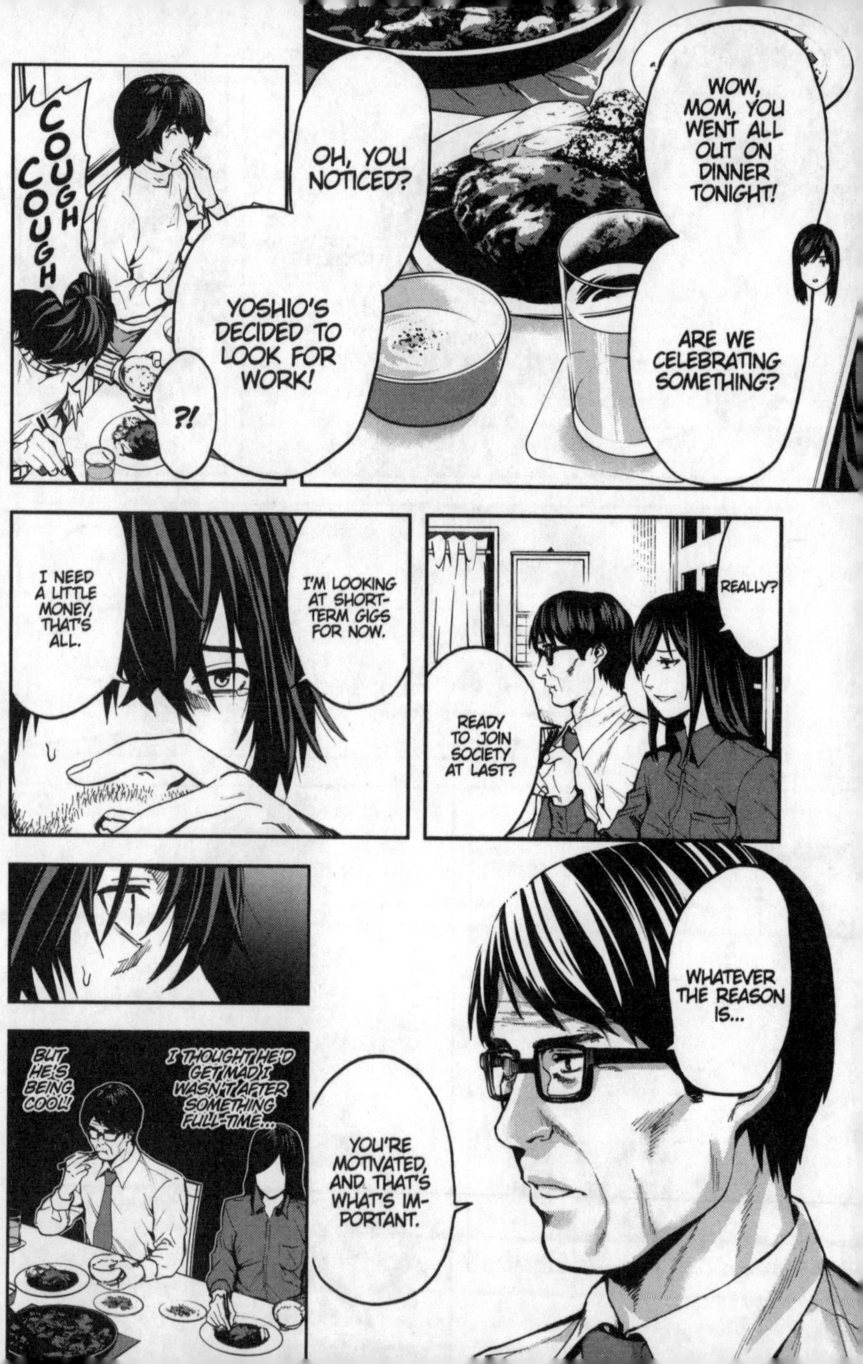
WOW, MOM, YOU WENT ALL OUT ON DINNER TONIGHT!
ARE WE CELEBRATING SOMETHING?
OH, YOU NOTICED?
YOSHIO'S DECIDED TO LOOK FOR WORK!
COUGH COUGH
?!
REALLY?
READY TO JOIN SOCIETY AT LAST?
I'M LOOKING AT SHORT-TERM GIGS FOR NOW.
I NEED A LITTLE MONEY, THAT'S ALL.
WHATEVER THE REASON IS...
YOU'RE MOTIVATED, AND THAT'S WHAT'S IMPORTANT.
I THOUGHT HE'D GET MAD I WASN'T AFTER SOMETHING FULL-TIME...
BUT HE'S BEING COOL!

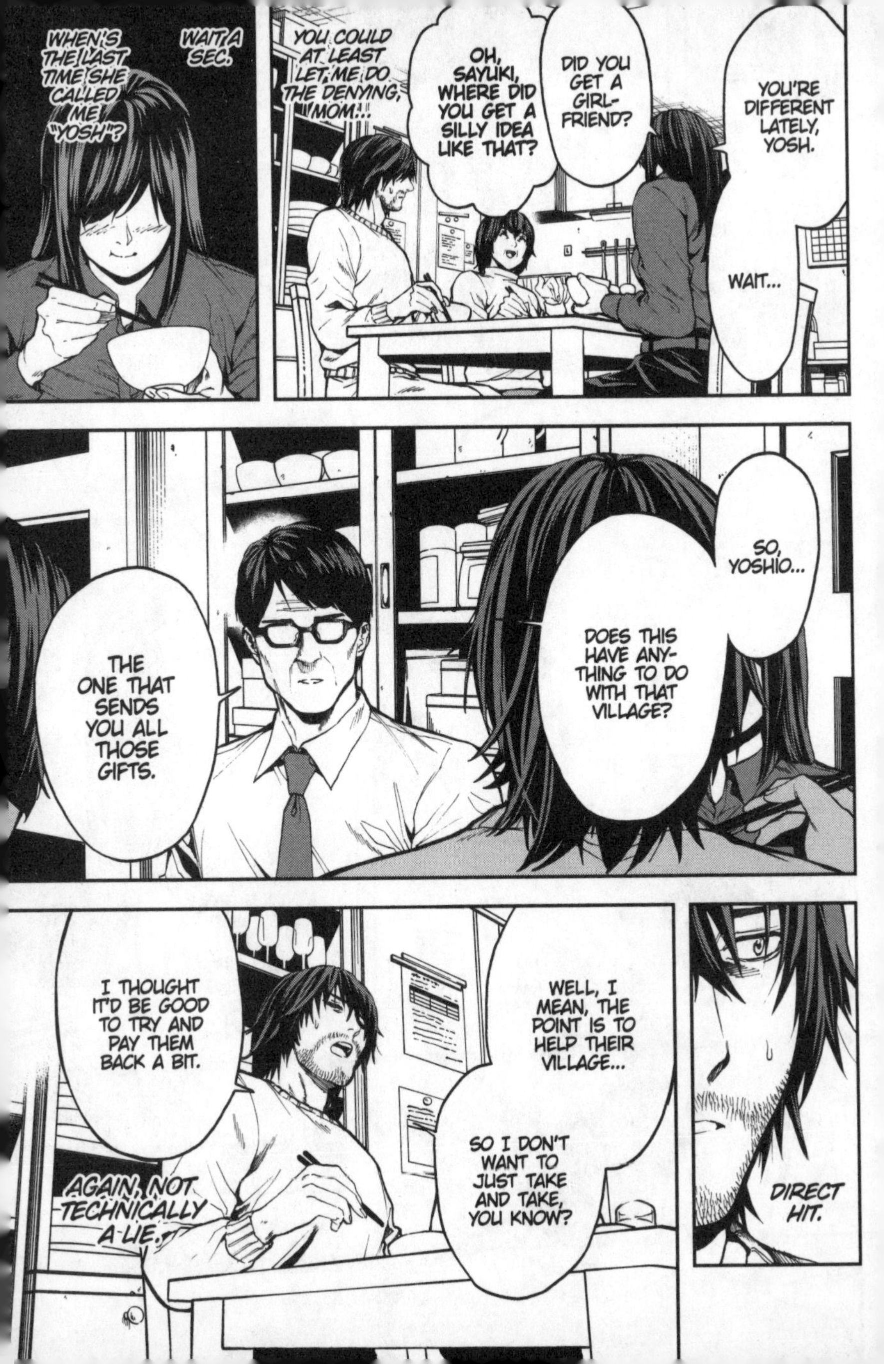
YOU'RE DIFFERENT LATELY, YOSH.
WAIT...
DID YOU GET A GIRL-FRIEND?
OH, SAYUKI, WHERE DID YOU GET A SILLY IDEA LIKE THAT?
YOU COULD AT LEAST LET ME DO THE DENYING, MOM...
WAIT A SEC.
WHEN'S THE LAST TIME SHE CALLED ME "YOSH"?
SO, YOSHIO...
DOES THIS HAVE ANY-THING TO DO WITH THAT VILLAGE?
THE ONE THAT SENDS YOU ALL THOSE GIFTS.
DIRECT HIT.
WELL, I MEAN, THE POINT IS TO HELP THEIR VILLAGE...
SO I DON'T WANT TO JUST TAKE AND TAKE, YOU KNOW?
I THOUGHT IT'D BE GOOD TO TRY AND PAY THEM BACK A BIT.
AGAIN, NOT TECHNICALLY A LIE.

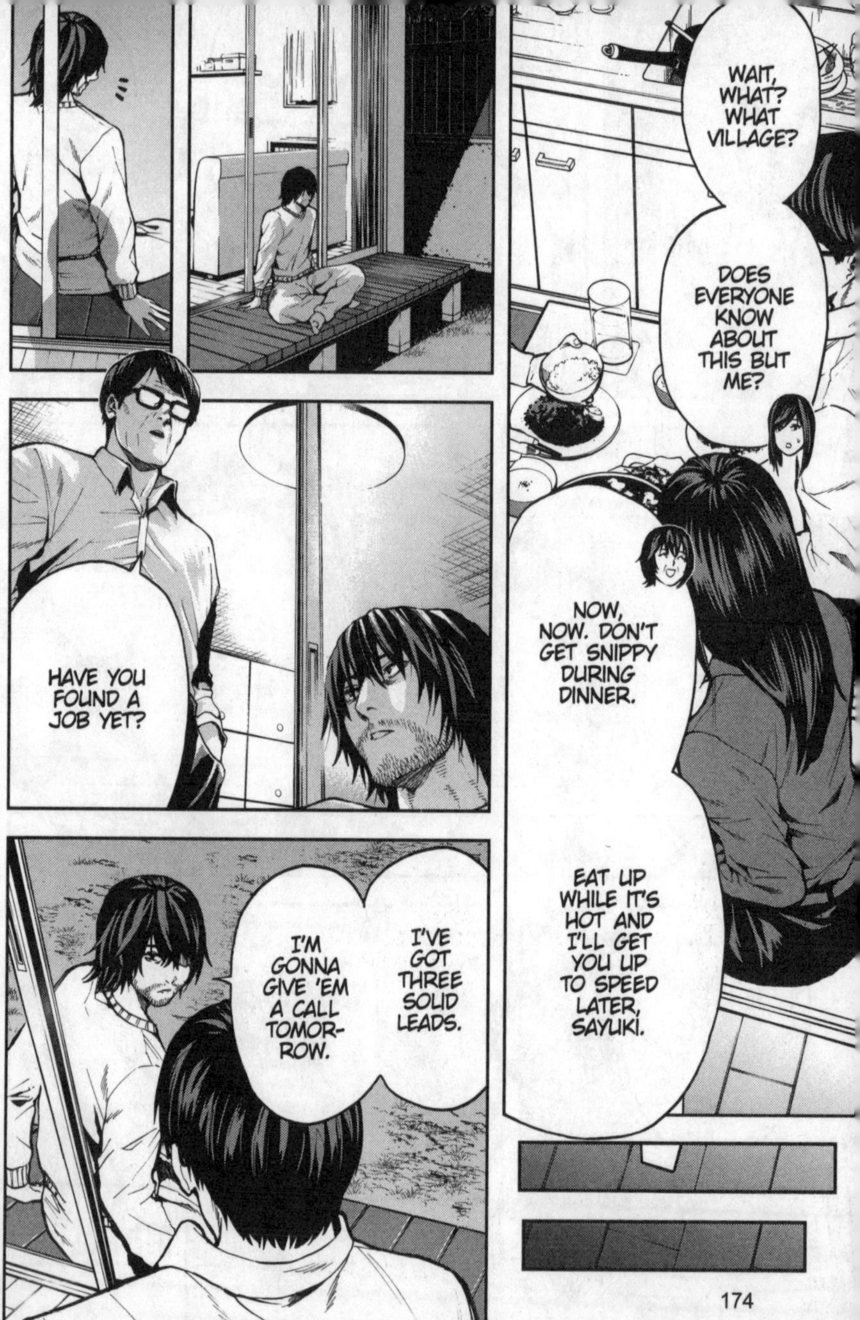
WAIT, WHAT? WHAT VILLAGE?
DOES EVERYONE KNOW ABOUT THIS BUT ME?
NOW, NOW. DON'T GET SNIPPY DURING DINNER.
EAT UP WHILE IT'S HOT AND I'LL GET YOU UP TO SPEED LATER, SAYUKI.
HAVE YOU FOUND A JOB YET?
I'VE GOT THREE SOLID LEADS.
I'M GONNA GIVE 'EM A CALL TOMOR-ROW.

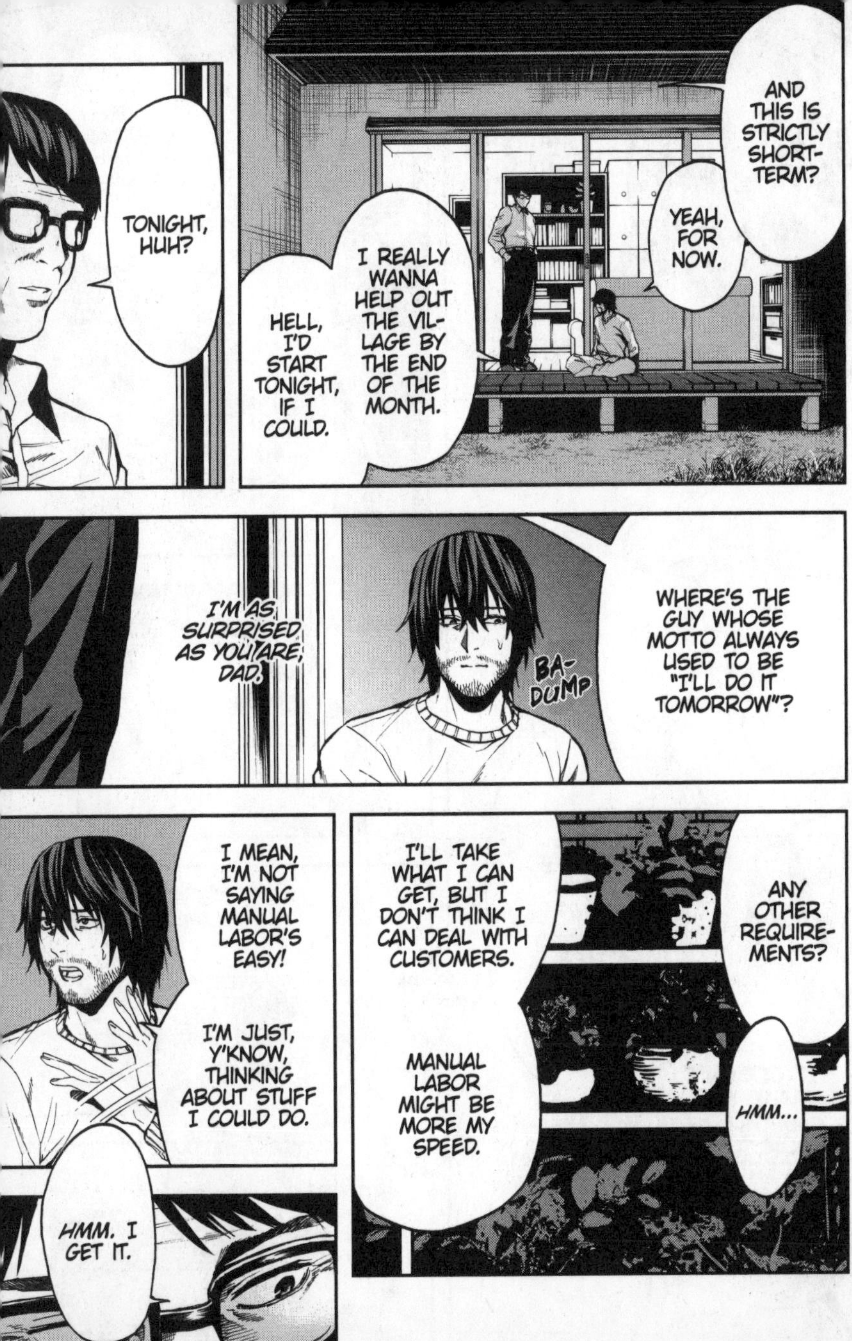
AND THIS IS STRICTLY SHORT-TERM?
YEAH, FOR NOW.
I REALLY WANNA HELP OUT THE VILLAGE BY THE END OF THE MONTH.
HELL, I'D START TONIGHT, IF I COULD.
TONIGHT, HUH?
WHERE'S THE GUY WHOSE MOTTO ALWAYS USED TO BE "I'LL DO IT TOMORROW"?
BA-DUMP
I'M AS SURPRISED AS YOU ARE, DAD.
ANY OTHER REQUIREMENTS?
I'LL TAKE WHAT I CAN GET, BUT I DON'T THINK I CAN DEAL WITH CUSTOMERS.
MANUAL LABOR MIGHT BE MORE MY SPEED.
HMM...
I MEAN, I'M NOT SAYING MANUAL LABOR'S EASY!
I'M JUST, Y'KNOW, THINKING ABOUT STUFF I COULD DO.
HMM. I GET IT.

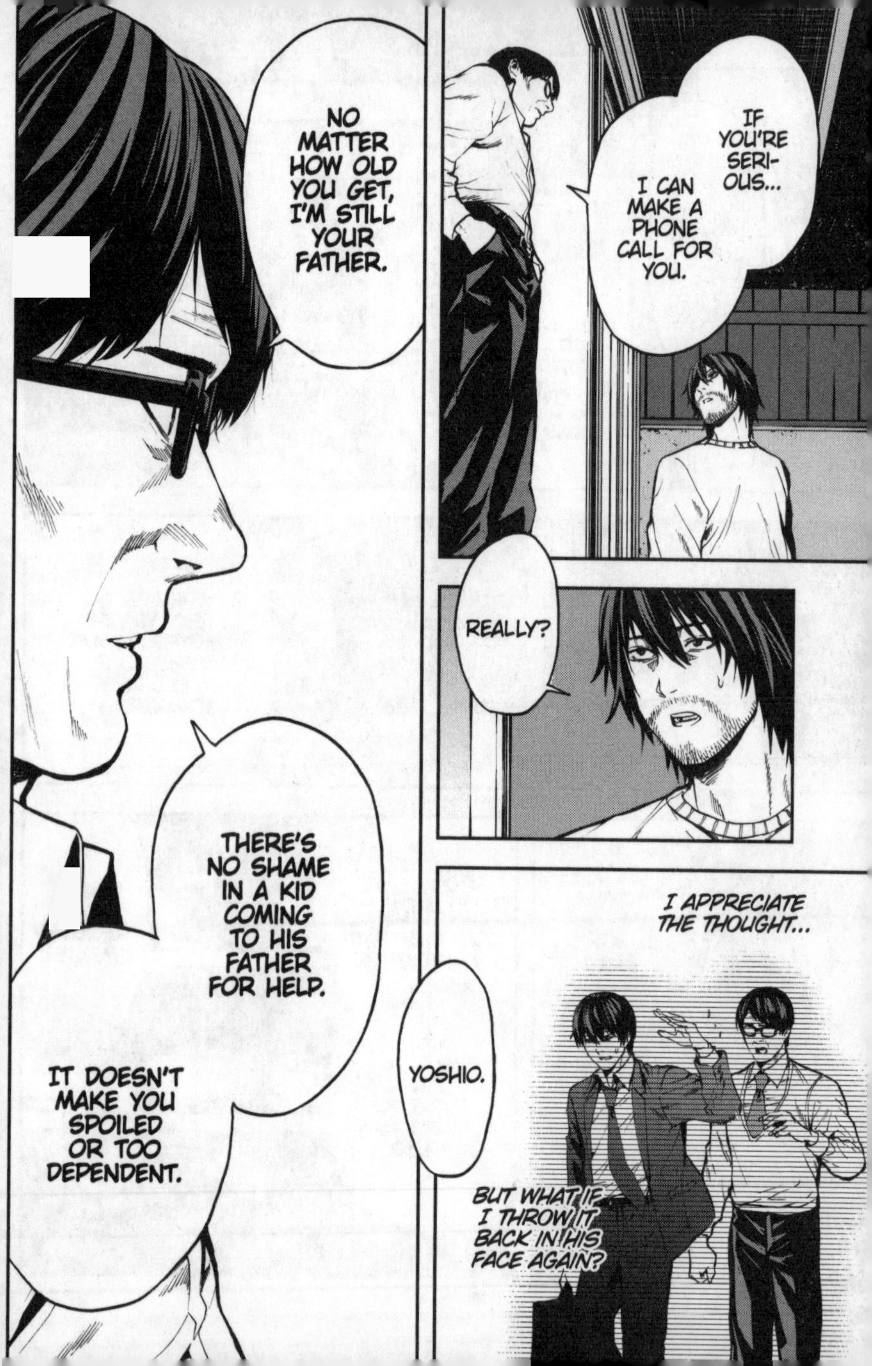
IF YOU'RE SERIOUS... I CAN MAKE A PHONE CALL FOR YOU.
REALLY?
I APPRECIATE THE THOUGHT...
YOSHIO.
BUT WHAT IF I THROW IT BACK IN HIS FACE AGAIN?
NO MATTER HOW OLD YOU GET, I'M STILL YOUR FATHER.
THERE'S NO SHAME IN A KID COMING TO HIS FATHER FOR HELP.
IT DOESN'T MAKE YOU SPOILED OR TOO DEPENDENT.

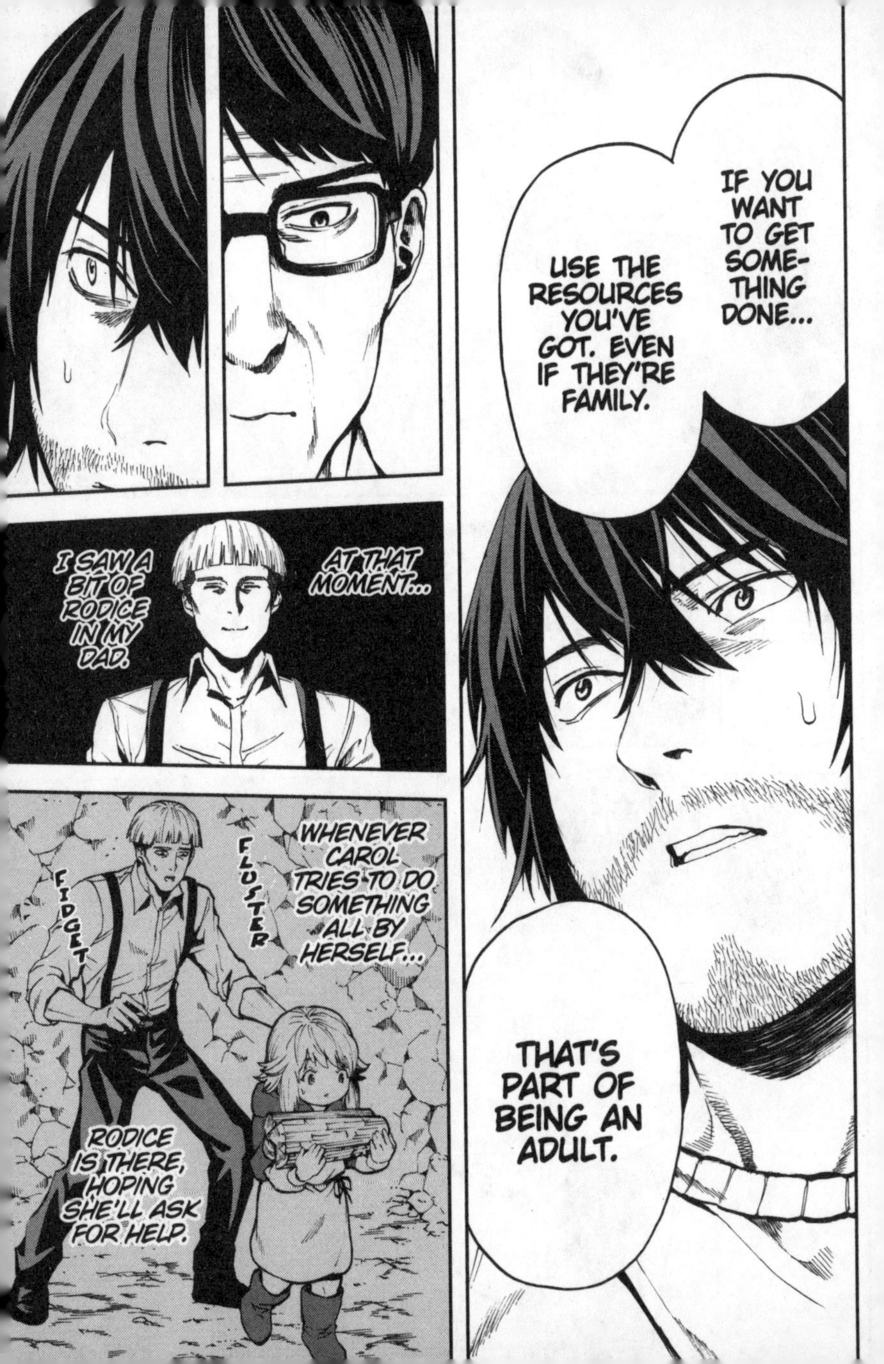
IF YOU WANT TO GET SOME-THING DONE...
USE THE RESOURCES YOU'VE GOT. EVEN IF THEY'RE FAMILY.
THAT'S PART OF BEING AN ADULT.
AT THAT MOMENT...
I SAW A BIT OF RODICE IN MY DAD.
WHENEVER CAROL TRIES TO DO SOMETHING ALL BY HERSELF...
FLUSTER
FIDGET
RODICE IS THERE, HOPING SHE'LL ASK FOR HELP.

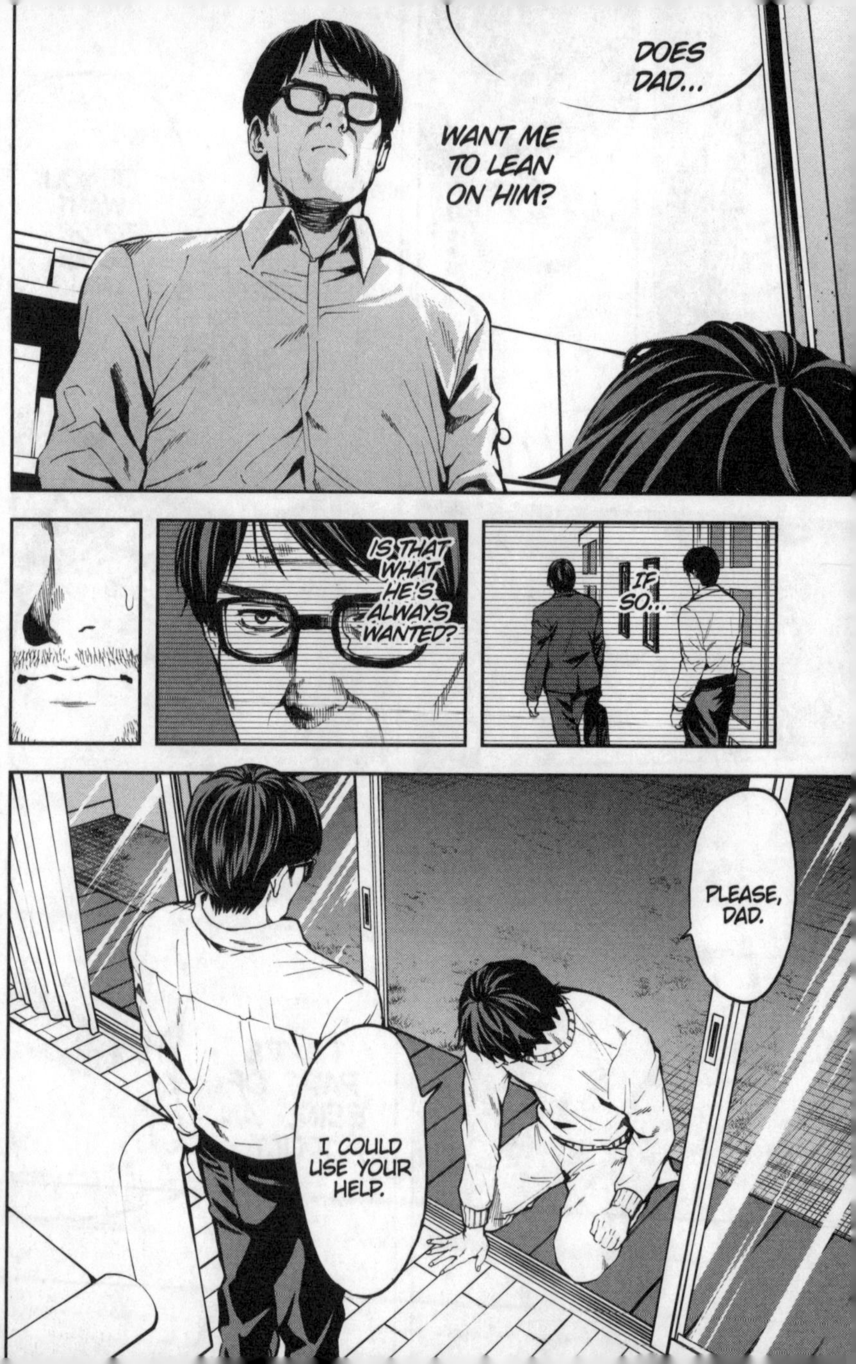
DOES DAD...
WANT ME TO LEAN ON HIM?
IF SO...
IS THAT WHAT HE'S ALWAYS WANTED?
PLEASE, DAD.
I COULD USE YOUR HELP.

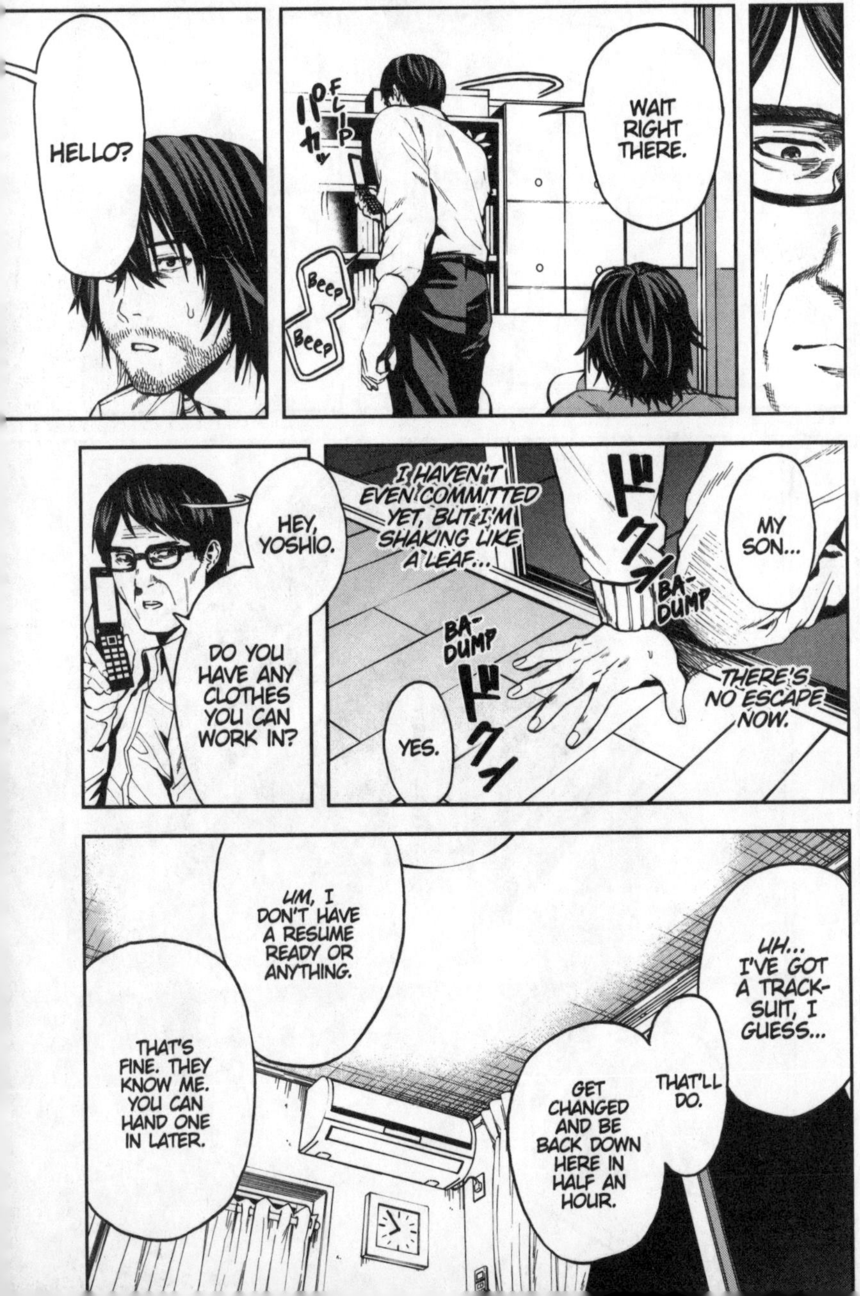

WAIT RIGHT THERE.
FLIP
Beep
Beep
HELLO?
MY SON...
I HAVEN'T EVEN COMMITTED YET, BUT I'M SHAKING LIKE A LEAF...
BA-DUMP
BA-DUMP
THERE'S NO ESCAPE NOW.
YES.
HEY, YOSHIO.
DO YOU HAVE ANY CLOTHES YOU CAN WORK IN?
UH... I'VE GOT A TRACK-SUIT, I GUESS...
THAT'LL DO.
GET CHANGED AND BE BACK DOWN HERE IN HALF AN HOUR.
UM, I DON'T HAVE A RESUME READY OR ANYTHING.
THAT'S FINE. THEY KNOW ME. YOU CAN HAND ONE IN LATER.

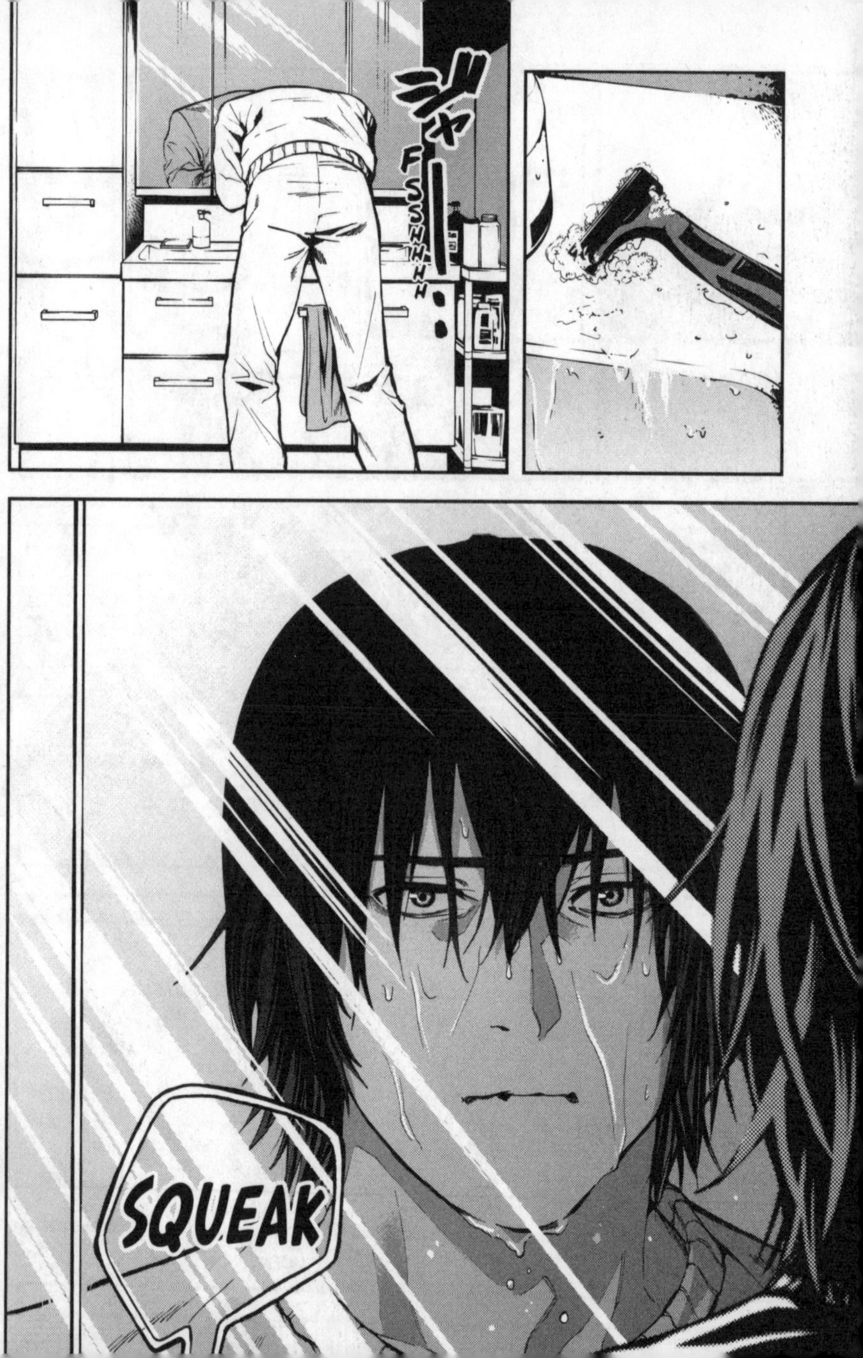
ジャー
FSSHHHH
SQUEAK

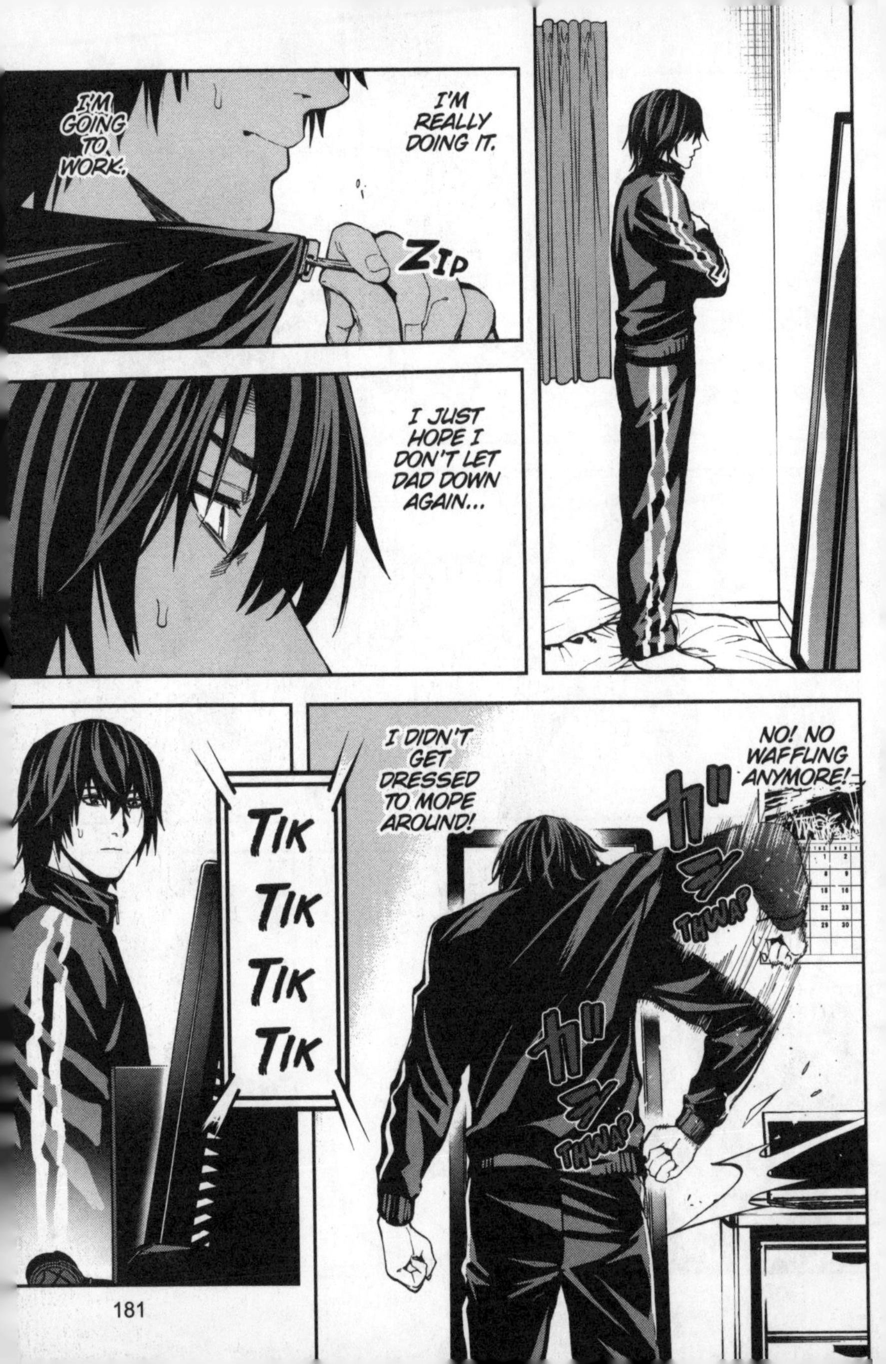
I'M REALLY DOING IT.
I'M GOING TO WORK.
ZIP
I JUST HOPE I DON'T LET DAD DOWN AGAIN...
NO! NO WAFFLING ANYMORE!
I DIDN'T GET DRESSED TO MOPE AROUND!
THWAP
THWAP
TIK TIK TIK TIK

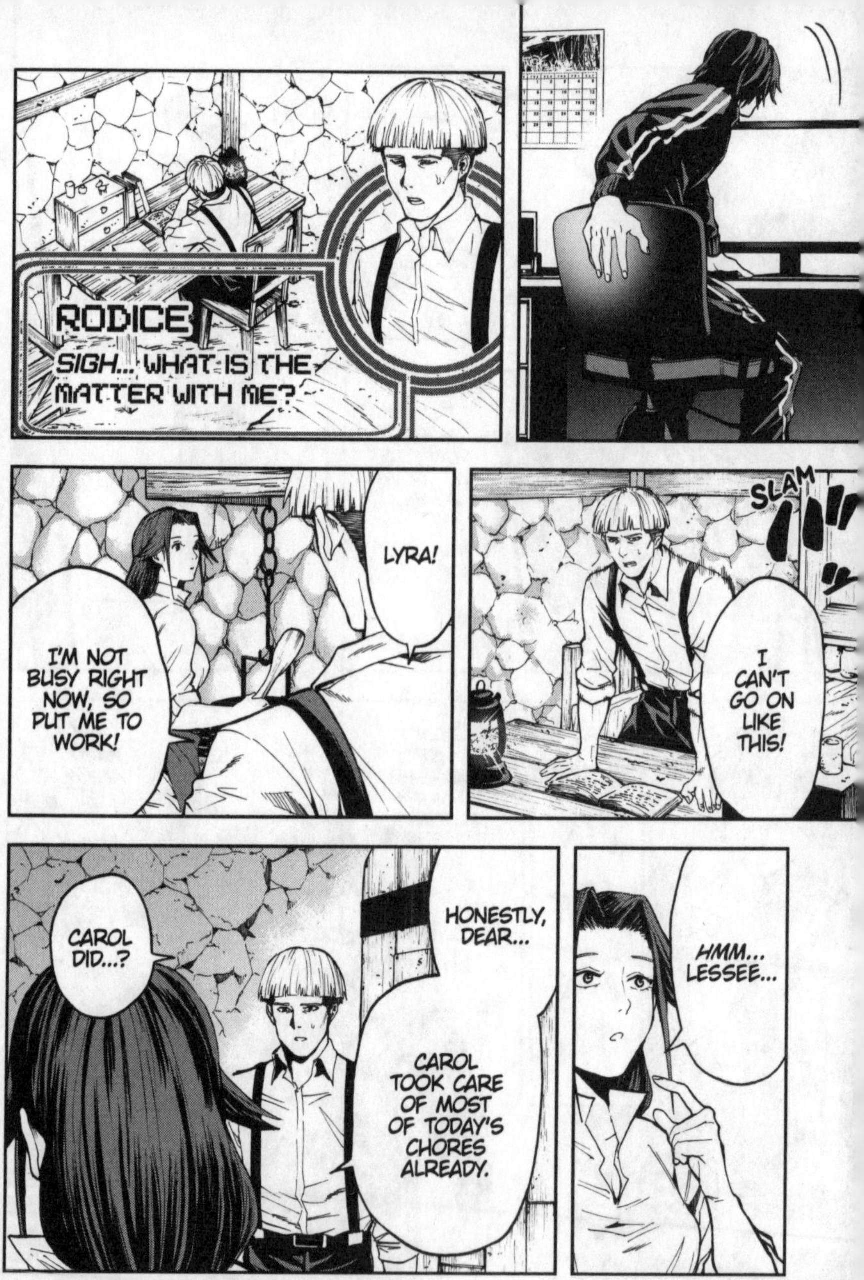
RODICE
SIGH... WHAT IS THE MATTER WITH ME?
SLAM
I CAN'T GO ON LIKE THIS!
LYRA!
I'M NOT BUSY RIGHT NOW, SO PUT ME TO WORK!
HMM... LESSEE...
HONESTLY, DEAR...
CAROL TOOK CARE OF MOST OF TODAY'S CHORES ALREADY.
CAROL DID...?

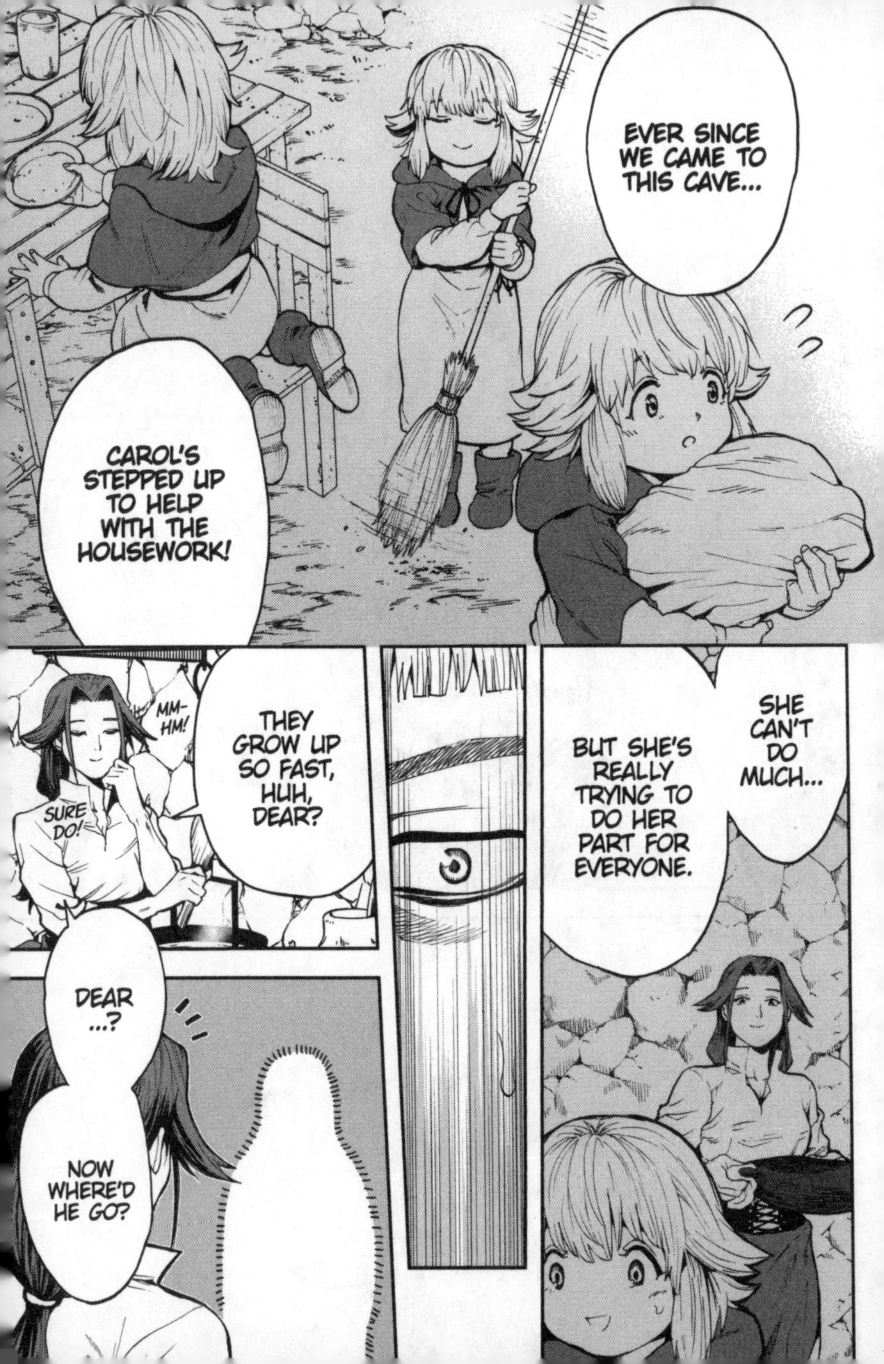
EVER SINCE WE CAME TO THIS CAVE...
CAROL'S STEPPED UP TO HELP WITH THE HOUSEWORK!
SHE CAN'T DO MUCH...
BUT SHE'S REALLY TRYING TO DO HER PART FOR EVERYONE.
THEY GROW UP SO FAST, HUH, DEAR?
MM-HM!
SURE DO!
DEAR ...?
NOW WHERE'D HE GO?

DADDY?

CAROL!

I'M SO SORRY ABOUT THIS MORNI--

HUH?

NO, DADDY, I'M SORRY!

EVERYONE'S ALWAYS TELLIN' ME...

Y'KNOW...

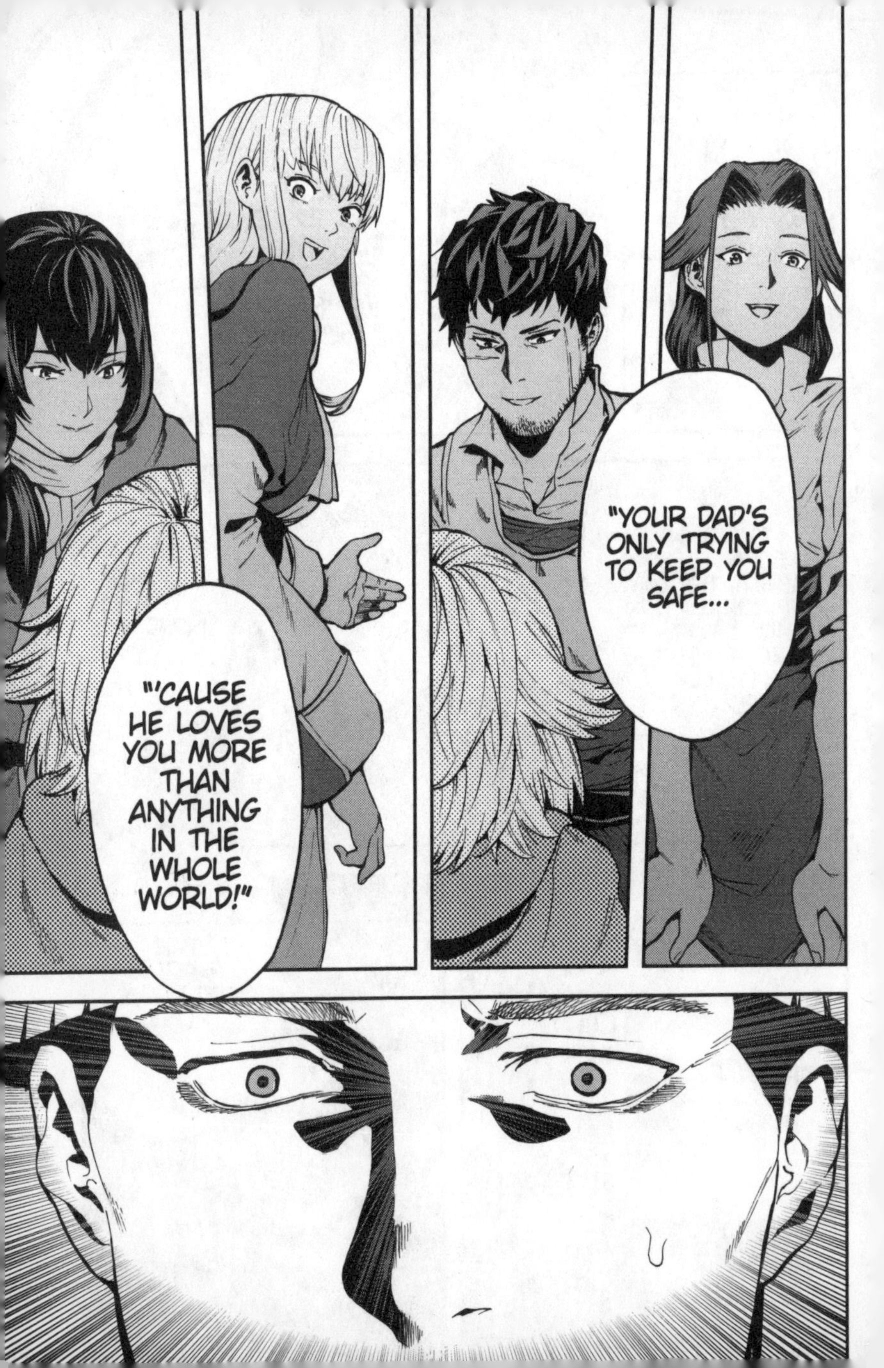
"YOUR DAD'S ONLY TRYING TO KEEP YOU SAFE...
"'CAUSE HE LOVES YOU MORE THAN ANYTHING IN THE WHOLE WORLD!"

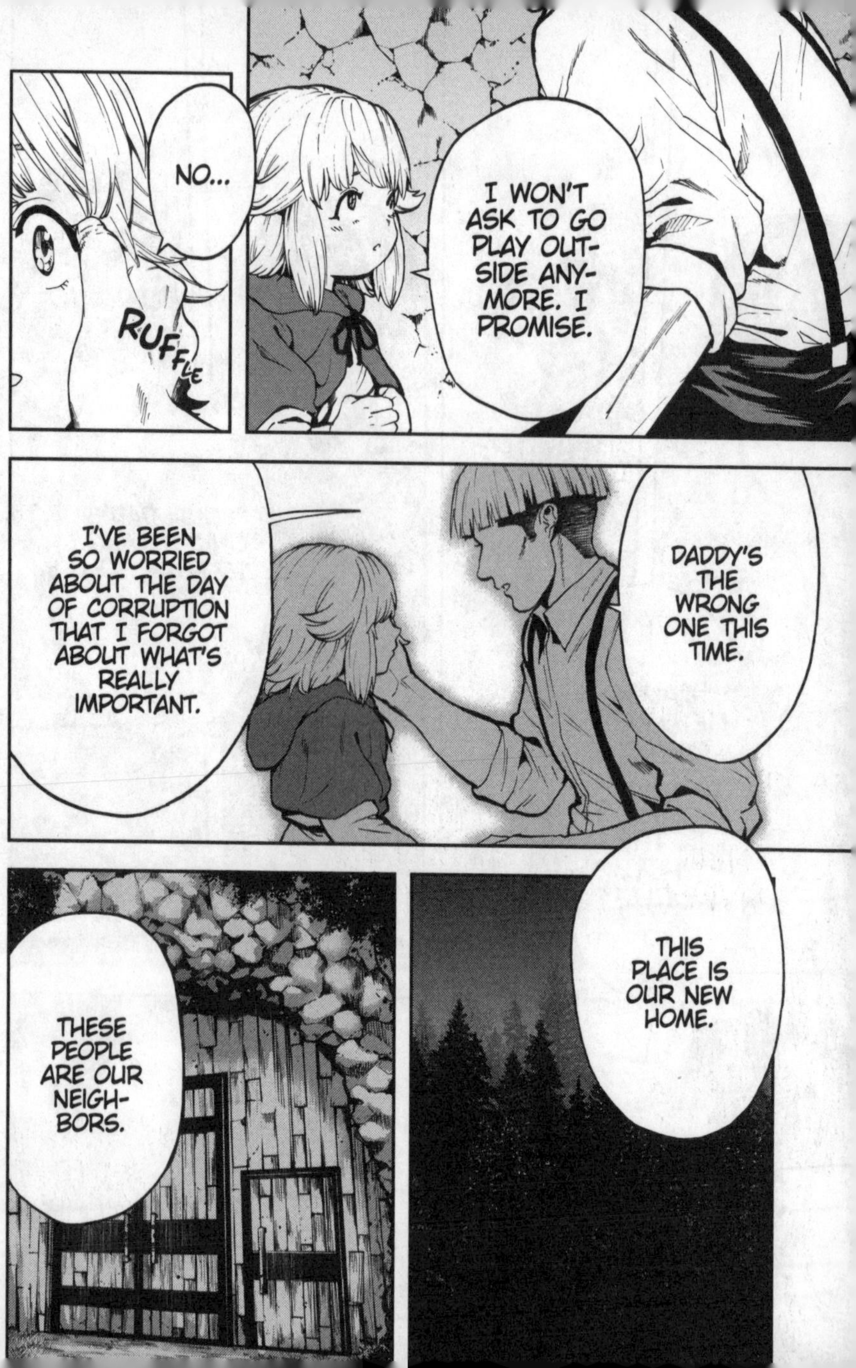
I WON'T ASK TO GO PLAY OUT-SIDE ANY-MORE. I PROMISE.
NO...
RUFFLE
DADDY'S THE WRONG ONE THIS TIME.
I'VE BEEN SO WORRIED ABOUT THE DAY OF CORRUPTION THAT I FORGOT ABOUT WHAT'S REALLY IMPORTANT.
THIS PLACE IS OUR NEW HOME.
THESE PEOPLE ARE OUR NEIGH-BORS.

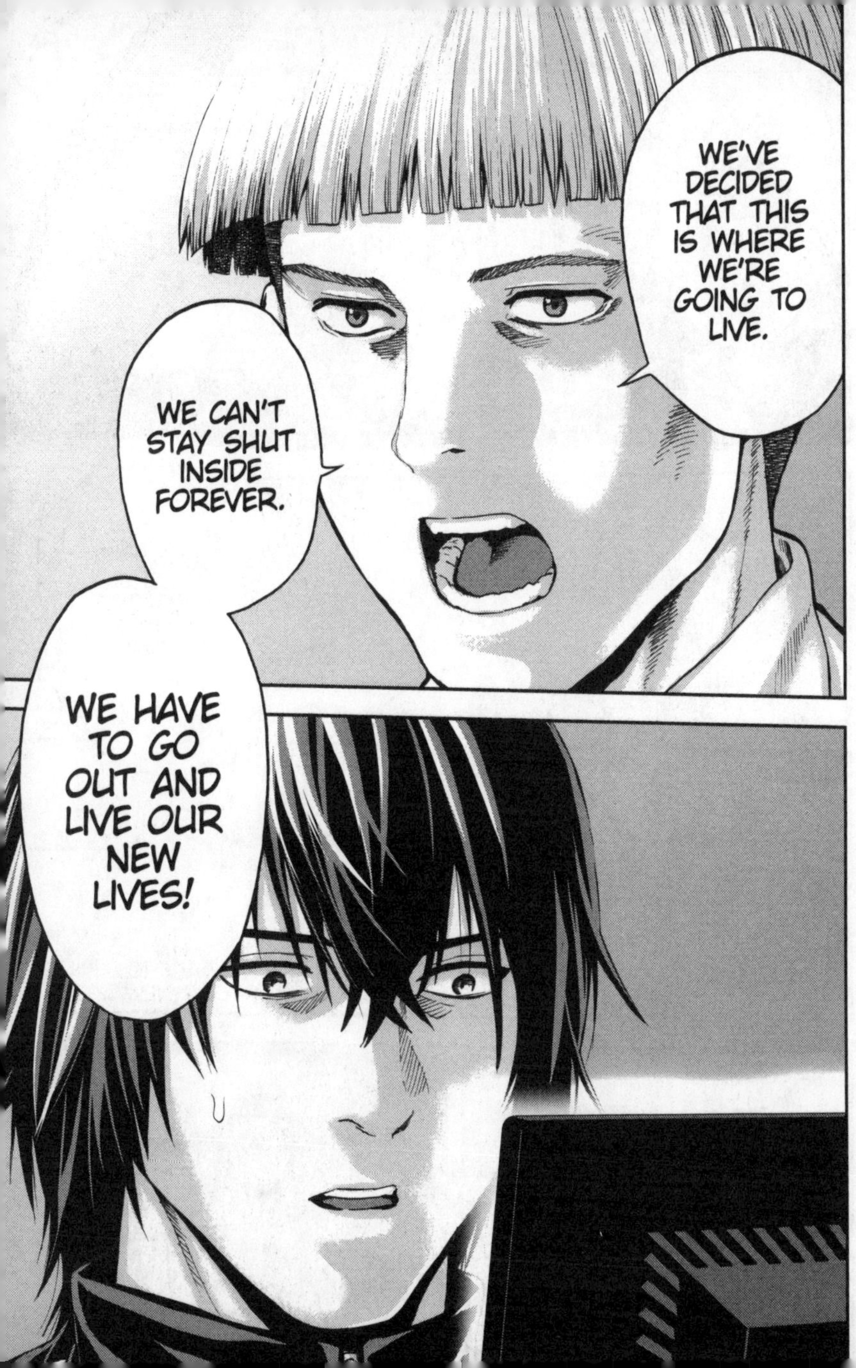
WE'VE DECIDED THAT THIS IS WHERE WE'RE GOING TO LIVE.
WE CAN'T STAY SHUT INSIDE FOREVER.
WE HAVE TO GO OUT AND LIVE OUR NEW LIVES!

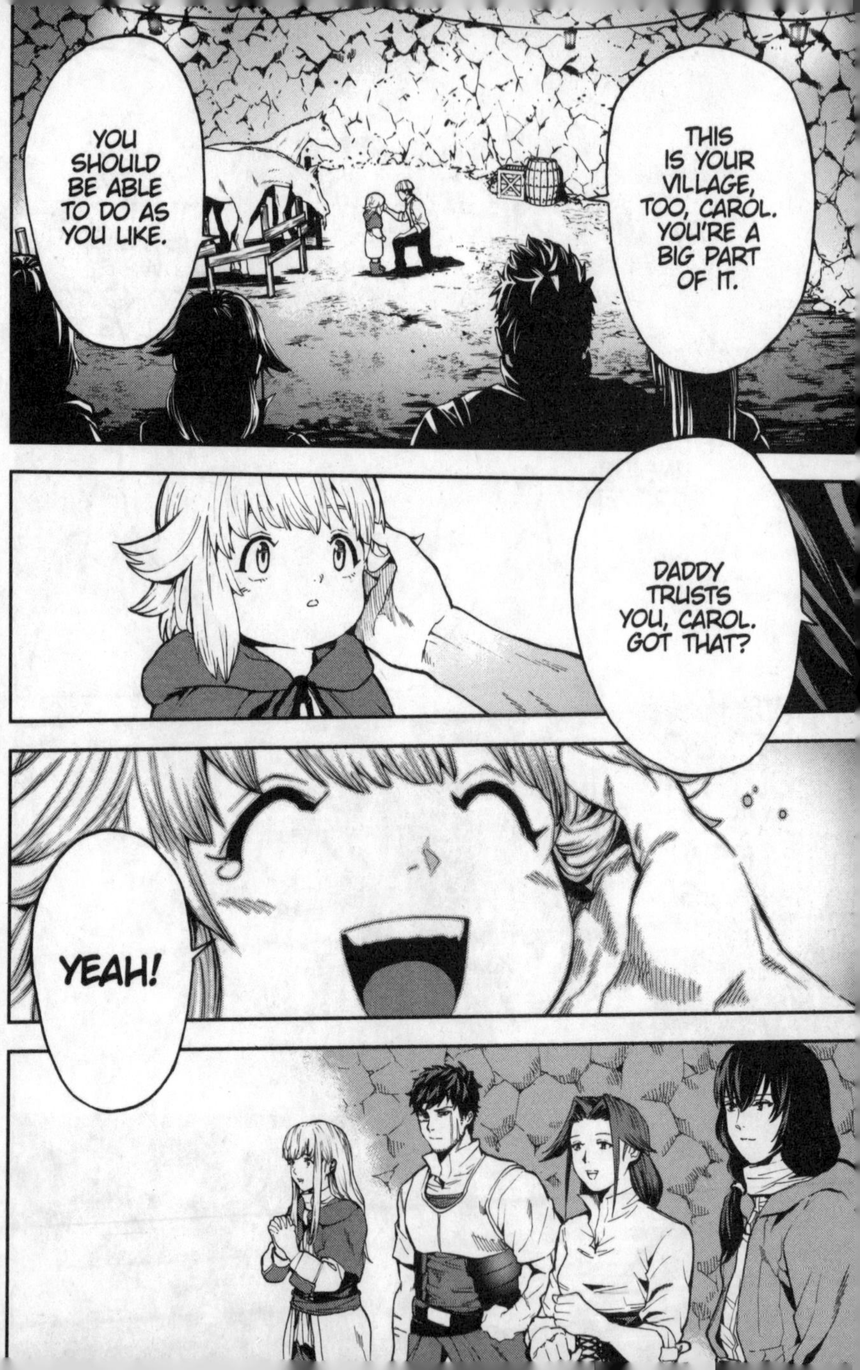
THIS IS YOUR VILLAGE, TOO, CAROL. YOU'RE A BIG PART OF IT.
YOU SHOULD BE ABLE TO DO AS YOU LIKE.
DADDY TRUSTS YOU, CAROL. GOT THAT?
YEAH!

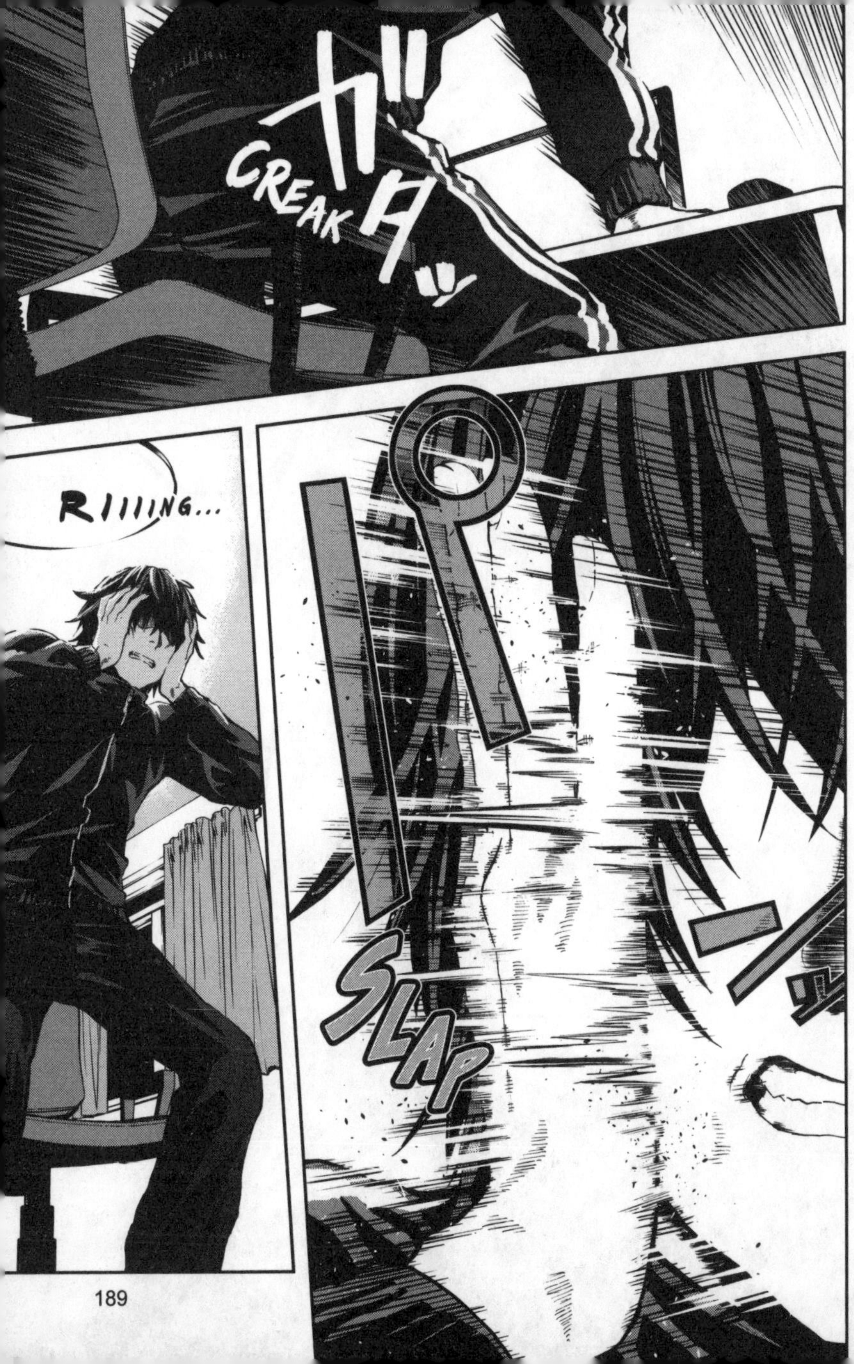
ガタッ
CREAK
SLAP
RIIIING...

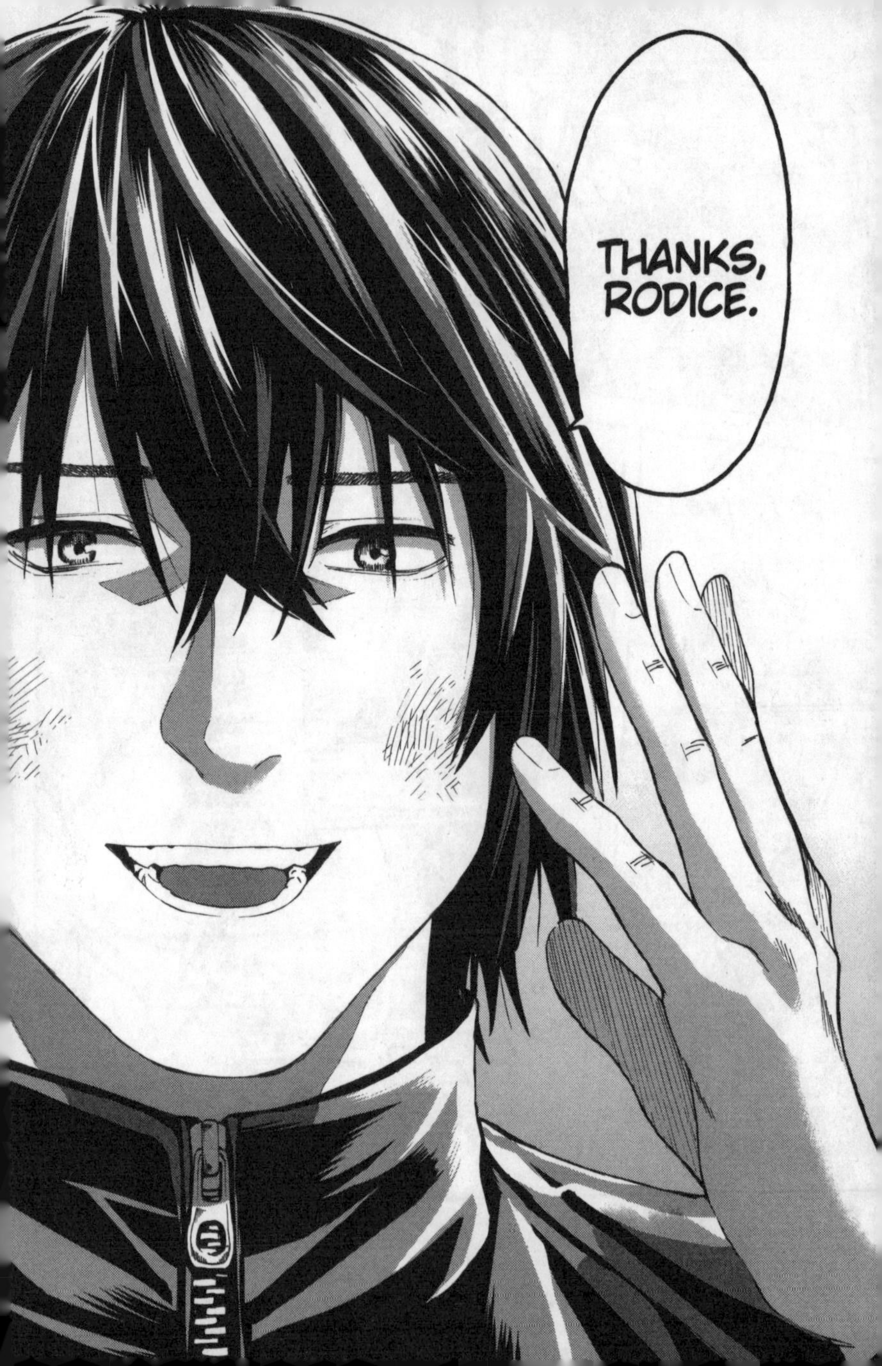
THANKS, RODICE.

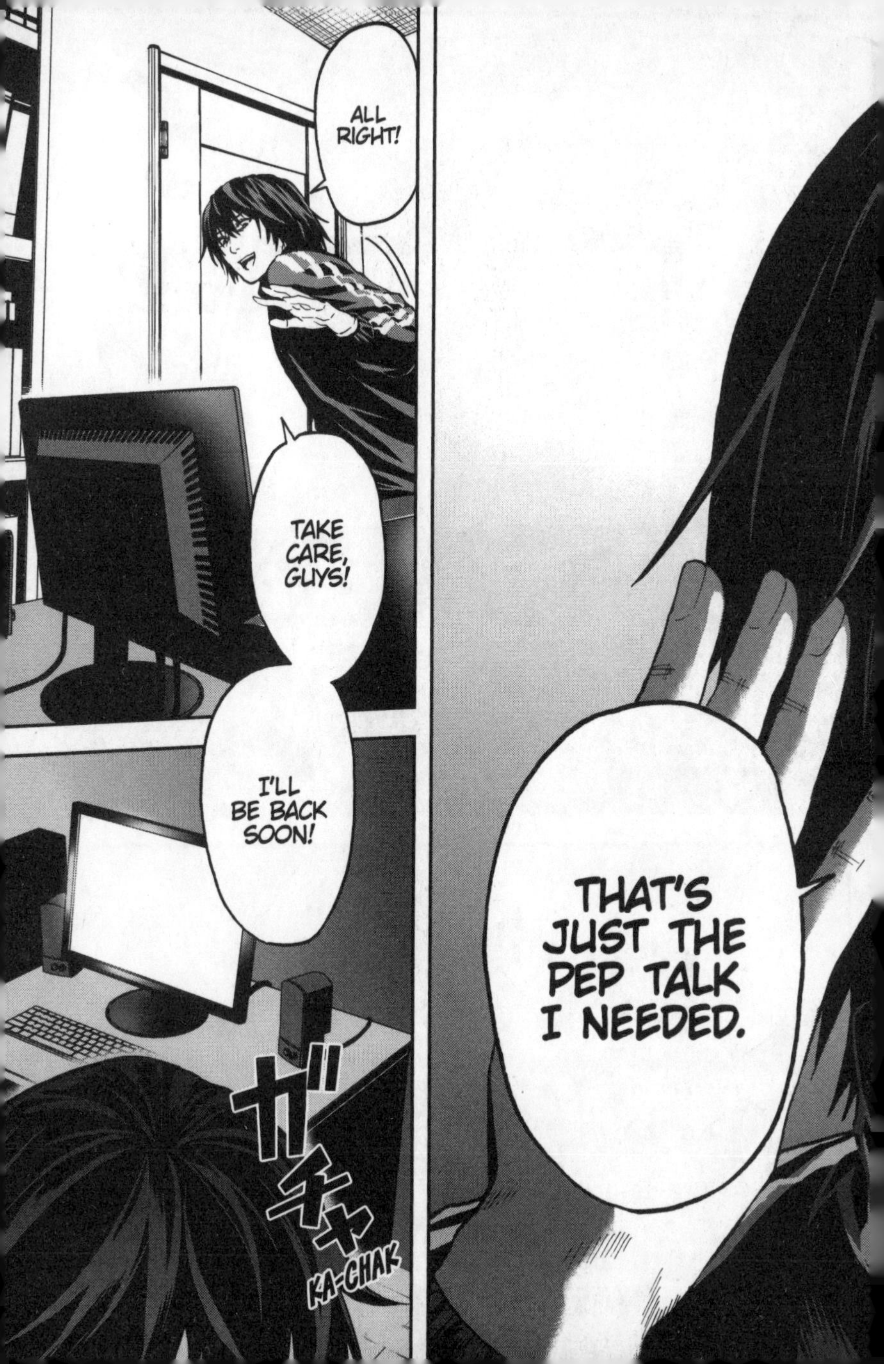
THAT'S JUST THE PEP TALK I NEEDED.
ALL RIGHT!
TAKE CARE, GUYS!
I'LL BE BACK SOON!
KA-CHAK

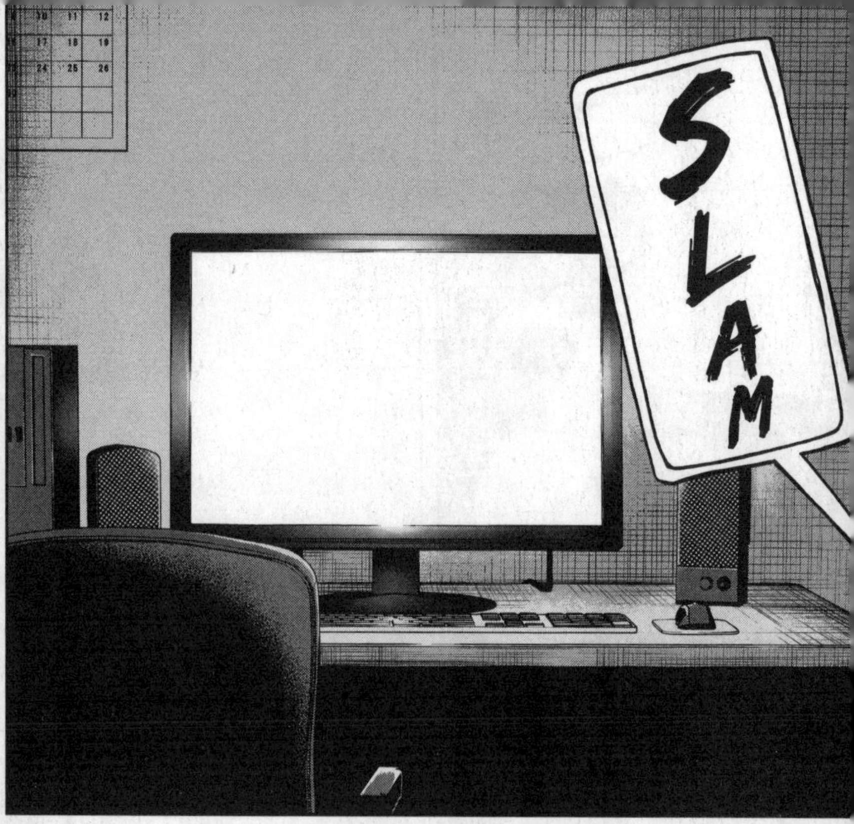
SLAM

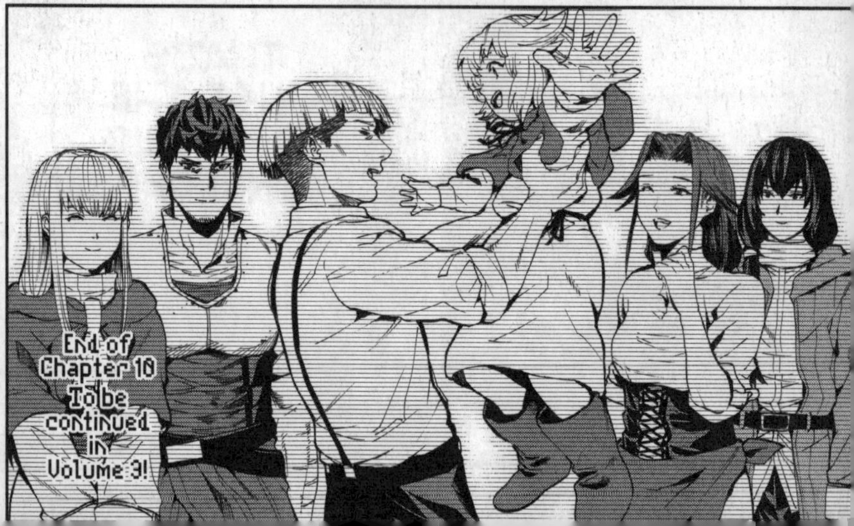
End of Chapter 10
To be continued in Volume 3!

THE NPCs IN THIS VILLAGE SIM GAME MUST BE REAL!

THE NPCs IN THIS
VILLAGE SIM GAME
MUST BE REAL! ↵

SEVEN SEAS ENTERTAINMENT PRESENTS

THE NPCs IN THIS VILLAGE SIM GAME MUST BE REAL!

Vol. 2

story by **HIRUKUMA** art by **KAZUHIKO MORITA** character design by **NAMAKO**

TRANSLATION
John Neal

LETTERING
Ochie Caraan

COVER DESIGN
Hanase Qi

LOGO DESIGN
George Panella

PROOFREADER
Brett Hallahan

COPY EDITOR
Dawn Davis

EDITOR
J.P. Sullivan

PREPRESS TECHNICIAN
Melanie Ujimori

PRINT MANAGER
Rhiannon Rasmussen-Silverstein

PRODUCTION ASSOCIATE
Christa Miesner

PRODUCTION MANAGER
Lissa Pattillo

MANAGING EDITOR
Julie Davis

ASSOCIATE PUBLISHER
Adam Arnold

PUBLISHER
Jason DeAngelis

Seven Seas press and purchase enquiries can be sent to Marketing Manager Lianne Sentar at press@gomanga.com. Information regarding the distribution and purchase of digital editions is available from Digital Manager CK Russell at digital@gomanga.com.

ISBN: 978-1-64827-642-2
Printed in Canada
First Printing: January 2022
10 9 8 7 6 5 4 3 2 1

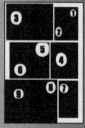

READING DIRECTIONS

This book reads from ***right to left***, Japanese style. If this is your first time reading manga, you start reading from the top right panel on each page and take it from there. If you get lost, just follow the numbered diagram here. It may seem backwards at first, but you'll get the hang of it! Have fun!!

1
2
3
4
5
6
7
8
9

Follow us online: www.SevenSeasEntertainment.com